SAP HANA® 2.0 Installation and Administration

A Practical Guide

Rajarajeswari Kaliyaperumal

Thank you for purchasing this book from Espresso Tutorials!

Like a cup of espresso coffee, Espresso Tutorials SAP books are concise and effective. We know that your time is valuable and we deliver information in a succinct and straightforward manner. It only takes our readers a short amount of time to consume SAP concepts. Our books are well recognized in the industry for leveraging tutorial-style instruction and videos to show you step by step how to successfully work with SAP.

Check out our YouTube channel to watch our videos at *https://www.youtube.com/user/EspressoTutorials*.

If you are interested in SAP Finance and Controlling, please join us at *https://forum.espresso-tutorials.com/* to get your SAP questions answered and contribute to discussions.

Related titles from Espresso Tutorials:

- Julie Hallett, Sarah Hallett Reeves:
  A Practical Guide to Cybersecurity Governance for SAP®
  https://es-tu.de/hDcMR1
- Fernando Roque:
  A Practical Guide to SAP S/4HANA® Administration: Monitoring and Optimizing Performance
  https://es-tu.de/Zsgopy
- Aušra Gustainienė, Damian Jordan:
  SAP S/4HANA® Rollout Strategies and Best Practices
  http://5518.espresso-tutorials.com
- Anurag Barua:
  Robotics Process Automation in SAP S/4HANA®
  https://es-tu.de/UWuJ7y
- Aušra Gustainienė, Domantas Mincė:
  Practical Guide to Using Focused Build for SAP® Solution Manager
  https://es-tu.de/L9c8
- Santosh Kumar, Kai Zhang:
  Practical Guide to SAP® Entitlement Management with SAP S/4HANA®
  https://es-tu.de/cC89ho

Rajarajeswari Kaliyaperumal
SAP HANA® 2.0 Installation and Administration—A Practical Guide

ISBN: 978-3-960124-42-9

Editor: Karen Schoch

Cover Design: Olesia Donchenko

Cover Photo: iStockphoto.com | lamontak590623 No. 838476220

Interior Book Design: Johann-Christian Hanke

1st Edition 2025, Gleichen

URL: *www.espresso-tutorials.com*

Feedback
We greatly appreciate any feedback you may have concerning this book. Please send your feedback via email to: *info@espresso-tutorials.com*.

Table of Contents

Preface **7**

1 HANA architecture and deployment options **9**

1.1 HANA versus traditional databases 9
1.2 SAP HANA—capabilities and use cases 12
1.3 HANA hosting options 15
1.4 Understanding the HANA database 17
1.5 Server components 29
1.6 Deployment options 38

2 HANA installation and upgrades **45**

2.1 Available deployment mode and types 45
2.2 HANA database file system layout 47
2.3 HANA database sizing 51
2.4 Preparing for HANA installation 60
2.5 HANA installation and configuration tools 76
2.6 HANA installation 91
2.7 HANA uninstallation 118
2.8 Performing a HANA database update 120

3 Administration and monitoring tools **129**

3.1 Available administration tools 129
3.2 SAP HANA Studio 129
3.3 HANA Cockpit 140
3.4 SAP HANA HDBSQL 151
3.5 SAP HANA XS administraton tools 158
3.6 Additional tools 158

4 Database administration **161**

4.1 Table management 161
4.2 HANA memory and its types 199
4.3 Managing tenants 206
4.4 HANA system properties 216
4.5 Persistent data storage 221

4.6 Workload management 228
4.7 HANA alert monitoring and scheduling 240
4.8 System views 244
4.9 Limitations 245

5 Security administration and user management 247
5.1 User management 247
5.2 Password policy 250
5.3 HANA authorization—privileges and roles 252
5.4 Encryption 254
5.5 Handling encrypted backup and restore 261
5.6 Auditing 263
5.7 Authentication in HANA database 265
5.8 Monitoring security settings 267

6 Backup, restore and refresh 269
6.1 Basics of HANA backup 269
6.2 Executing a HANA database backup 276
6.3 Restoring a HANA database 281
6.4 Refreshing a HANA database 282

7 Troubleshooting 309
7.1 Classifying the issue 309
7.2 HANA Studio "Overview" 310
7.3 SQL statement collection 311
7.4 "Guided Answers" and FAQs 312
7.5 Analyzing disk-full situations 313
7.6 Collecting and analyzing database dumps 314
7.7 Analyzing SQL statement issues 320
7.8 Traces in HANA database 322
7.9 Troubleshooting tools 324
7.10 Raising a support case with SAP 331

A About the Author 332

B Index 333

C Disclaimer 336

Preface

Introduction

This book aims to provide readers with a solid understanding of HANA database administration. It is designed for students, beginners, and intermediate-level HANA database administrators. This practical guide offers valuable insights and tips that administrators will find useful for their daily work.

Chapter 1 explores the architecture of the HANA database and the various deployment options.

Chapter 2 provides detailed information about installing and upgrading HANA databases.

Chapter 3 gives a concise overview of the tools available for administration and monitoring.

Chapter 4 dives into essential database administration tasks, and Chapter 5 covers security and administrative items.

Chapter 6 covers backup and restore processes, and Chapter 7 focuses on how to troubleshoot HANA database issues efficiently.

Acknowledgements

My sincere thanks go to Alice Adams and the team at Espresso Tutorials for providing me with the opportunity to write this book.

I would like to dedicate this book to my HANA mentor, Todd Pierce, who not only provided me with the opportunity to work on HANA but also taught me the right way to work with it.

In addition, I wish to thank my family, all my current and former managers, and my colleagues, who supported me in every possible way. Special thanks to my managers, Sreedhara Padmanabhuni and Prabakaran Subbarayalu, and my colleagues, Ramya Vijaykumar and Sourabh Chordiya for encouraging and supporting me throughout this journey.

Thanks also to AWS, and Venkat Tatvarthy from AWS, for helping me with AWS credits. All the servers used in this book are AWS EC2 instances.

The source of all the information available in this book is from the following URL:

https://help.sap.com/docs/SAP_HANA_PLATFORM

We have added a few icons to highlight important information. These include:

Tips

Tips highlight information that provides more details about the subject being described and/or additional background information.

Examples

Examples help illustrate a topic better by relating it to real world scenarios.

! Attention

Attention notices highlight information that you should be aware of when you go through the examples in this book on your own.

1 HANA architecture and deployment options

SAP HANA (High-performance Analytic Appliance) is an in-memory database (IMDB) with a column-oriented structure. It was developed by SAP (Systems, Applications, and Products in Data Processing) and is designed to efficiently handle advanced analytics and high-speed transactions. SAP HANA is a groundbreaking solution that seamlessly integrates Online Analytical Processing (OLAP) and Online Transaction Processing (OLTP), while effectively utilizing the latest hardware advancements.

Introduced in 2010, SAP HANA was meticulously crafted from the ground up to meet the latest business and data requirements. With HANA, users can receive query responses in under a second, delivering speeds up to 3600 times faster than traditional databases. Additionally, it can execute 3.5 billion scans per second per core and 15 million aggregations per second per core.

We should take pride in our ability to comprehend and manage such an intelligent database.

1.1 HANA versus traditional databases

1.1.1 Traditional databases

Traditional databases are obsolete in design and have several significant issues associated with them:

- The foundational design and operational principles of traditional databases are outdated when compared to current business and market trends.
- Traditional databases struggle to cope with the increasing volume of data and evolving data requirements. This prevents companies from fully leveraging real-time data and hinders their modernization efforts.

- Incompatibility with new data types (such as unstructured data, spatial data, graph data, etc.), which is prevalent in the digital market, is a major problem for traditional databases. They can only handle basic data requests and need application intelligence for further data processing.
- Partners encounter additional challenges in helping customers integrate with modern technologies such as data science, artificial intelligence, and IoT (Internet of Things). This introduces an additional layer of complexity.
- Traditional database designs often segregate transactional and analytical databases. The former focuses on record-level data processing (OLTP—online transaction processing) and the latter prioritizes batch loading, aggregation, and read-intensive queries (OLAP—online analytical processing). Moreover, bridging the gap between OLTP and OLAP systems requires an additional interface.

SAP developed HANA to address these limitations by leveraging cutting-edge innovations and technologies.

1.1.2 High-level comparison—traditional databases versus HANA

Figure 1.1 illustrates a typical traditional database versus the HANA database. In the conventional database model, data resides on disk and is only transferred to memory when requested by an application. As data processing intensifies, some of the information in memory must be evicted to create space for new data. This process leads to increased wait times before the requested information becomes available for the application or the end user. Moreover, due to hardware constraints relating to memory and CPU, there is constant back-and-forth communication between the application, disk, and memory, which ultimately results in performance degradation.

With HANA, the allocated memory is substantial enough to accommodate the entire database, thereby eliminating the need for frequent data transfers between disk and memory. This significantly enhances data processing speed. For the HANA database, memory and CPU are no longer bottlenecks. The use of a 64-bit operating system enables large amounts of memory to be addressed. Additionally, the evolution of multi-core CPU architecture enables parallel processing of application data. All these facilitate real-time analysis with HANA in a fraction of a second.

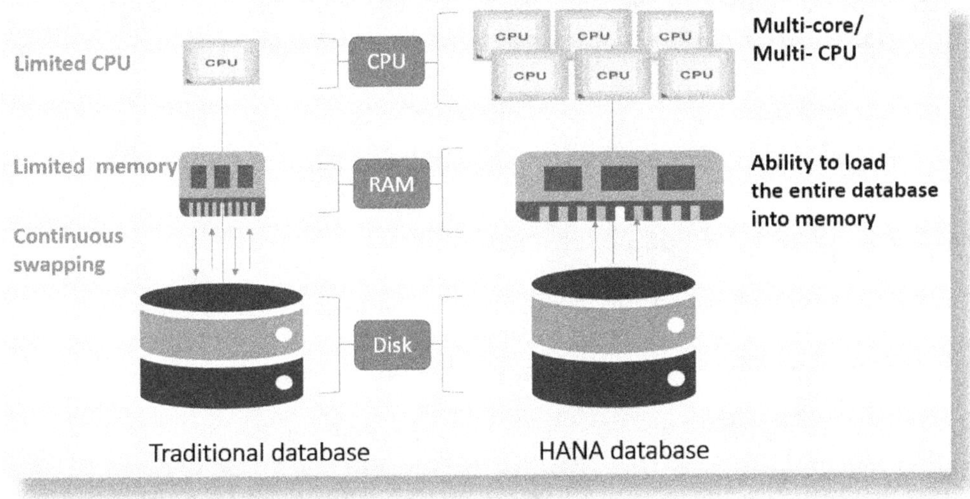

Figure 1.1: Traditional databases versus HANA

1.1.3 HANA as an intelligent database

HANA transcends the conventional definition of a database. In addition to fulfilling data requests like a traditional database does, it takes on the responsibility of processing data for applications, such as aggregating and disaggregating data, generating forecasts, cleansing data, filtering, sorting, ranking data, and much more.

With HANA, companies now have the ability to construct intricate data models using straightforward tools, empowering them to extract valuable insights from the vast reservoir of available data.

Unlike traditional databases, HANA can serve as both an OLTP and OLAP system. Consequently, companies can utilize a single database to manage both transactional processing and analytical processing, earning HANA the designation of HTAP (hybrid transaction/analytical processing).

HANA significantly minimizes the data footprint by eliminating unnecessary tables and indexes, employing various compression techniques, and implementing data aging strategies. Its column-based storage facilitates maximum compression and expedites the categorization of data based on its usage/temperature (such as hot data, warm data, and cold data).

SAP developed HANA from scratch, taking into consideration the latest business trends, customer needs, and hardware innovation.

1.2 SAP HANA—capabilities and use cases

1.2.1 SAP HANA database capabilities

The HANA database encompasses a myriad of capabilities, ranging from database management and application development to advanced analytical processing and flexible data virtualization, as outlined in Figure 1.2.

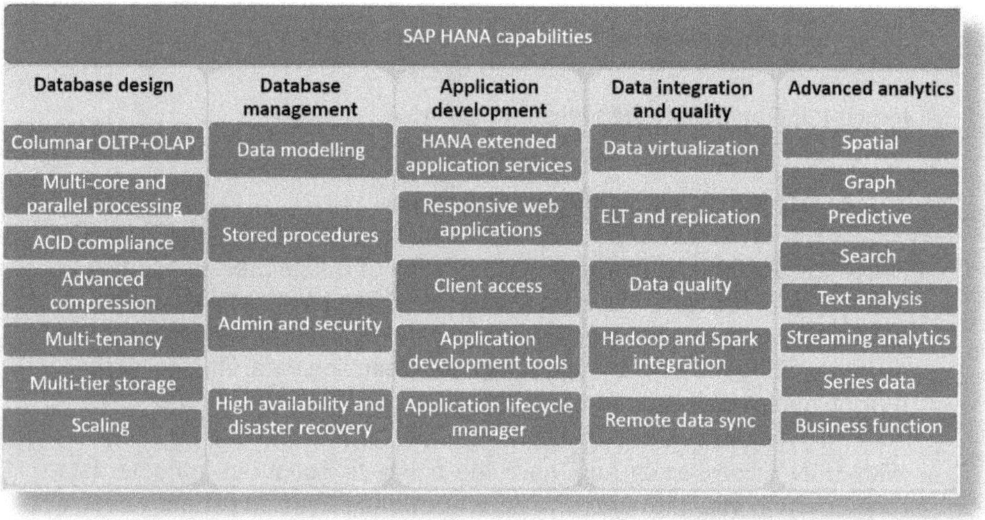

Figure 1.2: SAP HANA capabilities

HANA database design capabilities

The HANA in-memory database adheres to ACID (atomicity, consistency, isolation, and durability) principles, ensuring that a set of database operations, grouped together at transaction level, leaves the database in a consistent state in the event of any unexpected error.

In HANA, data stored in memory is predominantly organized based on columns. Column-store tables can be partitioned and distributed across servers (in a scale-out scenario) to enhance the speed of query processing using parallel processing. In this way, HANA can efficiently deliver queries faster than the aggregate data. This also avoids full-table scans, which can be rather costly.

HANA can host multiple tenants within one database system, where the system's memory and CPU are shared between tenants, while ensuring proper isolation of users and data within each tenant.

The HANA database also supports multi-tier storage. Utilizing SAP HANA's native storage extension (NSE), the database intelligently manages data between memory and persistent layer by identifying and classifying the data based on its temperature, such as hot, warm, and cold storage.

HANA database management capabilities

SAP HANA offers graphical modelling tools that facilitate the creation of intricate business logic and real-time data transformations.

Stored procedures in HANA are employed for building sophisticated logic which can be directly executed in the database.

HANA is equipped with a comprehensive array of administrative tools that cover various platform lifecycle, performance, and management operations, including automation, and more.

HANA ensures high availability and supports a wide range of recovery point objective (RPO) and recovery time objective (RTO) options for disaster recovery. The techniques which enable these capabilities include backup, snapshots, synchronous and asynchronous replication, multitarget system replication, hot standby, auto-restart, and auto-failover.

Application development capabilities

HANA features an integrated application server known as SAP HANA Extended Application Services (XSA), which enables the development of services such as REST (Representational State Transfer) and OData. It facilitates the creation of web-based applications suitable for on-premise, cloud, and mobile devices.

Responsive web applications can also be developed with the help of HTML5 and the JavaScript framework available in HANA. This framework is based on the SAP Fiori UI (user interface) that provides users with a consistent look and feel, irrespective of the device, and screen size, being used.

HANA can be accessed from other application platforms and languages such as JavaScript, Python, R, Java and Go, with the help of client libraries provided by HANA.

Along with application development, HANA also takes care of end-to-end application lifecycle management, starting from packaging applications and transporting them across landscapes to deploying and upgrading them.

HANA includes numerous lightweight application development tools for data modelling and application development both on-premise and in the cloud.

Data integration and quality capabilities

SAP HANA has built-in data consumption options such as ETL (Extract, Transform, Load), streaming data analysis, remote data source access, read data from Hadoop, and so on.

Advanced analytical processing capabilities

SAP HANA is equipped with native in-memory engines which are capable of real-time handling and processing of various types of data. Its advanced analytics features enable functionalities such as full-text searches and advanced fuzzy searches. Additionally, HANA can support spatial processing, conduct analysis using machine learning on data streams, and various other capabilities.

1.2.2 Solutions powered by HANA

Some of the critical applications that are hosted on HANA are:

- **S/4 HANA**—HANA serves as the primary persistence (storage) for robust enterprise suites such as S/4 HANA (SAP for HANA) and SAP Business Suite.
- **SAP Data Intelligence**—this platform seamlessly integrates data orchestration, metadata management, and powerful data pipelines with advanced machine learning capabilities.
- **SAP Data Warehouse Cloud**—this application facilitates the extraction of valuable insights from trusted data by providing a common semantic layer for data integration.

- **SAP Analytics Cloud**—this application is powered by artificial intelligence and machine learning, and enables access to business intelligence, predictive and augmented analytics, and enterprise planning.

1.3 HANA hosting options

HANA can be deployed or installed either on-premise or in various cloud environments such as AWS, Azure, GCP, etc., as shown in Figure 1.3.

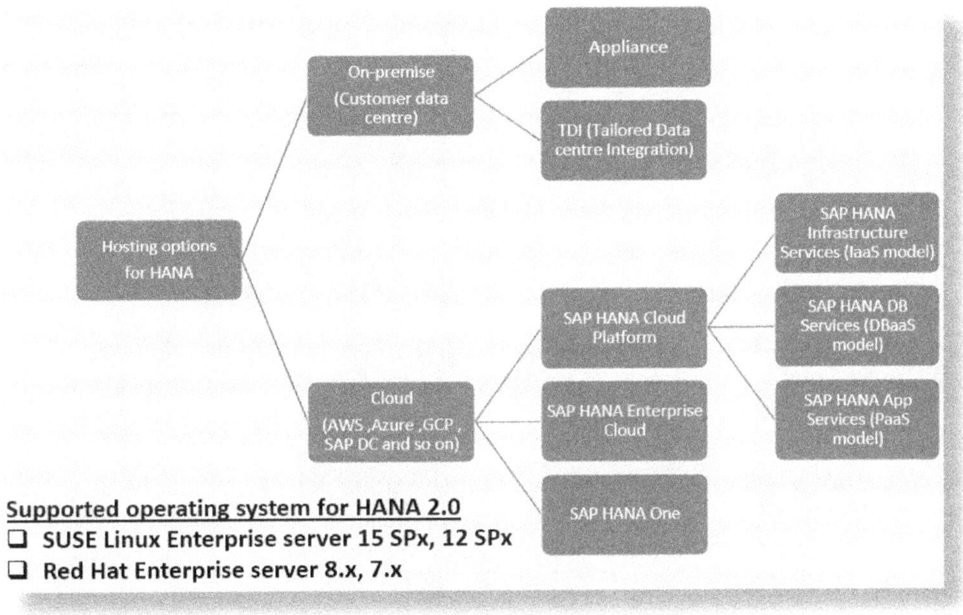

Figure 1.3: Hosting options for HANA Database

1.3.1 On-Premise hosting model

For on-premise hosting, companies have the option to deploy HANA in their own datacenter, known as the *customer-owned data center*, using either an appliance or the SAP HANA Tailored Data Center Integration (TDI) model.

In the appliance model, companies receive a pre-installed HANA system from an SAP-approved vendor hosted on the vendor's hardware. In this model, the vendor offers these appliances in the form of '*t-shirt sizes*' (e.g., small, medium, large), with predefined CPU and RAM configurations. This model therefore offers the fastest implementation due to pre-configured hardware and pre-installed software, eliminating the need for explicit sizing.

Alternatively, the TDI model enables companies to select the required amount of memory, CPU, storage, and server configurations from HANA-certified solutions. This model provides greater flexibility for HANA installation, as the installation can be carried out by the company or a hardware partner with a valid SAP HANA installation certificate (E_HANAINS). It also enables companies to reuse existing infrastructure, thereby potentially reducing costs. However, the chosen server must be certified and listed in the hardware directory. For further information on the hardware directory, see Section 2.4.1.

In addition, SAP also provides the SAP HANA Hardware Configuration Check Tool (HWCCT) to ensure optimal configuration of the HANA database on the chosen hardware.

1.3.2 Cloud hosting model

SAP offers several options in the cloud hosting model:

SAP HANA Cloud Platform

Within *SAP HANA Infrastructure Services*, SAP offers infrastructure for hosting the HANA database via a monthly subscription. However, companies need to possess a valid license to host their database on this infrastructure.

In the *SAP HANA Database services* model, companies can subscribe to a fully featured HANA database, hosted on a public cloud on a monthly subscription basis. Unlike the previous model, this model includes the HANA database license.

With *SAP HANA App Services*, companies are provided with a HANA Platform-as-a-Service (PaaS) model in the cloud, available on a monthly subscription basis, and inclusive of licenses.

SAP HANA Enterprise Cloud (HEC)

SAP HEC is a premium private cloud solution for HANA, offering infrastructure and managed services via a monthly subscription model. The HANA license is not included in this subscription. Instead, SAP enables its customers to either reuse their existing license under the Bring Your Own License (BYOL) model, or to purchase a new one.

SAP HANA One

SAP HANA One delivers a full-featured HANA database on a public cloud infrastructure, with a license available on an hourly subscription basis.

1.4 Understanding the HANA database

The HANA database revolves around the following key concepts:

- Column-store and row-store tables
- Delta merges and memory management
- Savepoints

1.4.1 Row-store tables and column-store tables

Row-store and *column-store* represent two distinct methods of organizing table cells in contiguous memory locations. In contrast to conventional databases that adopt a row-based model for storing table cells, HANA predominantly employs a column-store for its table content. While most tables in HANA are column-store tables, some continue to be row-store tables. As an HTAP database, HANA relies on both types of tables for optimal functionality.

Row-store and column-store tables in HANA

In the HANA database memory, row-store tables are organized by rows, whereas column-store tables are organized by columns. Table 1.1 contains sample rows of a database table which is used to demonstrate the difference between row store and column store.

Country code	Product	Sales
IND	A	1000
FR	A	900
GE	B	1000
GE	A	900

Table 1.1: Sample table and its data

Figure 1.4 illustrates this table and its organization in HANA's memory when saved as table type 'row-store' versus table type 'column-store'.

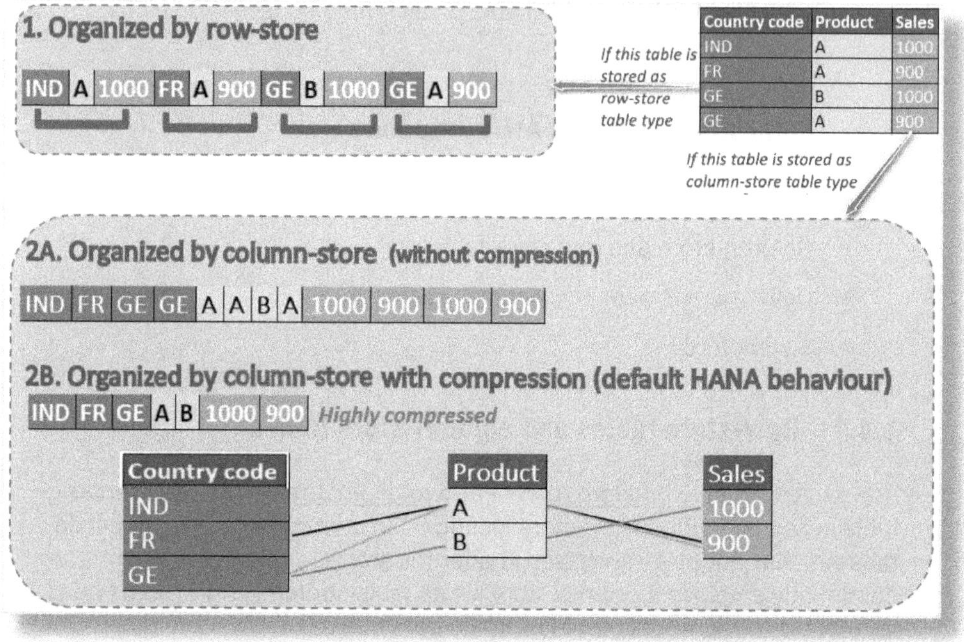

Figure 1.4: Table organization—row store versus column store

If the data from Table 1.1 is stored as table type 'column-store', the table contents are stored in a compressed format in memory, as depicted in part 2B in Figure 1.4 . When the same data is stored as table type 'row-store', there is no compression, as depicted in part 2A in Figure 1.4.

Compression in HANA is achieved by eliminating duplicate values in memory for column-store tables. In the example shown, HANA avoids storing duplicate values between record sets and instead uses pointers to reference a record set. This means that column values duplicated across different record sets are stored only once, with pointers distinguishing each of the record sets. This approach significantly reduces the overall memory footprint. However, for row-store tables, duplicate values between record sets are not taken into consideration and are stored individually in memory, thus preventing any possible compression.

Read operations on row-store and column-store tables

Figure 1.5 demonstrates how HANA reads the sample table data in memory, when created as a row-store table versus a column-store table.

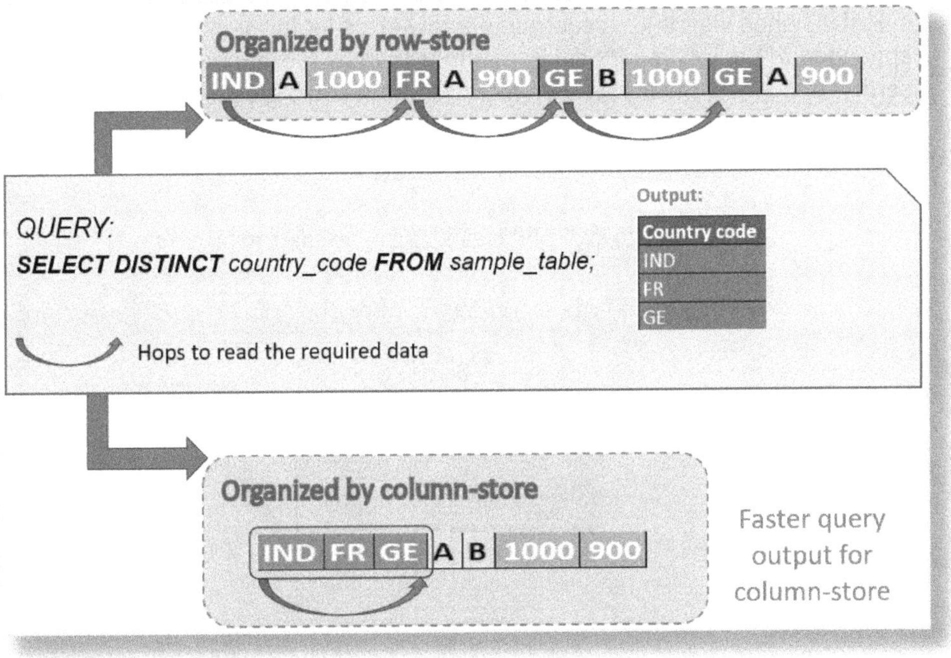

Figure 1.5: Reading a row-store table versus a column-store table

For a row-store table, the sequence and number of steps required to execute the query `SELECT DISTINCT country_code FROM sample_table;` are significantly higher compared to a column-store table. While a column-store table can achieve the desired result by reading adjacent pages in memory, a row-store table must navigate between pages to achieve the same outcome, as shown in Figure 1.5.

! Operation in HANA

Figure 1.5, Figure 1.6 and Figure 1.7 are for illustrative purposes only and do not depict the complete sequence of operations in HANA. For more detailed information refer to Section 1.4.2 and 4.1.5.

Inserts in row-store and column-store tables

Insert operations in column-store tables are complex and costly compared to row-store tables, where they are more straightforward.

In HANA, when inserting a record into a row-store table, the pointer can be appended to the last record set in memory, thereby facilitating a simple insertion of the new record set. Figure 1.6 illustrates this process.

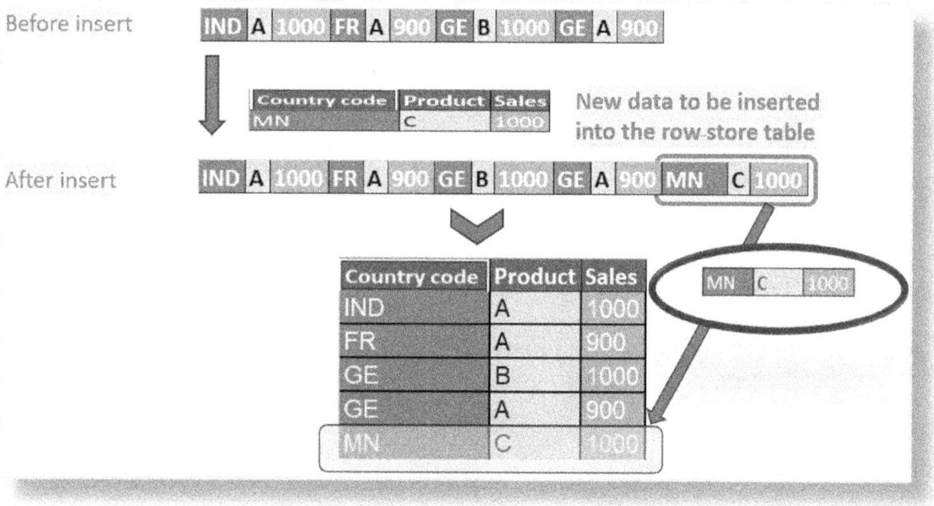

Figure 1.6: Row-store table insert operation

However, inserting a record into a column-store table is more challenging due to the highly compressed nature of this table type in HANA memory. Unlike a row-store table, a simple insert is not possible. To successfully perform an insert, the table must first be decompressed, and the required data must be inserted, before proceeding with recompression, as shown in Figure 1.7.

Nevertheless, HANA efficiently manages inserts into column-store tables by employing the concepts of *delta merge* and *delta memory area*. For more in-depth understanding of delta merge operations, refer to Section 1.4.2.

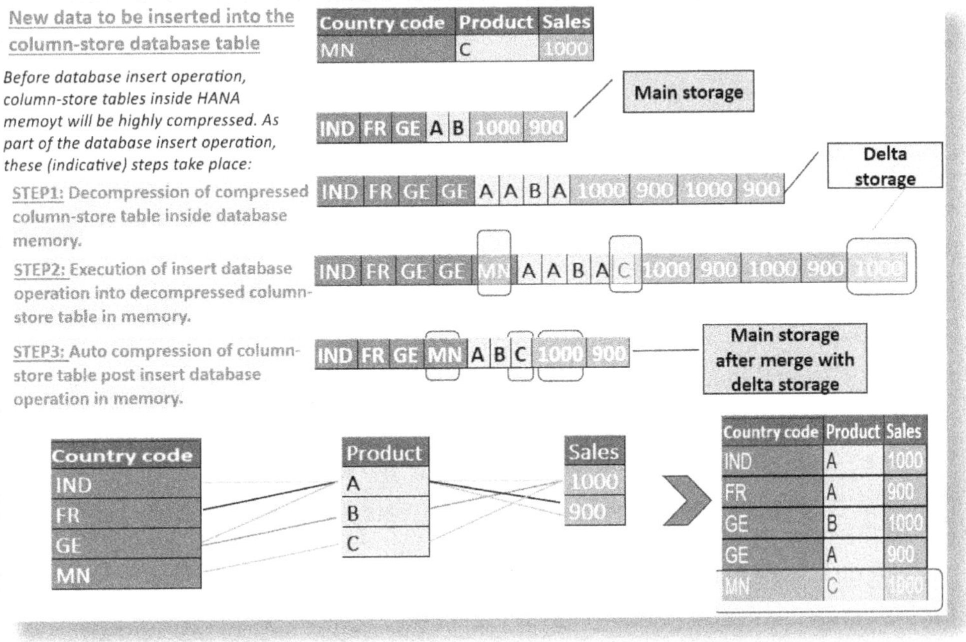

Figure 1.7: Complex insert operation in column-store tables

Relationship between HANA startup sequence and row-store tables

HANA, as an in-memory database, holds frequently used column-store tables in memory. However, row-store tables always reside in memory regardless of their usage. Row-store tables are loaded into memory as part of the startup procedure and remain there until the HANA database is shut down. Consequently, the number of row-store tables impacts the HANA startup duration, because loading all the row-store tables into memory marks the successful startup of the HANA database.

In the case of a column-store table, once the database is started, HANA reloads the tables that were in memory at the time of the last shutdown. Any additional tables required later, during the database operation, are loaded into memory in an on-demand basis from the persistence layer. In addition, these column-store tables might be evicted from memory, based on the least recently used (LRU) algorithm, when more memory is needed to load a different column-store table into memory.

Use cases for row-store and column store tables

While HANA supports both row-store and column-store table types, developers and administrators must carefully choose between them, based on specific needs. Row-store tables are advantageous in the following scenarios:

- The application processes individual records, performing frequent selects or updates on a single record.
- The application needs access to the entire data set (complete record).
- The table columns mainly contain distinct values, leading to inefficient compression.
- Operations such as aggregations and fast searches are not needed.
- The tables are small (such as configuration tables) with few rows.

Column-store tables are more suitable for the following scenarios:

- Computations focus on individual, or a limited number of, columns.
- Search operations concentrate on only a few columns.
- Tables have a large number of columns.
- Tables undergo extensive operations such as aggregation and scanning, involving both rows and columns.
- Tables have a limited number of distinct values, which allows for efficient data compression.

1.4.2 Concept of delta merge for column-store tables

As shown in Figure 1.7, writing to a column-store table can be challenging due to its highly compressed nature. To overcome this challenge, HANA utilizes column-store segments in its memory in order to manage these tables. This in-memory segment consists of two main components—main storage and delta storage—which together provide optimized read operations and efficient write operations.

Whenever a column-store table is modified, HANA uses its main storage and delta storage for a successful execution of a write operation in the following sequence:

1. The column-store table is either partially loaded (for partitioned tables) or fully loaded into the main memory, forming the main storage of the column-store table.
2. When a write operation begins, the contents of the main storage are copied to the delta storage, where the data is uncompressed to facilitate an efficient write database operation.
3. Write operations are performed in the delta storage.
4. Because HANA is an ACID-compliant database, all read operations for that table during this period are served by both the main storage and delta storage. This ensures that the application reads only consistent, committed data for the table. The in-memory computing engine (IMCE) uses multi-version concurrency control (MVCC) to maintain read consistency. See Figure 4.6.
5. Once the write operation is complete, the table's delta storage is merged back into the table's main storage. This process of merging delta storage into the main storage of a column-store table is referred to as a *delta merge* (see Figure 1.8).
6. After the delta merge, the updated table contents are persisted to disk.

A delta merge is an operation within the HANA database memory where the delta storage, which holds a column-store table's newly modified data, is merged back into the table's main storage within HANA memory, as shown in Figure 1.8.

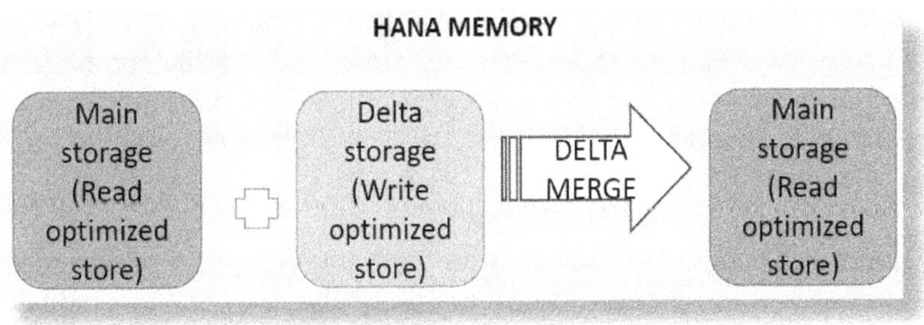

Figure 1.8: Column-store table delta merge

Table 1.2 summarizes the high-level differences between HANA database memory's main storage and delta storage.

Main storage	Delta storage
▶ Contains the main part of the table data. ▶ Table data here is fully compressed. ▶ This storage in memory is read optimized. ▶ Read operations on the table happens from both the main storage (actual data) and also from the delta storage (modified data). See Figure 1.8. ▶ Write operations cannot be executed in this part of main storage.	▶ Write operations happen only in this storage. ▶ Only has basic compression. ▶ This storage in memory is write optimized

Table 1.2: Main storage versus delta storage in HANA memory

! Delta merge for column-store tables

The concept of delta merge applies exclusively to column-store tables and not to row-store tables.

1.4.3 HANA persistence layer

HANA operates as an in-memory database, with memory capacity sufficient to accommodate the entire database. However, data is not solely stored in RAM; it is also durably persisted at the operating system level in data volumes and log volumes. Given that memory is a volatile component (dynamic RAM), its contents are erased when the HANA database is shut down. Therefore, a persistent layer or storage medium is essential to handle mission-critical workloads.

HANA stores the complete data dump to the data volume on the storage media. However, when a commit operation is executed for the modified data in memory, it triggers the creation of a redo log, which is then stored in the log volume as log segments. The modified data in memory is automatically transferred or flushed into the data volume at periodic intervals (the default interval value is five minutes)—this is referred to as a *savepoint* operation.

Persistence into data and log volumes

Every database has two primary folder structures for persistence:

- *Log volume*—stores transaction logs that record changes made to the data.
- *Data volume*—holds the actual database content, such as tables, indexes, and other data structures.

Changes made by an end-user are initially captured as log segments in the log volume and are then persisted from memory to the data volume using a savepoint operation.

When a data change is committed in HANA, a log segment is created and must be stored in the log volume in order for the corresponding database operation to succeed. In the case of a failure, the changes are reverted, and the user is notified to retry. A transaction is successful only when the corresponding log segment reaches the log volume—this is a synchronous process. The end-user must wait for a log segment creation and storage before proceeding with the next operation.

These changes must now also be persisted into the data volume, but not immediately, as is the case with a log volume. For this purpose, HANA uses the concept of a *savepoint*. A savepoint is an automatic, regular process that flushes all data changes from HANA memory to the data volume at configurable intervals—the default interval is five minutes. If this write operation from memory to data volume fails, it can be retried at the next savepoint without marking the corresponding transaction or database operation as a failure. Since the corresponding user/application does not need to wait for a successful savepoint before proceeding with the next transaction, this is considered *asynchronous* from an end-user/application perspective. Figure 1.9 illustrates these commit operations at the persistence layer.

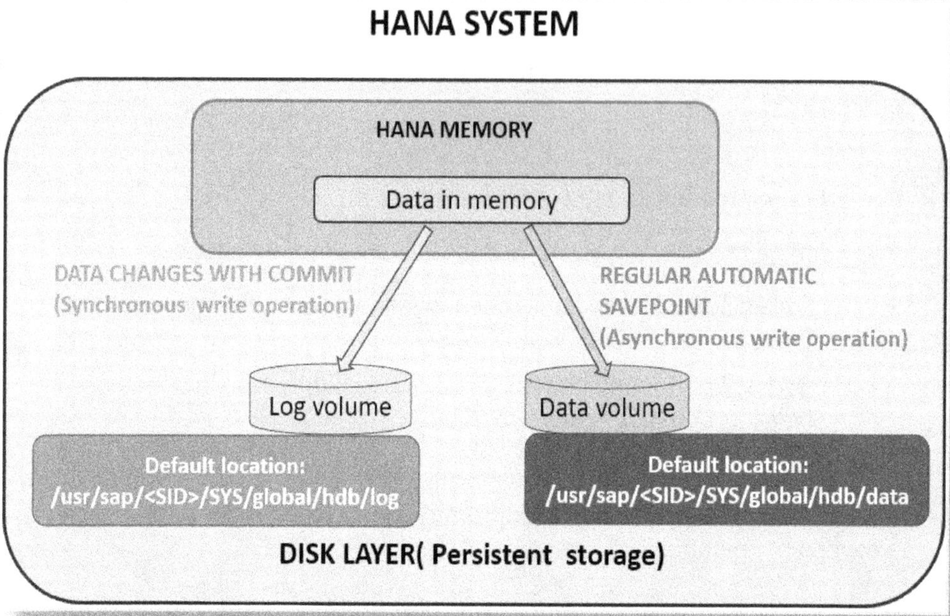

Figure 1.9: HANA database persistence layer

Consider a scenario where a table resides in memory. When a DDL (Data Definition Language—modify, update, or delete a table data column) or DML (Data Manipulation Language—insert, delete, or append table data) operation is performed on the table, the following process occurs before this change is reflected in the data volume of the storage layer:

1. The table is loaded into memory from the storage layer if not already present in the memory (lazy loading of column-store table).
2. An application or an end user executes a data insert into the table.
3. After making changes at memory level, a commit operation is triggered on that table:
   - A redo log segment is generated, containing the data changes for that table (known as *redo logs*).
   - This log segment is saved to the log volume in the persistence layer.
   - The application or user is notified of the successful completion of the above step.

! Log segments

If a log segment fails to reach the log volumes, HANA initiates the rollback of changes, marks the commit operation as unsuccessful, and rolls back the entire transaction. Consequently, the process of flushing data changes from memory to the log segment (in log volume) is a synchronous operation.

4. At regular intervals, as per the configured value (configuration parameter name '*savepoint_interval_s*'), the HANA database initiates an automatic savepoint, leading to the following sequence of operations:

    - Data changes from the memory are flushed into the data volume at the file system layer (persistence).

! Data segment

The transfer of data changes from memory to the data volume is an asynchronous operation. If this data transfer fails, the flush operation is retried during the next auto-triggered savepoint. Since neither the application nor the user need to wait for this task to complete or for the transaction to be marked as successful, writing data changes to the data volume is considered asynchronous.

- Once the changes reach the data volume from the memory, the corresponding data changes that were recorded as a log segment earlier (in log volume) are no longer necessary.
- This log segment is cyclically overwritten with or without executing the log backup, depending on the value of configuration parameter *log_mode*. (See Section 6.1.1 for further details).

! HANA—redo and undo logs

For transactions that have not reached the commit state, HANA records an undo log. These logs are stored in the data volume and help HANA maintain database consistency by undoing the uncommitted changes in the case of a failure. While redo logs (stored in the log volume) are used to replay committed transactions to bring the database to its most recent consistent state, undo logs revert any uncommitted changes during failures. Therefore, both redo and undo logs play a critical role in maintaining database consistency and ensuring the ACID properties.

HANA database after restart or crash

Figure 1.10 illustrates the state of a database both before and after a crash.

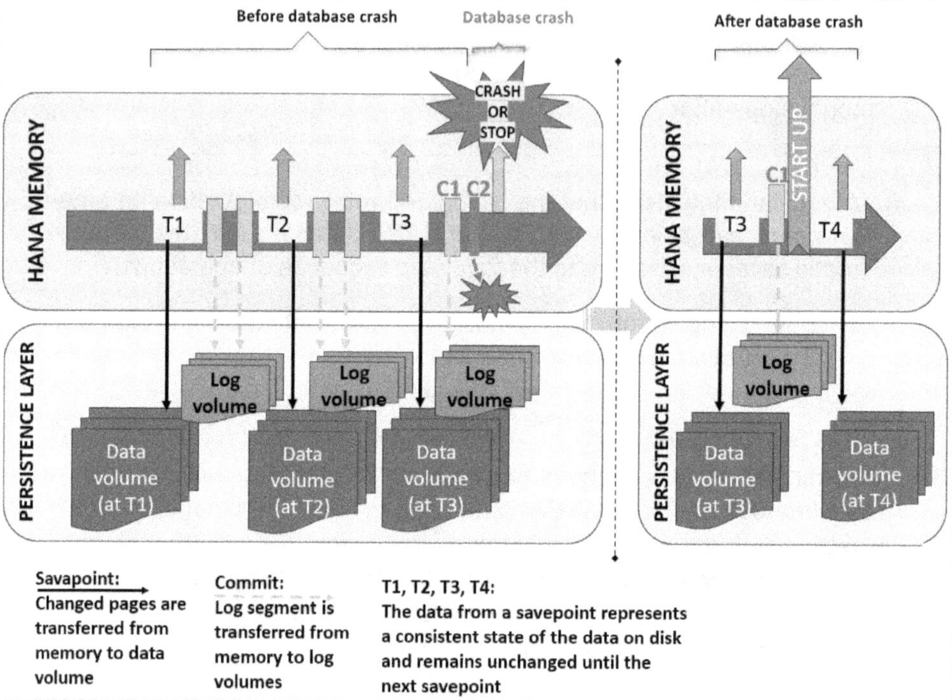

Figure 1.10: HANA database—consistency

In this representation, T1, T2, and T3 indicate savepoints, and C1 and C2 denote application/user changes. Prior to the crash, the database was operating normally, with the last savepoint triggered at T3, ensuring consistency of the data volume state. Subsequently, changes C1 and C2 were made before reaching the next savepoint. Change C1 was successfully committed, resulting in the log segment reaching the log volume, but the database crashed before committing the transactional change at C2.

When a HANA database crashes or shuts down, the following sequence of steps is executed automatically by the database as part of the subsequent startup:

1. Following the database crash, transactions that failed to write the redo log segment into the log volume will be lost.

2. The database initiates the startup process with the last consistent state reached at T3 and applies the one redo log segment holding change

C1, which is present in the log volume. However, change C2 is lost since there is no redo log segment in the log volume, leading to their rollback using the undo log.

3. Immediately upon the start of the HANA database, a save point is automatically triggered, bringing the data volume to a consistent state that includes all the data committed up to C1.

Shadow paging

If a HANA database crashes during an on-going savepoint operation, HANA can still be restored from the previous savepoint and redo logs. This is mainly because a HANA write operation writes to a new physical page to persist a changed logical page, and the physical page created during the previous savepoint is kept undisturbed as a shadow page until the next successful savepoint operation. This concept of having two physical pages for one logical page is known as *shadow paging*.

With shadow paging, physical disk pages written by the last savepoint are not overwritten until the successful completion of the next savepoint. Hence, a high number of shadow pages can increase the persistence (disk) size unexpectedly. The possible reasons for such cases might be due to long-running savepoints, low savepoint frequency, mass changes, or table optimizations of large tables.

1.5 Server components

HANA databases are generally identified by SID (system identifier), and consist of a system database (SystemDB) and zero or more tenant databases. These tenant databases are multiple isolated databases that can run on one SAP HANA system. The SID can be hosted on a single server or multiple servers, respectively known as *scale-up* or *scale-out* scenarios.

In a HANA database, the SystemDB and tenant databases host different sets of default and optional server components, as illustrated in Figure 1.11.

Some server components, such as the index server and XS engine, are exclusively for tenant databases; others, such as the nameserver and preprocessor, are managed by the SystemDB and are shared among the tenant databases.

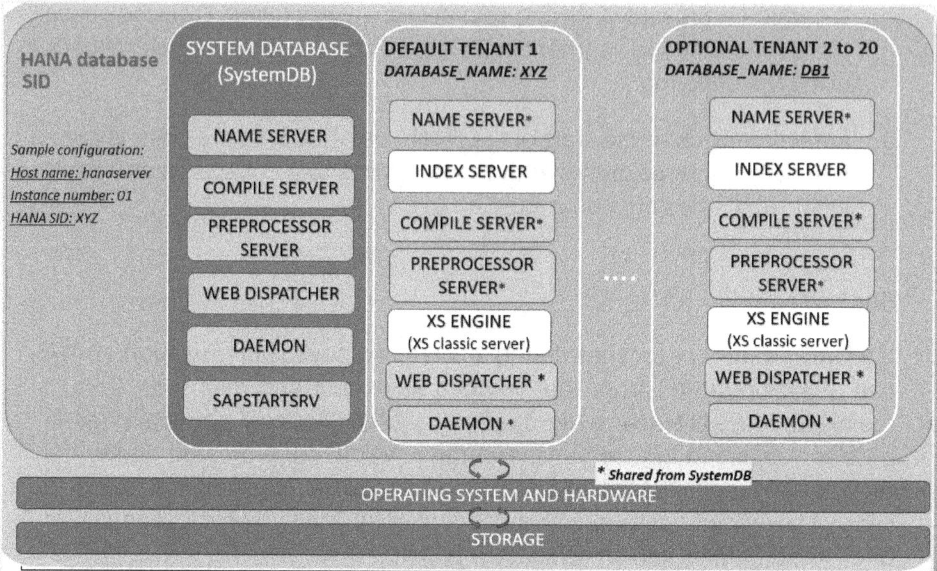

Indicative configuration

Description	SystemDB	Default tenant	Optional tenant
HANA SID	XYZ	XYZ	XYZ
Host name	hanaserver	hanaserver	hanaserver
HANA instance number:	01	01	01
SQL port	3nn03 <nn=01>	3nn15 <nn=01>	3nn41 <nn=01>

Figure 1.11: HANA database components

Figure 1.11 illustrates a multi-tenant HANA database with SID *XYZ* and instance number *01* hosted on the server *hanaserver*. This system includes one SystemDB and a default tenant database with database name *XYZ*. There is another tenant database with database name *DB1*, hosted on the same HANA SID (*XYZ*).

! SystemDB services versus tenant database services

In Figure 1.11, note the components marked with an asterisk (*) in the tenant databases—these components are originally owned by the SystemDB and are shared across the tenant databases.

The core server components of a HANA database include the nameserver, index server, compile server, preprocessor server, SAP web dispatcher, and SAP start service. There are also optional servers such as the script server, document store server, XS classic server (XS engine), and XS advanced runtime. For more information, refer to Section 1.5.3.

> **Name server and index server**
>
> A *name server* maintains the HANA system's landscape information.
>
> An *index server* stores data and performs all the database operations.

1.5.1 SystemDB

SystemDB is a mandatory component created during the installation of the HANA database. It is primarily used for centralized administration of the HANA system and contains the necessary data and users for performing administrative tasks. While it holds the data required for tenant administration and monitoring, it does not contain tenant database topology information. *Database topology* refers to details about the tables and their partitions within a database. Therefore, the SystemDB is unaware of tenant database objects such as tables, procedures, and indexes.

Some key features of the SystemDB are as follows:

- Each HANA database system can have only one SystemDB.
- Administrative tasks performed in the SystemDB can apply to the entire system, including tenants, or are specific to a particular tenant.
- The SystemDB does not provide full SQL support; a full-featured HANA database is only available in a tenant database.
- The SystemDB can only access or read monitoring data from tenant databases. Cross-database access to actual data between the SystemDB and tenant databases is not possible.

> **Cross database access**
>
> *Cross database access* means accessing the data of one database from another database.

- From the SystemDB, global configurations can be set that apply across all tenants. However, tenant-specific configurations cannot be set from the SystemDB; only global settings are allowed.
- The SystemDB is permanently assigned to the host server where it was originally installed and cannot be relocated to a different host.

1.5.2 Tenant database

SAP HANA tenant databases (a tenant database is also known as *TenantDB*) represent the basis for multi-tenancy in SAP HANA. This concept is based on SAP HANA with one SID, which contains one SystemDB and zero to 20 tenant databases. All these tenant databases share the same installation of the database software and the underlying operating system. However, each tenant database is self-contained and fully isolated, featuring its own set of database users, repositories, database catalogs, persistence, backups, traces, and logs.

Tenant databases were previously known as MDCs (multitenant database containers). MDC is now referred to as *multiple database container* and has been the only default operation mode for HANA databases since HANA 2.0 SP01. Prior to this, the default operation mode for the HANA database was SDC (*single database container*). For more details, refer to Section 2.1.1. See also SAP Note 2423367—"Multitenant database containers will become the standard and only operation mode".

> **! Cross-database access**
>
> While cross-database access from the SystemDB to tenant databases is not possible, it is permitted between tenant databases if enabled.

1.5.3 Server components of the SAP HANA database

In a HANA database installation, the SystemDB and tenant databases host different combinations of server components, such as the index server, the name server, the preprocessor, and more (See Figure 1.11). One of the crucial server components is the index server, which houses the actual data store and the necessary engine for data processing. This is a mandatory server component of the tenant database and operates within each tenant database. Another critical component is the name server, which stores landscape information. The name server operates from the SystemDB and contains the landscape information for itself and the tenant databases.

> **SystemDB and index server**
>
> The SystemDB does not have an index server component. Instead, its name server takes on the role of the index server and stores the SystemDB's landscape information.

Core server components of HANA

Table 1.3 outlines the core server components of the HANA database along with its OS level process name, service name, persistence layer, etc.

Core server component	OS process	Service name	Persist data	Runs on
Name server	hdbnameserver	nameserver	Yes	SystemDB
Index server	hdbindexserver	indexserver	Yes	Tenant database
Compile server	hdbcompileserver	compile-server	No	SystemDB
Preprocessor server	hdbpreprocessor	prepro-cessor	No	SystemDB
SAP web dispatcher	hdbwebdispatcher	webdis-patcher	No	SystemDB
SAP start service	sapstartsrv	sapstartsrv	No	Operating system level

Table 1.3: List of HANA database core server components

Persistence layer

The file system layer or storage layer is also known as the persistence layer. *Yes* in the 'Persist data' column in Table 1.3 refers to the presence of a dedicated folder structure for the corresponding database services.

Each of these services has its own responsibilities within a HANA database, as listed below:

- **Name server**—only runs on the SystemDB. It contains information about the topology of the SAP HANA system, such as the number of tenant databases. It does not have any information on the location of tenant database tables, table partitions, and so on. The name server persists data and has its own folder structure in the persistence layer.
- **Index server**—runs in every tenant database. It contains the actual data stores and the engines for processing the data. The index server is not present in the SystemDB, as this role is taken over by the name server of the SystemDB itself. This service persists data and has its own folder structure in the persistence layer.

- **Compile server**—performs the compilation of stored procedures and programs. It runs on every host associated with a HANA system. It does not persist data and, therefore, does not have a folder structure in the persistence layer. It runs in the SystemDB and serves all tenant databases.
- **Preprocessor server**—is used by the index server to analyze text data and extract the information on which the text search capabilities are based. It does not persist data and, hence, does not have a folder structure in the persistence layer. It runs in the SystemDB and serves all tenant databases.
- **SAP web dispatcher**—processes inbound HTTP and HTTPS connections to XS classic services. This does not persist data and therefore does not own a folder structure in the persistence layer. It runs in the SystemDB and serves all tenant databases.
- **SAP start service**—is responsible for starting and stopping the other services in the correct order. It also monitors their runtime state.

OS—operating system

OS is an abbreviation for *operating system*, or host server.

Optional server components

The optional server components for SAP HANA are outlined in Table 1.4.

Optional server components	Description
Script server	OS process: hdbscriptserver Service name: Scriptserver The script server is used to execute C++ application function libraries.
Document store server	OS process: hdbdocstore Service name: Docstore This document store enables native operations on JSON documents, and joins are possible with other columns or row-store tables.

Optional server components	Description
XS Advanced runtime (XSA)	OS process 1: hdbxscontroller Service name 1: xscontroller OS process 2: hdbxsexeagent Service name 2: xsexeagent OS process 3: hdixsuaaserver Service name 3: hdixsuaaserver SAP HANA provides a run-time environment for web-based application development—SAP HANA extended application services, advanced model (XS advanced).
SAP HANA Deployment Infrastructure (HDI) server	OS process: hdbdiserver Service name: diserver SAP HANA Deployment Infrastructure (HDI) server handles the deployment of design-time artifacts into the SAP HANA database.
XS classic server	OS process: hdbxsengine Service name: xsengine SAP HANA Extended Application Services, classic model (XS, classic) is the application server for native SAP HANA-based web applications. This enables developers to write and run SAP HANA-based applications without the need to run an additional application server. It is installed with the SAP HANA database and can run as a separate server process or embedded within the index server. SAP HANA XS, classic is deprecated as of SAP HANA 2.0 SPS 02. For further information, refer to SAP Note 2465027—"Deprecation of SAP HANA extended application services, classic model and SAP HANA Repository".
Extended store server	OS process: hdbesserver Service name: esserver This provides a high-performance, disk-based column-store for very big data up to peta byte and is part of SAP HANA dynamic tiering.

Optional server components	Description
Data provisioning server	OS process: hdbdpserver Service name: dpserver This is part of SAP HANA smart data integration (SDI), and provides capabilities such as data provisioning in real time and batch mode, real-time data transformations, data quality functions, adapters for various types of remote sources, and so on.
Streaming cluster	OS process: hdbstreamingserver Service name: streamingserver Streaming analytics extends SAP HANA with SAP Event Stream Processor capabilities for consuming data streams and complex event processing, and is part of SAP HANA streaming analytics.
Accelerator for SAP ASE	OS process: hdbetsserver Service name: etsserver This provides SAP Adaptive Server Enterprise (ASE) users with the ability to use SAP HANA on SAP ASE data for real-time analytics and is part SAP HANA accelerator.

Table 1.4: HANA database optional server components

These optional components are not included by default in the standard HANA database installation and need to be installed or enabled specifically for use. Certain servers, such as XS advanced runtime, also have the capability to be hosted on a dedicated server or alongside other HANA components.

The SAP HANA XS Advanced (XSA) server is a crucial optional server that offers a runtime environment for application development on HANA. Upon installation in HANA, the SystemDB gains access to platform services and the ability to execute applications. Table 1.5 offers a high-level overview of the XS Advanced services.

Server component	Description
SAP HANA XS Controller	OS process: hdbxscontroller Service name: xscontroller This service acts as a cockpit for the central management of components and applications running on SAP HANA XS Advanced. It provides end-to-end details on the applications that are deployed and/or running, and persists the configuration and status of these applications in the database. It also manages the platform router instance which is used by an SAP web dispatcher instance, exposing the public endpoint for the entire system.
SAP HANA XS Execution Agent	OS process: hdbxsexeagent Service name: xsexecagent The execution agent is responsible for managing processes such as starting, keeping alive, and stopping.
SAP HANA XS User Authentication and Authorization (UAA)	OS process: hdixsuaaserver Service name: hdixsuaaserver The UAA service manages user logon and logoff requests in SAP HANA XS advanced.

Table 1.5: SAP HANA XS Advanced services

1.5.4 Administration of tenant databases

Administration tasks for tenant databases can be executed either from the SystemDB or directly in the tenant database. Not all the administration tasks that can be carried out from the SystemDB are possible from a tenant database, and vice versa.

Let's look at some examples of administration tasks that can be performed from the SystemDB:

- Starting and stopping the whole system, including SystemDB and all the tenant databases.
- Monitoring the entire system.
- Configuring parameters in configuration (*ini) files at system level.

- Setting up and configuring tenant databases; for example:
  - Creating and dropping tenant databases
  - Disabling features on tenant databases
  - Configuring system-specific and database-specific parameters in configuration (*ini) files
  - Scaling out tenant databases by adding services
- Backing up tenant databases.
- Recovering tenant databases.

Examples of administration tasks that can be performed directly on a tenant database and that are specific to that respective tenant database include:

- Monitoring the database.
- Provisioning database users.
- Creating and deleting schemas, tables, and indexes in the database.
- Backing up the database.
- Configuring database-specific parameters in configuration (*ini) files.

1.6 Deployment options

The SAP HANA database can be installed on one or more servers and is capable of hosting multiple tenant databases within a single HANA database installation. The available deployment options for HANA are outlined in the following sections.

1.6.1 HANA on IaaS/virtualized platform/physical server

HANA on IaaS server in public cloud

The HANA database can be deployed on an Infrastructure as a Service (IaaS) setup on public clouds such as AWS, Azure, GCP, etc. Each public cloud platform offers a set of certified machines suitable for hosting the HANA database. Additional details can be found in SAP Notes provided by the cloud providers.

For AWS (Amazon web service), refer to the following:

- SAP Note 1656250–"SAP on AWS: Support prerequisites"
- SAP Note 1656099–"SAP Applications on AWS: Supported DB/OS and AWS EC2 products"

For Microsoft Azure, refer to the following:

- SAP Note 2015553–"SAP on Microsoft Azure: Support prerequisites"
- SAP Note 1928533–"SAP Applications on Microsoft Azure: Supported Products and Azure VM types"

For Google cloud (GCP), refer to the following:

- SAP Note 2456406–"SAP on Google Cloud Platform: Support prerequisites"
- SAP Note 2456432–"SAP Applications on Google Cloud: Supported Products and Google Cloud machine types"
- SAP Note 3000343–"SAP Applications on Google Cloud: Supported Products on Google Cloud Bare Metal Solution"

For additional information, refer to SAP Note 1380654–"SAP support in IaaS environments".

HANA on virtualized platforms

Previously, SAP HANA was approved to be hosted only on physical servers. However, with recent technological advancements, the SAP HANA database can now be hosted on virtualized platforms, subject to certain restrictions at the hypervisor layer. Figure 1.12 represents HANA databases on virtualized platforms.

Platforms where HANA can be hosted include VMware vSphere, Hitachi LPAR, Huawei FusionSphere, Red Hat Enterprise Virtualization (RHV), SUSE Linux Enterprise Hypervisor, and IBM PowerVM. For more information, refer to the following:

- SAP Note 1788665–"SAP HANA Support for virtualized/partitioned (multi-tenant) environments"
- SAP Note 2230704–"SAP HANA on IBM Power Systems with multiple - LPARs per physical host"

- SAP Note 2024433—"Multiple SAP HANA VMs on VMware vSphere in production on vSphere 5.5"

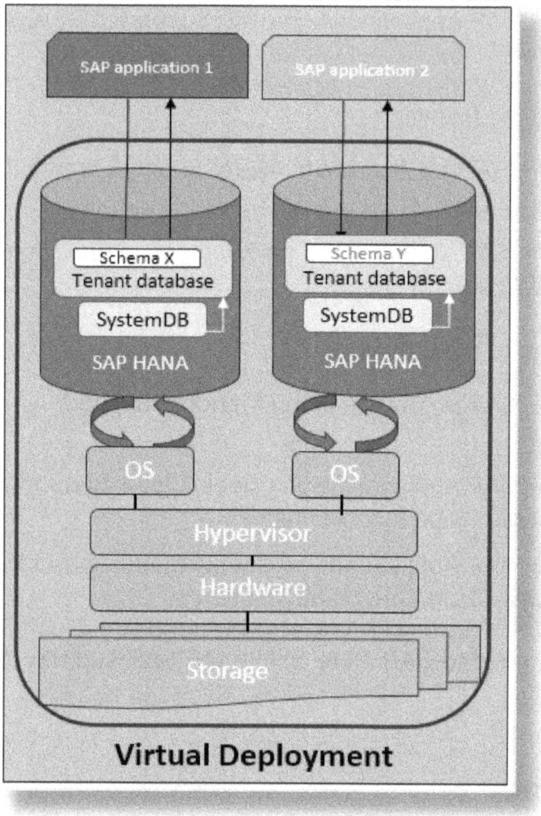

Figure 1.12: HANA virtual deployment

HANA on physical servers

The list of certified and supported SAP HANA physical servers can be found in the "Certified and Supported SAP HANA® Hardware Directory", at *https://www.sap.com/dmc/exp/2014-09-02-hana-hardware/enEN/index.html.*

1.6.2 SCOS, MCOD, MCOS deployment options

HANA database deployment can be classified based on the number of components implemented in one HANA system, as shown in Figure 1.13.

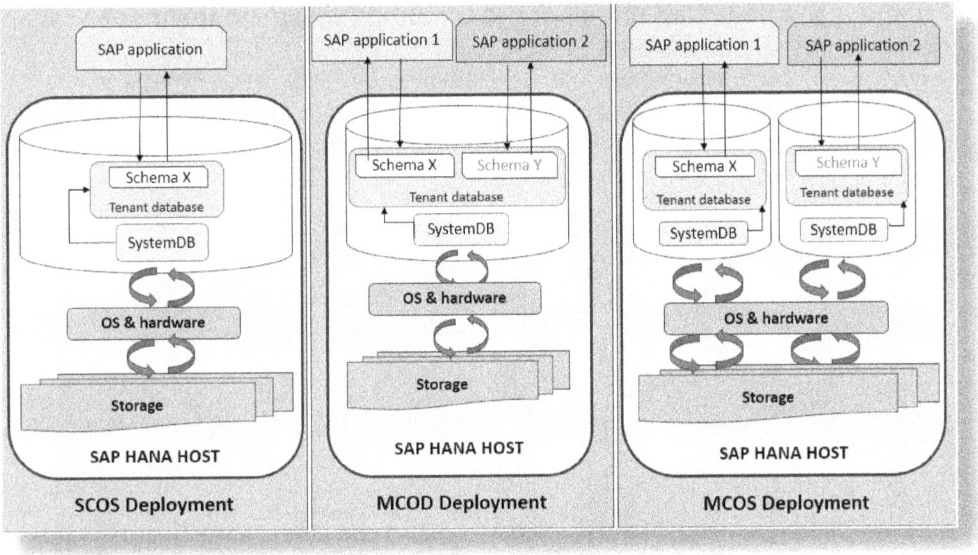

Figure 1.13: SCOS, MCOD and MCOS deployment options

SCOS (Single Component on One System) is a straightforward installation of a HANA database and is applicable for use in all scenarios. In this setup, an SAP HANA installation hosts a single application that operates within one schema.

MCOD (Multiple Components on One Database) refers to the installation of multiple applications or components on a single HANA system, each with its own dedicated schema. These applications share the underlying operating system and hardware resources from a single host server. This setup is limited to specific production scenarios that run packaged. For the list of supported production applications, refer to SAP Note 1661202—"Support multiple applications one SAP HANA database / tenant DB".

MCOS (Multiple Components on One System) enables multiple SAP HANA systems (SIDs) to run on a single SAP HANA host server. This configuration is supported for production systems and is limited to single host or scale-up scenarios. However, users should be aware of potential performance impacts due to shared computing resources (CPU, memory, I/O (input/output), etc.). This setup requires careful workload management in order to control memory allocation and CPU core usage for optimal performance. It provides an alternative to running multiple HANA SIDs on a virtual machine hosted on a single underlying hardware.

1.6.3 Single tenant and multiple tenant database deployment

HANA database deployment can be classified as single tenant database deployment or multiple tenant database deployment, depending on the number of tenants running on a single HANA database system, as illustrated in Figure 1.14.

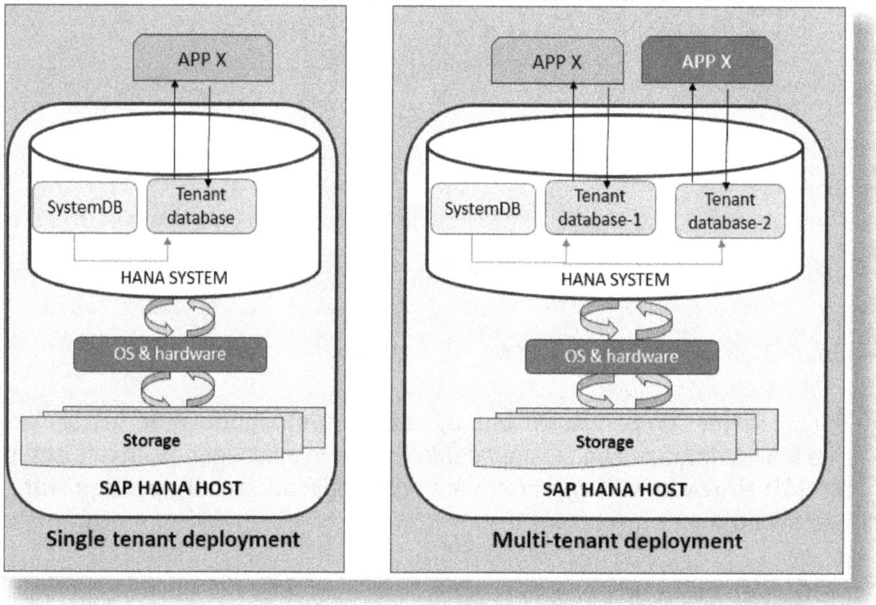

Figure 1.14: Single tenant and multiple tenant database deployment

Single tenant database deployment involves installing one SAP HANA database, with only one tenant, on one or more hosts.

! System database

A SystemDB cannot be distributed across multiple hosts; a tenant database can.

A *multiple tenant (multi-tenant) database* includes multiple tenants within a single SAP HANA database installation. It is a better alternative to MCOS deployment because each schema can be hosted on separate, well-isolated tenant databases.

! Production deployment

Single tenant and multi-tenant database options are supported for production deployments. These can be hosted on a single host or distributed across multiple hosts.

1.6.4 Single host deployment and multiple host deployment

HANA database deployment can also be classified as either single host deployment or multiple host deployment, depending on the number of hosts per database, as shown in Figure 1.15.

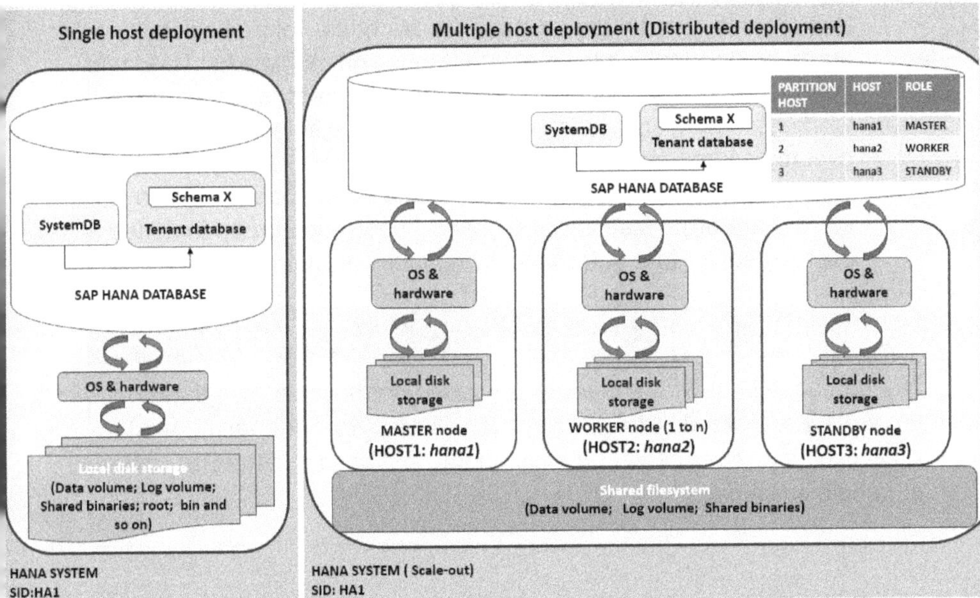

Figure 1.15: Single host and multiple host deployment

Single host (single node) deployment also known as *scale-up deployment* involves installing a HANA system on a single server. In this setup, if the HANA database needs additional memory, the server's memory can be increased or *scaled up* to the server's maximum capacity. As a result, the memory available for the HANA database in this configuration is limited by the hardware constraints of the underlying physical server.

Multiple host deployment (also known as distributed deployment and scale-out deployment) involves installing a HANA system with one SID on more than one host server (see Figure 1.15).

Use cases for this type of deployment focus on scalability and availability:

- *Scale-out scenarios* are used to address memory or RAM requirements that exceed the hardware limits of a physical server. In such cases, a new host can be added to the existing HANA database to increase CPU and RAM availability for the HANA SID. This enables the database to distribute its load across multiple servers by partitioning and assigning parts of tables to different index servers. This enhances parallel processing and query performance.
- *High availability and failover scenarios* are employed in environments where continuous availability is critical. High availability is achieved by installing the HANA database on multiple hosts. In this configuration, different hosts serve specific roles, such as master, worker, standby, and slave. If one server fails, a standby server takes over to ensure uninterrupted availability for connected applications. Additionally, HANA supports host groups, where hosts within a single SID are organized into multiple groups—each group includes a standby server that automatically replaces any unresponsive host.

Standby host role

The database host with a *standby* role does not have its own data and log volumes. Instead, it takes over the volumes from the failing hosts. As a result, the index server on the standby host does not store any data or handle any requests.

2 HANA installation and upgrades

This chapter provides comprehensive technical information about installing a single host and multi-host (distributed/scale-out) HANA database with a standby node. It also covers technical aspects of upgrading a HANA database using the SAP HANA Lifecycle Management tool.

2.1 Available deployment mode and types

2.1.1 Choosing a HANA database deployment

There are two models for installing HANA:

- *Appliance model*—only certified hardware partners can install HANA components on validated hardware on a specific operating system.
- *SAP HANA Tailored Datacenter Integration (TDI)*—certified administrators or official SAP HANA hardware partners can install HANA on approved hardware (from the hardware directory).

Once the deployment model has been selected, one of the technical deployment options, such as SCOS, MCOD, or MCOS, can be chosen.

These options can be deployed as a single tenant (scale-up) or multi-tenant (scale-out) setup across one or more hosts.

The chosen underlying server for the HANA database can be a physical server, an IaaS, or a virtualized environment.

Sample HANA deployment options

- The HANA database can be installed on a single host with a single tenant in an SCOS model, either as an appliance-type deployment or as an SAP HANA TDI deployment.
- The HANA database can be installed on multiple hosts with multiple tenants in an MCOS model, either as an appliance-type deployment or as an SAP HANA TDI deployment. This model of deployment is

only supported for the production database, with certain restrictions. For more information, refer to SAP Note 1681092–"Multiple SAP HANA databases on one appliance".

2.1.2 Understanding multi-container HANA database mode

The HANA database offers two deployment modes–*single container mode* and *multiple container mode*. In other words, SCOS, MCOS, MCOD and similar configurations can only be assigned to one of these two modes on a single host or on multiple hosts.

From HANA 1.0, and all versions prior to HANA 2.0 SP01, the default database mode was single container. However, as of HANA 2.0 SPS01, all the technical deployments mentioned in the previous sections can only be installed in multiple container mode (the default mode), also known as the *tenant database mode*.

Multiple container mode enables the HANA SID to accommodate more than one tenant database under the control of a SystemDB. Moreover, it does not always necessitate the existence of more than one tenant database. Note that the presence of a SystemDB within a HANA SID inherently implies this mode. As shown in Figure 2.1, multiple container mode always has a SystemDB component, whereas single container mode does not.

The benefits of multiple container mode include simplification and reduced capital expenditure on hardware. When a company requires additional HANA databases, this mode enables them to host new SIDs as isolated tenant databases on the same hardware, using the same database installation software and sharing some server components (RAM, CPU, etc.).

Conversely, in single container mode, any additional SIDs must be installed with their own database software and server components on the same or different hardware, without reusing components from existing HANA installations.

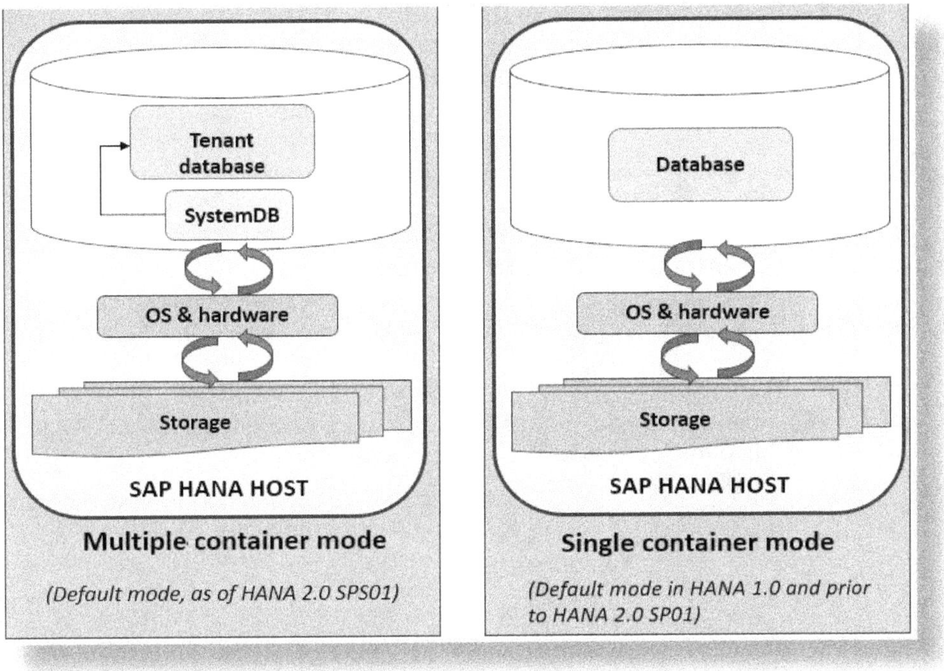

Figure 2.1: Multiple container and single container mode

! MDC mode

All subsequent topics discussed in this book are limited to the HANA multiple container database (MDC) mode.

2.2 HANA database file system layout

Despite functioning as an in-memory database, HANA requires disk storage (known as the persistence layer/storage layer) to maintain ACID compliance. In addition to the data and log volumes, which were covered in the previous chapter, other file systems are required, such as installation media, backup volume, root, etc.

2.2.1 HANA default file systems

The key file systems involved in any basic HANA installation are outlined in Table 2.1 and illustrated in Figure 2.2.

File system	Default path	Details
Root	*/root*	Base file system
Installation path (sapmnt)	*/hana/shared* This mount directory must be shared across all hosts in a multiple host scenario (scale-out) and must be accessible to each of the servers in the SAP HANA cluster.	Subdirectories: ▶ */hana/shared/<SID>*—contains executable programs (exe), globally shared data (global), instance profiles (profile), and SAP HANA configuration files ▶ */hana/shared/<SID>/hdbclient*—SAP HANA client installation path */hana/shared/<SID>/hdbstudio*—HANA Studio installation path (optional)
System instance	*/usr/sap* 60GB minimum (includes 10GB for OS installation)	Subdirectories: ▶ */usr/sap/hostctrl*—SAP Host Agent directory ▶ */usr/sap/<SID>*—contains symbolic links to system executables (SYS) and the home directory (home) of the <sid>adm user Note that */usr/sap/<SID>* cannot serve as a mount point, because this folder is fully managed by the SAP HANA database lifecycle manager tool (HDBLCM). Files should not be saved or mounted within this directory, as they might be deleted.
Data volume	*/hana/data*	*/hana/data/<SID>*—default data volume path
Log volume	*/hana/log*	*/hana/log/<SID>*—default log volume path

Table 2.1: HANA database default file systems

While file system paths to data, log, shared, and local file systems (*/usr/sap/**) are common between the SystemDB and tenant databases, there are specific folders dedicated to tenant databases and to the SystemDB. These specific folder structures have been indicated with '**' in Figure 2.2.

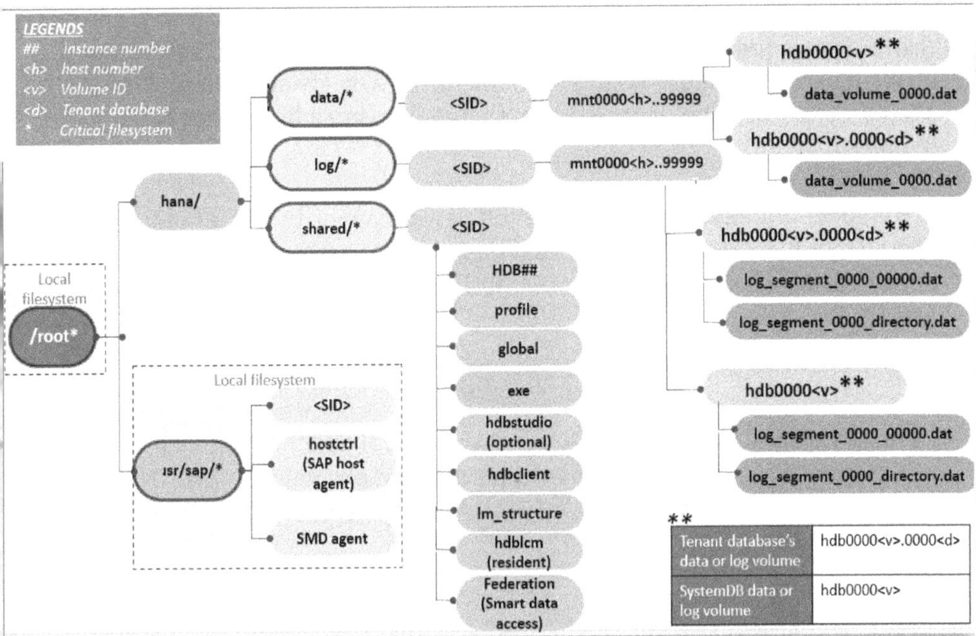

Figure 2.2: HANA file system layout

Figure 2.3 shows a list of the specific folder structures in HANA database installations for the SystemDB and tenant database.

Type	SystemDB	TenantDB
Data volume	/hana/data/<SID>/mnt000<h>..999999/hdb0000<v>	/hana/data/<SID>/mnt000<h>..999999/hdb0000<v>**.0000<d>**
Log volume	/hana/log/<SID>/mnt000<h>..999999/hdb0000<v>	/hana/log/<SID>/mnt000<h>..999999/hdb0000<v>**.0000<d>**
DB configuration files	/hana/shared/<SID>/global/hdb/custom/config	/hana/shared/<SID>/global/hdb/custom/config/DB_<SID>
Trace files	/usr/sap/WIP/HDB<nn>/work/SYSTEMDB	/usr/sap/WIP/HDB<nn>/work/DB_<SID>

Figure 2.3: Folder structures—SystemDB and tenant database

> **HANA database persistence services**
>
> Each of the SystemDB's and tenant database's persistence services (services which persist data at file system level) will have its own folder, labeled *hdb000**, within the data volume and log volume. Refer to Table 1.3 to identify which HANA core services persist data at file system level.

The folder structures including */hana/shared*, */hana/data*, */hana/log*, and */hana/backup* are provisioned through mount points using SSD (solid-state drive) disks in a single host environment. In a scale-out setup, */hana/shared/<SID>* must be accessible or shared across all hosts that belongs to one HANA SID.

In a master and slave setup with auto-failover capability, it is essential to ensure that the data volume, log volumes and */hana/shared/<SID>* file system are available across all hosts. For further details, refer to Sections 2.6.1 and 2.6.8.

> **! Altering file system layout**
>
> Proper design of the HANA file system is critical during the installation phase, as it cannot be modified after installation. Refer to SAP Note 2504196—"Can I change my SAP HANA file system layout after installation?".

2.2.2 Temporary files from SAP HANA

In addition to the default file systems mentioned in the previous section, the HANA database also stores multiple temporary files in the following folder structures after installation:

- SAP HANA DB files:
  - */tmp - .hdb_*_lock* (HANA 1.0 and prior to SPS09) and */var/lib/hdb* (HANA 1.0 and prior to SPS10) are used by HANA as read/write locks for shared memory segment access and are volatile in nature. Deleting these files will result in a HANA database crash, which can be fixed by a restart.
  - */var/tmp* –installer log files, *HDB_alive_**. This folder structure functions as a temporary directory during HANA database installation and upgrades, and contains all trace and log files.
- sapstartsrv files:
  - */etc/init.d/sapinit** –operating system related boot script.
  - */tmp/.sap** –operating system sockets, lock files (volatile in nature)

2.3 HANA database sizing

Sizing involves translating business needs into hardware requirements. The outcome of the sizing process determines the resources necessary (CPU, memory, disk space for data growth, disk I/O, frontend network) for hosting a customer application. However, it is important to recognize that sizing is an iterative process rather than a one-time activity.

Sizing holds significant importance in every installation. Inadequate sizing can result in a sluggish and unusable database, while excessive sizing can lead to higher costs for the company. Achieving the right sizing is therefore a critical part of any installation.

The critical components of HANA sizing are:

- Memory sizing
- Disk sizing (persistent layer or storage layer sizing)
- CPU (SAPS)
- Network

SAP provides various tools tailored to specific HANA database installation scenarios, which effectively determine target sizing.

Figure 2.4 outlines various scenarios and SAP-provided tools used to determine the corresponding target sizing.

Customer scenario	**Sizing for suite in HANA and S/4 HANA (OLTP)**	**Sizing for BW on HANA or BW/4 HANA (OLAP)**	**Sizing non- netweaver (Example: native HANA database)**
Greenfield / new implementation	❑ SAP QuickSizer ❑ Sizing guidelines	SAP QuickSizer	❑ Sizing guides ❑ Expert sizing service
Migration or conversion of SAP on AnyDB (Oracle, DB2, MSSQL, and so on) to HANA DB (Suite on HANA(SoH) or S/4 HANA or BW/4HANA) / brownfield conversion	**SAP Notes:** ❑ *1872170 - ABAP on HANA sizing report (S/4HANA, Suite on HANA...)* ❑ *1793345 - Sizing for SAP Suite on HANA* ❑ *1799449 - Sizing report ERP on SAP HANA database* ❑ *2758146 - SAP Readiness Check for SAP S/4HANA*	**SAP Notes:** ❑ *1736976 - Sizing Report for BW-on-HANA* ❑ *1637145 - SAP BW on HANA: Sizing SAP In-Memory Database* ❑ *2296290 - New Sizing Report for SAP BW/4HANA* ❑ *2610534 - HANA BW Sizing Report (/SDF/HANA_BW_SIZING)* ❑ *2363248 - SAP BW/4HANA Hardware Sizing*	**SAP Notes:** *1514966 - SAP HANA 1.0: Sizing SAP In-Memory Database*

Figure 2.4: Sizing scenarios and tools

A *greenfield* scenario refers to the implementation of a new HANA database, potentially incorporating S/4 HANA, Suite on HANA (SoH), BW/4HANA, native HANA, and similar systems.

A *brownfield* migration or conversion involves migrating or converting existing systems into Suite on HANA or S/4 HANA, respectively.

2.3.1 SAP sizing tools

SAP sizing tools include:

- Quick Sizer, for greenfield implementations
- Sizing reports (delivered via SAP Notes), for brownfield migrations or conversions.

Sizing HANA for greenfield implementations

Let's take a brief look at the Quick Sizer tool provided by SAP for greenfield implementations.

Quick Sizer tool

The Quick Sizer online tool enables user-based and throughput-based sizing, using structured questionnaires for key SAP applications to determine the target sizing. The Quick Sizer can be accessed directly via:

https://www.sap.com/about/benchmark/sizing.quick-sizer.html#quick-sizer.

Figure 2.5 describes three types of Quick Sizer that can be used, depending on the chosen implementation scenario:

- HANA-BASED QUICK SIZER
- HANA-BASED CLOUD QUICK SIZER
- NON-HANA-BASED CLASSIC QUICK SIZER

To determine the target sizing for an SAP application, in the case of a greenfield implementation, the tool requires answers to specific questions before suggesting the indicative target sizing. The process is outlined in Figure 2.6 and Figure 2.7.

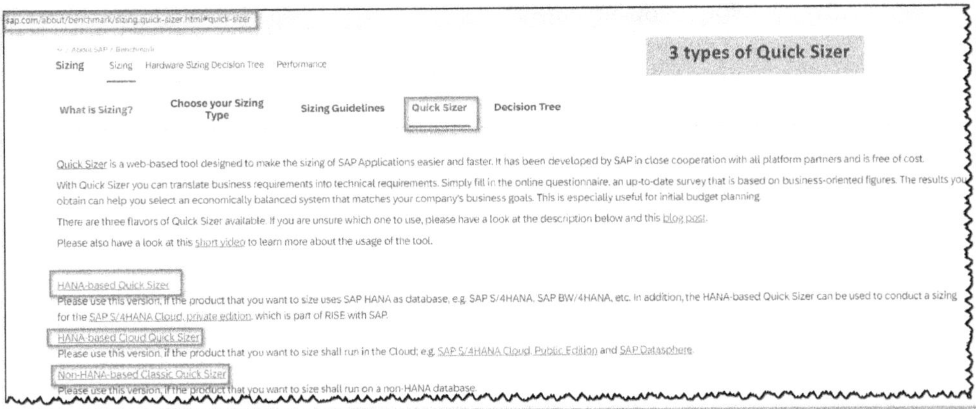

Figure 2.5: Types of Quick Sizer

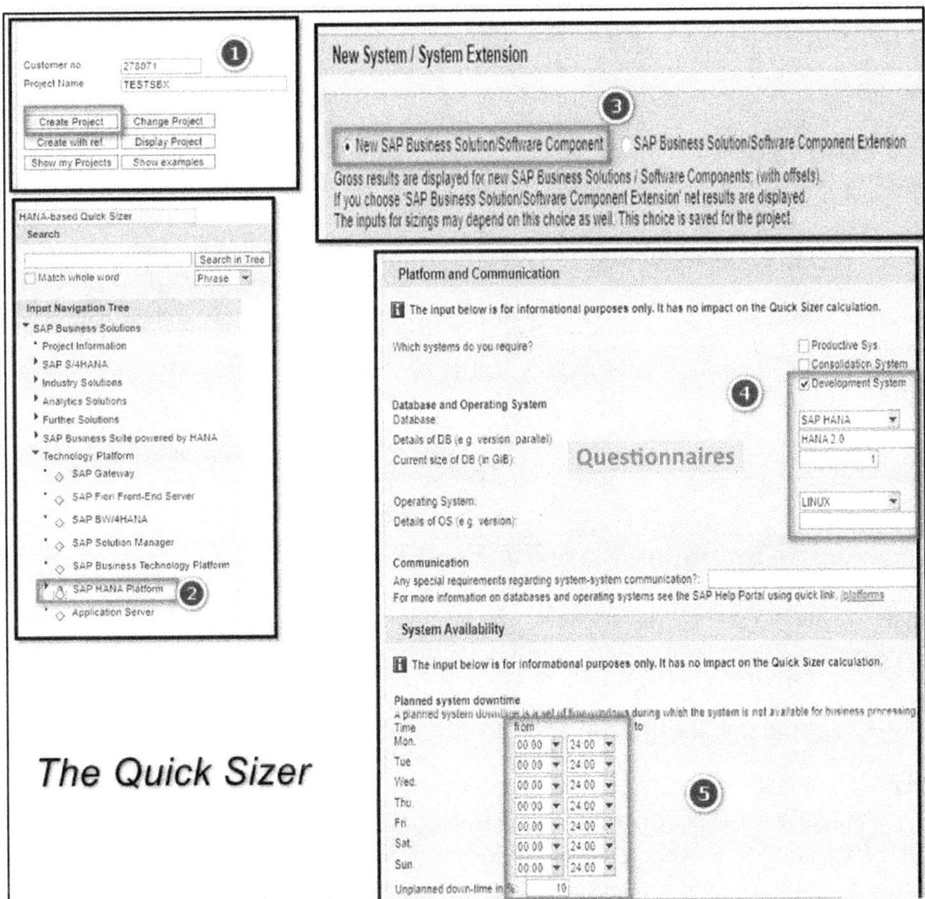

Figure 2.6: Quick Sizer tool (image 1 of 2)

Figure 2.6 shows the following steps:

❶ Select CREATE PROJECT to begin a sample project in Quick Sizer.

❷ Select the appropriate technology platform.

❸ Choose NEW SAP BUSINESS SOLUTION/SOFTWARE COMPONENT.

❹–❺ Proceed to answer the questions to determine the target sizing.

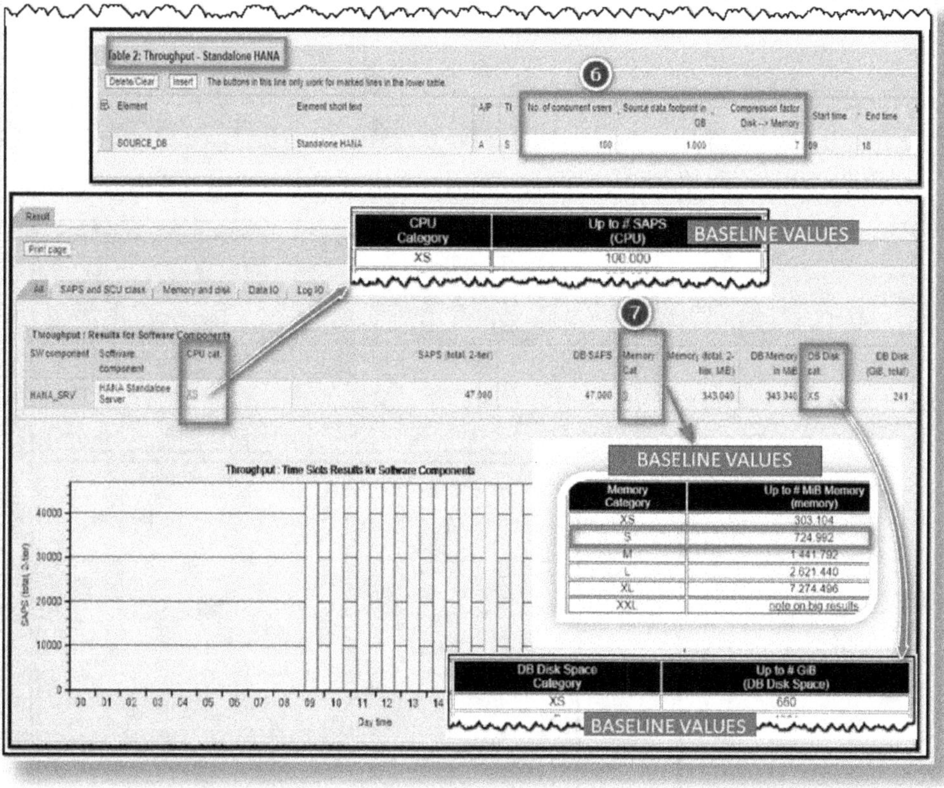

Figure 2.7: Quick Sizer tool (image 2 of 2)

Figure 2.7 shows the remaining steps:

❻ Complete the questionnaire to determine the target sizing.

❼ The Quick Sizer output provides details of the required target size and includes information such as RAM size ('S'), CPU size ('XS'), disk size ('XS'), and other relevant parameters.

Sizing Guidelines

Sizing Guidelines are online documents that offer insights into architecture and functionality, for target sizing according to selected business scenarios, and can be accessed at: *https://www.sap.com/about/benchmark/sizing.quick-sizer.html#sizing-guidelines*.

This is shown in Figure 2.8.

These documents provide guidance on selecting the appropriate "t-shirt size" in SAPS (SAP Application Performance Standard), CPU and GB (memory and disk) for deployment.

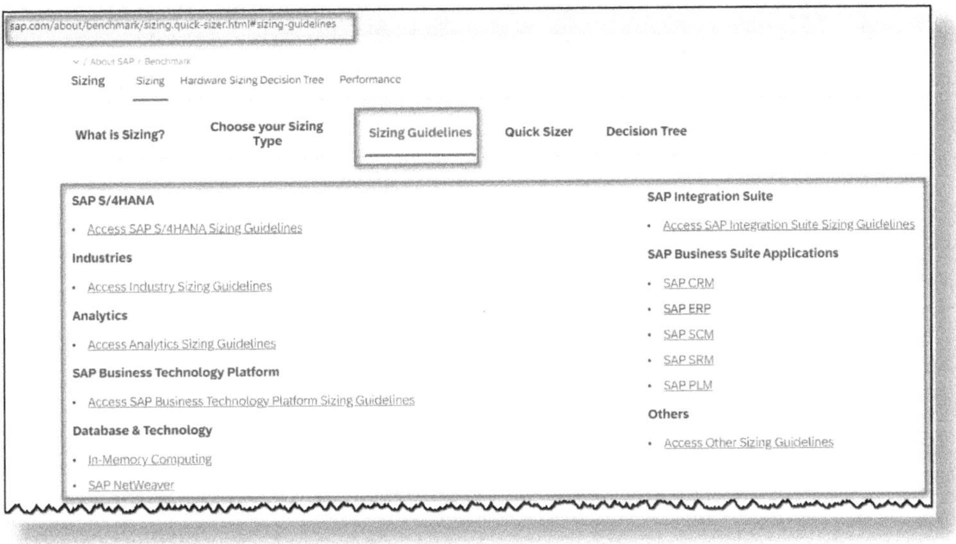

Figure 2.8: Sizing Guidelines

Sizing for brownfield conversion of SAP on HANA

As outlined in Figure 2.4, SAP offers several SAP Notes that provide reports for HANA target sizing for an existing SAP environment. These notes need to be applied to the company's SAP landscape. These reports are available and executable using transaction-code (T-code) SE38.

The reports include:

- Suite on HANA sizing report (*/SDF/HDB_SIZING*)
- Readiness check report (*RC_COLLECT_ANALYSIS_DATA*)
- Sizing report for BW on HANA and BW4/HANA (*/SDF/HANA_BW_SIZING*)

Figure 2.9 shows the steps to execute a sizing report along with its output for a company landscape. According to the report, if the company migrates their existing ERP system to HANA, the target HANA database memory requirement will be 35 TB, and the target disk size requirement will be 21 TB.

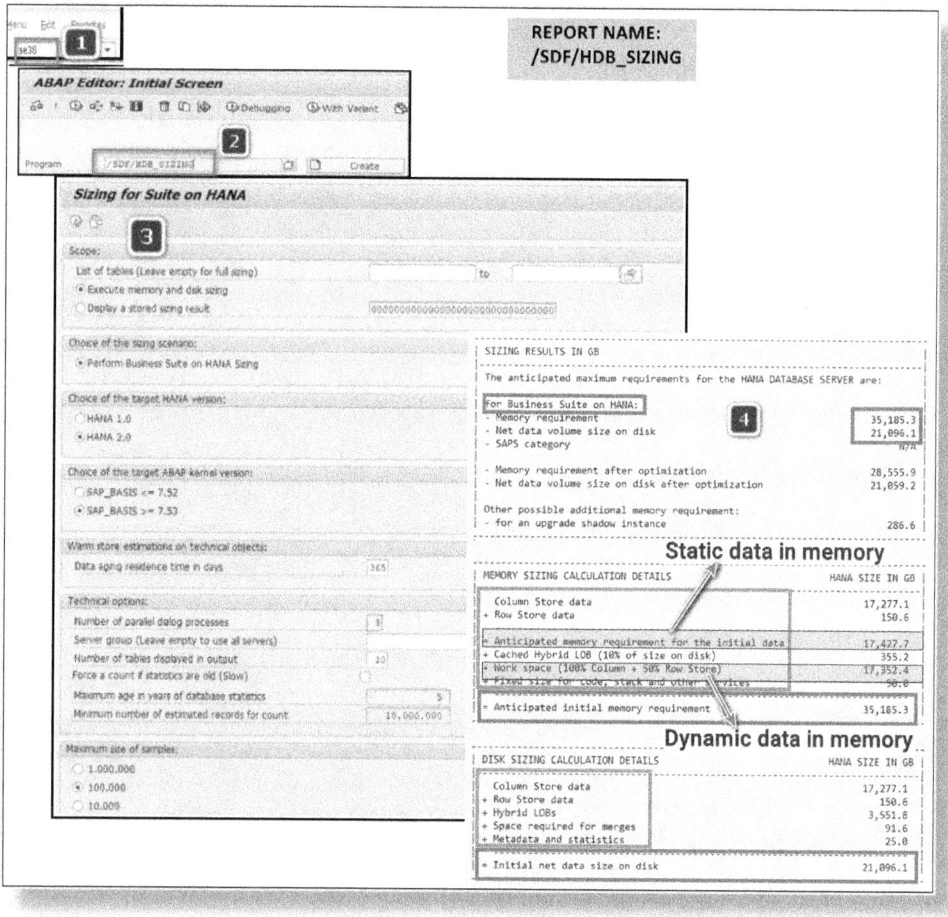

Figure 2.9: Sizing report for Suite on HANA: /SDF/HDB_SIZING

Numbers ❶, ❷ and ❸ show the process flow, starting with execution of the sizing report '/SDF/HDB_SIZING' via t-code SE38. The required values are then entered.

Number ❹ shows the resulting target HANA sizing from the report.

This sizing report indicates that the memory size is influenced by various factors, including memory consumed by column-store tables, row-store tables, cached hybrid LOB, workspace, etc. It also shows that the disk size is influenced by factors such as the disk space occupied by column-store tables, row-store tables, hybrid LOB, and additional space required for delta merges, etc.

Sizing HANA for SAP Java-based source systems

In contrast to SAP ABAP, there are no pre-existing standard reports from SAP for determining the target sizing of an SAP JAVA system. In these cases, the expert SIZING GUIDELINES (see Figure 2.8) must be used. Depending on the chosen SAP JAVA application, SAP provides comprehensive guidelines on the input to be supplied to the SAP Quick Sizer tool. The outcome will be a t-shirt-based recommendation for target sizing. We saw some SAP Quick Sizer input and output in Figure 2.6 and Figure 2.7.

2.3.2 Formula-based sizing for TDI environments

Formula-based memory sizing

Memory allocation in the HANA database is divided into two areas:

- Static memory area—stores static data,
- Dynamic memory area—manages dynamic data.

Refer to Figure 2.9 which shows the static and dynamic memory requirements contributing to the total HANA memory size. These segments determine the overall memory requirements for hosting the HANA database. As previously mentioned, SAP offers various reports to determine the target HANA sizing.

In general, the target HANA database's anticipated memory size depends on:

- Static data stored in row-store and column-store tables, including indexes.
- Dynamic database objects created temporarily at runtime.
- Cached records of hybrid LOBs (although hybrid LOBs are primarily stored on disk—it is assumed that 20% of them are cached in memory).
- 50GB (approx.) of additional allocation for database code, stack, and other services.

As a general guideline, it is recommended to allocate as much memory for dynamic memory as is needed for static memory, or to double the value of data stored in tables, including indexes. In essence, this allocation should be at least twice the total size of the row-store and column-store tables. The guiding principle is shown in the following equation:

```
Static memory = Dynamic memory = RAM
```

Therefore, the anticipated total memory required to host the HANA database is:

```
Static memory + Dynamic memory = >RAM+RAM= >2RAM.
```

The memory size should optimally be at least two times the total size of row store and column store, as per SAP Note 3307794—"How to judge if the available memory is sufficient for the current system".

Formula-based disk sizing (persistence sizing)

Data volume disk size recommendation

Savepoint, delta merge operations, and snapshots trigger flushing of data from memory to the data volume at */hana/data/<SID>* (see Figure 2.2). The anticipated net data on disk can usually be calculated using application-specific programs and the result should be increased by 20% to arrive at the target data volume size. The formula is:

```
Size of data volume = 1.2 * anticipated net data on disk.
```

This data volume size must be sufficient to hold all database tables and indexes, as well as the disk space required for delta merge operations on the column-store tables. However, it does not account for year-on-year growth and must be adjusted accordingly.

In cases where it is not feasible to determine the anticipated net data on disk, it is advisable to have a data volume size equivalent to the anticipated total memory (RAM), as follows:

```
Size of data volume = 1 * Anticipated memory (Single host)
```

For a distributed environment (multiple host), the size of data volume per host is calculated using the following formula:

```
Size of data volume per host = (1 * Anticipated memory) / number
                               of hosts
```

Log volume disk size recommendation

The minimum size for the log volume file system (*/hana/log/<SID>*) is determined by the number of data changes between two consecutive savepoints. This size must also be large enough to hold log segments until a successful savepoint and subsequent log backup. However, there is no direct relationship between the database size and the required log volume size. The general recommended value is shown in Figure 2.10, and is based on best practices and experience.

[systems ≤ 512GB] $Size_{Redo\ log}$ = 1/2 x RAM

[systems > 512GB] $Size\ (min)_{Redo\ log}$ = 512 GB

Figure 2.10: Formula for data volume size calculation

Disk space required for SAP HANA installation

The HANA database installation directory (*/hana/shared/<SID>*) stores all the binary, trace, and configuration files. In the case of a scale-out installation, this file system must be exposed to all the nodes. The recommended size is shown in Figure 2.11.

Recommended size for /hana/shared/<SID> :

$Size_{Installation}$ = MIN(1 x RAM; 1 TB) for **single host/node installation**

$Size_{Installation}$ = 1 * RAM_of_worker per 4 worker node for **multi-node / scale-out installation**

Figure 2.11: Formula for sizing HANA shared file system

Disk space required for SAP HANA backups

Backups play a critical role in business continuity. In the event of storage corruption on data and log volumes, backups are essential for restoring the database to its last consistent state. Therefore, it is necessary to have a separate, adequately sized backup volume, not only to store backups encompassing the entire database payload, but also to store multiple full backups and regular log backups. These backups must align with the adopted backup strategy and its retention period. The recommended value for this size is shown in Figure 2.12.

$$Size_{Backups} \geq Size_{data} + Size_{Redo\ log}$$

Figure 2.12: Formula for sizing HANA backup volumes

Detailed information on this is covered in Chapter 6.

Disk space required for exports

In root-cause analysis scenarios, it is necessary to export certain database content to the file system, which requires ample disk space to store these binary exports. As a rule of thumb, you need to reserve space that is approximately twice the size of the largest database table in order to store these exports.

> **! Network requirements**
>
> Note that network related requirements are not covered in this book. For more information, refer to: *https://www.sap.com/documents/2016/08/1cd2c2fb-807c-0010-82c7-eda71af511fa.html.*

Formula-based CPU sizing

There is generally no standardized approach to determine the CPU requirements for a HANA database. However, it is usually acknowledged that an active user consumes approximately 300 SAPS (SAP Application Performance Standard). In addition, it is advisable to ensure that the CPU load does not exceed an average of 65% at any given time on the HANA database server.

2.4 Preparing for HANA installation

Before installing a HANA database, to ensure seamless installation, the target server must be prepared correctly.

2.4.1 Preparing the target server

The following sections cover the activities required to prepare the target server for HANA installation.

Supported hardware platform and operating system

SAP HANA 2.0 is compatible with hardware platforms which are based on both Intel and IBM Power series. The supported versions include:

- SUSE Linux Enterprise Server 15 SPx and 12 SPx
- Red Hat Enterprise Server 8.x and 7.x .

For more details, refer to the following:

- SAP Note 2235581—"SAP HANA: Supported Operating Systems"
- SAP Note 2622671—"SAP HANA Certified and Supported Hardware"

Hardware directory and the Product Availability Matrix

SAP has certified specific combinations of hardware and operating systems to support the HANA database. These certified configurations are listed in the SAP HANA Hardware Directory, which can be accessed at: *https://www.sap.com/dmc/exp/2014-09-02-hana-hardware/enEN/index.html*.

Figure 2.13 illustrates the hardware directory and its various filters, such as DEPLOYMENT, VENDORS, CPU ARCHITECTURE, and MEMORY SIZE, which assist in selecting a certified server configuration capable of hosting a production HANA database.

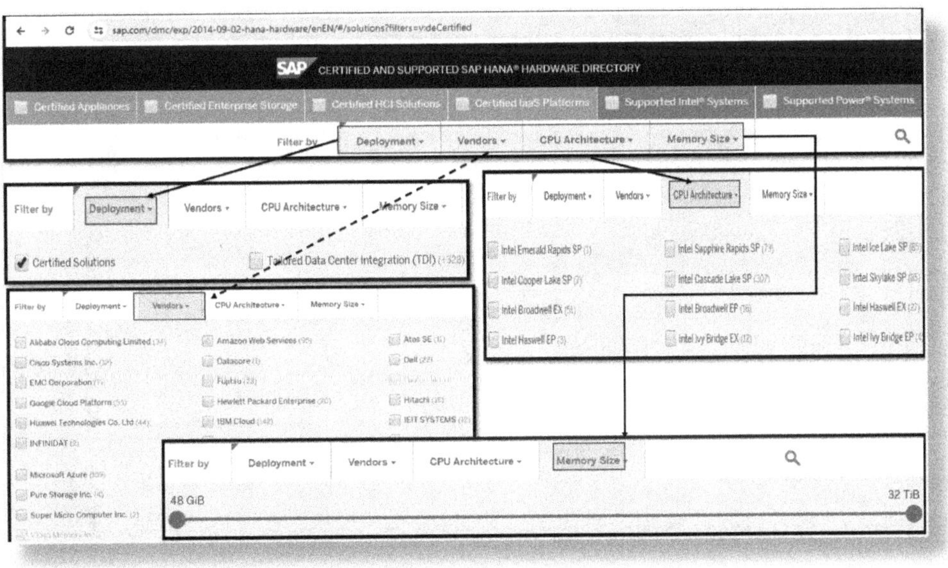

Figure 2.13: SAP HANA Hardware Directory

Figure 2.14 shows a list of SAP-certified AWS EC2 instances that are suitable for hosting a production HANA database when the AMAZON WEB SERVICES checkbox is selected.

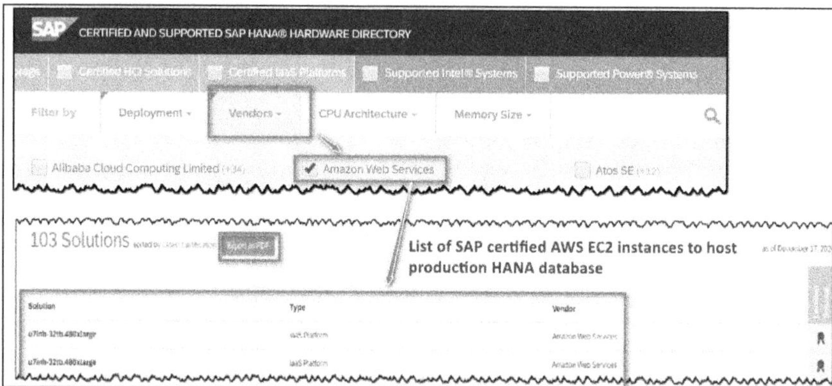

Figure 2.14: List of certified AWS EC2 instances to host HANA

In addition to the SAP HANA Hardware Directory, SAP also offers the Product Availability Matrix (PAM). The PAM includes a comprehensive list of all SAP HANA components along with their compatible hardware, kernels, and other software prerequisites. It can be accessed at: *https://support.sap.com/pam.*

Figure 2.15 shows a sample PAM output for S/4HANA 2023, detailing the list of compatible operating systems, databases, and other requirements needed to host this product.

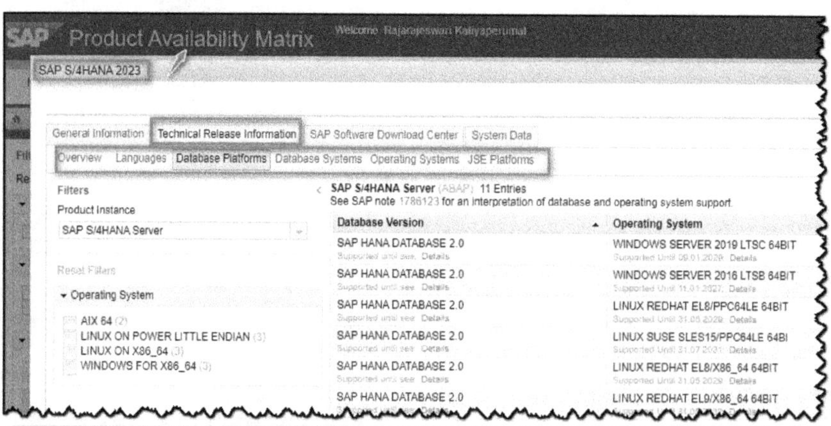

Figure 2.15: SAP Product Availability Matrix

Recommended operating system settings

Once the hardware and OS version have been finalized, the OS parameters need to be adjusted according to the guidelines provided in the SAP Notes listed in Figure 2.16.

Supported Operating System for SAP HANA on Intel- Based Hardware Platforms	Supported Operating System for SAP HANA on IBM Power Servers
▸ SAP Note 1944799 : SAP HANA Guidelines for SLES Operating System Installation ▸ SAP Note 2578899 : SUSE Linux Enterprise Server 15 : Installation Note ▸ SAP Note 2684254 : SAP HANA DB: Recommended OS settings for SLES 15 / SLES for SAP Applications 15 ▸ SAP Note 2205917 : SAP HANA DB: Recommended OS settings for SLES 12 / SLES for SAP Applications 12 ▸ SAP Note 2772999 : Red Hat Enterprise Linux 8.x: Installation and Configuration ▸ SAP Note 3108316 : Red Hat Enterprise Linux 9.x: Installation and Configuration ▸ SAP Note 3108302 : SAP HANA DB: Recommended OS Settings for RHEL 9 ▸ SAP Note 2777782 : SAP HANA DB: Recommended OS Settings for RHEL 8 ▸ SAP Note 2292690 : SAP HANA DB: Recommended OS settings for RHEL 7	▸ SAP Note 2055470 : HANA on POWER Planning and Installation Specifics – Central Note ▸ SAP Note 2188482 : SAP HANA on IBM Power Systems: Allowed Hardware ▸ SAP Note 2554012 : FAQ: SAP HANA big-endian to little-endian Migration for IBM Power ▸ SAP Note 2537080 : Migrate SAP HANA 1.0 on IBM Power Systems big-endian to SAP HANA 2.0 on IBM Power Systems little-endian ▸ SAP Note 2684254 : SAP HANA DB: Recommended OS settings for SLES 15 / SLES for SAP Applications 15 ▸ SAP Note 2205917 : SAP HANA DB: Recommended OS settings for SLES 12 / SLES for SAP Applications 12 ▸ SAP Note 3108302 : SAP HANA DB: Recommended OS Settings for RHEL 9 ▸ SAP Note 2777782 : SAP HANA DB: Recommended OS Settings for RHEL 8 ▸ SAP Note 2292690 : SAP HANA DB: Recommended OS settings for RHEL 7

Figure 2.16: Configuration guidelines for hosting HANA on Intel or IBM Power-based hardware

File systems supported by HANA

The file systems used for HANA databases—such as data volume, log volume, and backup volume—are certified, tested, and supported only on specific storage types. At the time of writing, the supported file systems for HANA database include GPFS, MPFS, NFS, OCFS2, XFS, and Ext3. However, it is important to note that while MPFS and OCFS2 are supported, their certification status expired on September 23, 2020.

For more information on supported file systems, refer to the following:

- SAP Note 2972496—"SAP HANA File system Types"
- SAP Note 1999930—"FAQ: SAP HANA I/O Analysis"
- SAP Note 405827—"Linux: Recommended file systems"

SAP HANA hardware and cloud measurement tools

Once the hardware with the chosen operating system and settings is ready, the HANA database file systems must be mounted. As a next step, SAP customers and partners should validate the hardware or virtual machine's capability to host a production HANA database. For this purpose, SAP provides SAP HANA hardware and cloud measurement tools, which include the following sub-tools:

- *SAP HANA hardware and cloud measurement tool*—for measurement
- *SAP HANA hardware and cloud measurement analysis*—for analysis.

Let's look at these in a little more detail.

SAP HANA hardware and cloud measurement tool

The SAP HANA hardware and cloud measurement tool (HCMT) can be downloaded and installed on the target hardware. It is used to execute tests, measure performance, and collect various KPIs (Key Performance Indicators) from the target hardware in order to verify its compliance for hosting a HANA database. It also evaluates whether the system planned for SAP HANA deployment meets the minimum performance requirement and can provide satisfactory overall performance based on the intended SAP HANA usage. The collected measurement results are then saved as a *zip* file on the local file system.

Figure 2.17 shows how to download and install HCMT on the HANA database server.

The steps highlighted in the figure are as follows:

❶ Log in to the SAP software center at *https://me.sap.com/softwarecenter* and navigate to SUPPORT PACKAGES & PATCHES.

❷–❸ Search for HANA OPTIM.

❹–❺ Download the SAR file containing the tool, according to the target OS type (HCMT*.SAR).

❻ Transfer the downloaded file to the target server.

❼ Extract the downloaded SAR file using *SAPCAR*. This action creates a folder structure named SETUP in the current location.

❽ Install the tool using the command `./hcmtsetup`. The command `./hcmt -l` is used to list all available tests from SAP HANA hardware and cloud measurement tools.

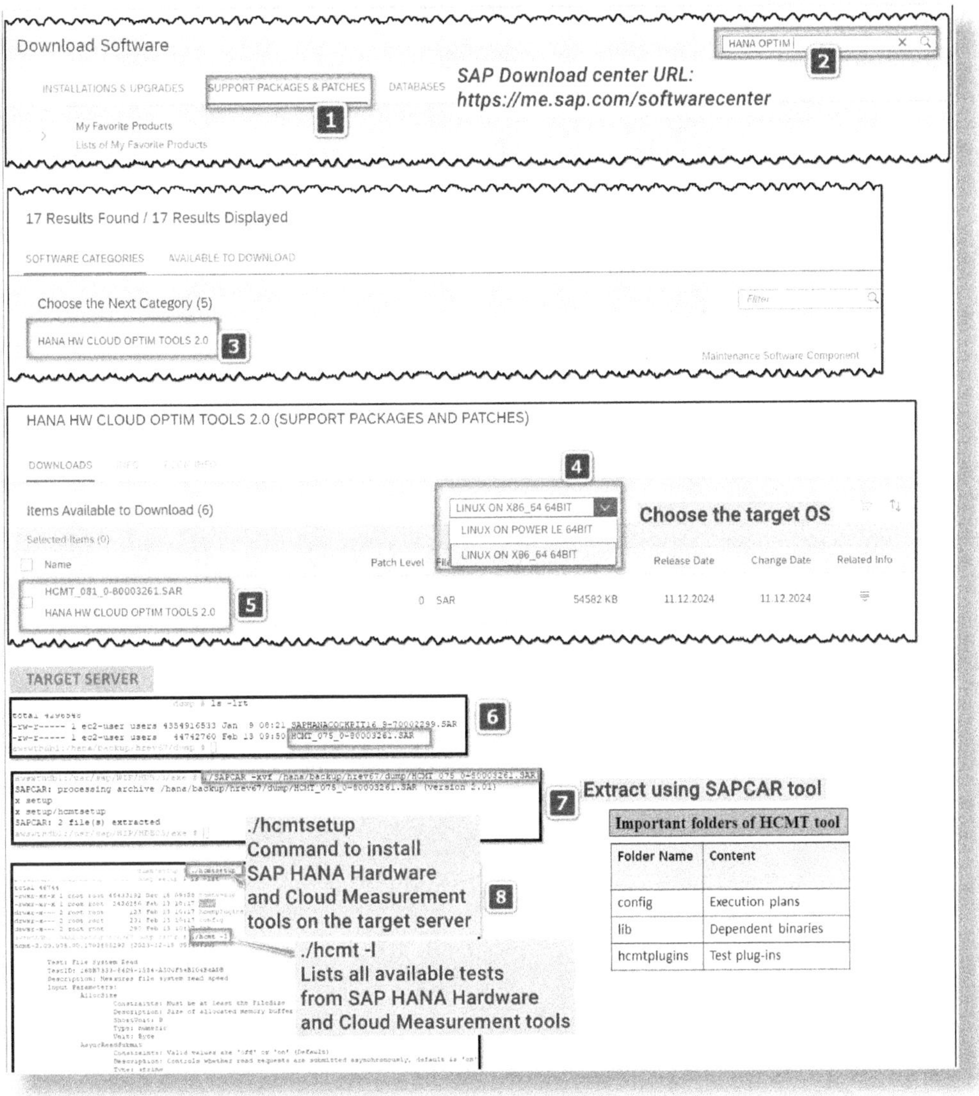

Figure 2.17: Installing HCMT on target server

Figure 2.17 also shows the key folder structures created on the target server after the tool is installed, including *-config, lib, and hcmtplugIns*. The *config* folder contains execution plans such as *executionplan.json* (default) or *full_executionplan.json*, which determine the series of automated tests performed by the measurement tool.

These execution plans typically include test cases that evaluate the hardware's CPU, memory, network, IOPS, file systems, and other factors in order to verify the server's capability against standard KPIs for hosting a HANA database. Each test case has a unique identifier, number of iterations, default input value, and other specifications.

Before executing the report, the host must have at least 20GB of free storage space to store the output. If the target already has a HANA database installed and running, it has to be stopped while the report is executing. In addition, ports 50000 and 50001 must be opened for communication.

The tool can be executed on both scale-up and scale-out systems. With scale-out systems, the measurement tool must be started on the master host, and additional worker hosts can be supplied as additional inputs for execution.

Figure 2.18 shows how to execute tests and download the results from the HCMT tool.

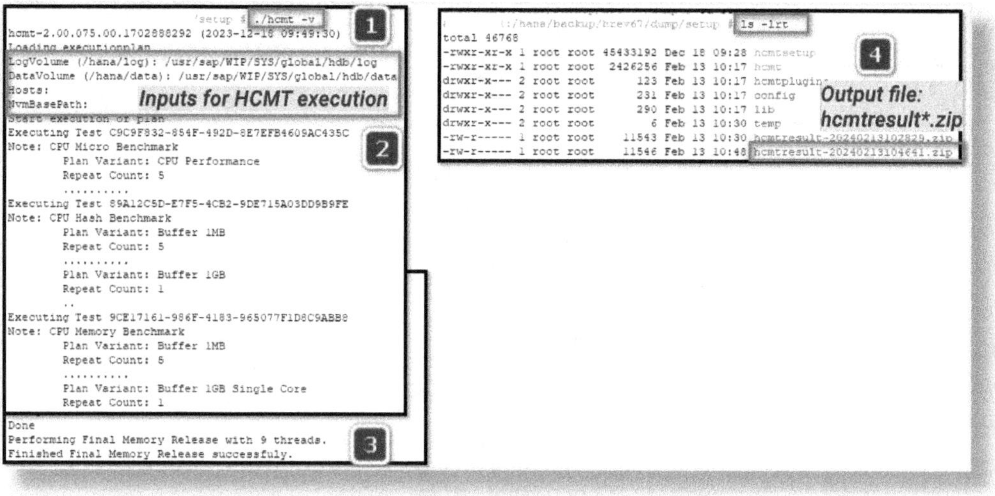

Figure 2.18: Executing and uploading into the analysis tool

The numbers in the figure highlight the following steps:

❶ Execute the HCMT tool in default mode (execution plan is *executionplan.json*) using the command `./hcmt -v`.

❷ Supply the mandatory input for the tool such as log and data volume path, hosts, etc.

❸-❹ Successful execution of this tool is marked, and the output is stored as *'hcmtresult-*.zip'*.

Some of the key inputs for the tool are:

- LOGVOLUME—location of the log volume for the target HANA database.
- DATAVOLUME—location of the data volume for the target HANA database.
- HOSTS—list of host names (scale-out system).
- NVMBASEPATH—location of the persistent memory, separated by commas (if available). If no persistent memory is available, this value can be left empty.

In the case of a scale-out system, the tool reads the execution plan, starts the test locally, and delegates tests marked for scale-out to the worker hosts. The tool waits for the completion of the tests on the worker hosts before starting the next test in the execution plan. All test measurement data and host manifests are collected into one file written by the master host instance.

This output file must be uploaded to the SAP HANA hardware and cloud measurement tool online for interpretation purposes.

SAP HANA hardware and cloud measurement analysis

For further analysis and reporting, the previously generated zip file must be uploaded to the online SAP HANA hardware and cloud measurement analysis tool at: *https://hotui-supportportal.dispatcher.hana.ondemand.com/index.html.*

To log in to this online tool, a valid S-user ID, with the appropriate permissions, is required. Before uploading the measurement output to the tool, the server needs to be added to the portal along with its configuration, as shown in Figure 2.19

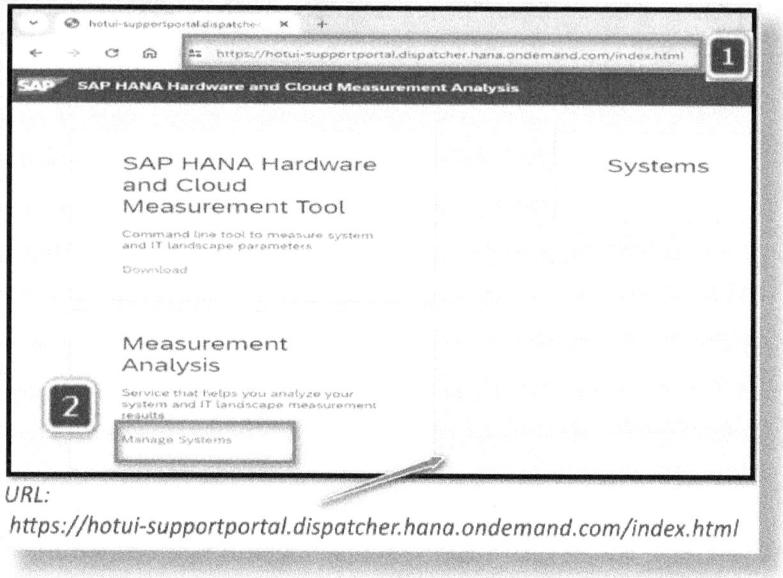

Figure 2.19: SAP HCMT tool

Referring to the screenshot, the steps are as follows:

❶ Open the SAP HANA Hardware and Cloud Measurement Analysis tool.

❷ Continue via Manage Systems to register the target server in order to interpret the analyzed result.

Next, proceed to add the system for further analysis, as shown in Figure 2.20.

Referring to the image, the steps are as follows:

❶ Click on Add system.

❷ Add the System Name and other details of the system to be analyzed.

❸–❹ Upload the zip file that was generated in the HCMT tool that was generated earlier.

❺ The analysis tool provides the output of the analysis in graphic and textual representation.

❻ The output can be downloaded.

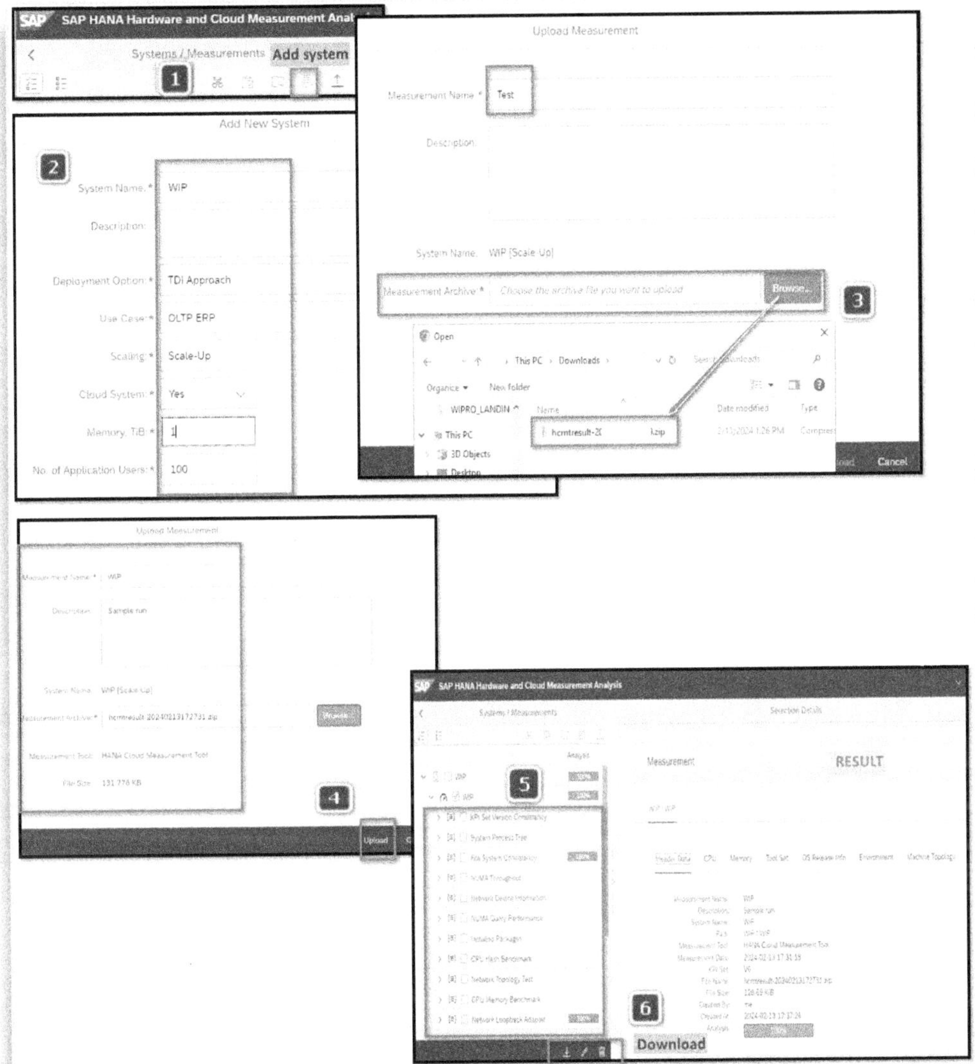

Figure 2.20: Analysis tool—executing, uploading and analysing

The tool provides a graphical and textual representation of the measurement results, as shown in Figure 2.21.

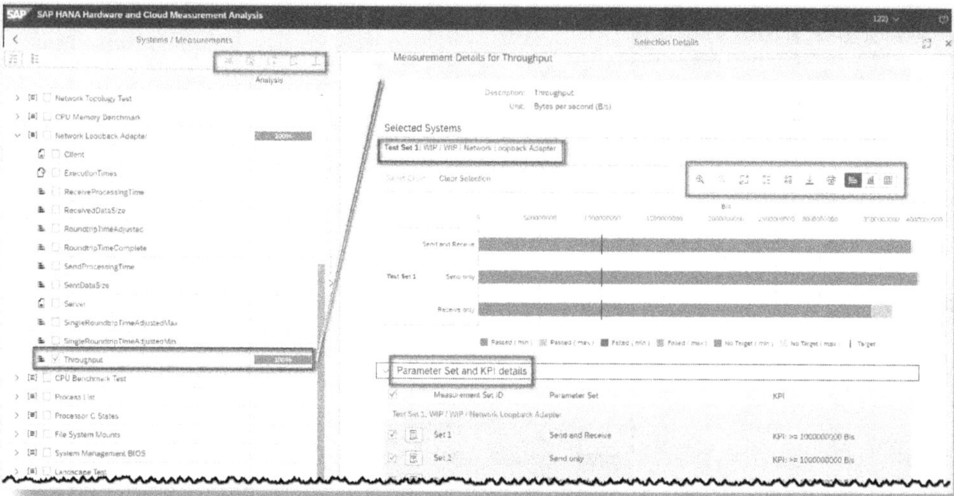

Figure 2.21: Navigating through the Analysis report

This helps to identify problematic areas in the hardware that need to be adjusted in order to achieve the required performance. A positive result from the analysis indicates that the server that is intended to host the HANA database meets the minimum performance criteria and KPIs required to run SAP HANA production database. This analysis report can be shared with other users and can also be compared with existing reports.

Key commands from HCMT tool

Table 2.2 lists some of the key commands in the HCMT tool.

Important HCMT command	Details
`./hcmt -l`	Lists all the available tests
`./hcmt -v`	Executes the tool in verbose mode and displays the output. This uses the default execution plan *<path>/setup/config/ executionplan.json*.
`./hcmt -v -S`	Starts the execution on worker host (scale-out setup) rather than master node in verbose mode.
`./hcmt -v -p <path>/setup/config/full_executionplan.json`	Executes the tool in verbose mode using *full_executionplan.json* as the execution plan.

Table 2.2: HCMT key commands

> **Verbose mode**
>
> *Verbose mode* provides detailed, comprehensive output or information about the operations being performed.

For more information, refer to SAP Note 2493172—"SAP HANA Hardware and Cloud Measurement Tools".

2.4.2 Downloading HANA media

The *SAP HANA Platform Edition* serves as the technical foundation of the SAP HANA platform and encompasses various components, including the SAP HANA database, SAP HANA client, SAP HANA Studio, SAP HANA XS engine, and SAP HANA Local Secure Store (LSS), among others. For the purpose of easier download, most of these components are bundled together as one zip file and are accessible for download from the SAP portal, in the INSTALLATION & UPGRADES function (see ❶ in Figure 2.22). However, if there is a need to upgrade these components individually, they can be selectively downloaded under SUPPORT PACKAGES & PATCHES (see ❷ in Figure 2.22).

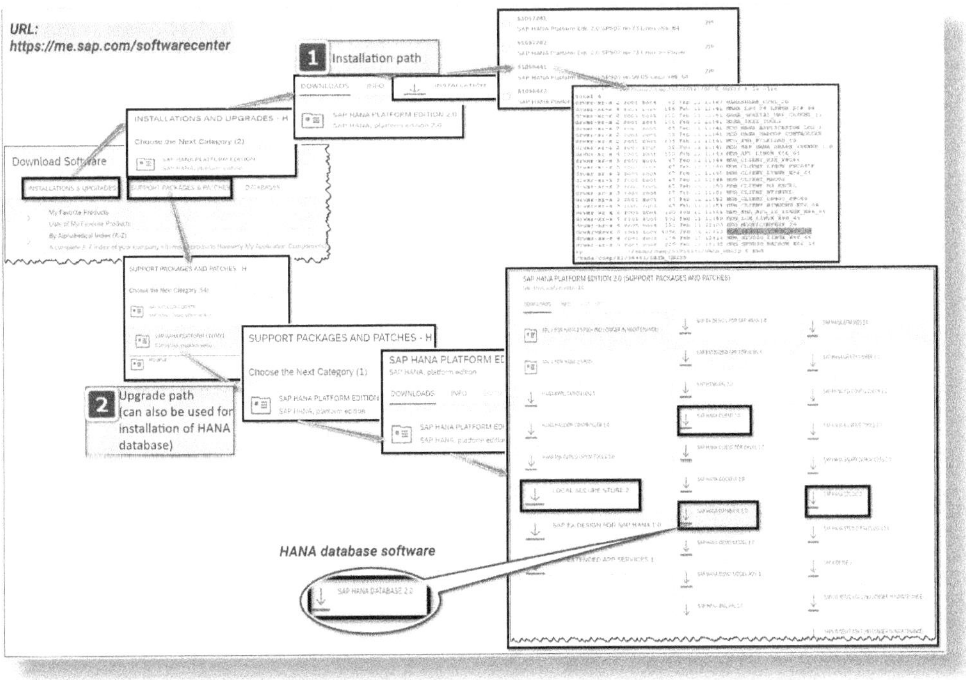

Figure 2.22: HANA Platform edition download

To download the required SAP HANA database software and its components from SAP's download center, a valid S-user ID with appropriate download authorization is needed.

INSTALLATION & UPGRADES includes media for the initial revision of a Support Package Stack (SPS), and SUPPORT PACKAGES & PATCHES contains all the latest SPS revisions. You can download from either of these sections, regardless of whether you are performing a HANA installation or an upgrade. This is because SAP HANA media are self-contained full installation packages.

The download paths for these components are outlined below.

Under INSTALLATIONS & UPGRADES (see path ❶ in Figure 2.22):

- Open BY ALPHABETICAL INDEX (A-Z)
- Choose H
- Choose SAP HANA PLATFORM EDITION
- Go to DOWNLOADS
- Choose SAP HANA PLATFORM EDITION 2.0
- Download the SAP HANA PLATFORM ED*.

Under SUPPORT PACKAGES & PATCHES (see path ❷ in Figure 2.22):

- Open BY ALPHABETICAL INDEX (A-Z)
- Choose H
- Choose SAP HANA PLATFORM EDITION
- Go to DOWNLOADS
- Choose SAP HANA PLATFORM EDITION 2.0
- Download the following components:
  - SAP HANA DATABASE 2.0 as per the target OS
  - LOCAL SECURE STORE 2 as per the target OS
  - SAP HANA STUDIO 2 according to the target OS from Linux, MACOS, or WINDOWS
  - SAP HANA CLIENT 2.0 as per the target OS

The download path for other components is outlined below.

For SAP HOST AGENT:

- Go to SUPPORT PACKAGES & PATCHES
- Open By Alphabetical Index (A-Z)
- Choose H
- Choose SAP HOST AGENT
- Go to DOWNLOADS
- Choose SAP HOST AGENT 7.22
- Download the latest SAPHOSTAGENT*.SAR

For SAPCAR:

- Go to SUPPORT PACKAGES & PATCHES
- Open By Alphabetical Index (A-Z)
- Choose S
- Choose SAPCAR
- Go to DOWNLOADS
- Choose SAPCAR
- Choose the target HANA host operating system
- Download the SAPCAR*.EXE from the latest revision.

These downloaded files need to be transferred or copied to the target HANA server using tools such as *WinSCP*.

2.4.3 Extracting HANA media using SAPCAR

As previously mentioned, when downloading the SAP HANA database software media from the INSTALLATIONS & UPGRADES path, it will be in the form of a zip folder. In contrast, when downloading the media from the SUPPORT PACKAGES & PATCHES path, it will be in the form of an *IMDB_SERVER.SAR* file, which must then be unpacked.

SAP provides an OS-dependent tool called *SAPCAR*.EXE* to unpack files with the **.SAR* extension. This SAPCAR tool is also available for download from the SAP download center (as outlined in the previous section). It is important to note that SAPCAR media selection must align with the target HANA host operating system, which could be either *LINUX x86_64* or *LINUX POWER LE*. For convenience, it is recommended to rename *SAPCAR_*.EXE* to *SAPCAR* and place it alongside other **.SAR* file(s) intended for extraction.

Before unpacking the software components, it is essential to verify their authenticity and security, because they are being transferred from an external network to the target server. These files must then be extracted in the target host server.

Figure 2.23 shows a sample set of commands to verify and unpack the *SAPHOST*.SAR* file on the target host.

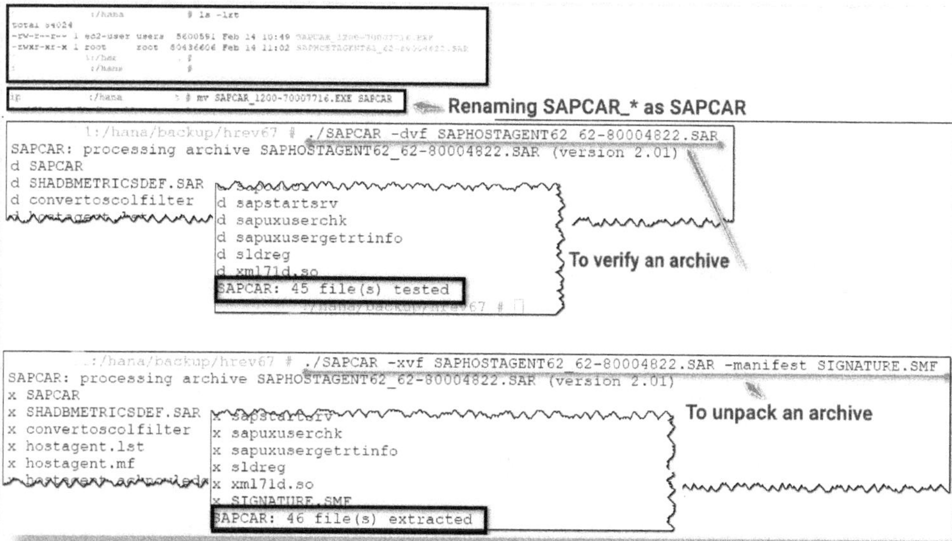

Figure 2.23: Using SAPCAR for verifying and unpacking

The command to verify an archive using SAPCAR is:

```
./SAPCAR -dvf <SAR File name>
```

The command to unpack an archive using SAPCAR *is*:

```
./SAPCAR -xvf <SAR_FileName> -manifest SIGNATURE.SMF
```

The *IMDB_SERVER*.SAR* file must also be verified and extracted in a similar way.

Using the option *-manifest SIGNATURE.SMF* during extraction generates the required signature file during the unpacking process. However, it is important to note that extracting more than one *.SAR file into the same directory will result in overwriting the SIGNATURE.SMF file from the previous extraction. To avoid this, SIGNATURE.SMF must be relocated to a different directory, such as SAP_HANA_DATABASE, SAP_HANA_CLIENT, etc., before extracting the next SAR file. For further details, refer to SAP Note 2577617—"Verifying software authenticity and integrity during SAP HANA installation and update".

To verify the authenticity of an already extracted SAR file or the zip file from the installation media of the HANA database, use the *sapdsigner* tool. This executable can be found in the Host Agent folder */usr/sap/hostctrl/exe*, or in *<installation path>/<SID>/global/hdb/saphostagent_setup*.

Note that the HANA database lifecycle management tool (HDBLCM) can also be utilized to perform validation and extraction of the downloaded files from the SAP download center. Section 2.5.7 covers more information about this.

2.4.4 Host Agent installation

SAP Host Agent is a tool that performs various lifecycle management tasks, including system monitoring, database monitoring, system instance control, and provisioning in SAP application servers or the HANA database. After downloading the Host Agent SAR file from the SAP download center, it must be transferred to the target HANA database server and extracted there. The resulting folder structure contains the necessary executables for installing the Host Agent.

SAP Host Agent can be installed using the command `./saphostexec -install`, as shown in Figure 2.24

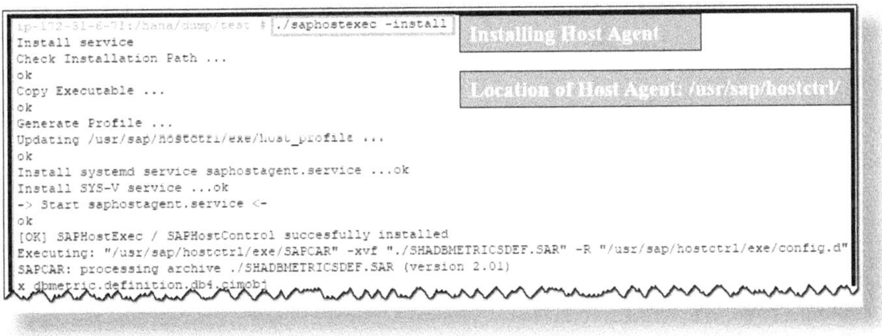

Figure 2.24: Installing SAP Host agent

Other important SAP Host Agent commands include:

- To update: `./saphostexec -upgrade`
- To stop: `./saphostexec -stop`
- To start: `./saphostexec -start`
- To validate the status: `./saphostexec -status`
- To check the version: `./saphostexec -version`

Figure 2.25 shows the Host Agent commands.

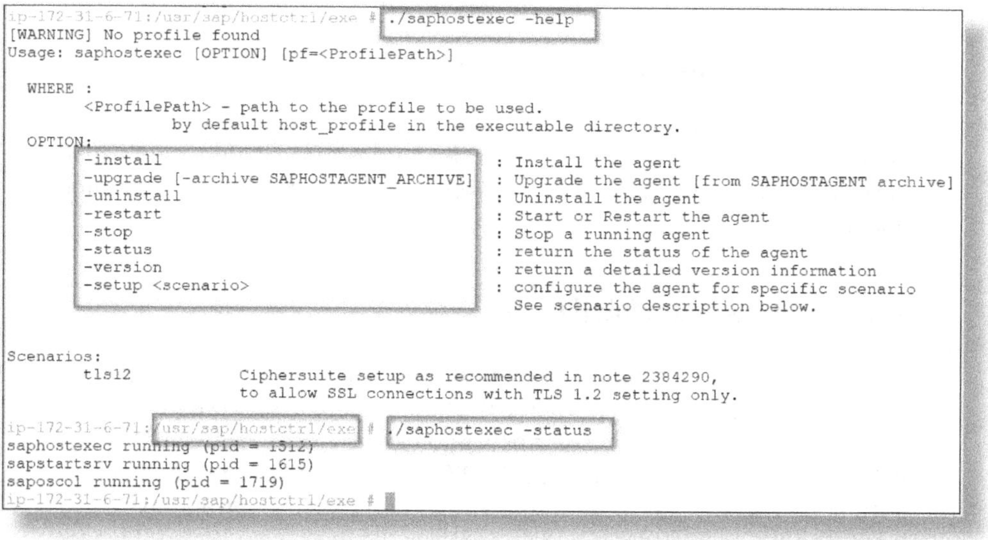

Figure 2.25: Host Agent commands

2.5 HANA installation and configuration tools

HANA employs lifecycle management tools for both platform and application management. These tools are categorized as *Application LCM (Lifecycle Management)* tools, which are used by developers, and *Platform LCM* tools, which are utilized by administrators.

! Platform LCM

This book will only cover Platform LCM from an administrator perspective.

2.5.1 Platform LCM—types and activities

Platform LCM can be further classified into *HDBLCM from installation media* and *resident HDBLCM*, each serving different roles in platform life cycle management, as illustrated in Figure 2.26. Also note that the resident HDBLCM can only be launched from */hana/shared/<SID>/hdblcm*, and the HDBLCM from installation media can only be launched from the installation media.

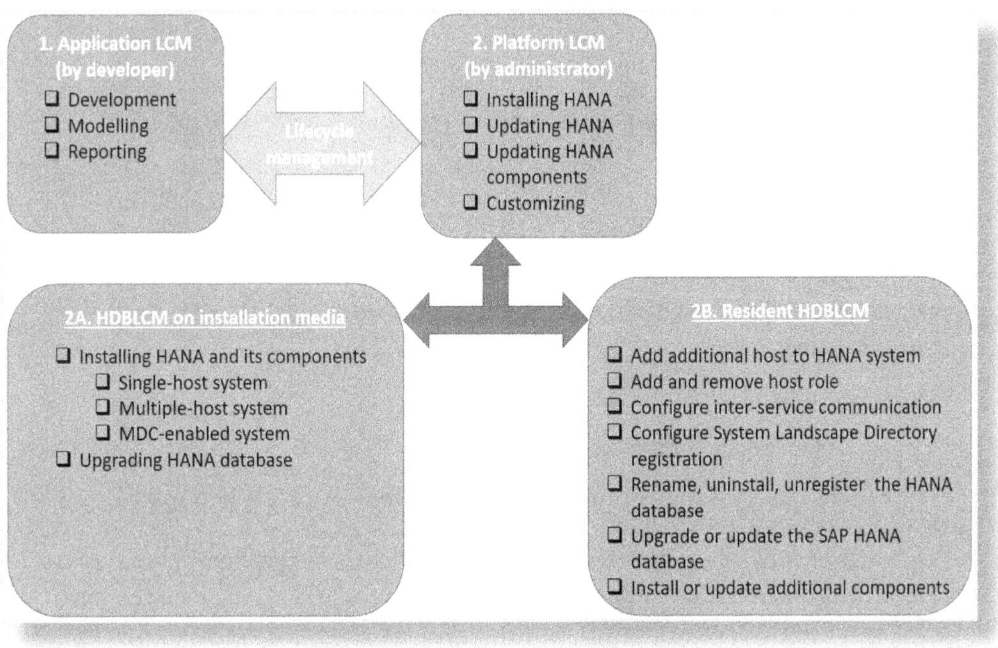

Figure 2.26: HANA database lifecycle management

It is important to understand that these tools have specific purposes and cannot generally be used interchangeably. Table 2.3 shows the list of activities that can be carried out by the respective HDBLCM.

HDBLCM from installation media	Resident HDBLCM
▶ Install HANA and its components ▶ Single host system ▶ Multiple host system ▶ MDC-enabled system ▶ Upgrade HANA database	▶ Add additional host to HANA system ▶ Add and remove host role ▶ Configure inter-service communication ▶ Configure System Landscape Directory registration ▶ Rename, uninstall, unregister the HANA database ▶ Update the SAP HANA database ▶ Install or update additional components

Table 2.3: HDBLCM from installation media versus resident HDBLCM

2.5.2 HDBLCM user interfaces and modes

Administrators can use both types of HDBLCM via three different user interfaces. They are:

- Graphical user interface (GUI)
- Command line interface
- Web user interface (not available for HDBLCM installation media)

Figure 2.27 provides executables and commands to trigger both types of HDBLCM according to the user interface.

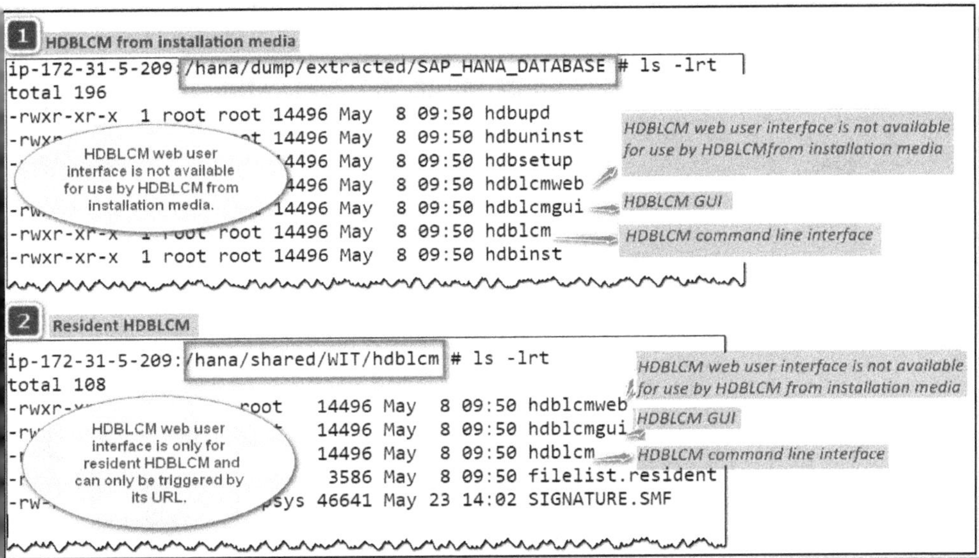

Variants of HDBLCM	Graphical User Interface	Command line interface	Web user interface
HDBLCM from installation media **Execution path:** cd <installation medium>/DATA_UNITS/HDB_LCM_LINUX_*	./hdblcmgui	./hdblcm	Not Applicable
Resident HDBLCM **Execution Path:** /sapmnt/<SID>/hdblcm OR /hana/shared/<SID>/hdblcm	./hdblcmgui	./hdblcmgui	URL: https://<host_name>:1129/lmsl/HDBLCM/WIP/index.html OR http://<host_name>:1128/lmsl/HDBLCM/WIP/index.html (not recommended nor secure)

Figure 2.27: HDBLCM from installation media versus resident HDBLCM

2.5.3 User interfaces of HDBLCM from installation media

HDBLCM from installation media can be triggered either from GUI mode or command line mode. Unlike command line mode, GUI mode (*hdblcmgui*) requires external GUI software (such as MOBAXTERM_PORTABLE_V23.6) to launch. The steps involved in invoking the *hdblcmgui* are shown in Figure 2.28. External software MOBAXTERM_PORTABLE_V23.6 is downloaded and used here.

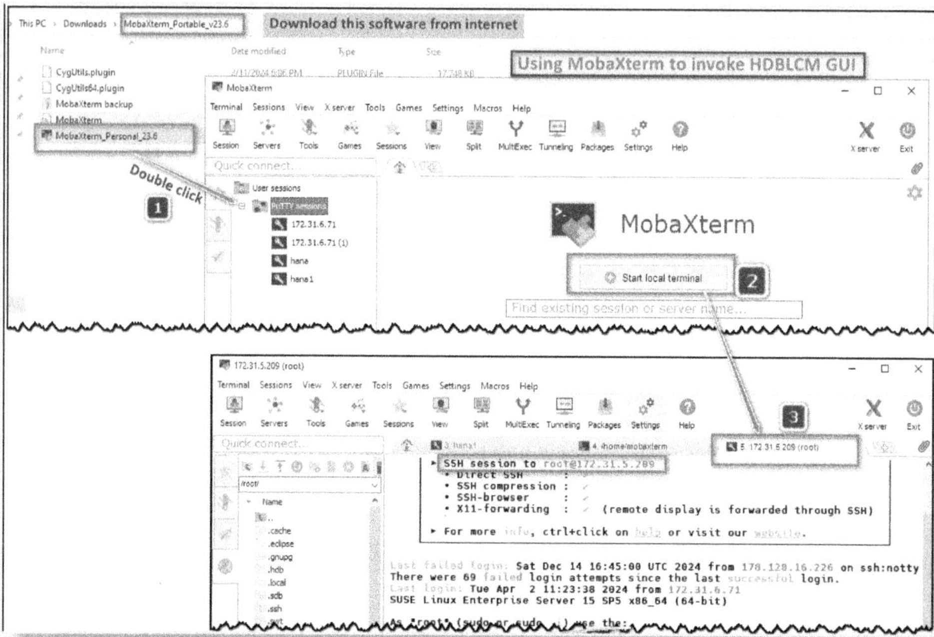

Figure 2.28: MobaXterm to invoke HDBLCM GUI mode

The steps involved in invoking the target database server are:

❶ To invoke *hdblcmgui*, external software MOBAXTERM_PORTABLE_V23.6 can be downloaded and used. Double click on the executable.

❷ Click on START LOCAL TERMINAL.

❸ Connect to the target server using the command `ssh <os_user_name>@<target_server>`.

Figure 2.29 shows screenshots of both HDBLCM modes from installation media:

❶ Database tasks possible from the GUI mode—install a new database or update an existing system.

❷ Database tasks possible from command-line mode—install a new database or update an existing system; Extract SAR files.

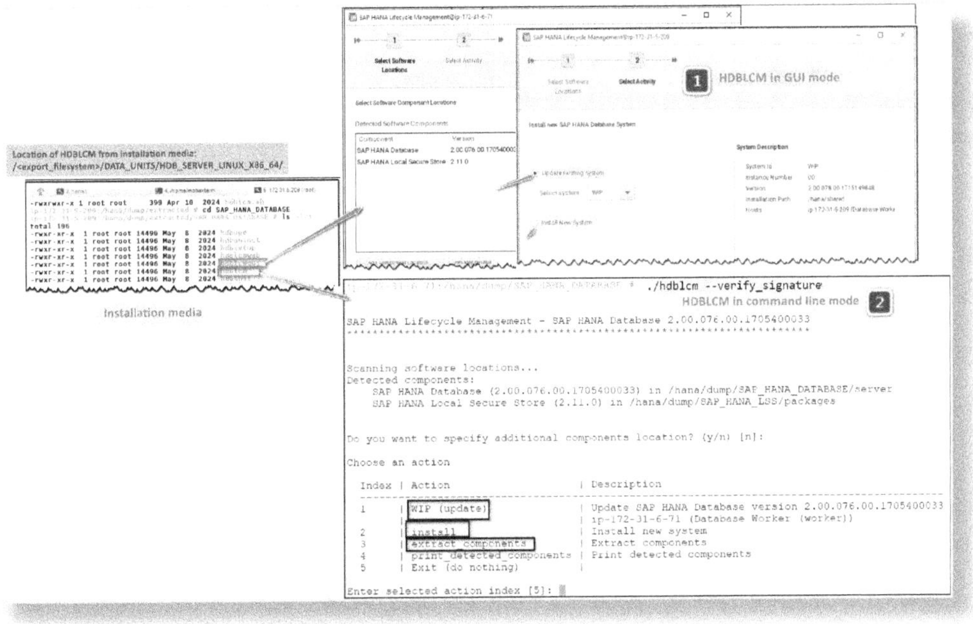

Figure 2.29: HDBLCM from installation media—GUI modes

2.5.4 Resident HDBLCM—user interfaces

Figure 2.30 displays screenshots of the resident HDBLCM GUI mode and command line mode, along with a list of tasks that can be performed using each tool.

> **! Resident HDBLCM**
>
> Resident HDBLCM is version-compatible because it is automatically installed as part of HANA database installation or upgrade.

2.5.5 Resident HDBLCM—web user interface

The web user interface, unlike the command line and GUI modes, cannot be directly invoked using the executable *hdblcmweb*. It is only accessible as part of the resident HDBLCM user interface. Unlike the other two user interfaces, this one is hosted by the SAP Host Agent and is auto-enabled during HANA database installation. Figure 2.31 shows a screenshot of the web user interface.

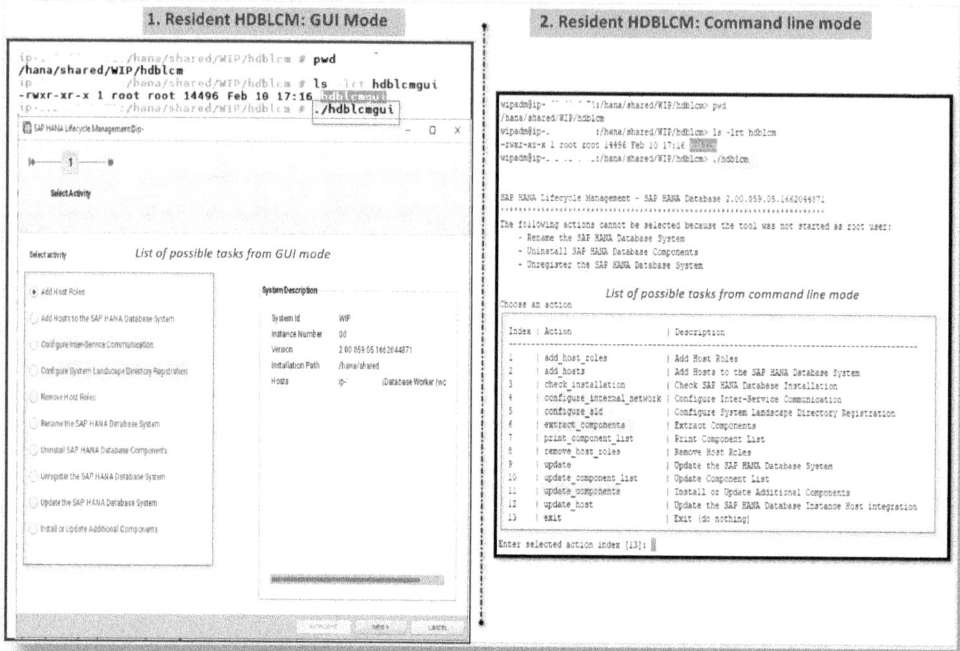

Figure 2.30: Resident HDBLCM user interfaces

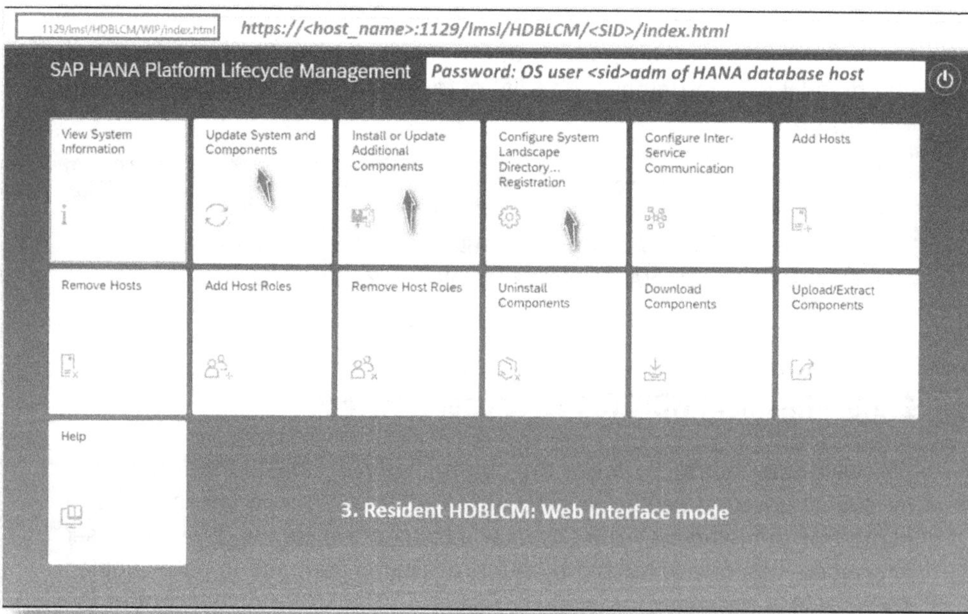

Figure 2.31: Web user interface of resident HDBLCM

When a user connects to the web interface URL using *<sid>adm* credentials, HDBLCM web is triggered automatically by the Host Agent. It is worth noting that web user interface actions are always executed on an existing HANA database, which is already installed and registered.

> **! HDBLCM web user interface**
>
> The web user interface always corresponds directly to the installed HANA database and can only be activated after the database has been installed. HDBLCM in web user interface mode cannot be used to install a HANA database.

2.5.6 Different modes to pass parameters to HDBLCM

HANA platform lifecycle management tasks need various mandatory and optional parameter inputs based on the database operations that are triggered through this tool.

Parameters can be supplied to platform LCM (Both HDBLCM from installation media and resident HDBLCM) in three different modes:

- **Interactive mode**—prompts the end user to provide only the mandatory parameters, leaving optional parameters unchanged with their default values.
- **Advanced interactive mode**—users can provide both mandatory and optional parameters, including those that override default values, either through the command line or a configuration file.
- **Batch mode**—used for automated installations, this mode requires the parameters to be supplied via either the command line or a configuration file. Default values will be used for any parameters which do not have a specific value in the configuration file.

Figure 2.32 outlines which HDBLCM user interface modes are valid against the indicated parameter modes.

HDBLCM INTERFACE/ MODE	INTERACTIVE MODE	ADVANCED INTERACTIVE MODE	BATCH OR AUTOMATED MODE
Graphical user interface	Available	Available	*Not available*
Command-line interface	Available	Available	Available
Web user interface	Available	*Not available*	*Not available*
	❑ Parameters in this mode will be entered as and when requested by the tool. ❑ No modification to default parameters.	❑ Parameters in this mode can be entered interactively, and can also be provided as CALL options or via a configuration file. ❑ Default values can be modified.	❑ All required parameters must be provided with CALL to the HDBLCM or via configuration file. ❑ Default values can be modified.

Figure 2.32: Ways to pass parameters to HDBLCM

Parameter mode and their preferences

Be aware that parameters specified in the command line, along with the HDBLCM command, override the parameter values specified through a configuration file. Similarly, parameters from the configuration file override default values.

Parameter precedence to HDBLCM is as follows: Command Line -> Configuration file -> Default values

Sample commands for these parameter modes are outlined below.

Interactive mode

Commands to pass the parameters in interactive mode to resident HDBLCM and HDBLCM from installation media are as follows:

- HDBLCM from installation media and from resident HDBLCM:
  - `./hdblcm` (command line interface)
  - `./hdblcmgui` (GUI interface)
- Resident HDBLCM for web interface (hdblcmweb cannot be triggered directly)

The URL is *https://<host_name>:1129/lmsl/HDBLCM/<SID>/index.html*

or

http://<host_name>:1128/lmsl/HDBLCM/<SID>/index.html

(Note that http is not secure and is therefore not recommended)

Advanced interactive mode

Commands to pass the parameter value in advanced interactive mode for resident HDBLCM and HDBLCM from installation media are:

- Call option via configuration file (command line interface):

```
./hdblcm --configfile=<file path>
```

- Call option via command line (GUI interface):

```
./hdblcmgui --<parameter key>=<parameter value>
```

A sample command to install WIP HANA SID with instance number 00 involves the HDBLCM usage shown below. These inputs can be passed directly in a command or by using a configuration file (HANA_install.cfg):

- `./hdblcm -s WIP -n 00 -G 110`
    - `-s` = system name
    - `-n` = instance number
    - `-G` = group ID
- `./hdblcm --configfile=/home/root/HANA_install.cfg`

The advanced interactive mode is not available for a web-based interface.

Batch mode

The commands to pass parameter values to HDBLCM from installation media and resident HDBLCM in batch mode are:

- Call option via command line:

```
cat ~/<passwords.xml> | ./hdblcm --batch --action=install --
components=server --sid=<SID> --number=<instance_number> --read_
password_from_stdin=xml
```

▶ Call option via configuration file:

```
./hdblcm --batch --configfile=/var/tmp/configfile
```

▶ Call option in batch mode via configuration file:

```
./hdblcm --configfile=/home/root/HANA_install.cfg -b
```

! User interface versus mode of passing parameter

GUI and web interfaces are not valid for passing the parameter in batch mode.

Generating template configuration file

The template configuration file, which can be used to pass parameters to HDBLCM (both from the installation media and resident), via either advanced interactive mode or batch mode, can be generated from the HANA database server using the following command:

```
./hdblcm --configfile=<file_path>/<file_name>.cfg
```

This command generates a blank template containing all the configuration parameters with their default values. These parameters can then be modified as needed and passed to HDBLCM through the configuration file option.

A sample installation command using the updated template parameter file is:

```
./hdblcm --action=install --dump_configfile_template=<file_
path>/<file_name>.cfg
```

This is shown in Figure 2.33.

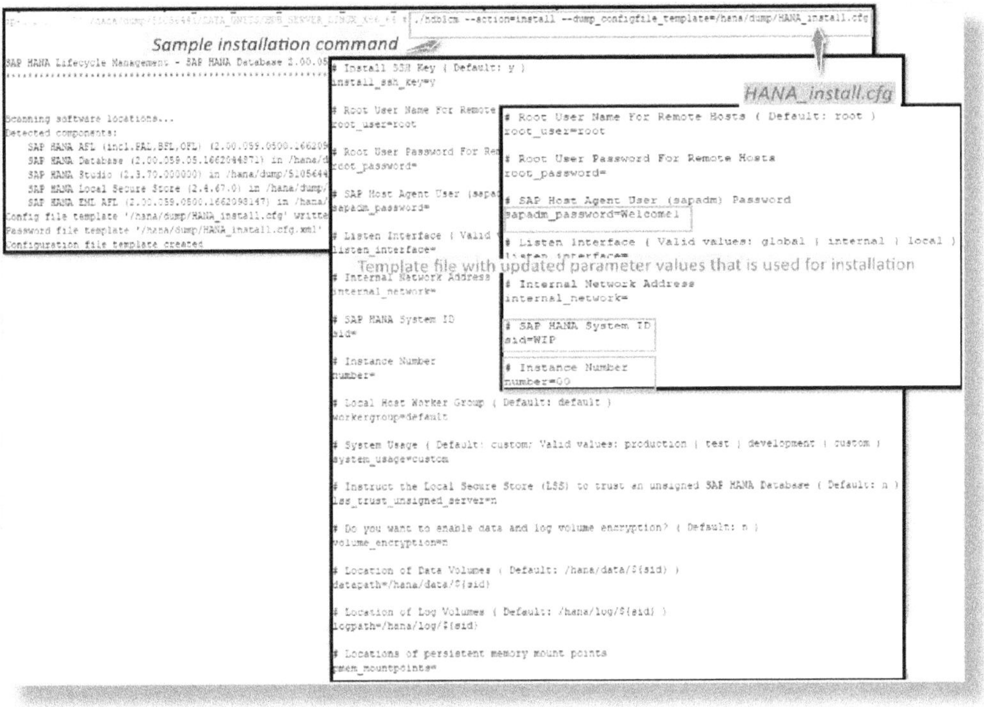

Figure 2.33: Generating template configuration file

2.5.7 Verifying and extracting SAR files using resident HDBLCM

The SAP HANA database installation dump in *.SAR format can also be extracted using HDBLCM. The HDBLCM options for extraction of these SAR files are:

- HDBLCM from installation media in command line mode (see Figure 2.29)
- Resident HDBLCM in command line mode (see Figure 2.30)
- Web user interface mode (see Figure 2.31)

Figure 2.34 shows SAR file extraction using resident HDBLCM.

```
ip-172-31-5-209:/hana/shared/WIP/hdblcm # ./hdblcm

SAP HANA Lifecycle Management - SAP HANA Database 2.00.078.00.1715149848
************************************************************************

Choose an action

  Index | Action                      | Description
  -----------------------------------------------------------------------------------------------
  1     | add_host_roles              | Add Host Roles
  2     | add_hosts                   | Add Hosts to the SAP HANA Database System
  3     | check_installation          | Check SAP HANA Database Installation
  4     | configure_internal_network  | Configure Inter-Service Communication
  5     | configure_sld               | Configure System Landscape Directory Registration
  6     | extract_components          | Extract Components
  7     | print_component_list        | Print Component List
  8     | print_detected_components   | Print Detected Components
  9     | remove_host_roles           | Remove Host Roles
  10    | rename_system               | Rename the SAP HANA Database System
  11    | uninstall                   | Uninstall SAP HANA Database Components
  12    | unregister_system           | Unregister the SAP HANA Database System
  13    | update                      | Update the SAP HANA Database System
  14    | update_component_list       | Update Component List
  15    | update_components           | Install or Update Additional Components
        |                             |   SAP HANA Cockpit: Install of version 2.0016.12 is pending (s
  16    | update_host                 | Update the SAP HANA Database Instance Host integration
  17    | exit                        | Exit (do nothing)

Enter selected action index [17]: 6

Enter Location of SAP HANA Database Component Archives: /hana/dump/test
Enter Temporary Extract Directory [/hana/dump/test/extracted]:
Overwrite Existing Files in the Extraction Directory [n]:
Enter Location of 'SAPCAR' Executable [/hana/shared/WIP/global/hdb/saphostagent_setup/SAPCAR]:

Summary before execution:
=========================

SAP HANA Database
   Extract Components Parameters
      Location of SAP HANA Database Component Archives: /hana/dump/test
      Temporary Extract Directory: /hana/dump/test/extracted
      Location of 'SAPCAR' Executable: /hana/shared/WIP/global/hdb/saphostagent_setup/SAPCAR
   Log File Locations
      Log directory: /var/tmp/hdb_WIP_hdblcm_extract_components_2024-12-19_04.50.05
      Trace location: /var/tmp/hdblcm_2024-12-19_04.50.05_12583.trc

Do you want to continue? (y/n): y

Extracting components...
```

Location of SAR files to be extracted

Verifies authenticity of the downloaded SAR files automatically

Figure 2.34: Extract SAR files using HDBLCM

As of SAP HANA 2.0 SP03, resident HDBLCM automatically verifies the authenticity of software updates during extraction. However, verification is disabled by default when using HDBLCM from installation media because the HANA database installation kit is considered untrusted. To enable verification in this case, include the `--verify_signature` command line parameter with the `hdblcm` command from the installation media.

2.5.8 HDBLCM—'--help' and '--pass_through_help'

For every database action performed using HDBLCM, a range of mandatory and optional input parameters are required. To gain a comprehensive list of these parameter values for a database task performed through HDBLCM, SAP provides the options `--help` and `--pass_through_help`. The `--action` parameter, together with `--help` or `-h`, must be specified in combination with `--pass_through_help`, as shown in Figure 2.35, in order to obtain a detailed understanding of all the possible input parameters that can be supplied.

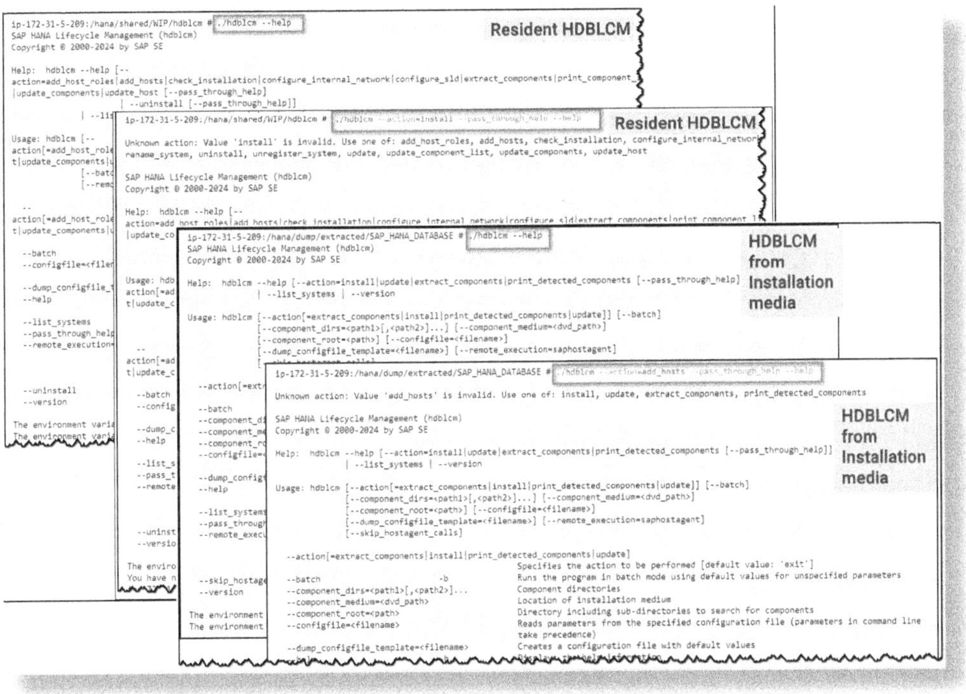

Figure 2.35: HDBLCM with '--help' and '--pass_through_help'

Some commands shown in this figure include:

- `./hdblcm -help`
- `./hdblcm --action=install --pass_through_help --help`

2.5.9 HDBLCM on multiple host environment

HDBLCM is initiated from the HANA database server in a single host scenario. However, in multiple host (distributed or scale-out) scenarios, these tasks can be triggered either from master node, known as *centralized execution,* or worker node, known as *decentralized execution*.

With decentralized execution, tasks are initially performed on a worker host and then manually repeated on each of the remaining hosts. In centralized execution, tasks are performed centrally from the master node, and are replicated to other hosts remotely using:

- SSH keys (*--remote_execution=ssh*) or
- SAP Host Agent.

With a centralized HDBLCM task execution using SSH keys, the HANA database scale-out installation must be performed with root user credentials. During installation, a secure shell (SSH) key is configured, enabling future platform LCM tasks to be performed remotely on multiple hosts without the need for a root user password. Additionally, HDBLCM installs and configures the SAP Host Agent on remote hosts by logging into the host via SSH. In general, as a prerequisite for a successful execution and completion of HDBLCM tasks on remote hosts, the root username and password can be identical across all the associated hosts. In the event of a password mismatch, SSH keys can be manually distributed between the database hosts in advance.

With a centralized execution using the SAP Host Agent (`--remote_execution=saphostagent`), platform LCM tasks are performed without root credentials through the SAP Host Agent. In this case, HDBLCM relies on the SAP Host Agent for the following functionalities:

- Execution as the system administrator user `<sid>adm`.
- Connectivity to remote hosts via HTTPS (when no SSH or root user credentials are available)
- Execution from the SAP HANA database lifecycle manager web user interface

As a prerequisite for this mode, the SAP Host Agent must be installed and configured on all hosts, in advance.

The steps to do this are as follows:

1. Install SAP Host Agent.
2. Configure a Secure Sockets Layer (SSL) certificate for the SAP Host Agent so that the HTTPS port 1129 is accessible. Refer to the "Configuring SSL for SAP Host Agent on UNIX" page in the SAP Help Portal (*help.sap.com*) for information about configuring the SSL certificate. Note that HDBLCM can also be forced to use HTTP in place of HTTPS by using the call option `--use_http`. It informs the HANA database lifecycle manager to communicate with the SAP Host Agent via HTTP.
3. When adding new hosts to an SAP HANA system, or during installation, the SAP Host Agent's HTTPS is automatically configured by the SAP HANA database lifecycle manager.

2.6 HANA installation

HDBLCM from installation media is the tool used to install the HANA database. As part of the HANA database installation process, this tool installs resident HDBLCM and automatically configures it with the installed HANA database. Subsequent upgrades to the system can be performed either through HDBLCM from installation media or from the resident HDBLCM.

2.6.1 Single host installation

The most straightforward method to install a HANA database involves deploying a single host system. The HDBLCM tool present in the installation media must be used to perform the database installation using either command line mode or GUI mode, as previously outlined. In addition, the parameters (mandatory and optional) required for installation can be supplied either in interactive mode or via automated batch mode, as discussed earlier.

Before starting the installation:

- The target server must already be provisioned with the chosen operating system on the designated hardware, along with the required amount of vCPU, RAM, and other necessary components and OS settings as specified previously.
- The HANA database file systems must already be provisioned and mounted.
- Optionally, the server can also be installed with the SAP Host Agent prior, as described earlier.
- The installation media must already be downloaded, transferred, validated, and extracted into the HANA database server, as shown in Figure 2.36.

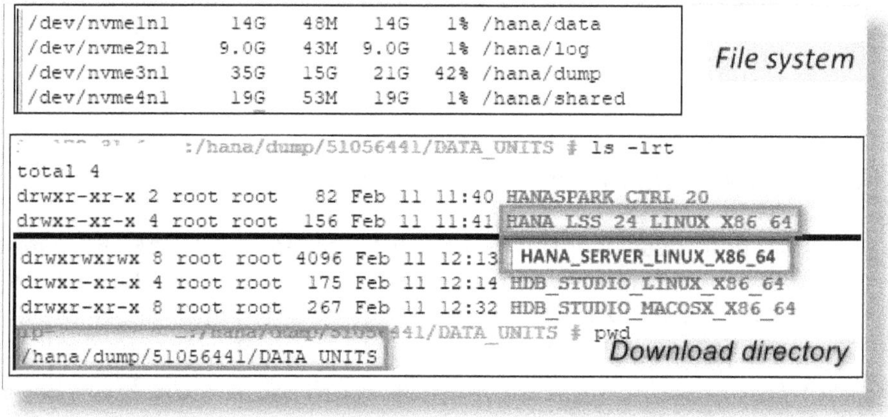

Figure 2.36: HANA Installation—file system and hdblcm path from the installation media

Table 2.4 provides a list of possible HANA database installation commands that can be used to install a HANA database of SID *WIP* with instance number *00* using various parameter modes.

Types of command line interface parameter mode	Commands Path from which the command must be executed: *<software_location>/DATA_UNITS/HDB_SERVER_LINUX_X86_64*
Interactive mode	`./hdblcm`
Advanced interactive mode	`./hdblcm --sid=`**WIP** `--number=`**00** `--groupid=`**110** `--sapmnt=/hana/shared --datapath=/hana/data/`**WIP** `--logpath=/hana/log/`**WIP** or `./hdblcm --configfile=/home/root/HANA_install.cfg`
Batch mode	`./hdblcm --configfile=/home/root/HANA_install.cfg -b`

Table 2.4: Commands for HANA DB installation from command line

Table 2.5 outlines the parameters that will be used in the installation that is covered in the coming sections.

System details	Specification	Command line
System Name (HANA SID)	WIP	`--sid=WIP`
Instance number	00	`--number=00`
Installation path	/hana/shared	`--sapmnt=/hana/shared`
Data path	/hana/data/WIP	`--datapath=/hana/data/WIP`
Log path	/hana/log/WIP	`--logpath=/hana/log/WIP`
User group ID	<default> or 1001	`--groupid=1001`
Command used for this installation	./`hdblcm -secure_store=localsecurestore`	

Table 2.5: Single host HANA system installation details

SAP HANA LSS

LSS (Local Secure Store) in HANA is a separate, lightweight utility designed for storing and securely managing encryption keys, encryption root keys, and other sensitive data. Section 5.4.2 provides further details on this.

A single node HANA database installation using interactive mode is depicted in Figure 2.37 and Figure 2.38 .

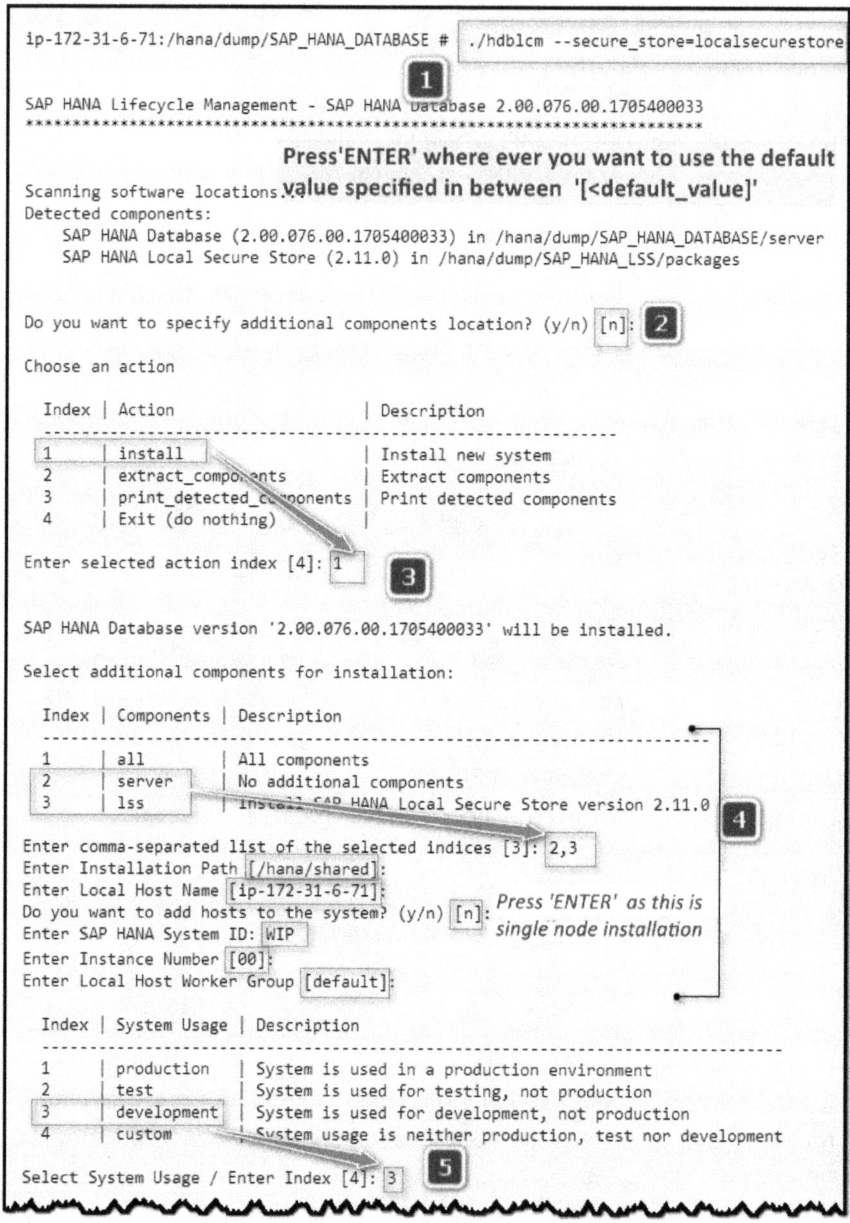

Figure 2.37: Single host HANA installation (1/2)

6

```
Do you want to enable backup encryption? [y]:
Do you want to enable data and log volume encryption? [y]:
Enter Location of Data Volumes [/hana/data/WIP]: /hana/shared/data
Enter Location of Log Volumes [/hana/log/WIP]: /hana/shared/log
Restrict maximum memory allocation? [n]:
Apply System Size Dependent Resource Limits? (SAP Note 3014176) [y]:
Enter System Administrator (wipadm) Password:
Confirm System Administrator (wipadm) Password:
Enter System Administrator Home Directory [/usr/sap/WIP/home]:
Enter System Administrator Login Shell [/bin/sh]:
Enter System Administrator User ID [1001]:
Enter System Database User (SYSTEM) Password:
Confirm System Database User (SYSTEM) Password:
Restart system after machine reboot? [n]:
Enter Installation Path for Local Secure Store [/lss/shared]:
Enter Local Secure Store User Home Directory [/usr/sap/WIP/lss/home]: /lss/WIP
Enter Local Secure Store User Login Shell [/bin/sh]:
Enter Local Secure Store Auto Backup Password:
Confirm Local Secure Store Auto Backup Password:

Summary before execution:
=========================

SAP HANA Database System Installation
   Installation Parameters
      Remote Execution: ssh
      Database Isolation: low
      Install Execution Mode: optimized
```

```
   Software Components
      SAP HANA Database
         Install version 2.00.076.00.1705400033
         Location: /hana/dump/SAP_HANA_DATABASE/server
      SAP HANA Local Secure Store
         Install version 2.11.0
         Location: /hana/dump/SAP_HANA_LSS/packages
   Log File Locations
      Log directory: /var/tmp/hdb_WIP_hdblcm_install_2024-02-19_08.23.50
      Trace location: /var/tmp/hdblcm_2024-02-19_08.23.50_4179.trc
```

```
Installing SAP HANA Local Secure Store...
  Preparing package 'LocalSecureStore'...
  Preparing package 'Installer'...
  Installing Local Secure Store to /lss/shared/WIP...
  Installing package 'LocalSecureStore'...
  Installing package 'Installer'...
  Configuring SAP HANA Local Secure Store across the SAP HANA landscape...
    Configuring Local Secure Store on local host...
Installing Resident hdblcm...
Registering SAP HANA Database binaries in Local Secure Store...
Configuring SAP HANA Database...
  Configuring System...
  Configuring instance...
Starting instances...
```

Resident HDBLCM gets auto installed as part of database installation

```
Updating SAP HANA Database Instance Integration on Local Host...
  Deploying SAP Host Agent configurations...
Creating Component List...
SAP HANA Database System installed
Log file written to '/var/tmp/hdb_WIP_hdblcm_install_2024-02-19_08.23.50/hdblcm.log' on host 'ip-172-31-6-71'.
ip-172-31-6-71:/hana/dump/SAP_HANA_DATABASE #
```

Figure 2.38: Single host HANA installation (2/2)

The steps shown in the screenshots are as follows:

❶ Execute the HDBLCM command from installation media.

❷ To specify additional components apart from the one detected, enter the folder path that contains those component dumps.

❸–❹ Choose the INSTALL option and select specific indexes against the components that need to be installed.

❺ Select the SYSTEM USAGE type.

❻ Enter the required installation values as prompted, modifying the default suggested values within '[ ]' if necessary.

The installed HANA database can be accessed using HANA Studio. Further information about HANA Studio will be covered in Section 2.6.6.

2.6.2 Trace and log files

Trace files

In the event of a HANA database installation failure—whether due to an installer crash, an unexpected deadlock, or a loop—detailed tracing must be activated to identify the root cause. To do this, the environment variable *HDB_INSTALLER_TRACE_FILE* must be configured to point to a trace file before restarting the installation process, as shown in Figure 2.39.

```
ip-172-31-5-209:/hana/dump # HDB_INSTALLER_TRACE_FILE=/hana/dump; export HDB_INSTALLER_TRACE_FILE
ip-172-31-5-209:/hana/dump # echo $HDB_INSTALLER_TRACE_FILE
/hana/dump
ip-172-31-5-209:/hana/dump #
```

Figure 2.39: Setting the trace file path before installation

The generated trace file provides valuable information about the issue and can be attached to an SAP OSS (Online Service System) message for reporting to SAP for further analysis (see Section 7.10).

Log files

Tasks relating to HANA database actions executed through hdblcm generate logs that are stored either in */var/tmp/hdblcm.log* or */var/tmp/hdblcmgui.log*, depending on the user interface used. Additionally, copies of these logs are archived in the directory *hdb_<SID>hdblcm<action>_<date>* in the same location. Apart from these logs, specific action-related logs for hdblcm such as install, update, uninstall, add host, and others, are stored in the following path: */var/tmp/hdb_<SID>hdblcm<action>_<time_stamp>*, where *<action> ::= install | update | addhost | uninstall |*, and so on. The log files in this folder include:

- *<hdbcommand>.log* (readable using a text editor)
- *<hdbcommand>.msg* (XML format for display within the installation tool with the GUI.)
- *<hostname>_tracediff.tgz* (provides a delta analysis of the original trace files, making detailed analysis easier)

2.6.3 Database and operating system users

During the HANA installation process, users are created both in the database and at the operating system (OS) level. They are:

- **<sid>adm** (OS user)—an operating system user that is automatically created during the HANA database installation process using installation inputs such as user ID (UID), password, group ID (GID), etc. This user is responsible for executing administrative tasks such as starting and stopping the HANA database, as well as performing various other database-related activities at the operating system level. The user's primary group must be *sapsys*, with 79 as the default GID. In scenarios involving multiple hosts (distributed hosts), both the UID and GID of this user must remain the same across all the associated hosts within the HANA database system.
- **sapadm** (OS user)—serves as the administrator user for the SAP Host Agent. During installation of the HANA database, this user is created if it does not already exist. If it is already present on the installation host, neither sapadm nor its password are modified by the installer. The primary group for this user must be *sapsys*, with 79 as the default GID. Like <sid>adm, in a scenario involving multiple hosts (distributed hosts), the UID and GID of this user must remain the same across all hosts within the HANA database system.
- **SYSTEM**—a database superuser that has maximum privileges. During installation, two *SYSTEM* users are created—one for the SystemDB and the other for the tenant database. The passwords for these users are supplied during installation (through parameter name *system_user_password*).

- **<sid>crypt** (OS user)—a trusted local secure store (LSS) user. This user owns the storage of encryption keys and other sensitive data.

2.6.4 Key ports

Each HANA server component or service runs as a separate operating system process and is initiated during the HANA database start-up. Most of these services can be accessed individually through their own network ports. Table 2.6 lists some critical HANA database services along with their network ports.

Service	Multiple container xx=HANA system instance number	Function
daemon	3xx00	Monitors and controls the state of SAP HANA instance
Nameserver	3xx01 (SQL: 3xx13)	Used for administrative tasks such as handling topology information, collecting load history, and monitoring system replication
Indexserver	3xx03 (SQL: 3xx15)—for default tenant 3xx40 or higher (SQL: 3xx41 and higher)—for additional tenant databases	Primary HANA service responsible for managing row and column-store tables.
Webdispatcher	3xx06	Handles HTTP based requests
Sapstartsrv	5xx13 5xx14	Used to start and stop SAP HANA services and monitor their state

Table 2.6: HANA—key ports

For an end-user or application to log in to the SystemDB or a tenant database, the corresponding SQL port must be open and accessible from the source application server or the end-user's desktop. As part of standard HANA database installation, the SystemDB and tenant databases are assigned specific ports for SQL, internal communication, HTTP, etc. The ports for the SystemDB and default tenant database (the first tenant installed by default) adhere to a predetermined port number format as shown in Table 2.6 and Table 2.7. However, additional tenant databases are assigned ports starting from 3<instance number(xx)>40 with an increment of three up to 3<instance number>99. Consequently, the default maximum number of tenant databases that can be created per HANA database system is 20.

Type of port	SystemDB	Default tenant	Additional tenant (1)	Additional tenant (2)	Additional tenant (20)
Internal communication	3xx01	3xx03	3xx40	3xx43	3xx97
SQL	3xx13	3xx15	3xx41	3xx44	3xx98
HTTP	3xx14	3xx08	3xx42	3xx45	3xx99

Table 2.7: HANA database ports format

For further information, refer to SAP Note 2477204—"FAQ: SAP HANA Services and Ports".

2.6.5 Starting and stopping the HANA database

The HANA database can be restarted either from the operating system or by using administration tools such as HANA Studio or the HANA Cockpit. Table 2.8 lists the OS commands used to restart the HANA database by logging in as a <sid>adm OS user. The restart command varies depending on whether it is a single host or multi-host (scale-out) system.

Command	Single node OS User : *<sid>adm*	Scale-out OS User : *<sid>adm* *<nn> = instance number*
To start the database	`HDB start`	From master node: `/usr/sap/hostctrl/exe/sapcontrol -nr <nn> -function StartSystem HDB`
To stop the database	`HDB stop`	From master node: `/usr/sap/hostctrl/exe/sapcontrol -nr <nn> -function StopSystem HDB`
To view database status	`HDB info`	From master node: `/usr/sap/hostctrl/exe/sapcontrol -nr <nn> -function GetSystemInstanceList`

Table 2.8: HANA database start, stop and status commands

Figure 2.40 shows the commands to start, stop, and check the status of a single host HANA database.

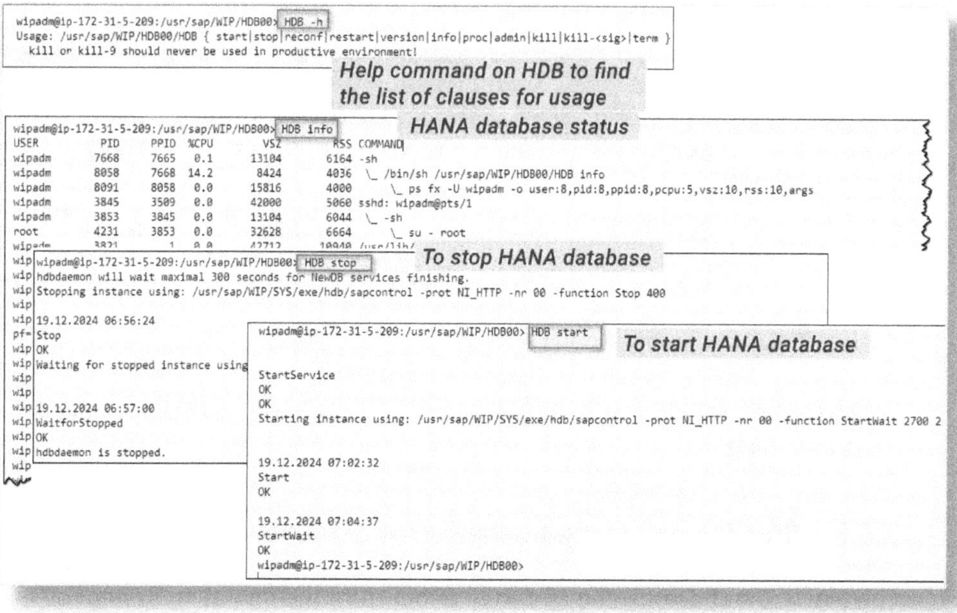

Figure 2.40: Single node—start, stop, and status commands

Figure 2.41 shows the commands to start, stop, and check the status of a multi-host (scale-out) HANA database.

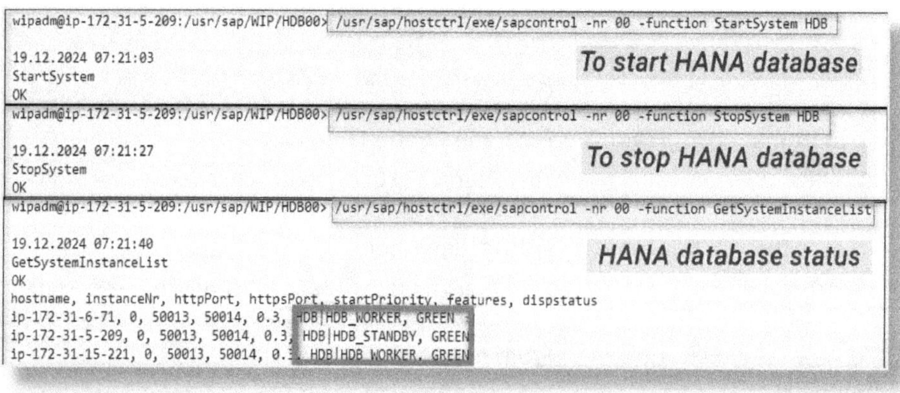

Figure 2.41: Scale-out node—start, stop, and status commands

2.6.6 HANA Studio installation

HANA Studio serves as a simple user-friendly administration tool for the HANA database. It can be installed either on the HANA database server (Linux) or on an end user's remote desktop.

Downloading the HANA Studio software from the SAP portal involves a process similar to that outlined in Section 2.4.2. Refer to SAP Note 2902153—"How to download HANA Studio"—and download the required software. Note that the SAPCAR used to unpack this software must match the user desktop's operating system in the case of a desktop-based studio installation.

Figure 2.42 and Figure 2.43 show the steps involved in unpacking and installing a HANA Studio on a Windows RDP (remote desktop).

Figure 2.42: HANA Studio: Extracting IMC_STUDIO.SAR*

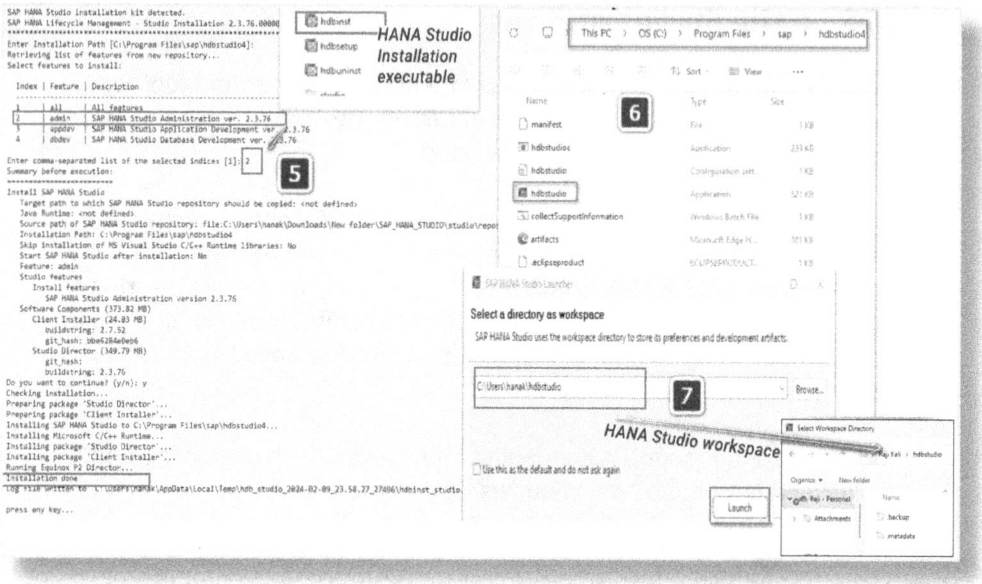

Figure 2.43: HANA Studio: Installing and launching HANA Studio

The steps shown in the screenshots are as follows:

❶ Download HANA Studio and Windows' SAPCAR and place them on the target desktop where the studio is to be installed.

❷ Extract HANA Studio using SAPCAR.

❸ A folder is created, labelled SAP_HANA_STUDIO

❹ Navigate to the folder and double-click on HDBINST to start the HANA Studio installation.

❺ Select the index based on the HANA Studio feature to be installed. For administrators, the ADMIN feature is generally recommended

❻ After installation, navigate to the target installation folder and double-click on HDBSTUDIO.

❼ When launched, HANA Studio will prompt you to specify a HANA Studio workspace. Enter a folder location and click on the LAUNCH button.

HANA Studio workspace

A workspace is a dedicated directory or folder where SAP HANA Studio stores all the files and metadata related to development, modeling, and administrative tasks

Once the installation is complete, HANA Studio can be launched, as shown at step 7 in Figure 2.43, and can be used to connect to an installed HANA database.

To connect the HANA database to HANA Studio on an RDP (remote desktop), the following ports from the HANA server must be accessible from the RDP:

- SystemDB SQL port: 3xx13
- Tenant database SQL port: 3xx15 (default tenant) or 3xx41 (tenant1), 3xx41+3 (tenant2), and so forth.
- sapstartsrv port: 5xx13, 5xx14 (to enable start and stop of DB from the studio).

The `telnet` command can be used to verify the HANA server's reachability from the end user's RDP server. Examples of telnet commands are as follows:

- From a linux server to HANA database server using *putty*:

```
telnet <hana_server> <port>
```

- From a Window's server to HANA database server using *PowerShell*:

```
Test-NetConnection <hana_server> -Port <sql_port>
-InformationLevel "Detailed"
```

An example command is as follows:

```
PS C:\Users\ra20214445> Test-NetConnection XX.XX.XXX.XX -Port
30015 -InformationLevel "Detailed"
```

(Port number 3<nn>15 indicates the SQL port of the default tenant database.

After installing HANA Studio on the end-user's local desktop, the installed HANA database can be connected for database administration and management, as shown in Figure 2.44.

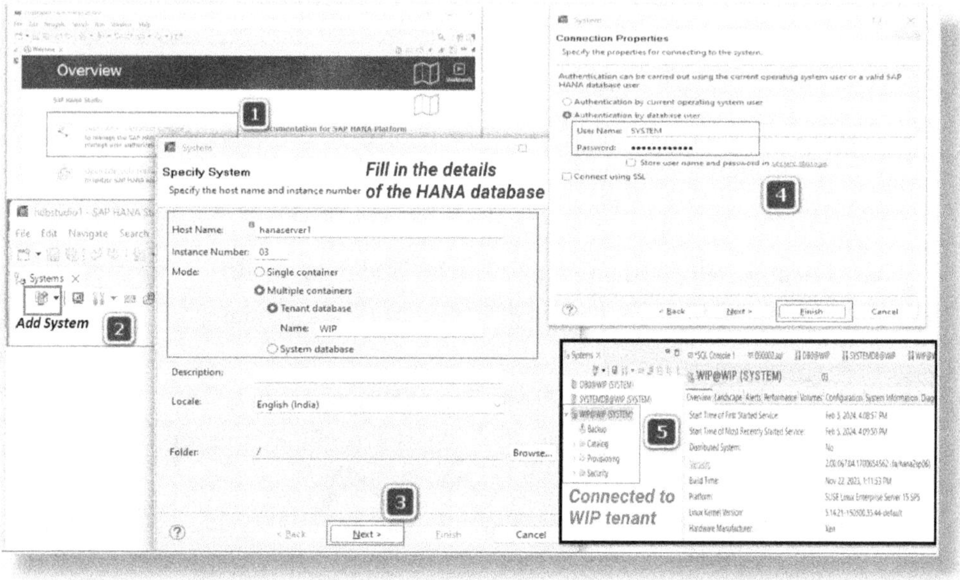

Figure 2.44: HANA Studio—launching HANA Studio and connecting to HANA database

Figure 2.44 is a continuation of Figure 2.42 and Figure 2.43. The steps in the image are as follows:

❶ Click on OPEN ADMINISTRATION CONSOLE

❷ Click on the "add system" icon as highlighted in the image.

❸ Enter the details of the target HANA database which is to be connected. It can be either a SystemDB or a tenant database.

❹ Enter the database credentials.

❺ shows a HANA database which has been successfully connected through HANA Studio.

2.6.7 Adding standby node to single host installation

Integrating a standby node into an existing single node installation provides the HANA system with an auto-failover capability—a crucial high-availability feature that ensures swift recovery in the event of primary host failure. In cases where the host handling end-user requests fail, the standby node seamlessly assumes the responsibilities of the failing node and starts to serve all new user requests. This is illustrated in Figure 2.45. Here, a single node setup can be converted to a master-slave (standby) setup by adding a standby node to the former single node.

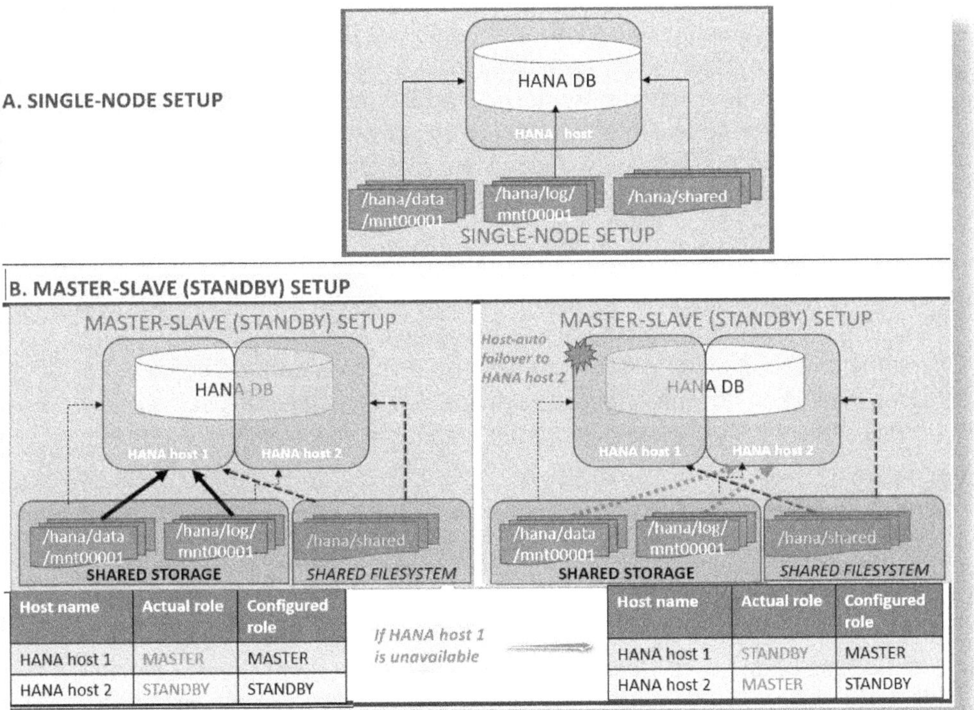

Figure 2.45: Concept of master-standby setup

After a standby node addition, one HANA node will act as a MASTER node and another acts as a STANDBY node.

HANA database installations with more than one host will have the configuration that is illustrated in Figure 2.46:

- Host role is either *WORKER* or *STANDBY*.
- Name server is either *MASTER* or *SLAVE*.
- Index server is *MASTER, SLAVE* or *STANDBY*.

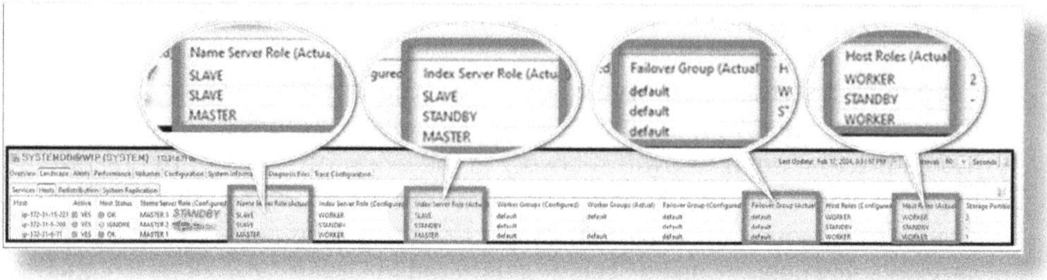

Figure 2.46: Possible roles for HANA host, name server, and index server

When the index server with the master role becomes unavailable, the index server with the standby role seamlessly assumes the data and log volumes of the failing master node, transitioning into the new master to handle end-user requests and minimize downtime. The failing node then becomes the new standby node. Note that only one host with the role of worker can function as the master node, hosting the master name server and master index server. All other worker nodes act as slave nodes, each hosting a slave index server.

Both the master index server and slave index server have their own data and log volumes and collaborate to serve end-user requests. However, a host with a standby role does not have its own data and log volume, nor does it serve end-user requests. It remains as a standby index server/slave name server in passive, dormant mode, without handling end-user requests, unless a worker host fails. In the event of a failed worker host (master or slave node), the standby node assumes the host role of the former worker host by taking over its data and log volume and automatically converting itself from a standby host role to a worker host role. The failed node is then assigned the standby host role.

In the case of an *active-standby* setup, HANA has an out-of-the-box capability to identify an unresponsive host and to trigger an auto-failover. For this purpose, one of the name servers functions as the *cluster manager*, regularly pinging all hosts to check their availability (heartbeat). If an unresponsive host is detected, the cluster manager ensures that the standby host takes over the role of the failing host by converting it into a worker host. Additionally, the failed host is no longer allowed read/write access to its former data and log volumes (called *fencing*), thereby preventing corruption. It is crucial to note that the failure of a single service does not automatically trigger failover because HANA's hdbdaemon generally restarts and auto-heals failing services.

! M_LANDSCAPE_HOST_CONFIGURATION

The system view M_LANDSCAPE_HOST_CONFIGURATION can be used to determine if a node is active or standby using the following SQL query:

```
select * from M_LANDSCAPE_HOST_CONFIGURATION;
```

For the standby host to seamlessly take over the data and log volumes from the failing node, it is imperative to configure all the HANA system hosts to share or have access to all the data and log volumes, regardless of their master, slave or standby status. Note that in case of a multi-node setup (distributed setup), it is mandatory to ensure that the */hana/shared* file system is shared between all the hosts of the HANA database, irrespective of whether a slave node host role is a worker or a standby.

The screenshot in Figure 2.47 demonstrates the addition of a standby host to an existing single host HANA database installation using the resident HDBLCM tool.

The steps are as follows:

❶ Trigger the resident HDBLCM from */hana/shared/<SID>/hdblcm/*.

❷ Choose ADD_HOSTS.

❸ Enter the details of the new host.

❹ Choose the STANDBY host role and configure it with the DEFAULT host failover group.

❺ Configure the HANA database LISTEN INTERFACE as INTERNAL

❻ Set up passwords for *<sid>adm* and *<sid>crypt* in the new host.

❼ This results in successful addition of the standby host to the HANA database and writes the installation log file to the location specified.

To facilitate this addition, the */hana/shared, /hana/data, and /hana/log* volumes were shared between both the hosts. Identical root passwords were also configured on both servers. As part of this addition, the installer has created the required operating system users similar to those in the master node and has enabled the required configuration for auto-failover.

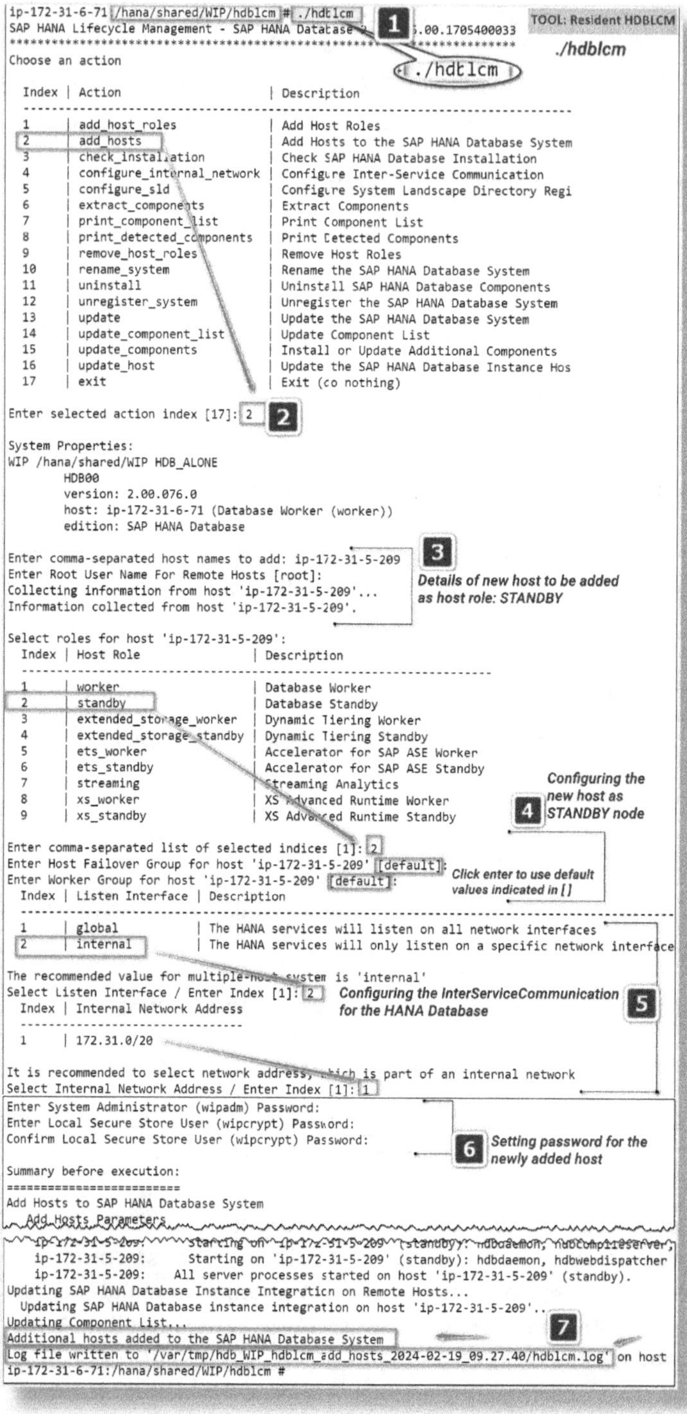

Figure 2.47: Adding a standby node to previously installed HANA database

> **☛ Inter-service communication settings**
>
> Note that when adding standby node, HDBLCM prompts you to set up the inter-service communication (if not already set) to *internal*. Setting this value to *global* results in the HANA service listening on all network interfaces, an *internal* value allows HANA services to only listen on a specific network interface. This setting can be configured via RESIDENT HDBLCM • CONFIGURE INTER-SERVICE COMMUNICATION (see Figure 2.30) or by using the HANA Cockpit.

2.6.8 Multiple host installation (distributed installation)

The distributed deployment of a HANA database, also known as scale-out deployment, was discussed previously, and I highlighted various reasons for adapting such a setup.

To convert a single node HANA database into a distributed or scale-out installation, an additional host with a worker host role must be added to the database. After adding a new host with this role, it is recommended to redistribute or transfer some of the tables from the original host to the newly added worker host. This sequence is shown in Figure 2.48. From a table redistribution perspective, further details will be covered in Section 4.1.8.

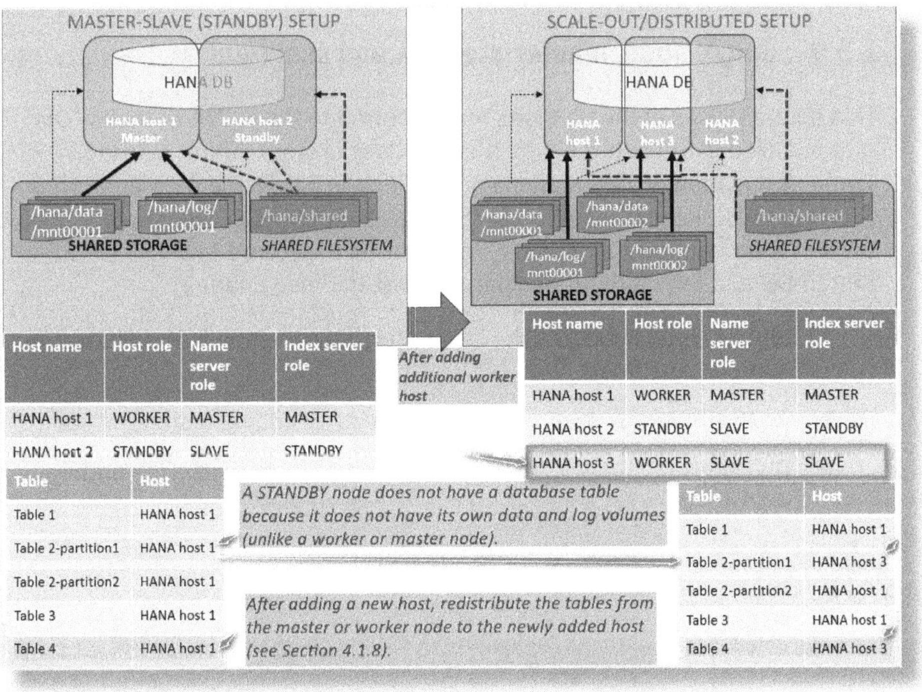

Figure 2.48: Before and after adding an additional worker node

Figure 2.49 shows the addition of a worker host to an existing master-standby setup, using resident HDBLCM. To facilitate this addition, the */hana/shared* volume has been shared among all hosts. Furthermore, identical root passwords were configured on all the associated servers. Note that sharing */hana/data* and */hana/log* volumes across all nodes is not required if the database does not have a standby node.

The steps are as follows:

❶ Trigger the resident HDBLCM from */hana/shared/<SID>/hdblcm/*.

❷ Choose ADD_HOSTS.

❸ Enter the details of the new host.

❹ Choose the WORKER host role and configure it with the DEFAULT host failover group.

❺ Set up passwords for *<sid>adm* and *<sid>crypt* in the new host.

❻ Confirm the input variables and type *y* to proceed further.

❼ This results in successful addition of the worker host to the HANA database and writes the installation log file to the location specified.

2.6.9 Single node, master-standby, and scale-out

This section looks at the changes that occurred to the HANA database that was installed in Section 2.6.1 as a single host system, which was then followed by the addition of a standby node (Section 2.6.7) and the transformation to a multiple host installation (Section 2.6.8). The screenshots in this section were captured at various stages of this system's evolution, from a SystemDB and tenant database perspective. In these images:

- SINGLE NODE indicates the basic installation of the HANA database with a single host.
- ACTIVE-STANDBY means the database after adding a standby node.
- DISTRIBUTED HANA DB refers to the same database after adding a worker node.

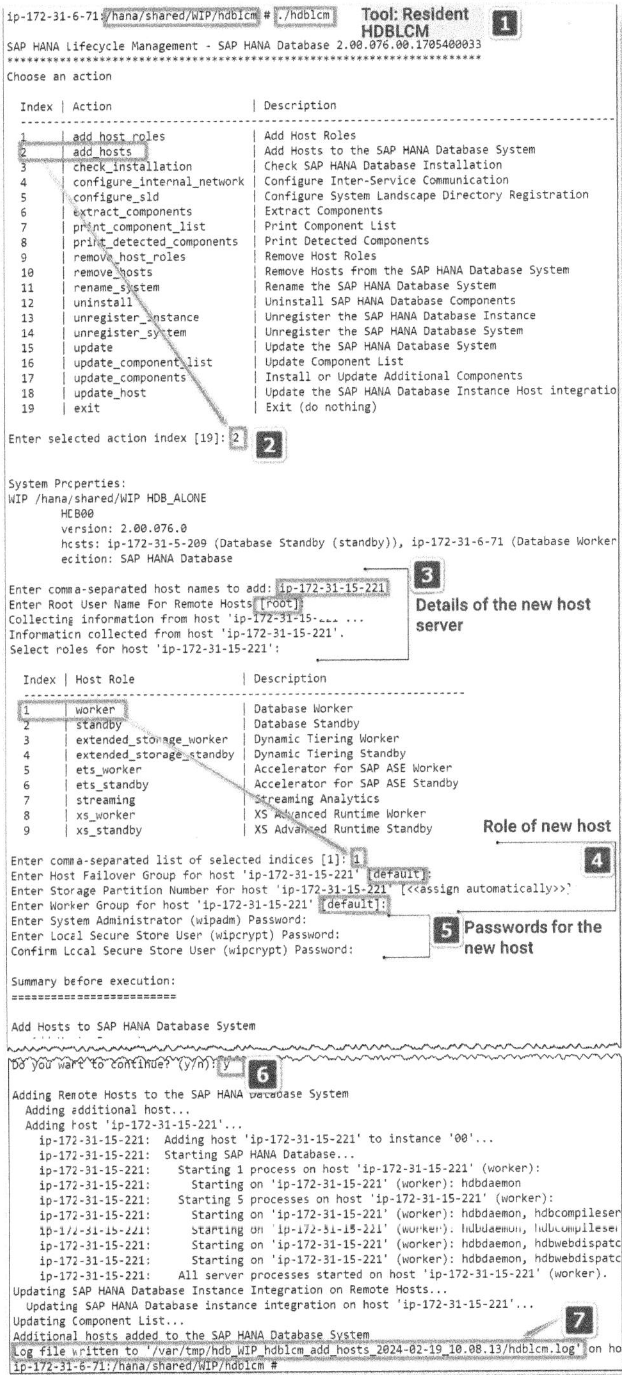

```
ip-172-31-6-71:/hana/shared/WIP/hdblcm # ./hdblcm

SAP HANA Lifecycle Management - SAP HANA Database 2.00.076.00.1705400033
************************************************************************
Choose an action

  Index | Action                      | Description
  -----------------------------------------------------------------------------------------
  1     | add_host_roles              | Add Host Roles
  2     | add_hosts                   | Add Hosts to the SAP HANA Database System
  3     | check_installation          | Check SAP HANA Database Installation
  4     | configure_internal_network  | Configure Inter-Service Communication
  5     | configure_sld               | Configure System Landscape Directory Registration
  6     | extract_components          | Extract Components
  7     | print_component_list        | Print Component List
  8     | print_detected_components   | Print Detected Components
  9     | remove_host_roles           | Remove Host Roles
  10    | remove_hosts                | Remove Hosts from the SAP HANA Database System
  11    | rename_system               | Rename the SAP HANA Database System
  12    | uninstall                   | Uninstall SAP HANA Database Components
  13    | unregister_instance         | Unregister the SAP HANA Database Instance
  14    | unregister_system           | Unregister the SAP HANA Database System
  15    | update                      | Update the SAP HANA Database System
  16    | update_component_list       | Update Component List
  17    | update_components           | Install or Update Additional Components
  18    | update_host                 | Update the SAP HANA Database Instance Host integratio
  19    | exit                        | Exit (do nothing)

Enter selected action index [19]: 2


System Properties:
WIP /hana/shared/WIP HDB_ALONE
        HDB00
        version: 2.00.076.0
        hosts: ip-172-31-5-209 (Database Standby (standby)), ip-172-31-6-71 (Database Worker
        edition: SAP HANA Database

Enter comma-separated host names to add: ip-172-31-15-221
Enter Root User Name For Remote Hosts [root]:
Collecting information from host 'ip-172-31-15-... ...
Information collected from host 'ip-172-31-15-221'.
Select roles for host 'ip-172-31-15-221':

  Index | Host Role                | Description
  -------------------------------------------------------------------
  1     | worker                   | Database Worker
  2     | standby                  | Database Standby
  3     | extended_storage_worker  | Dynamic Tiering Worker
  4     | extended_storage_standby | Dynamic Tiering Standby
  5     | ets_worker               | Accelerator for SAP ASE Worker
  6     | ets_standby              | Accelerator for SAP ASE Standby
  7     | streaming                | Streaming Analytics
  8     | xs_worker                | XS Advanced Runtime Worker
  9     | xs_standby               | XS Advanced Runtime Standby

Enter comma-separated list of selected indices [1]: 1
Enter Host Failover Group for host 'ip-172-31-15-221' [default]:
Enter Storage Partition Number for host 'ip-172-31-15-221' [<<assign automatically>>]:
Enter Worker Group for host 'ip-172-31-15-221' [default]:
Enter System Administrator (wipadm) Password:
Enter Local Secure Store User (wipcrypt) Password:
Confirm Local Secure Store User (wipcrypt) Password:

Summary before execution:
=========================

Add Hosts to SAP HANA Database System

Do you want to continue? (y/n): y

Adding Remote Hosts to the SAP HANA Database System
  Adding additional host...
  Adding host 'ip-172-31-15-221'...
    ip-172-31-15-221:  Adding host 'ip-172-31-15-221' to instance '00'...
    ip-172-31-15-221:  Starting SAP HANA Database...
    ip-172-31-15-221:    Starting 1 process on host 'ip-172-31-15-221' (worker):
    ip-172-31-15-221:      Starting on 'ip-172-31-15-221' (worker): hdbdaemon
    ip-172-31-15-221:    Starting 5 processes on host 'ip-172-31-15-221' (worker):
    ip-172-31-15-221:      Starting on 'ip-172-31-15-221' (worker): hdbdaemon, hdbcompileser
    ip-172-31-15-221:      Starting on 'ip-172-31-15-221' (worker): hdbdaemon, hdbcompileser
    ip-172-31-15-221:      Starting on 'ip-172-31-15-221' (worker): hdbdaemon, hdbwebdispatc
    ip-172-31-15-221:      Starting on 'ip-172-31-15-221' (worker): hdbdaemon, hdbwebdispatc
    ip-172-31-15-221:    All server processes started on host 'ip-172-31-15-221' (worker).
Updating SAP HANA Database Instance Integration on Remote Hosts...
  Updating SAP HANA Database instance integration on host 'ip-172-31-15-221'...
Updating Component List...
Additional hosts added to the SAP HANA Database System
Log file written to '/var/tmp/hdb_WIP_hdblcm_add_hosts_2024-02-19_10.08.13/hdblcm.log' on ho
ip-172-31-6-71:/hana/shared/WIP/hdblcm #
```


Figure 2.49: Adding worker node to the HANA system

Figure 2.50 provides detailed information about this evolution, from a SystemDB perspective. It showcases the SystemDB's OVERVIEW, LANDSCAPE, and VOLUME tabs during its transition from a single node to active-standby setup, and finally as a distributed system (scale-out).

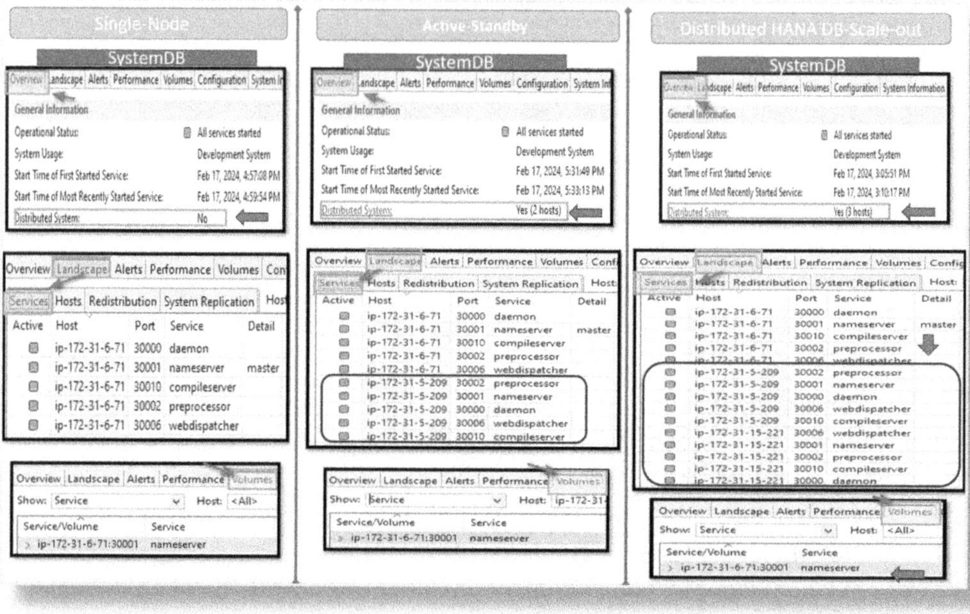

Figure 2.50: SystemDB—single node, master-standby, and distributed setup (scale-out)

Let's look at this SystemDB transition in more detail.

Single Node (SystemDB)

On the OVERVIEW tab, DISTRIBUTED SYSTEM is shown as No, which indicates that the system consists of only one host.

Note the list of services under the LANDSCAPE • SERVICES tab, including MASTER NAMESERVER, and also note the VOLUMES tab.

Because this is a SystemDB, it primarily maintains nameserver-related persistence. The index server, responsible for holding the actual data, is found only in the tenant database.

Active-Standby (SystemDB)

On the OVERVIEW tab, DISTRIBUTED SYSTEM is shown as YES (2 HOSTS), which indicates that the system consists of two hosts.

Note the list of services under the LANDSCAPE • SERVICES tabs, along with its MASTER NAMESERVER. Also note the additional SERVICES from the newly added standby node—from server IP-172-31-5-209. You can also see that the VOLUMES tab has the same details as the single node setup.

Distributed HANA DB-Scale-out (SystemDB)

On the OVERVIEW tab, DISTRIBUTED SYSTEMS is shown as YES (3 HOSTS), which indicates that the system consists of three hosts.

Note the list of services under LANDSCAPE • SERVICES, which includes additional services due to the presence of an additional worker node—from server IP-172-31-15-221—along with the MASTER NAMESERVER.

The VOLUMES tab remains the same as the previous two sections.

Figure 2.51 provides detailed information about this evolution, from a tenant database perspective. It showcases the tenant database's OVERVIEW, LANDSCAPE, and VOLUME tabs during its transition from a single node to active-standby setup, and finally as a distributed system (scale-out).

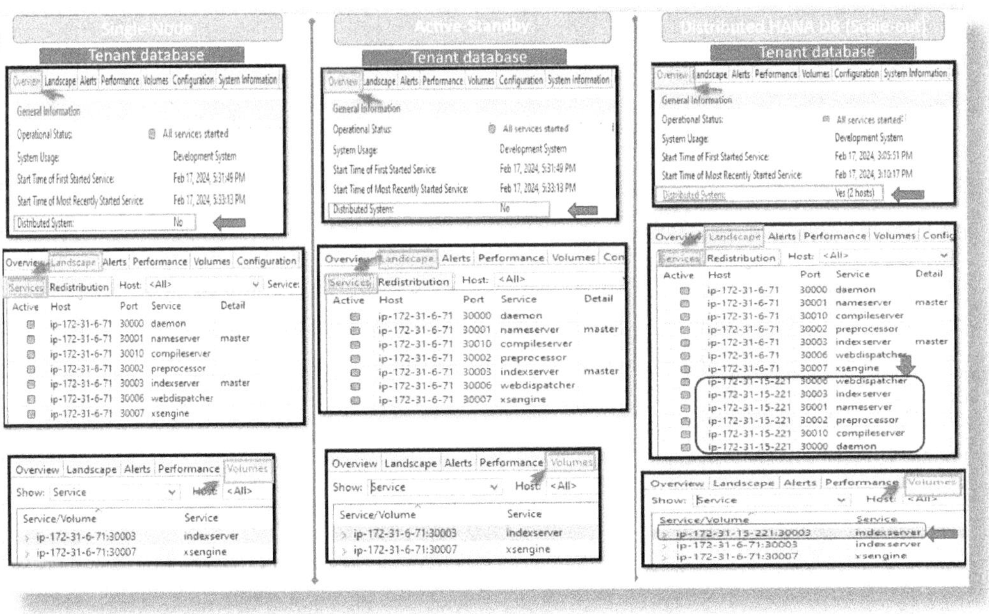

Figure 2.51: Tenant DB—single node, active-standby, and distributed setup

Single Node (tenant database)

On the OVERVIEW tab, DISTRIBUTED SYSTEM is shown as No, indicating that the system consists of only one host.

Note the list of services under LANDSCAPE • SERVICES, which includes one MASTER NAMESERVER and one MASTER INDEXSERVER.

The VOLUMES tab shows two persistence rows from the master node IP-172-31-6-71, which belong to the INDEXSERVER and XSENGINE.

Active-Standby (tenant database)

On the OVERVIEW tab, DISTRIBUTED SYSTEM is shown as No, meaning that the system consists of only one host, even though it now has a standby node. This is because the tenant database is more restricted to the index server service. Because standby hosts do not have an index server or persistence, the tenant database does not consider the latter to be an additional host.

Note the list of services under LANDSCAPE • SERVICES, which is the same as the single node tenant database. There are also no changes on the VOLUMES tab.

Distributed HANA DB-(Scale-out)

On the OVERVIEW tab, DISTRIBUTED SYSTEM – YES (2 HOSTS) indicates that the system consists of two index servers from two different hosts.

Note the list of services under LANDSCAPE • SERVICES, which includes additional services due to the presence of an additional worker node from server IP-172-31-15-221.

The VOLUMES tab now shows additional INDEXSERVER persistence from server IP-172-31-15-221.

2.6.10 Testing a failover to standby node

Figure 2.52 illustrates HANA's out-of-the-box auto-failover capabilities.

In this example scenario, the unavailability of worker node IP-172-31-15-221 results in a seamless transfer of data and log volume to the standby node IP-172-31-5-209, thereby changing the former failed node into a standby node.

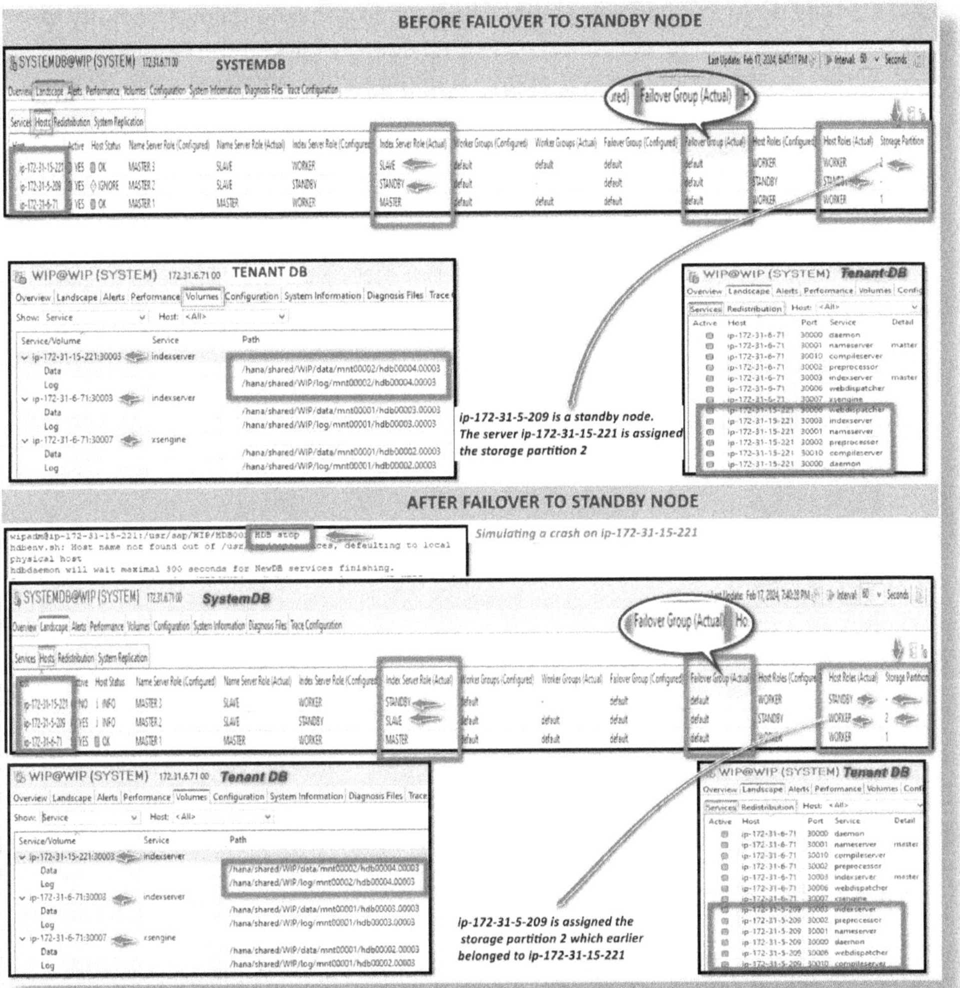

Figure 2.52: Simulating an auto-failover to standby node

2.6.11 Host group

In Figure 2.52, note the FAILOVER GROUP (host group) value, which is set to DEFAULT. The HANA database incorporates the concept of *host groups*, whereby multiple worker nodes are grouped, and each group is assigned a standby node. When there is failure within a group, failover is directed to that group's designated standby node. However, if there is no standby node available for that group, the database attempts a failover to the standby node of another host group. The primary objective of configuring a dedicated standby node to a specific group of hosts is to enhance failover security. It is important to understand that this setup does not affect the distribution of workload among the worker nodes. In Figure 2.53, note that each host group includes one or more standby hosts, which serve as backup for the active worker nodes in the event of their failure.

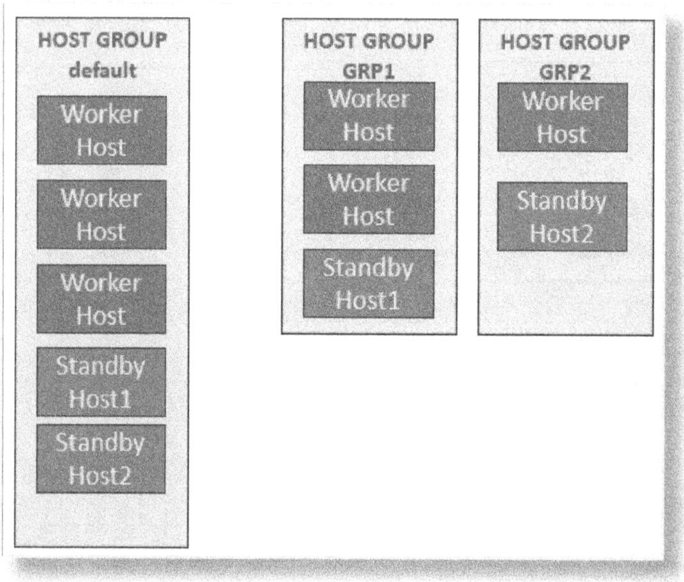

Figure 2.53: Host groups

2.6.12 HANA license key

After completing database installation, the next step is to apply the HANA license. HANA database licenses are determined by the total main memory consumption across all services on non-standby nodes and can be installed either globally within the SystemDB or locally, specific to a tenant database.

Figure 2.54 depicts two types of HANA database license keys—*temporary* and *permanent*. The permanent license key can be further classified into *unenforced* and *enforced*.

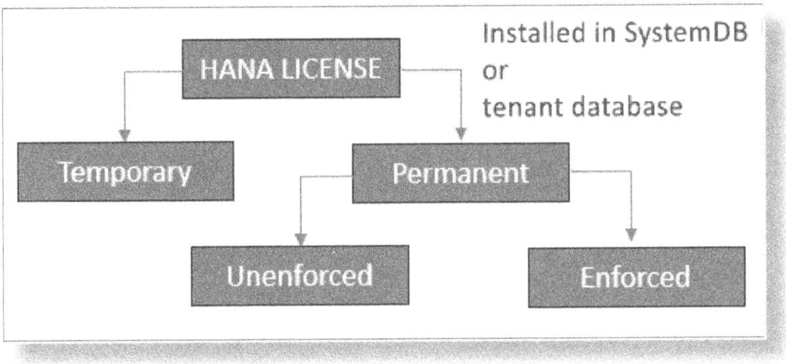

Figure 2.54: HANA license key

Temporary license keys are automatically installed with a newly installed SAP HANA database and are valid for 90 days. Within this period, a new permanent license key with a predefined expiration date can be requested through the SAP Support Portal (*https://me.sap.com/systemsprovisioning/keys*), under "Request Keys", by specifying the amount of licensed memory. If a permanent license key expires, a second temporary key, valid for 28 days, is automatically installed.

Permanent license keys can be categorized as either *unenforced* or *enforced*. An unenforced license key does not affect the HANA database operation if the current memory consumption exceeds the licensed memory, unlike an enforced license. With an enforced license, the system is auto-locked if the current memory consumption exceeds the licensed amount. To unlock the database, a new license covering the additional consumption must be installed, followed by a database restart.

It is important to note that license keys installed at tenant database level are specific to that tenant and take precedence over licenses installed in the SystemDB. If a tenant-specific license is not installed, the license from the SystemDB applies to the tenant database as well.

Figure 2.55 shows the steps to install a HANA database license from HANA Studio.

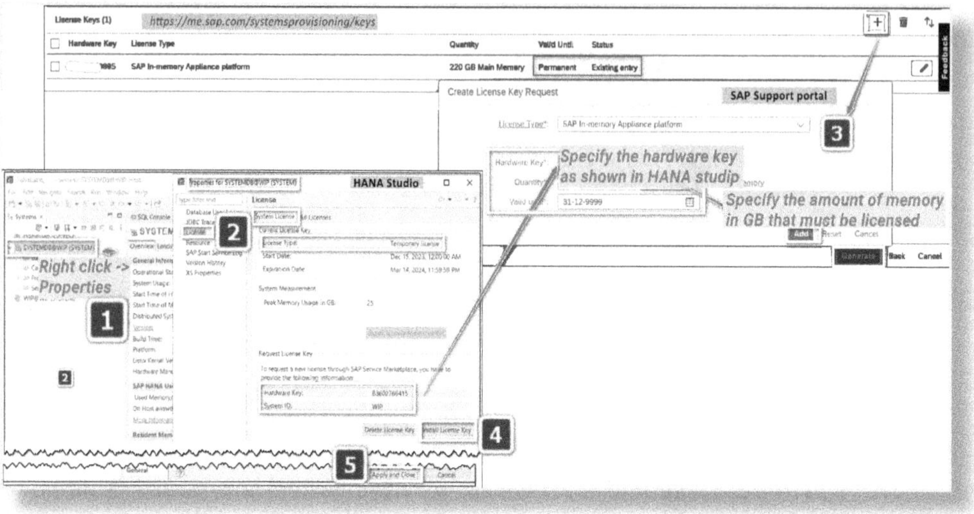

Figure 2.55: Requesting a HANA license

The steps shown in the image are as follows:

❶ Log in to the HANA database through HANA Studio and right-click on the HANA SID.

❷ Navigate to LICENSE and make a note of the system's HARDWARE KEY.

❸ Download the license key from the SAP portal by navigating to the system and clicking on the ADD button. Use the hardware key that was obtained from HANA Studio to request a new permanent license.

❹ Download the license from the previous step and upload it to the HANA Studio using the INSTALL LICENSE KEY button.

❺ Click on APPLY AND CLOSE.

2.7 HANA uninstallation

The HANA database can be uninstalled using the resident HDBLCM by logging in as a *root* OS user. This action facilitates a clean uninstallation of the HANA database by clearing up the file systems and deleting the operating system users created during the HANA database installation. Figure 2.56 shows the sequence involved with uninstalling a HANA database.

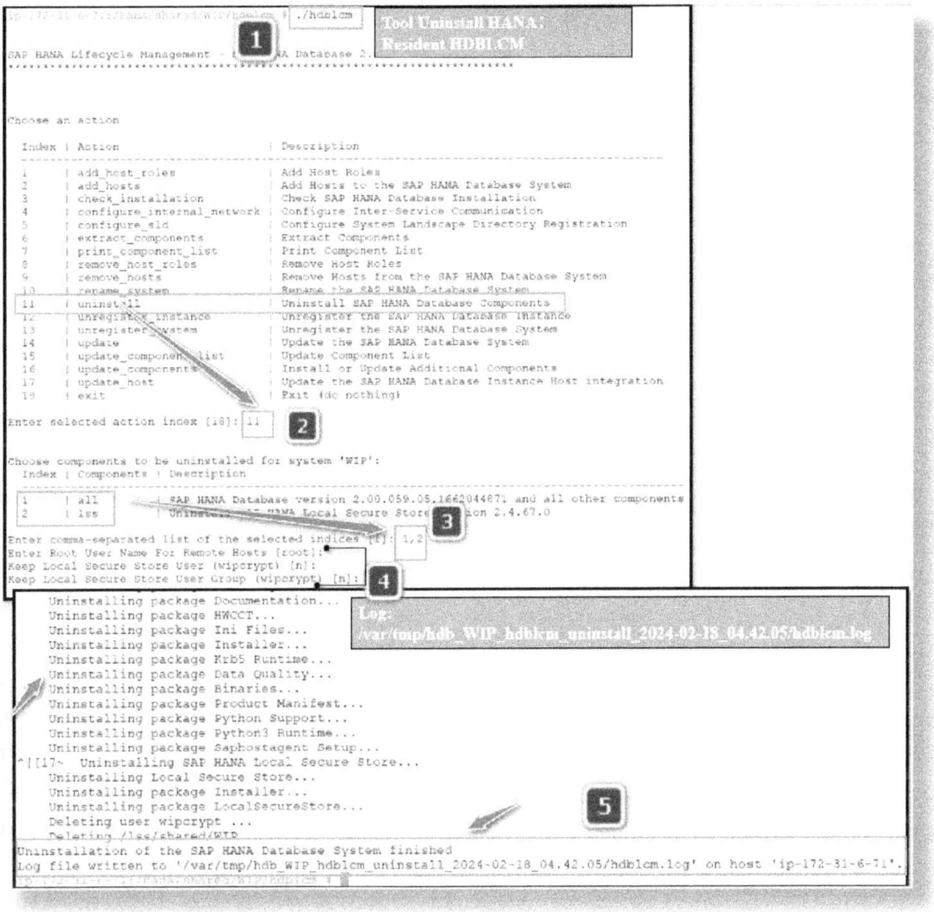

Figure 2.56: HANA database uninstallation

The steps shown in the image are as follows:

❶ Trigger the resident HDBLCM from */hana/shared/<SID>/hdblcm/*.

❷ Choose UNINSTALL.

❸ Choose the components that need to be uninstalled.

❹ Supply the password for *root* and *<sid>crypt* OS users.

❺ Proceed with uninstallation—the respective log is written to the indicated location.

2.8 Performing a HANA database update

HANA upgrades can be carried out using either resident HDBLCM from the HANA database or the HDBLCM available in the upgrade media.

Note that when resident HDBLCM triggers a database upgrade, it in turn calls the HDBLCM in the installation media to continue with the upgrade, as shown in Figure 2.57

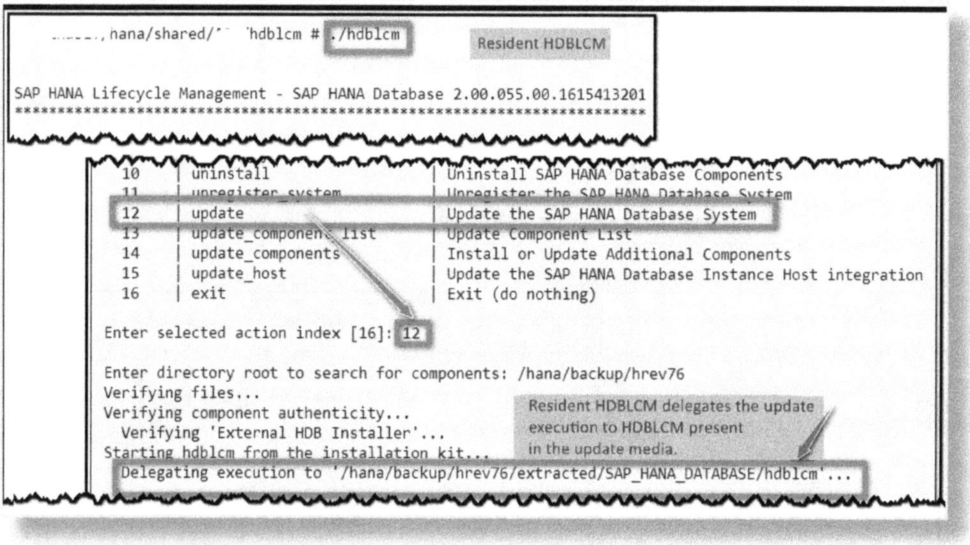

Figure 2.57: Resident HDBLCM and HDBLCM from installation media during upgrade

2.8.1 Determining HANA database version

Before proceeding with the HANA upgrade, it is important to determine the current database version.

Figure 2.58 shows the OVERVIEW tab from HANA Studio, which displays the HANA database version of the SID.

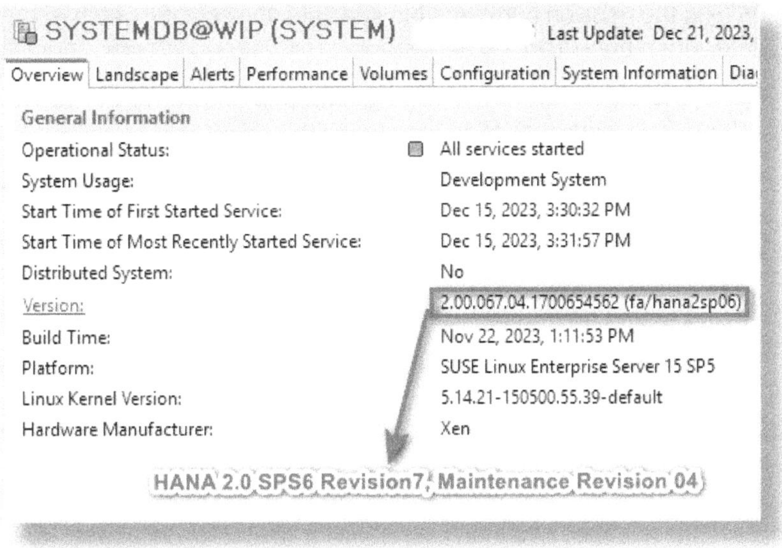

Figure 2.58: HANA database version from HANA Studio

Another means of determining the current database version is by executing the command `HDB version` from OS user *<sid>adm*, as shown in Figure 2.59.

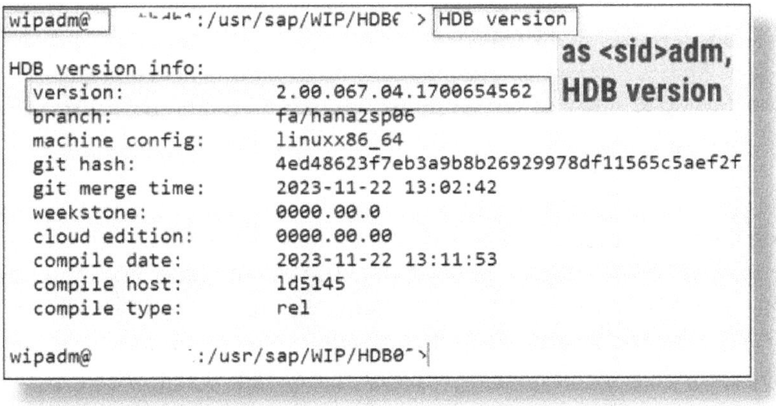

Figure 2.59: HANA database version from command line

The HANA database version string 2.00.067.04.1700654562 is made up of the following sections:

- 2.00—refers to the major version of the SAP HANA database. This indicates HANA 2.0.

- 067—is the revision number. This specifies the specific patch or update within the HANA 2.0 series.
- 04—is the patch level for this revision. This shows further refinement or bug fixes applied to the revision.
- 1700654562—is a unique build or internal identifier. This is often used by SAP for internal tracking and might correspond to the build timestamp or specific release artifact.

2.8.2 Determining HANA revision strategy

In addition to understanding the HANA database version, it is also important to understand the HANA revision strategy and its terminologies.

To date, SAP has released two major versions for the HANA database—SAP HANA 1.0 and SAP HANA 2.0. The various terms associated with the HANA maintenance strategy for these major versions are as follows:

- SAP HANA standard revision
- SAP HANA maintenance revision
- Support Pack (SP)
- Support Packs Stack (SPS)

While the revisions and the SP primarily address corrections to the SAP HANA platform, SPSs introduce new capabilities, updates, and enhancements for the respective HANA SPS stack.

Based on the requirements and current database version, the correct target (revision, SP, or SPS) needs to be determined for an upgrade. For more information on HANA 2.0 maintenance strategy, refer to SAP Note 2378962—"SAP HANA 2.0 Revision and Maintenance Strategy".

2.8.3 Software download and preparation

To perform an SAP HANA database upgrade, download the upgrade media from SUPPORT PACKAGES & PATCHES, as previously shown in the upgrade path in Figure 2.22. Along with the HANA database upgrade media file, the latest version of the additional components, such as SAP HANA LSS, SAP HANA Client, Host Agent media, etc., must also be downloaded. These files then need to be transferred to the target server using *WinSCP* or any other suitable means.

Remember to verify the authenticity of these downloaded files and to unpack them, as covered earlier.

2.8.4 Upgrading SAP Host Agent

When performing a HANA upgrade, it is recommended to upgrade the SAP Host Agent using the following command:

```
./saphostexec -upgrade
```

Figure 2.60 shows the extraction of the SAP Host Agent followed by the execution of an upgrade of the same.

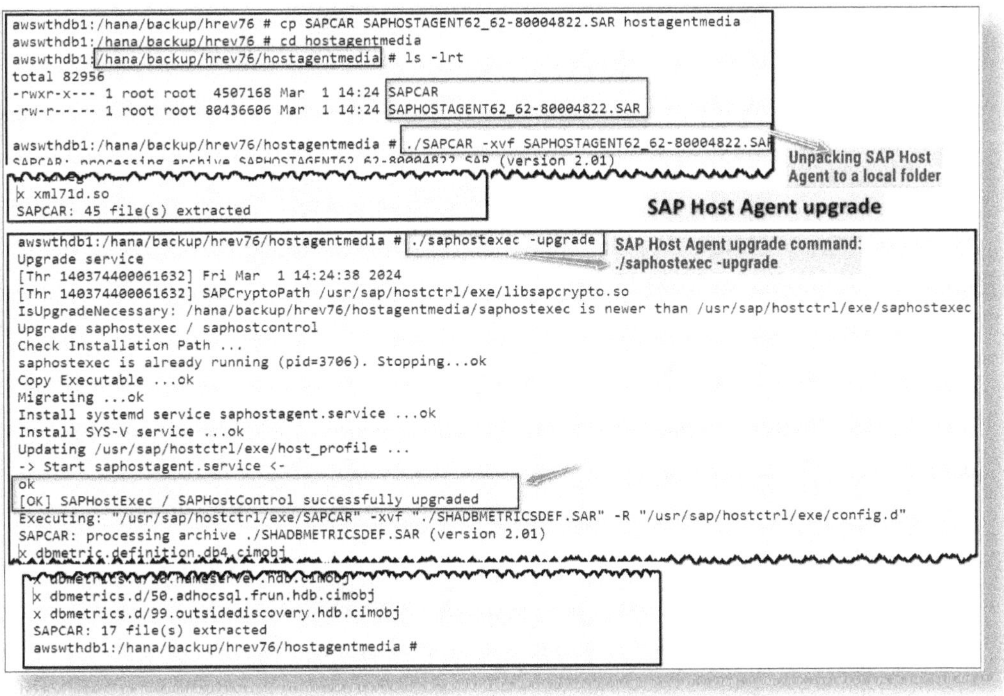

Figure 2.60: SAP Host Agent upgrade

2.8.5 Upgrading HANA

Preparing for the upgrade

The preparation activities required before upgrading a HANA database are as follows:

- **Download and prepare media**—to begin the HANA database upgrade process, it is crucial to download the necessary upgrade media, verify its authenticity, and unpack it on the target HANA database server.
- **Initiate full database backup**—before the upgrade, it is recommended to initiate a complete backup of the HANA database to ensure the preservation of its current state. Detailed instructions on performing backups will be covered in Section 6.2.
- **Ensure availability of database and OS passwords**—ensure that the passwords for *<sid>adm* (OS user) and database users (*SYSTEM* for SystemDB and tenant databases) are readily available. These passwords will be required at various stages of the upgrade process.
- **Execute upgrade from the database host**—it is highly recommended to initiate HANA database upgrades directly from the HANA database server. This approach minimizes the risk of upgrades failing due to network issues.

Upgrading/updating the HANA database

A HANA database upgrade involves a major transition of the database to a new version (e.g., from HANA 1.0 to HANA 2.0). In contrast, a HANA database update involves a minor modification within the same major version (e.g., from HANA 2.0 SPS 03 to HANA 2.0 SPS 05).

> **! HANA database "upgrade" versus "update"**
>
> In HANA, the core technical procedure for both a database update and a database upgrade is the same. Therefore, these words are used interchangeably in this section.

A HANA database update/upgrade can be performed using either a *single step* approach or a *phased* approach, as described in Figure 2.61.

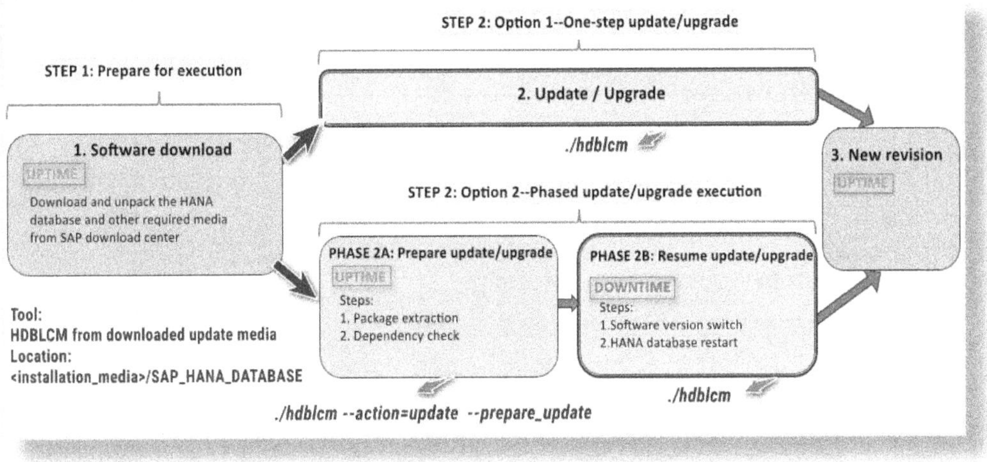

Figure 2.61: Upgrade/update execution options

With the single step approach, the HANA database is directly upgraded using HDBLCM (*./hdblcm*).

In the phased approach, the HANA database upgrade/update is divided into two phases:

- **Preparation** (online phase)—in this phase, the HDBLCM performs tasks such as package extraction and dependency checks, which do not alter or restart the HANA database:

```
./hdblcm -action=update -prepare_update
```

- **Execution** (offline phase)—in this phase, the HDBLCM completes the actual database upgrade:

```
./hdblcm
```

With a scale-out system, the HDBLCM can be initiated from the master node to execute the database upgrade.

- Note that the upgrade of HANA database components such as Application Function Libraries (AFLs), EML (Entity Manipulation Language) and the product-specific AFLs, SAP HANA XS Advanced Runtime, etc., can be carried out using either resident HDBLCM or HDBLCM from installation media.

The screenshots in Figure 2.62 and Figure 2.63 show an upgrade of a previously installed HANA database using the phased approach.

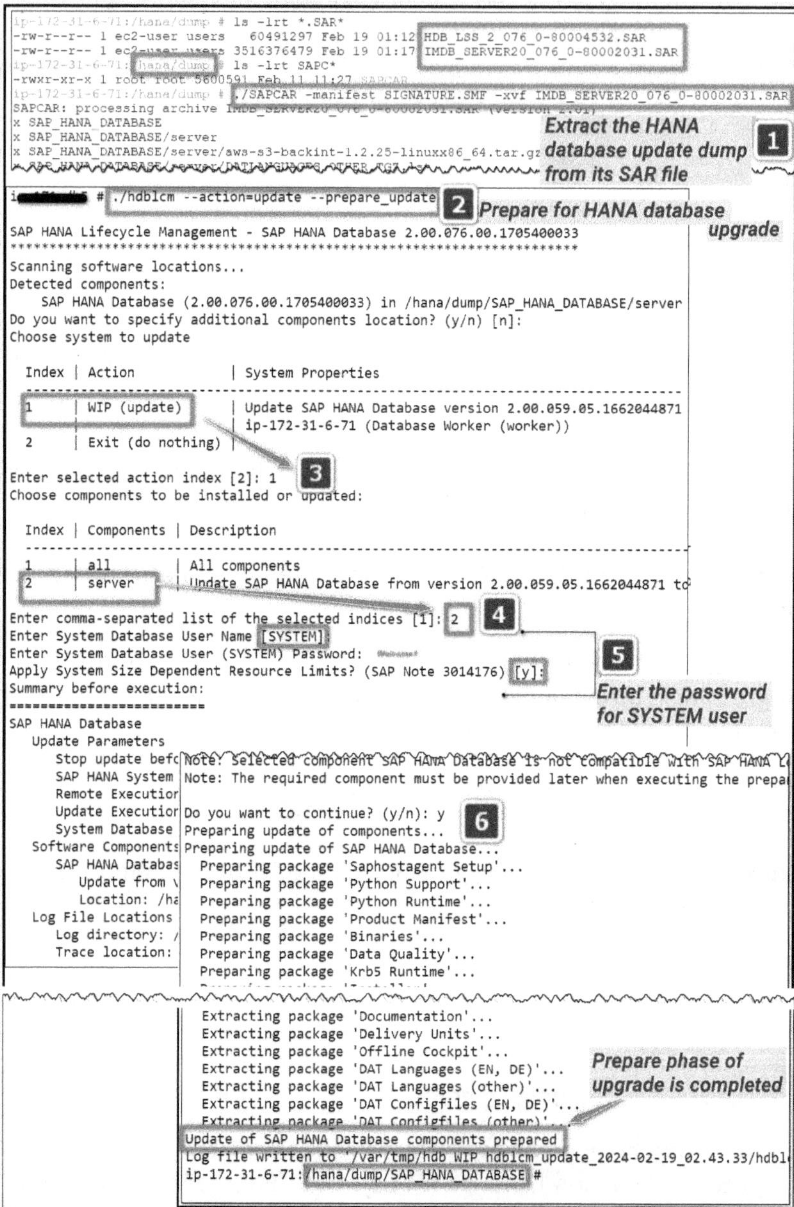

Figure 2.62: Phased approach—preparation

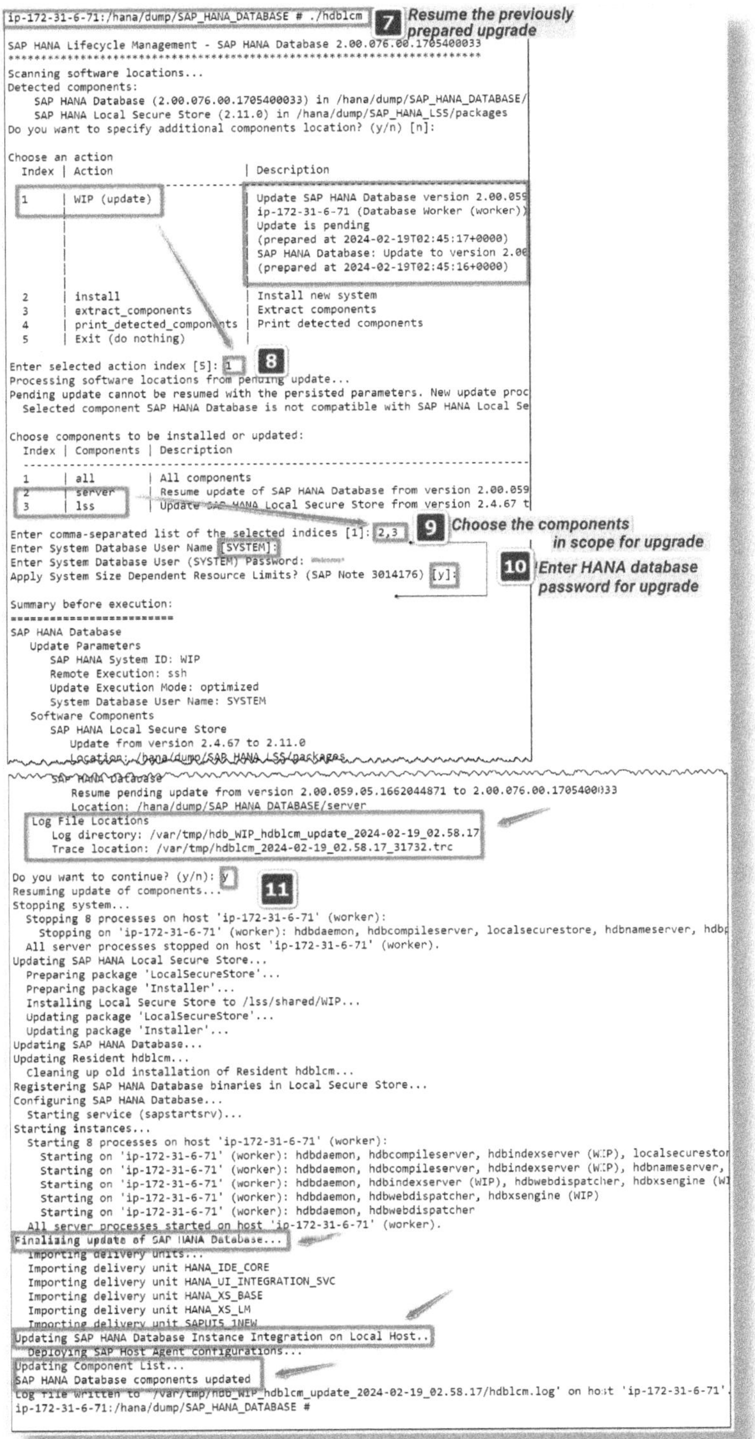

Figure 2.63: Phased approach—execution of update/upgrade

The process shown in these images is as follows:

❶ Extract the update/upgrade software dump for the HANA database using SAPCAR.

❷ Trigger the preparation phase of the database update/upgrade from the resident HDBLCM using the command `./hdblcm -action=update -prepare_update`.

❸ Select UPDATE.

❹ Choose the components to be updated/upgraded.

❺ Enter the SYSTEM database user password.

❻ Review the provided input and type *y* to proceed with the update/upgrade preparation.

❼ During the actual downtime phase, resume the previously prepared update/upgrade from the resident HDBLCM using the command `./hdblcm`.

❽ Select UPDATE.

❾ Choose the components to be updated/upgraded.

❿ Enter the SYSTEM database user password.

⓫ Review the provided input and type *y* to proceed with the update/upgrade execution.

3 Administration and monitoring tools

This chapter covers technical details about the HANA database administration and monitoring tools.

3.1 Available administration tools

SAP offers a range of administration and monitoring tools for managing the HANA database, as illustrated in Figure 3.1.

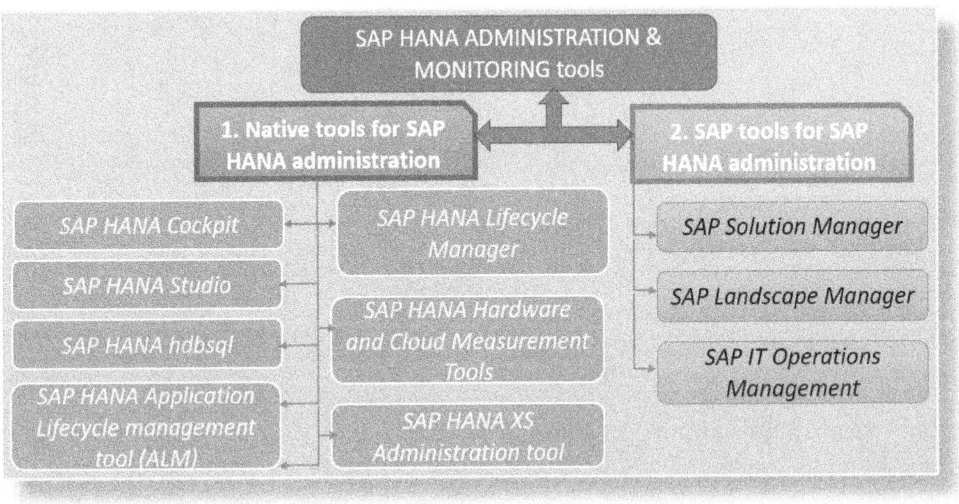

Figure 3.1: List of HANA administration and monitoring tools

3.2 SAP HANA Studio

SAP HANA Studio is an eclipse-based HANA development, administration and monitoring tool. Let's discuss how to administer the HANA database using this tool.

3.2.1 Connecting to the database via HANA Studio

As a first step towards database administration, HANA Studio must be configured to connect to the database using either:

- a database user (if the database is up and running—online), or
- the *<sid>adm* operating system user (if the database is offline).

HANA Studio provides login options, as shown in Figure 3.2, for both single container and multi-container (SystemDB or tenant database) HANA databases.

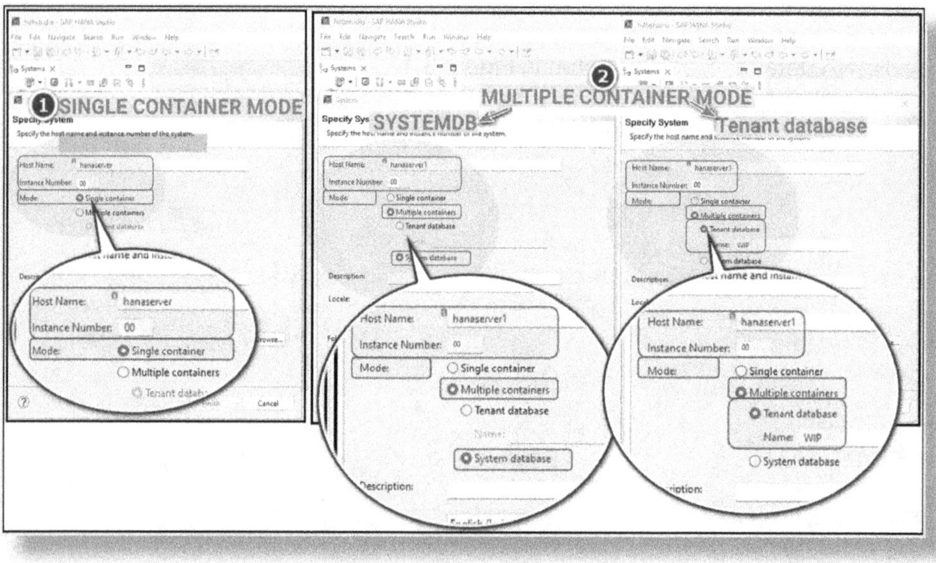

Figure 3.2: HANA Studio options—database mode

The installation of HANA Studio was covered previously in Chapter 2.

3.2.2 HANA Studio—workspace, perspectives and preferences

HANA Studio as a software consists of many key elements. We will now take a look at some of them.

Workspace

HANA Studio, like any other standard software, has its own menus, configuration, and settings that can be tailored to users' needs. These user-specific settings, configurations, database connections, and preferences are stored in a designated folder location called *workspaces* (see Figure 3.3 and also Figure 2.43). This is usually a local folder path on the user's machine where HANA Studio is installed.

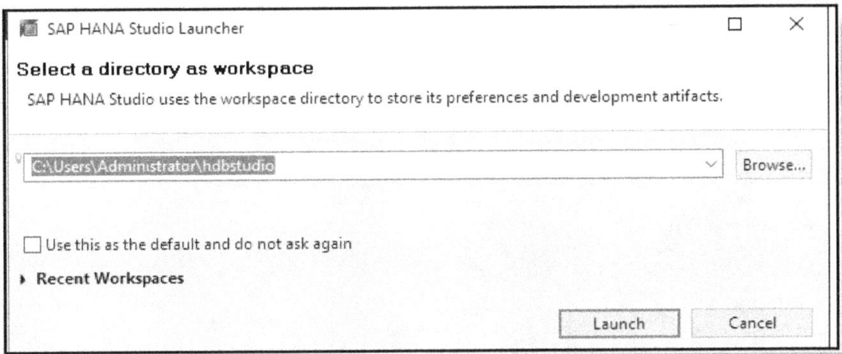

Figure 3.3: HANA Studio workspace

Perspectives

HANA Studio offers various *perspectives*, such as developer, administrator, and modeler, tailored specifically to cater to the needs and tasks of a developer, database administrator and database modeler respectively. It is possible to switch between the required perspectives, as shown in Figure 3.4.

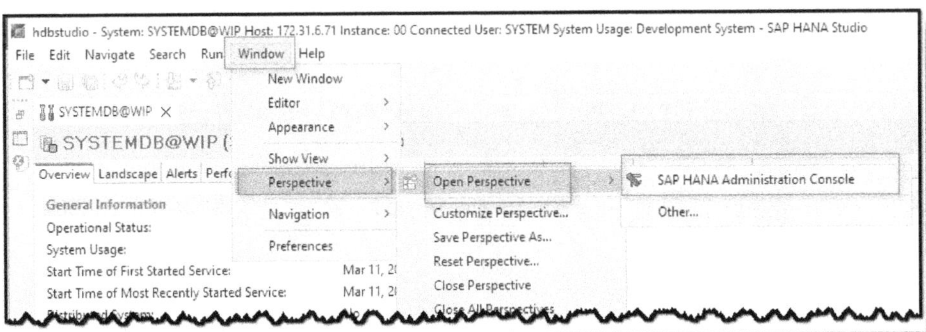

Figure 3.4: HANA perspectives

> **! HANA Studio perspectives**
>
> This book only covers HANA Studio's administrator perspective.

Preferences

HANA Studio also provides various settings, known as *preferences* that enable users to configure and customize their HANA Studio experience. A comprehensive list of these settings can be found under WINDOWS • PREFERENCES. One of the key HANA Studio preferences that users can customize is the number of table rows displayed when executing an SQL query against the database in HANA Studio. By default, the value is restricted to 1000 entries. This can be changed by navigating to menu path WINDOW • PREFERENCES • SAP HANA • RUNTIME • RESULT, as shown in Figure 3.5.

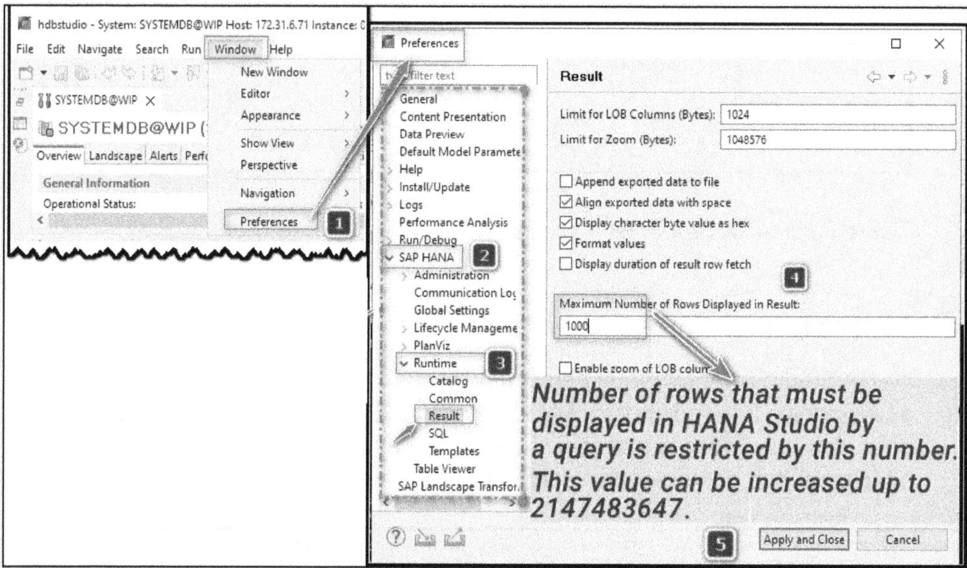

Figure 3.5: Altering the maximum number of rows displayed in results, using preferences in HANA Studio

The steps shown in the screenshots are as follows:

❶ Log in to HANA Studio, connect to the target database, and go to WINDOW • PREFERENCES.

❷–❸ Navigate to SAP HANA • RUNTIME • RESULT.

❹ Update the MAXIMUM NUMBER OF ROWS DISPLAYED IN RESULT field, as required.

❺ Click on APPLY AND CLOSE.

3.2.3 HANA database administration using HANA Studio

With HANA Studio, an administrator can perform a wide range of database administration and configuration tasks, such as database restart, backup and restore, table management, execution of SQL queries, access to system views, monitoring of database critical alerts, etc., using various consoles and tabs.

HANA Studio offers dedicated consoles for BACKUP administration, CATALOG administration (table administration), and SECURITY management for database administrators, as illustrated in Figure 3.6.

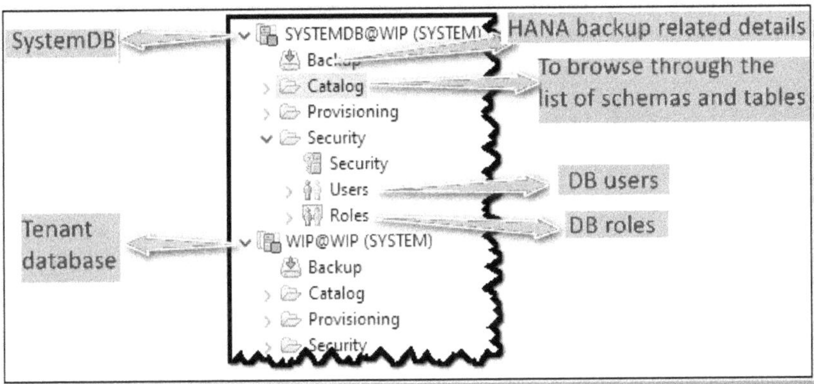

Figure 3.6: HANA Studio—backup, catalog, provisioning, security

In addition, HANA Studio includes various tabs, each representing a set of HANA administration tasks, as shown in Figure 3.7.

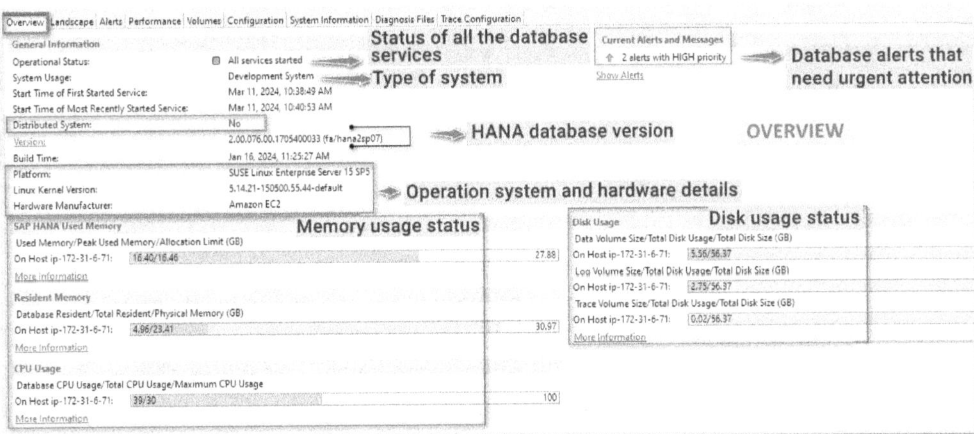

Figure 3.7: HANA Studio—overview

Let's examine these tabs in more detail.

The OVERVIEW tab contains a high-level summary of the database, including its status, version, operating system, underlying hardware, memory, disk usage, start time of first and last services, usage type, alerts, number of hosts, etc.

The LANDSCAPE tab includes several sub-tabs that provide detailed information about HANA database services, their status, the number of hosts, their roles (worker or standby), and the system replication status (see Figure 3.8). It also features a REDISTRIBUTION sub-tab, which is used to redistribute database tables between all the available HANA database index servers. For more information, see Section 4.1.8.

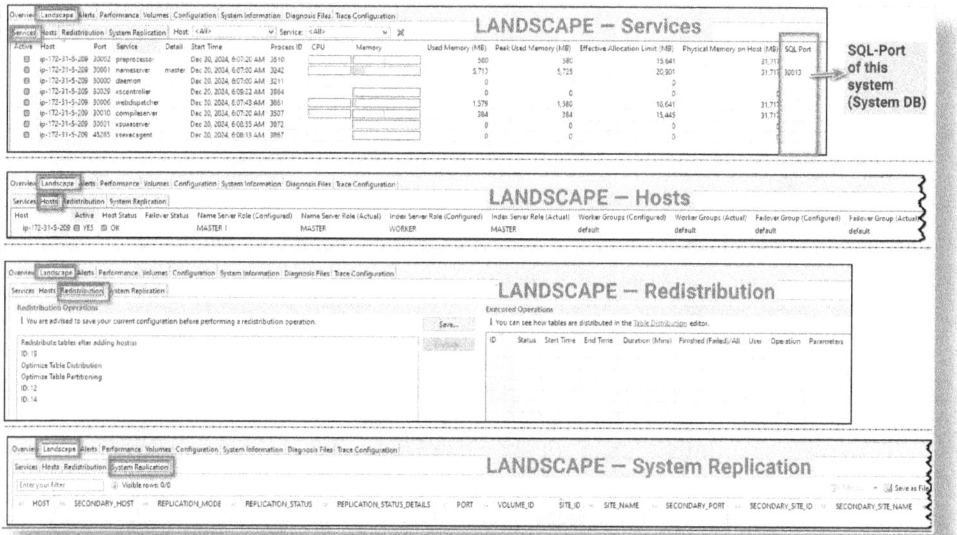

Figure 3.8: HANA Studio –Landscape tab

> **☛ HANA system replication (HSR)**
>
> The SYSTEM REPLICATION tab, shown in Figure 3.8, enables HANA system replication. This acts as a high-availability and disaster recovery feature in HANA. In this process, a primary database replicates its committed content, either synchronously or asynchronously, to a connected secondary (high-availability) or DR (disaster recovery) database. This is covered in more detail in Section 6.4.3.

The ALERTS tab in HANA Studio provides details relating to database alerts and their priority.

The PERFORMANCE tab helps us to understand HANA database transactions and database jobs along with their related threads, sessions, and blocked transactions. It also offers historical details of executed SQLs, such as SQL plan cache and expensive statements trace. All this information serves as a starting point for troubleshooting HANA database performance issues.

The VOLUMES tab provides information about the HANA database persistence layer. It helps with 1:1 mapping between the HANA database persistence service and its volumes. Refer to Table 1.3 for the list of database services that persist data at operating system level.

Figure 3.9 shows the HANA Studio ALERTS, PERFORMANCE, and VOLUMES tabs.

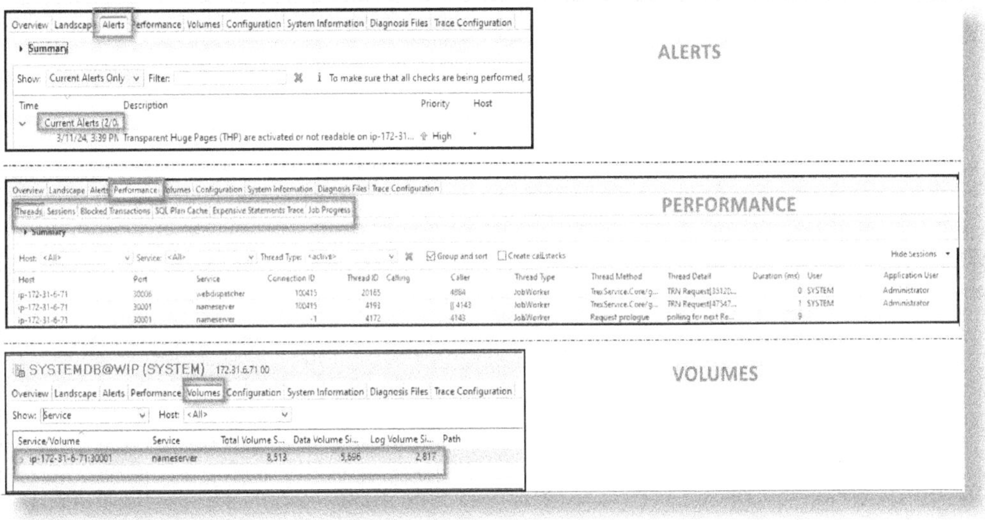

Figure 3.9: HANA Studio tabs (part 1)

Figure 3.10 shows the HANA Studio CONFIGURATION, SYSTEM INFORMATION and TRACE CONFIGURATION tabs.

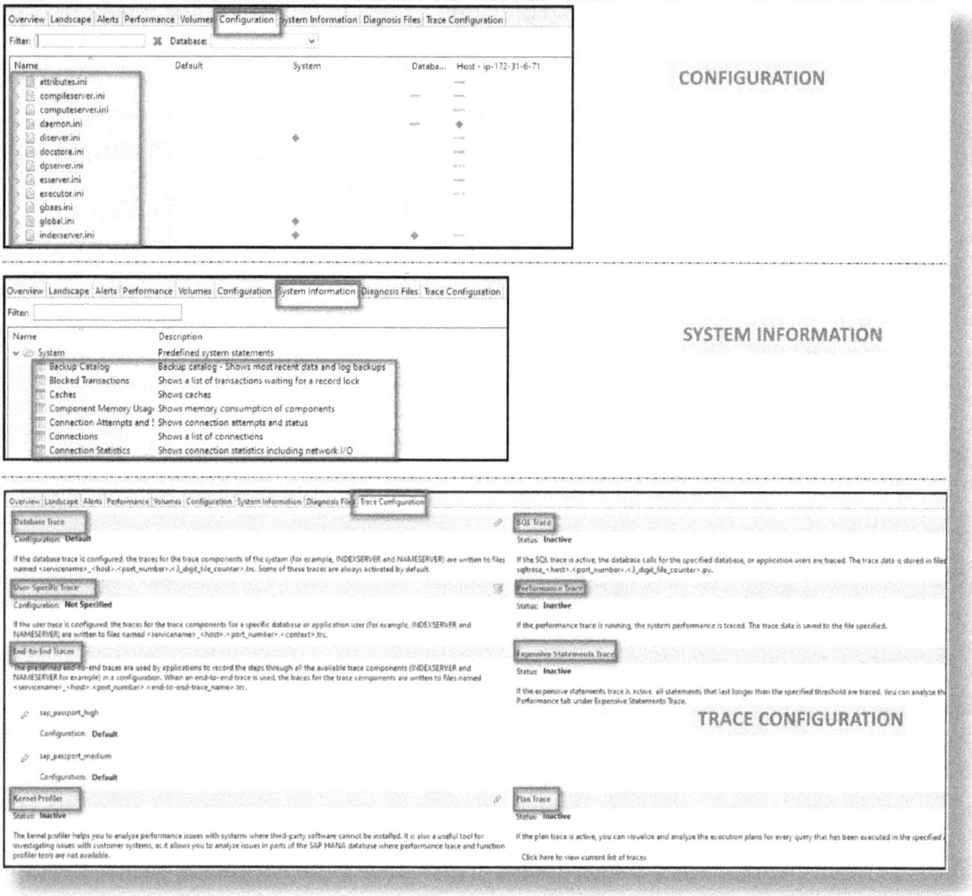

Figure 3.10: HANA Studio tabs (part 2)

The CONFIGURATION tab enables users to change the HANA database configurations.

The SYSTEM INFORMATION tab presents a list of predefined system views that can be used for day-to-day database administration.

The TRACE CONFIGURATION tab enables users to control the level of granularity for various types of database traces that can be captured.

The CATALOG in HANA Studio offers a detailed view of all schemas and their tables (see Figure 3.11).

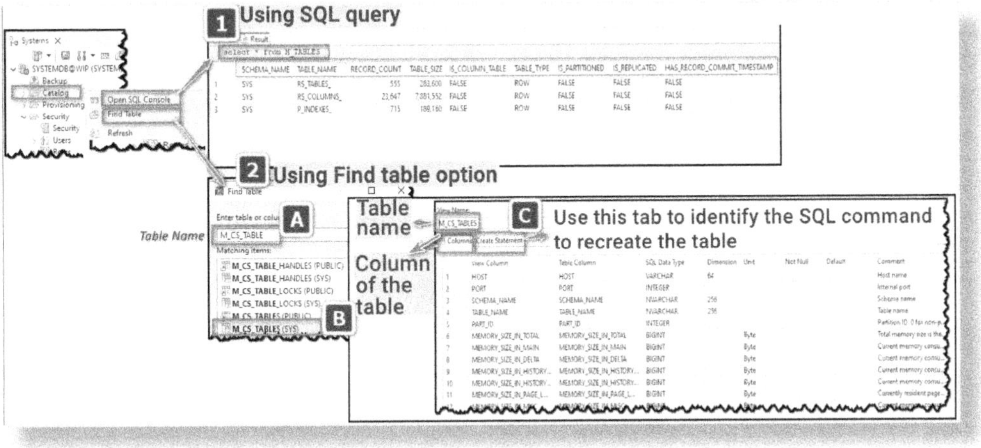

Figure 3.11: Displaying a table using SQL or "Find table" option

These tables can be accessed through the SQL console or by using the FIND TABLE option.

The SQL console option helps with the execution of both DDL and DML SQL queries and also helps with understanding the table contents. The steps using the SQL console, as shown in Figure 3.11, are as follows:

❶ Go to CATALOG • OPEN SQL CONSOLE and execute the select query on the desired table.

❷ The FIND TABLE option helps to understand the database table column and its properties:

A Search for the desired table using FIND TABLE.

B Double-click on the selected table to display its column details.

C The list of table columns and their properties is shown. In addition, the CREATE STATEMENT tab provides the SQL query required to re-create the table from the SQL console, if necessary.

Figure 3.12 shows the EXPORT and IMPORT OPTIONS AVAILABLE FOR THE HANA database table(s) from HANA Studio.

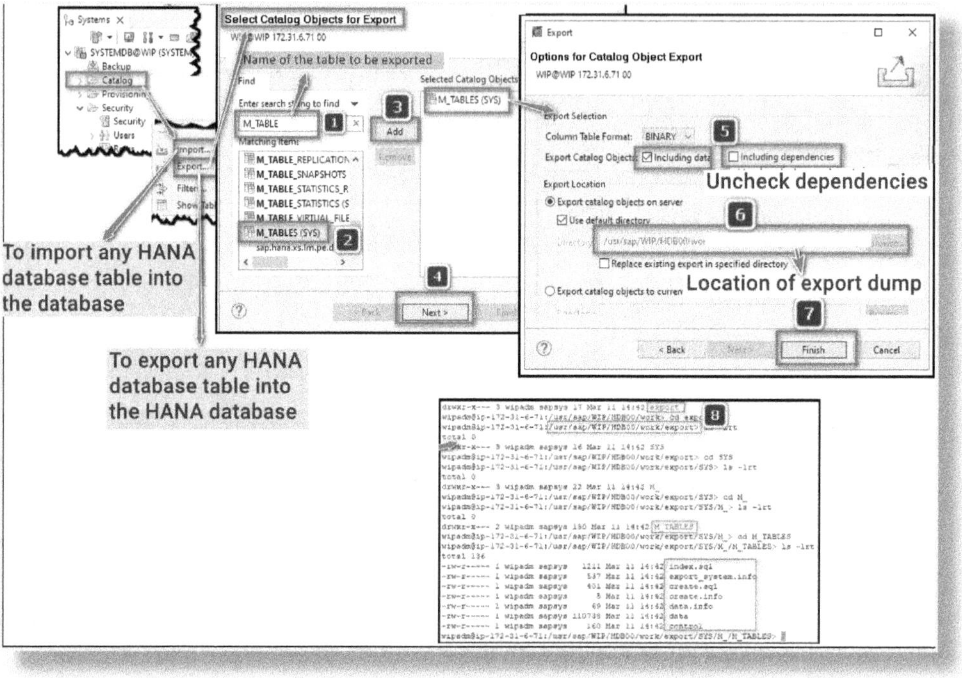

Figure 3.12: Exporting a table using Export option

The steps to export a table from HANA Studio are as follows:

❶–❷ Select the table to be exported.

❸–❹ Click on ADD and then on NEXT.

❺ Deselect the INCLUDE DEPENDENCIES checkbox, otherwise all the procedures/views associated with the associated table will be exported.

❻ Provide the file system path at OS level to store the table export dump.

❼ Click on FINISH to complete the process.

❽ Check for the successful export of the database table at OS level.

3.2.4 HANA Studio—SystemDB versus tenant database

While the administration tabs discussed in HANA Studio are identical for both the SystemDB and tenant database, certain administration tasks are restricted exclusively to the SystemDB. For instance, restarting the entire HANA database and initiating backup or restore operations for the SystemDB or any specific tenant database etc., can only be performed through the SystemDB, as shown in Figure 3.13. Note the difference between the SystemDB and tenant database's CONFIGURATION AND MONITORING option and the BACKUP AND RECOVERY option.

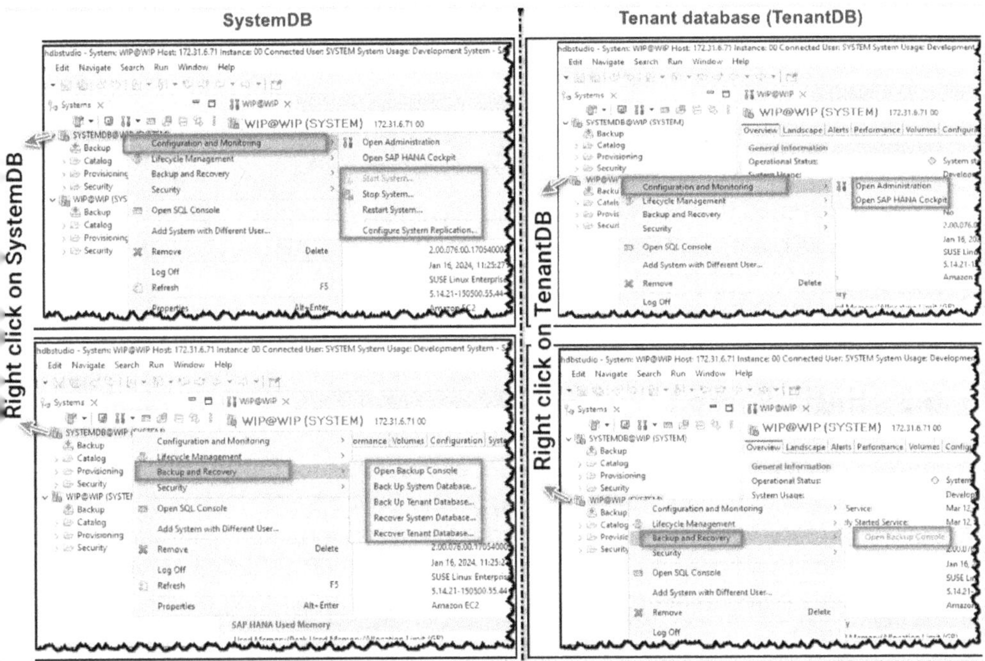

Figure 3.13: HANA Studio—SystemDB versus tenant database

! Restarting tenant database via SQL console

HANA database tenants can be stopped or started either from the SystemDB's SQL console (from HANA Studio, HANA Cockpit) or at the database operating system level (see Section 4.3.2).

The SQL to stop a tenant database is:

```
alter system stop database <tenant_DB>;
```

The SQL to start a tenant database is:

```
alter system start database <tenant_DB>;
```

! HANA Studio

It is anticipated that HANA Studio will eventually be replaced by HANA Cockpit, as mentioned in SAP Note 2073112—"FAQ: SAP HANA Studio".

3.3 HANA Cockpit

HANA Cockpit is a web-based, browser-accessible tool designed for administering and monitoring HANA databases. Built on SAP HANA XS Advanced, it features an HTML5 user interface and supports database administration and monitoring as of SAP HANA 1.0 SP12. HANA Cockpit provides functionality comparable to the administrative and monitoring features of HANA Studio.

Let's examine some of the details of HANA Cockpit.

3.3.1 Installing HANA Cockpit

The HANA Cockpit is an integral component of HANA Platform Edition and can be installed using one of the following deployment options:

- On a dedicated hardware
- On a shared hardware with another HANA database
- On a separate tenant database within an existing HANA database.
- The software for HANA Cockpit installation can be downloaded from SAP's software center, as follows:

From SUPPORT PACKAGES & PATCHES:

- Go to SUPPORT PACKAGES & PATCHES;
- Open > BY ALPHABETICAL INDEX (A-Z)
- Choose H
- Choose SAP HANA PLATFORM EDITION
- Go to DOWNLOADS
- Choose SAP HANA PLATFORM EDITION 2.0
- Download the following components:
  - SAP HANA COCKPIT 2.0 as per the target OS
  - Required support pack version of the SAPHANACOCKPIT<NNN>. SAR file

Once downloaded, this dump needs to be transferred to the target server and unpacked using the following command:

```
./SAPCAR -manifest SIGNATURE.SMF -xvf SAPHANACOCKPIT<nn>.SAR
```

The installation of HANA Cockpit is similar to any normal HANA database installation using the HDBLCM from installation media tool, as shown in Figure 3.14. Figure 3.14 shows an SAP HANA Cockpit installation on an already installed tenant database. Note that the HANA Cockpit can also be installed as a standalone HANA database.

Figure 3.14: HANA Cockpit installation

The steps shown in the image are as follows:.

❶ Execute the *hdblcm* command from the installation media.

❷ To specify additional components apart from those detected, enter the folder path containing the component dumps. Otherwise, leave it blank.

❸ Choose XS as the component to be installed on top of the already installed tenant database.

❹ Enter the SYSTEM DATABASE user password for the tenant database on which the HANA Cockpit will be installed. Also, provide the username and password that will be used to control and manage the HANA Cockpit post-installation. The XSA_ADMIN user serves as the superuser for HANA Cockpit.

❺ In HANA Cockpit, ROUTING MODE refers to how the system routes requests between Cockpit components and target databases. The ROUTING MODE chosen is PORTS in the example shown here. PORTS indicate specific network ports used for communication between the HANA Cockpit and target HANA databases.

❻ Configure the settings for the HANA Cockpit operating system user *sap<sid>xsa*.

❼ Choose the required XSA components to be installed.

❽ HANA Cockpit has been successfully installed, and the Cockpit URL has been provided in the installer output.

Note that the HANA Cockpit URL is recorded in the Cockpit installation log by HDBLCM. In addition, the port for HANA Cockpit is not standard and can vary depending on the available ports on the database host.

Be aware that the server hosting the HANA Cockpit should have a minimum of 32GB RAM, 150+ GB of disk space, and approximately 12,000 SAPS in terms of CPU capacity. For additional sizing guidelines specific to HANA Cockpit, refer to SAP Note 2780721—"SAP HANA 2.0 Cockpit Recommended Sizing Guidelines".

3.3.2 HANA Cockpit—post-installation

From the Cockpit installation log, we can identify the following URLs, as shown at step ❽ in Figure 3.14:

- HANA-COCKPIT—HANA Cockpit URL
- HANA-COCKPIT-ADMIN—HANA Cockpit admin URL

As the first step after installation, log in to the HANA Cockpit admin URL using the username *XSA_ADMIN* and the password provided during installation, as shown in Figure 3.15.

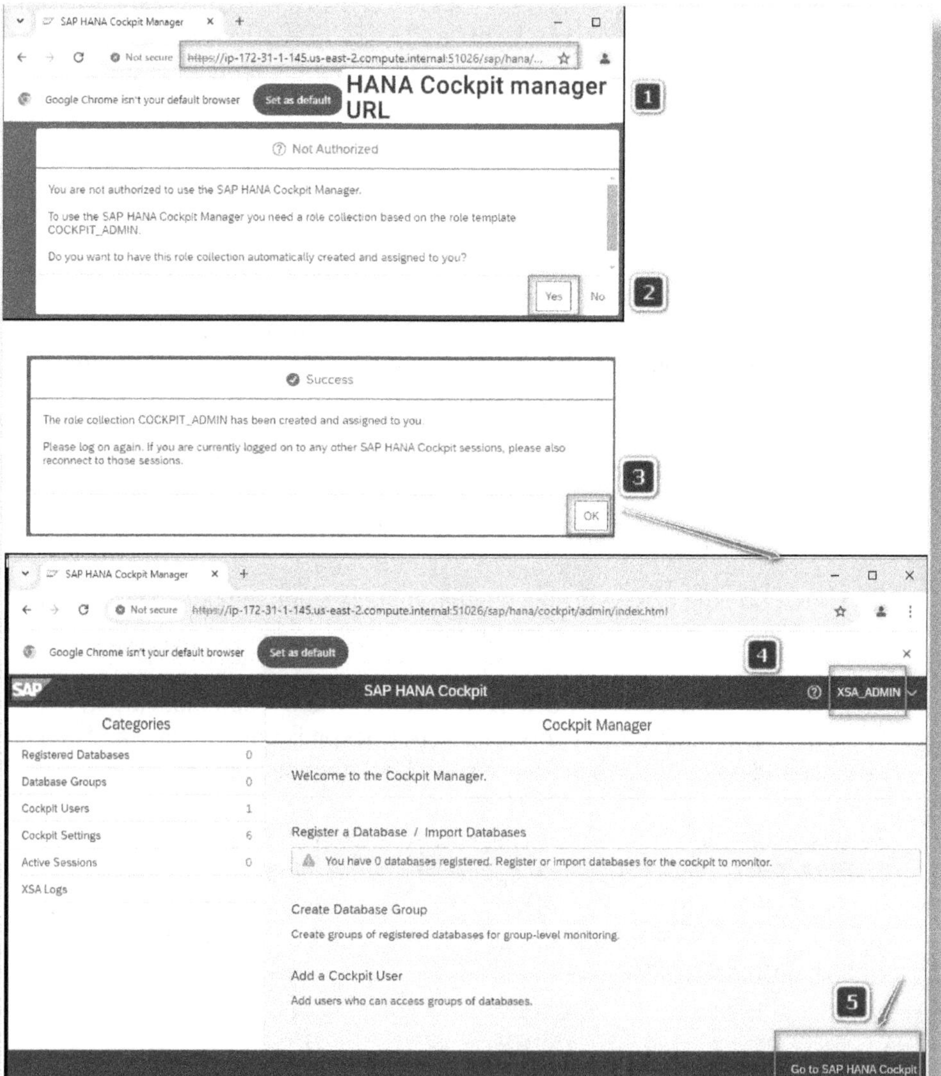

Figure 3.15: Enabling HANA Cockpit

The steps shown in the image are as follows:

❶ Log in to the HANA Cockpit admin URL.

❷-❸ You will see a prompt regarding the missing authorization. Click on YES and then OK to assign the required authorization. You will be prompted to log in again.

❹ Log in again using the username *XSA_ADMIN* and the password to access the HANA Cockpit URL.

❺ Click on GO TO SAP HANA COCKPIT.

3.3.3 Registering a HANA database in HANA Cockpit

Like HANA Studio, databases must specifically be added to the HANA Cockpit to enable monitoring and administration. Prior to adding a HANA database (SystemDB or tenant database), a HANA database group must be created from the HANA Cockpit Manager, as shown in Figure 3.16.

The steps shown in the image are as follows:

❶ Click on CREATE DATABASE GROUP.

❷ Enter the group name.

❸ Select the REGISTER DATABASES AFTER THE GROUP IS CREATED checkbox.

❹ Add the required user to the group. In the example shown, user XSA_ADMIN has been assigned to manage this database group.

❺ Click on CREATE GROUP.

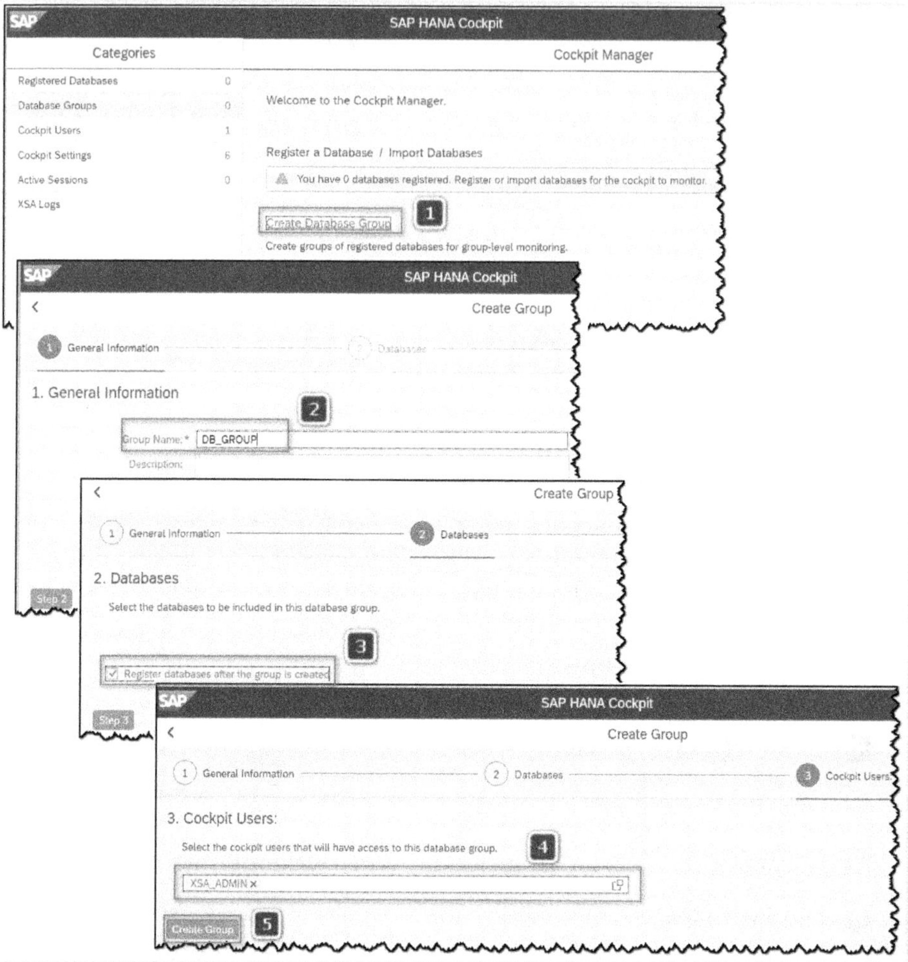

Figure 3.16: HANA Cockpit Manager—Database Group

As a next step, HANA databases that have to be monitored and administered from HANA Cockpit must be added to the DATABASE GROUP that we created earlier. The process to add a database to the HANA Cockpit is shown in Figure 3.17.

Follow menu path COCKPIT MANAGER • REGISTER A DATABASE and proceed with below steps:

❶ Enter the HANA DATABASE host details.

❷ Select the type of CONNECTION (encrypted or unencrypted).

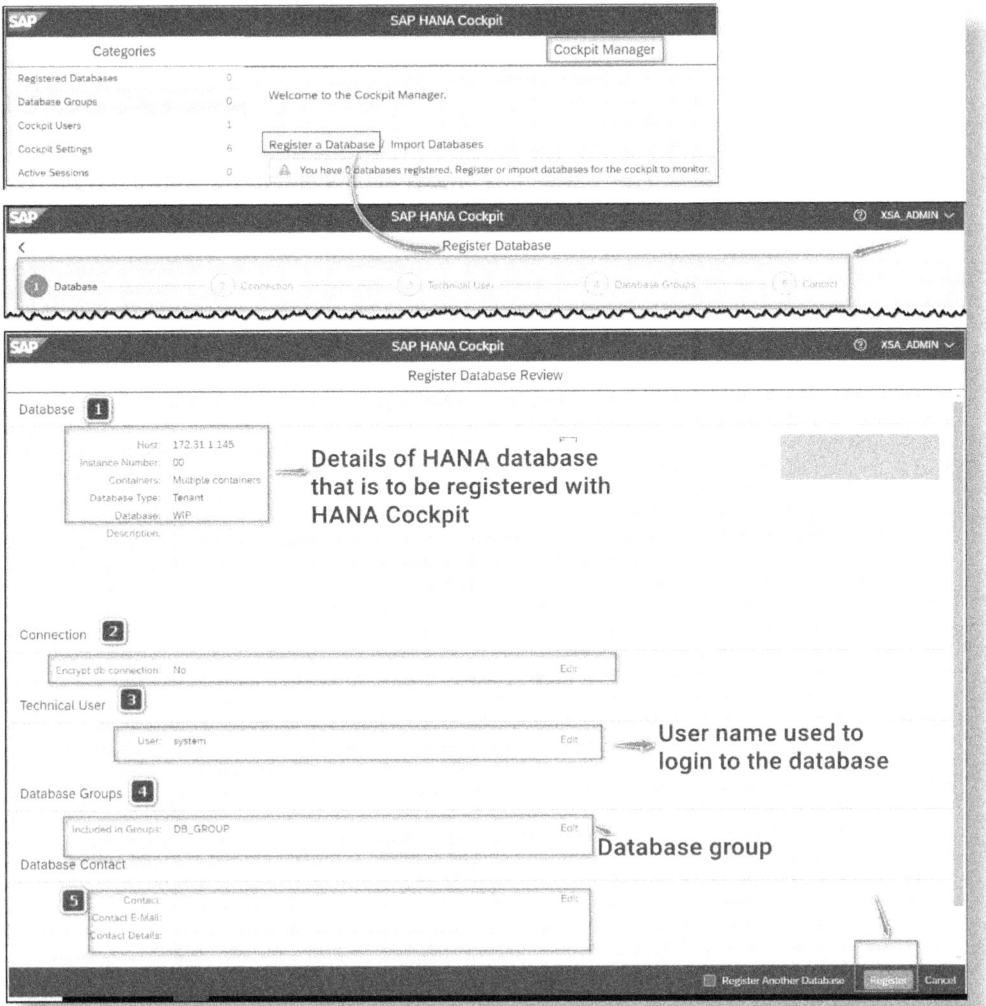

Figure 3.17: HANA Cockpit Manager—registering HANA databases

❸ Provide the TECHNICAL USER credentials for the database to be monitored.

❹ Assign a database group.

❺ Enter contact details for alerts.

Click on REGISTER to complete the process.

3.3.4 Monitoring the registered HANA database

Once HANA databases are registered with the HANA Cockpit, they can be monitored and administered through the HANA Cockpit web page. Figure 3.18 shows the high-level monitoring view available from the HANA Cockpit DATABASE DIRECTORY. This view helps you to monitor the system's current STATUS, including ALERTS, CPU usage, MEMORY usage, DISK usage, and active EXPENSIVE STATEMENTS.

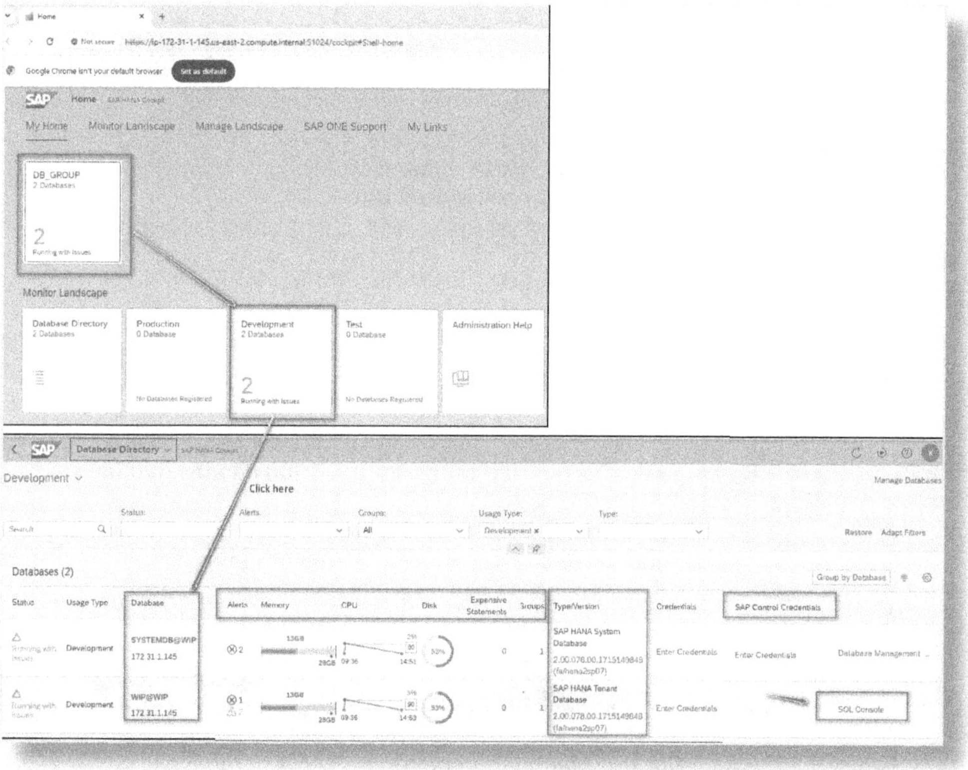

Figure 3.18: HANA Cockpit administration

Clicking on an individual system entry will take you to the administrative web page of the respective database. Figure 3.19 shows the HANA Cockpit database administration web page for both the SystemDB and the tenant database.

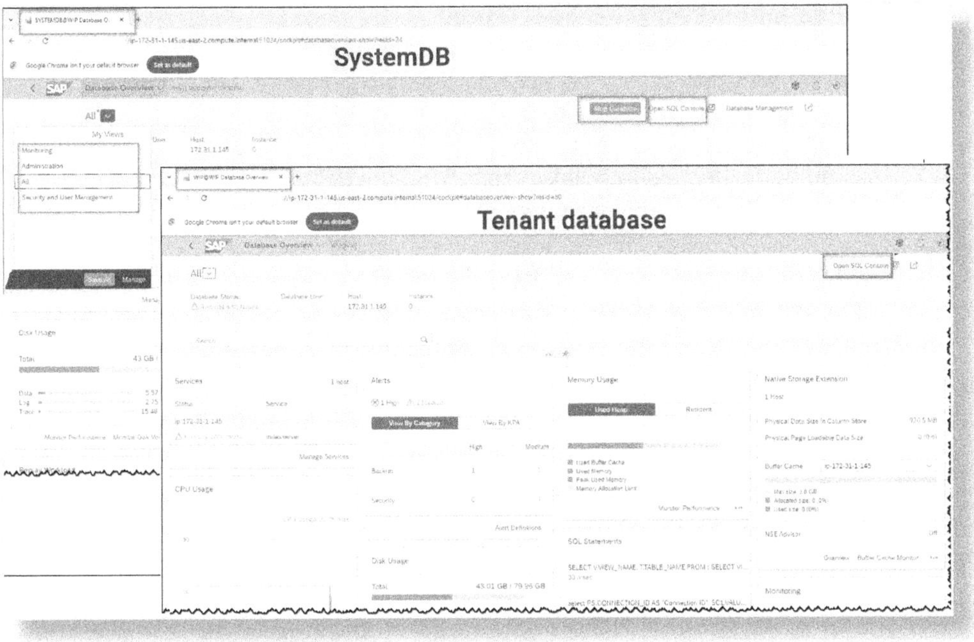

Figure 3.19: HANA Cockpit—SystemDB and tenant database

> **! HANA Studio versus HANA Cockpit**
>
> HANA Studio is a thick client that requires dedicated software to be installed on the end user's or administrator's computer. HANA Cockpit is a server-level product with its own database, specifically the HANA express edition. End users can access this via their web browser, without a dedicated installation of any software on their desktop or laptop.

Similar to HANA Studio, the HANA Cockpit also features various groups of database administration tasks, each represented as a Fiori tile in the Cockpit URL. Every tab, which we looked at earlier in this chapter, has an equivalent Fiori tile in HANA Cockpit. Some of the tiles available in HANA Cockpit include SERVICES, ALERTS, MEMORY USAGE, CPU USAGE, DISK USAGE, MONITORING, DATA ENCRYPTION, THREADS, DATA BACKUPS, MANAGING SQL PERFORMANCE, etc.

3.3.5 Administering the XSA tenant

Because HANA Cockpit runs on the XSA service, a basic understanding of XSA commands and tasks are essential. For instance, users and roles for HANA Cockpit must be created through SAP HANA XS Advanced Cockpit. XSA commands also aid in quickly identifying the URLs for both the HANA Cockpit and HANA Cockpit Manager.

Figure 3.20 illustrates how to get the URLs for HANA COCKPIT, HANA COCKPIT MANAGER, and SAP HANA XS ADVANCED COCKPIT. To do this, connect to the XS application at the server level by logging in as *<sid>adm*. Execute the command `xs-admin-login` and provide the required credentials. Then, use the `xs-apps` command to view the list of applications running on the XS Advanced engine. Based on the application name, locate the corresponding URL, as shown in Figure 3.20

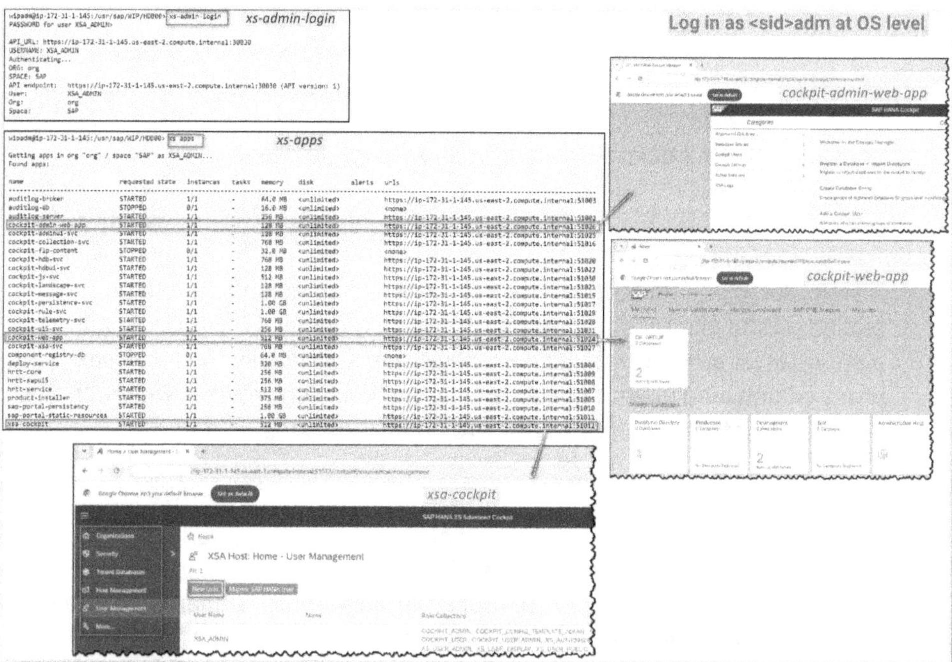

Figure 3.20: XS Advanced app for HANA Cockpit Manager, HANA Cockpit and SAP HANA XS Advanced Cockpit

3.4 SAP HANA HDBSQL

HDBSQL is a command-line tool designed for executing commands on the HANA database. It is typically installed as part of the SAP HANA database, enabling database access from the database server. It can also be accessed from the SAP HANA client package, enabling remote access to the database from the application hosting the database client.

In a standard HANA database installation, *hdbsql* can be found at */usr/sap/<SID>/HDB<nn>/exe*. This tool facilitates the execution of SQL statements/procedures and enables users to query information about the database and its objects.

3.4.1 Determining SQL port and DATABASE_NAME for HDBSQL

HDBSQL uses either the *SQL port* or *DATABASE_NAME*, together with the HANA database server, instance number, username, and credentials in order to connect to the target HANA database. The SQL port required for this connection can be determined by executing the following SQL query on the respective database (see Figure 3.21):

```
select SERVICE_NAME, SQL_PORT from M_SERVICES where SQL_PORT != '0' ;
```

Figure 3.21 shows that the SQL port of the SystemDB is 3<NN>13, the tenant database is 3<NN>15, and an additional tenant is 3<NN>41, where <NN> represents the database instance number.

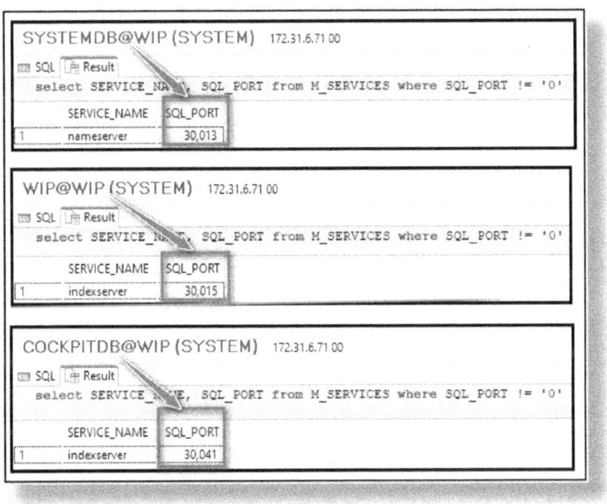

Figure 3.21: Determining SQL port

For more details on ports, refer to Table 2.6.

The SQL port can also be determined by connecting to the relevant database using HANA Studio and navigating to LANDSCAPE • SERVICES • SQL PORT COLUMN (see Figure 3.8).

The HANA *DATABASE_NAME* can be identified by executing the below SQL query from the SystemDB:

```
SELECT * FROM M_DATABASES;
```

Figure 3.22 shows that the DATABASE_NAME for a SystemDB is SYSTEMDB. It also lists the DATABASE_NAME for all the tenants in the HANA database.

> **! SID versus DATABASE_NAME**
>
> *SID* is different from *DATABASE_NAME*. Every HANA database has its own SID and zero to <n> number of tenant databases. Each tenant database has its own *DATABASE_NAME*.

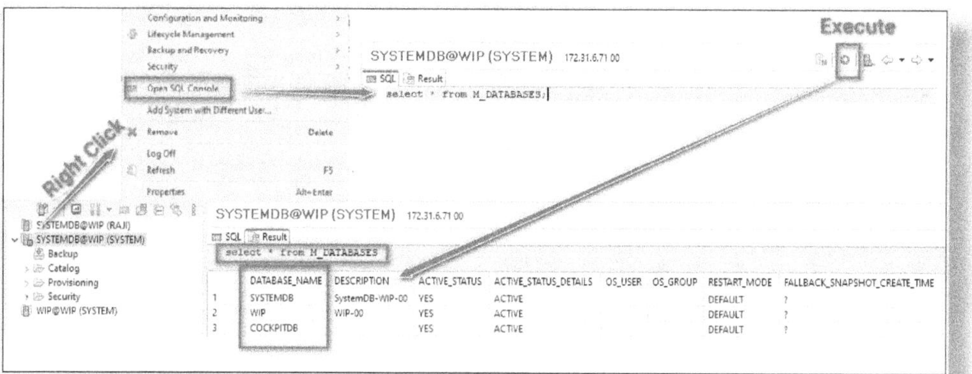

Figure 3.22: Executing SQL command from HANA Studio

3.4.2 Connecting the database using HDBSQL

A HANA database SystemDB can be connected using one of the following *hdbsql* commands:

- Using SQL port:

```
hdbsql -n <db_host>:3<nn>13 -u <DBuser_name> -p <password>
```

- Using *DATABASE_NAME*:

```
hdbsql -n <db_host> -i <nn> -u <DBuser_name> -p <password> -d
SYSTEMDB
```

Tenant databases can be connected using one of the following *hdbsql* commands:

- Using SQL port:

```
hdbsql -n <db_host>:<tenant_SQL_Port> -u <DB_user_name> -p
<password>
```

- Using *DATABASE_NAME*:

```
hdbsql -n <db_host> -i <nn> -u <DB_user_name> -p <password> -d
<tenant_DB_name>
```

Note that all the commands listed above can be executed without the *-p <password>* option. In these cases, the password must then be entered when prompted by the database.

Sample outputs are shown in Figure 3.23.

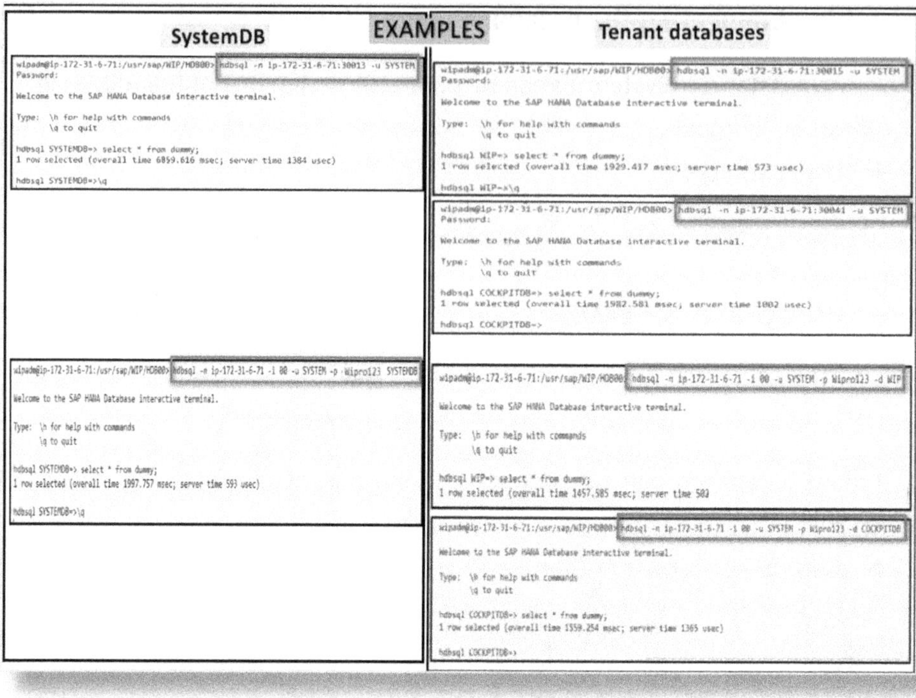

Figure 3.23 HDBSQL sample commands

3.4.3 Executing SQL commands from HDBSQL console

There are two distinct methods to execute database SQL queries through HDSQL:

- **Method 1** (see Figure 3.24)—incorporates the SQL to be executed along with the *hdbsql* login command. With this approach, upon executing the SQL, the console returns the query output and disconnects itself from the database.

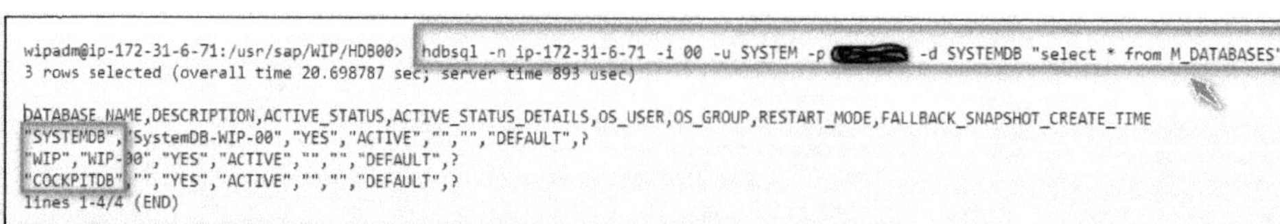

Figure 3.24: Executing SQL from HDBSQL—method 1

- **Method 2** (see Figure 3.25)—executes queries after establishing a database connection to the target database via the *hdbsql* console. To exit from this console, type the command /q .

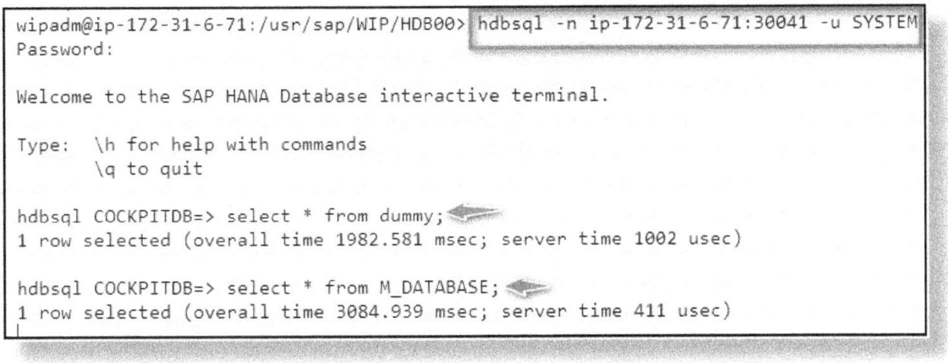

Figure 3.25: Executing SQL from HDBSQL—method 2

SQL console

The SQL console, which enables the execution of SQL statements, is accessible through:

- HANA Studio (see Figure 3.11),
- *hdbsql* console (see Figure 3.25), and
- HANA Cockpit (see Figure 3.18).

3.4.4 hdbuserstore

The HANA database user store (*--hdbuserstore)* enables secure storage of the database user name and password at the operating system level. This tool is automatically installed when the HANA database or database client software is installed. It facilitates seamless connections between the HANA database and its application, eliminating the need for repeated authentication by end users or applications when communicating with the database.

The default location of this tool is */usr/sap/<SID>/HDB<nn>/exe/*. For client applications, it is installed in the same location as the HANA database client.

Figure 3.26 shows an example of using command *hdbuserstore*. It shows how to store the database connection string along with the username and password, enabling a connection to the target database through the *User_Store_Name*, without specifically providing the username and password.

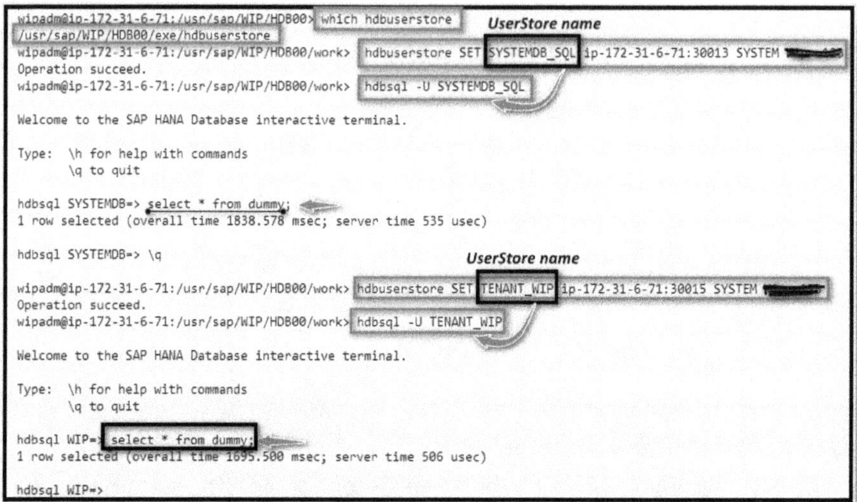

Figure 3.26: Secure storage using hdbuserstore

The command to store usernames and passwords using *hdbuserstore* at OS level is:

```
hdbuserstore SET <User_Store_Name> <DB_host>:<SQL_port>
<DBUsername> <Password>
```

To connect to the target database via *hdbsql,* using the previously created *hdbuserstore*, use the following command:

```
hdbsql -U <User_Store_Name>
```

Figure 3.26 shows the use of *hdbuserstore* for both the SystemDB and a tenant database, and the execution of SQL query `select * from dummy;` to test the database connection. A successful connection returns a dummy output.

Figure 3.27 shows some of the parameter options available with *hdbuserstore*:

- `hdbuserstore LIST`—lists the user stores that are stored on the current server.

- `hdbuserstore DELETE <User_Store_Name>`—deletes the saved user store with the name *User_Store_Name*.

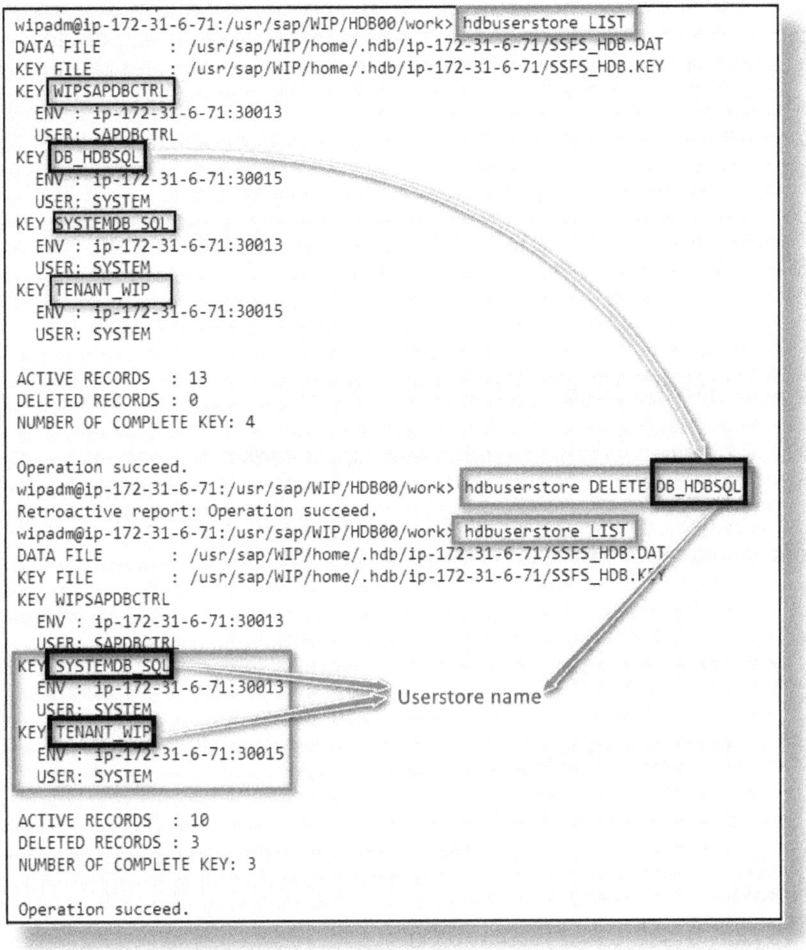

Figure 3.27: hdbuserstore sample commands

> **SAP ABAP system and HANA client software**
>
> For an SAP ABAP application hosted on a HANA database, the HANA client software is installed on all SAP application servers. This software serves as a bridge between the application server and the database, facilitating the connection using the SAP schema and password, which are stored in the *hdbuserstore* under the key name *DEFAULT* during the SAP HANA installation

3.4.5 hdbuserstore in master/slave (standby) setup

In a distributed HANA database with a standby node, the user store that is used by the application or end-user to communicate with the database must be configured on all hosts, including the standby node. This ensures a smooth transfer of end-user connections from a failing node to the standby node, using the user store password. The *hdbuserstore* command used in this scenario is:

```
hdbuserstore SET <User_Store_Name> "<host1>:<SQL_Port>;
<host2>:<SQL_Port>; <host3>:<SQL_Port>" <DB_User> <password>
```

3.5 SAP HANA XS administraton tools

The XS administration tool is used to develop, configure, and manage web-based applications. For this purpose, the SAP HANA XS advanced model offers command-line tools such as XSA and xs CLI. Refer to the commands outlined in Figure 3.20 for examples of xs commands.

3.6 Additional tools

3.6.1 SAP Solution Manager

SAP Solution Manager (SolMan) serves as a central infrastructure for alerting and monitoring. All SAP applications rely on Solution Manager for performing regular monitoring, EarlyWatch Alert (EWA), end-to-end root cause analysis, and so on.

The steps to integrate an installed HANA database with SolMan are as follows:

1. Install the Diagnostics Agent (DA) on the HANA database server using the SAP application installer tool—Software Provisioning Manager (SWPM). The menu path for this installation is: GENERIC OPTIONS • DIAGNOSTICS IN SAP SOLUTION MANAGER • INSTALL – DIAGNOSTICS AGENT. This is shown in Figure 3.28.

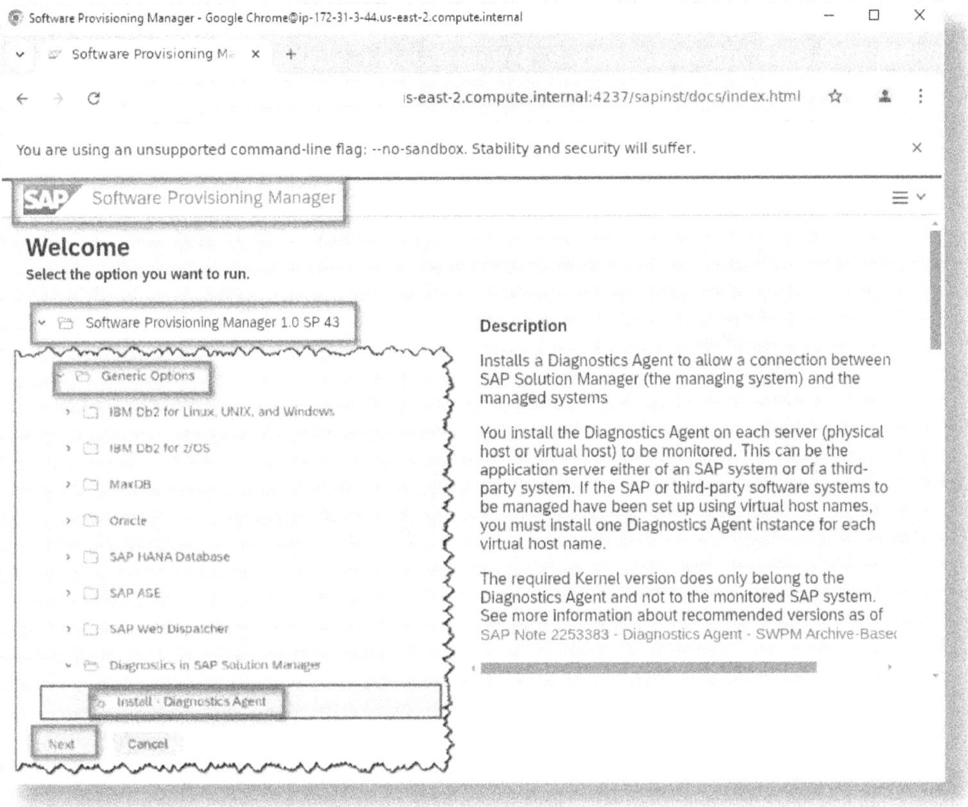

Figure 3.28: SWPM path to install Diagnostics Agent

2. Create a new database user for monitoring, with HANA database roles *DBA_COCKPIT* and *MONITORING*.

3. Securely store the database connection, user credentials, and password in hdbuserstore in HANA using the command:

```
hdbuserstore SET <SID>SAPDBCTRL <hana_host>:<SQLPort> <dbuser>
<password>
```

4. Register the HANA database in SLD (System Landscape Directory) and schedule periodic transfers of system information from the HANA database to SLD. Figure 3.29 shows the inputs required for SLD registration. Resident HDBLCM helps with this SLD registration, and the options are available through command-line, GUI, or web-user interface options (see Figure 2.30 and Figure 2.31).

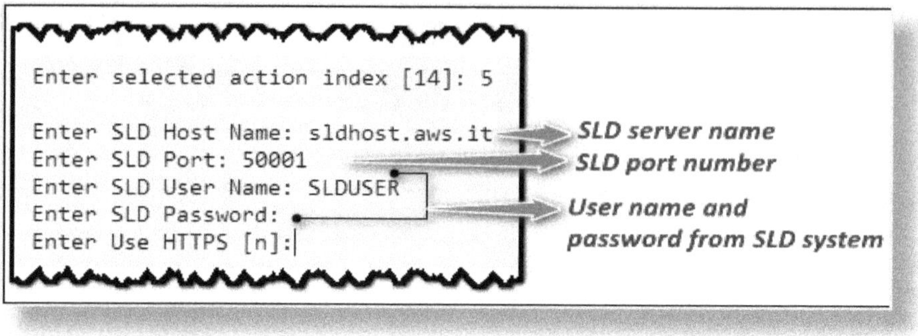

Figure 3.29: Resident HDBLCM (command line)—SLD registration

5. Verify that the SLD and Landscape Management Database (LMDB) content in SolMan are synchronized and contain the latest information regarding the HANA database.
6. Configure the newly discovered HANA database system as a managed system in SolMan.

For further information, refer to the following:

- *https://support.sap.com/en/alm/solution-manager/expert-portal/sap-hana-database-preparation.html*
- SAP Note 2362392—"How do you install the Diagnostic Agent for a HANA system?"

3.6.2 SAP Landscape Management

SAP Landscape Management (LaMa) is an SAP application that runs on SAP NetWeaver AS JAVA and can be used to automate many HANA operational tasks. For more information, refer to SAP Help Portal.

3.6.3 SAP IT Operation Analytics

SAP IT Operation Analytics (ITOA) is an SAP HANA XSA application that runs on the HANA platform with the SAP HANA Predictive Analysis Library. It provides a holistic, real-time overview of complex data center landscapes, aiding in root cause analysis, and predicting and preventing issues. For more information, refer to the SAP Help Portal.

4 Database administration

This chapter provides comprehensive technical information about HANA database administration and table management.

4.1 Table management

Table management is a critical aspect of any database administration. It refers to the process and techniques used to create, maintain, and manipulate tables within a database. These tables can be either column-store (predominantly) or row-store. Along with these table structures, the HANA database also supports document store for JSON artifacts and indexes to enable efficient table data access. Refer to SAP Note 2160391—"FAQ: SAP HANA Indexes"—for further details.

Schemas in the HANA database act as logical containers that organize database objects such as tables, views, indexes, procedures, and other database elements (see Figure 4.1).

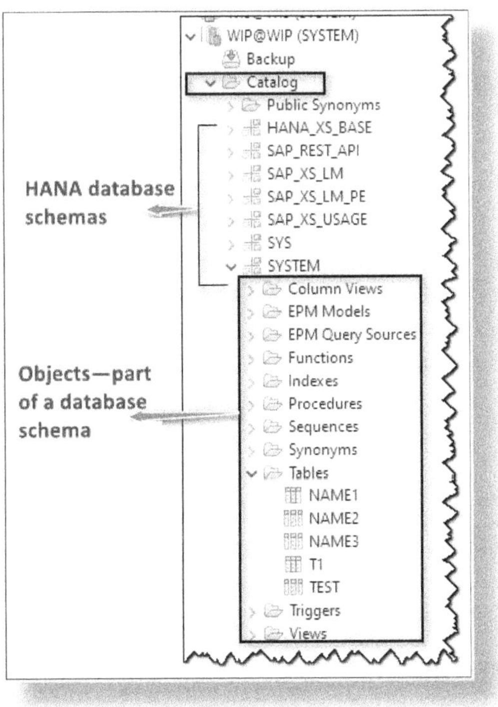

Figure 4.1: HANA database schemas and objects

> **CREATE TABLE statement**
>
> When a table is created using the CREATE TABLE statement without specifying a table type, a column-store table is created. This is as per the default value of the parameter *default_table_type* in the *indexserver.ini* configuration file.

> **! Semicolon (;) and SQL query**
>
> Every SQL query executed against the HANA database must end with a semicolon (;).

4.1.1 Interpreting row-store and column-store tables using system views

The key to HANA database administration is to have an overall understanding of the key database tables, table types and their properties. HANA provides various system views such as *M_TABLES, M_CS_TABLES, M_RS_TABLES, M_CS_COLUMNS*, etc., to understand the tables and their behavior. Some of the key SQL queries based on these system views are outlined in Table 4.1.

SQL query	Description
select * from SCHEMAS;	To identify the list of schemas in the HANA database.
select * from M_TABLES;	To identify the list of tables in the HANA database.
select * from M_TABLES where SCHEMA_NAME='<SCHEMA_NAME>';	To identify the list of tables in a particular schema of the HANA database.
select count(*) from M_TABLES;	To identify the total number of tables in the HANA database.
Row-store: ▶ select count(*) from M_TABLES where TABLE_TYPE='ROW'; Column-store: ▶ select count(*) from M_TABLES where TABLE_TYPE='COLUMN';	To identify the total number of column-store and row-store tables in the HANA database.

SQL query	Description
select * from M_CS_TABLES;	To obtain more details about column-store tables (e.g., memory consumed, memory loaded status, historical information, etc.)
select * from M_RS_TABLES;	To obtain more details about row-store tables.
select round (sum(memory_size_in-total)/1024/1024/1024,0) as mry_column_size_gb from M_CS_TABLES;	To identify the total amount of memory occupied by a column-store table at any point in time.
select top 10 * from M_CS_TABLES order by MEMORY_SIZE_IN_TOTAL desc;	To identify the top 10 column-store tables that are occupying maximum memory.
select * from M_CS_COLUMNS where TABLE_NAME=' <table_name>';	To identify the list of columns of all the column-store tables and their status in HANA memory.

Table 4.1: SQL queries

Some of the execution of SQL queries from Table 4.1 are shown in Figure 4.2.

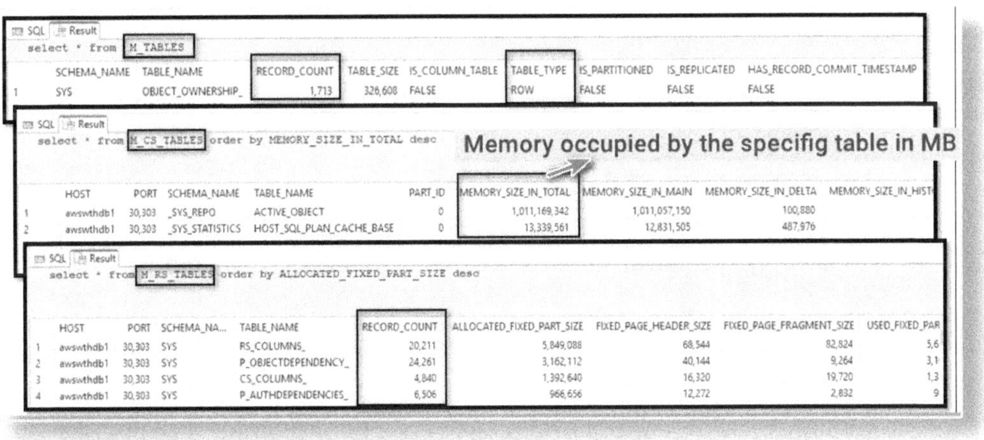

Figure 4.2: Sample query on the system tables

HANA table creation commands

- The SQL query to create a table in the HANA database is:

```
CREATE TABLE <schema_name>.<table_name>( <column_name1> <data_
type>, <column_name2> <data_type>);
```

- The SQL query to create a table in the HANA database as a copy of another table is:

```
CREATE TABLE <schema>.<new_table> AS (SELECT * FROM
<schema>.<table_to_be_copied>);
```

4.1.2 Loading and unloading column-store tables

The HANA database primarily operates on column-store tables. These tables and their columns are automatically loaded or unloaded into memory according to their usage by HANA's memory manager. However, this process can also be controlled manually through the following SQL queries:

- To load all the columns of a column store table into memory:

```
load <schema_name>.<table_name> ALL;
```

- To unload all columns of a column store table from memory:

```
unload <schema_name>.<table_name>;
```

- To load only specific columns of a column store table to memory:

```
load <schema_name>.<table_name> (<column_name>);
```

Column-store tables need not always have to be loaded fully into memory. Instead, they can be loaded at individual column level or partition level and can have the status of *partially* or *fully* loaded into memory. This is shown in Figure 4.3, using the following queries.

- To check whether a table is fully loaded into memory (all the table's columns are loaded into memory) or partially loaded (only some of the table's columns are loaded into memory):

```
select SCHEMA_NAME, TABLE_NAME, LOADED from M_CS_TABLES where
TABLE_NAME='<table_name>';
```

- To check the table's column status (loaded or unloaded) in memory:

```
select SCHEMA_NAME, TABLE_NAME,COLUMN_NAME, LOADED from M_CS_
COLUMNS where TABLE_NAME='<table_name>';
```

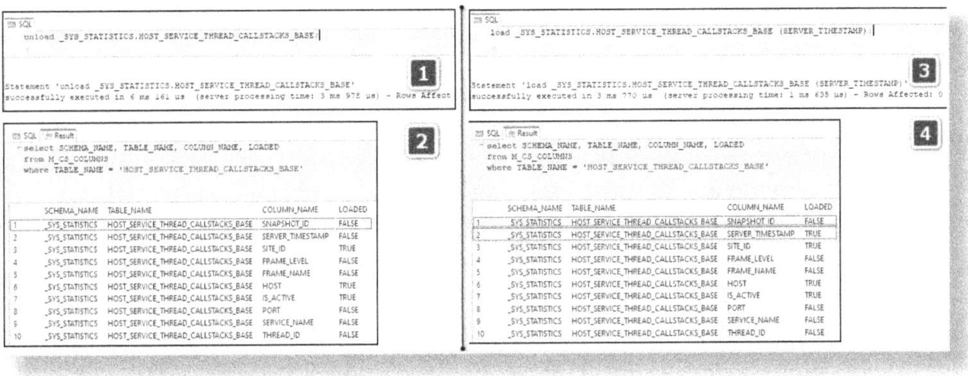

Figure 4.3: Loading and unloading column-store table or its column

The numbers in Figure 4.3 indicate the following:

❶ Unload a column-store table.

❷ Check the status of its columns in HANA memory by querying the system view M_CS_COLUMNS for the table.

❸ Load a column of a column-store table into memory.

❹ Verify this column's status in memory by querying the system view M_CS_COLUMNS.

> **! Row-store table**
>
> Row-store tables remain in memory and are loaded during the start-up of the HANA database. However, they cannot be specifically loaded or unloaded like a column-store table.

4.1.3 Managing column-store priority and eviction

The HANA database's memory manager—that controls the loading and unloading of column-store tables—can be controlled and configured directly (at database level) or indirectly (at table level) using the following parameters:

- *unused_retention_period*—this parameter in *global.ini*, determines the duration after which a table or data is evicted from memory when not used. This parameter can also be configured at individual table level using the following query:

```
ALTER TABLE "<table_name>" WITH PARAMETERS('UNUSED_RETENTION_
PERIOD'='60');
```

- *unused_retention_period_check_interval*—this parameter in *global.ini*, determines how often the system checks for the in-memory unused data that can be safely removed in accordance with its defined retention period.
- *Table priority*—helps with managing memory at an individual column-store table level by setting the unload priority. This priority is a numerical value ranging from 0 to 9. Value 0 indicates that the object can never be automatically unloaded, while 9 indicates the earliest possible unload. The SQL query to alter the table priority is as follows, where <n> is a numerical value between 0 to 9:

```
ALTER TABLE "<table_name>" UNLOAD PRIORITY <n>;
```

- The unload priority for all the column-store tables can be viewed from the *TABLES* table using the query below:

```
SELECT UNLOAD_PRIORITY FROM TABLES WHERE TABLE_NAME = "<table_
name>";
```

Figure 4.4 shows a sample configuration of parameters and sample execution of the queries specified in this section.

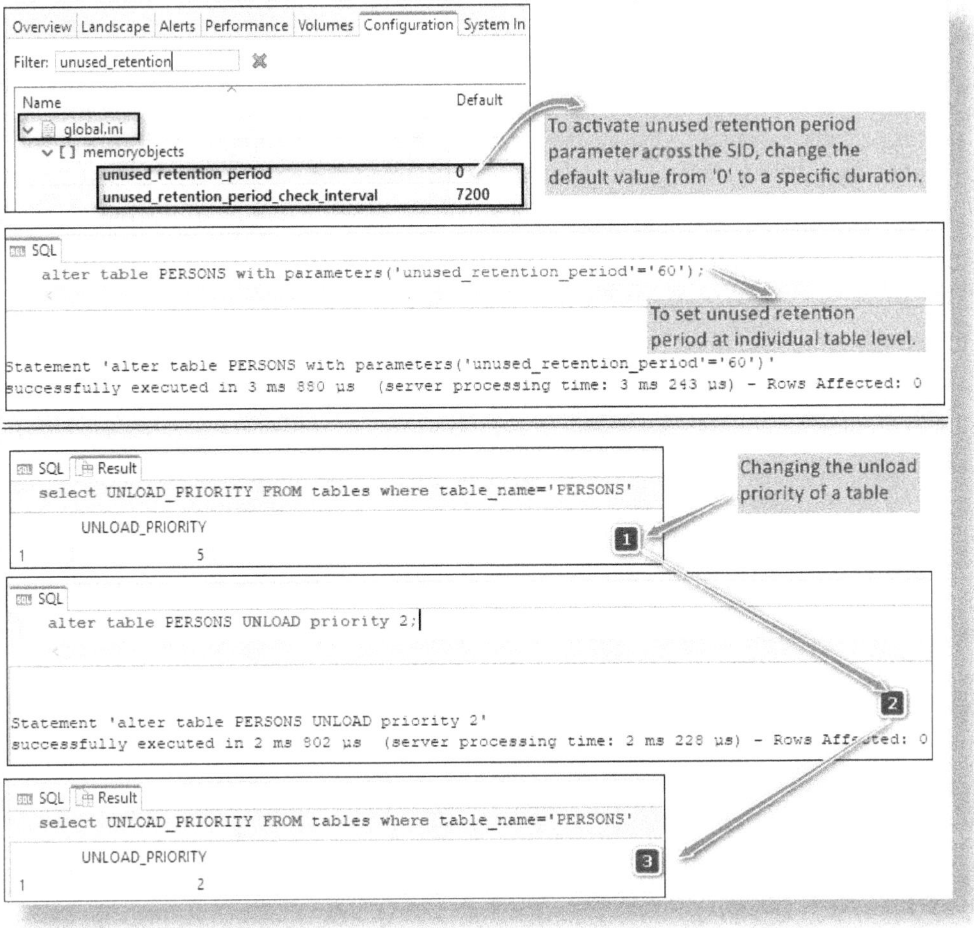

Figure 4.4: Unused retention period and unload priority

The numbers in this image relate to the following functions:

❶ Displays the UNUSED_RETENTION_PERIOD and UNUSED_RETENTION_PERIOD_CHECK_INTERVAL parameters from the GLOBAL.INI configuration file, which together help manage the periodic removal of unused data from memory.

❷ Demonstrates setting the unused retention period for an individual table using an SQL query.

❸ Illustrates how to modify the unload priority of a table through an SQL query.

4.1.4 Managing large objects in HANA

HANA manages not only standard data but also large objects (LOBs), such as videos and images. This type of data has a short-term disposition setting and is the first to be evicted from memory in the case of a memory shortage. These LOBs can be stored entirely in memory (up to 1 GB supported), entirely on disk (with a virtual file created per LOB), or in a hybrid model where smaller LOBs are in memory, larger ones on disk, and medium-sized ones in LOB containers.

> **! LOBs and startup times**
>
> Be aware that the number of LOBs directly affects the database start-up duration.

To identify memory consumption by hybrid LOB data, use the following SQL query:

```
select * from M_HEAP_MEMORY where CATEGORY = 'Pool/
PersistenceManager/LOBContainerDirectory';
```

This is shown in Figure 4.5.

SQL | Result

`SELECT * FROM M_HEAP_MEMORY WHERE CATEGORY = 'Pool/PersistenceManager/LOBContainerDirectory'`

	HOST	PORT	VOLUME_ID	STATISTICS_ID	CATEGORY	DEPTH	INCLUSIVE_SIZE_IN_USE	INCLUSIVE_COUNT_IN_USE
1		30,303	3	19,603	Pool/PersistenceManager/LOBContainerDirectory	3	752	2
2		30,307	2	18,100	Pool/PersistenceManager/LOBContainerDirectory	3	752	2

Figure 4.5: LOB memory consumption in main memory

4.1.5 Delta merge operations

As a quick recap, the HANA database has the ability to store table data in a compressed form in memory. Because the column-store table in memory is highly compressed, direct write operations are costly. To address this, HANA uses the delta store area in memory. In this part of memory, table data is uncompressed, enabling easy writes. The table data in main memory is read-optimized, and the table data in the delta store is write-optimized. To ensure consistent data reads during a parallel write operation, the table data is read from both the main and delta stores. However, table writes continue to take place in the delta store. Once the write operation is successful, the data changes from the delta store are merged back with the main store, followed by data compression. This operation is known as a *delta merge*. Delta merge operations move data from write-optimized delta store to the compressed, read-optimized main store, after a certain configurable threshold.

Main store and delta store in a delta merge

- The main store and delta store of a column-store table are part of HANA database memory.
- Delta merge operations are initiated and performed at the individual table level, meaning that they are specific to each table and depend on the data changes impacting that particular table.

The delta merge operation is asynchronous and is decoupled from the transaction that makes the data changes to the table. The sequence of events in a merge operation are illustrated in Figure 4.6.

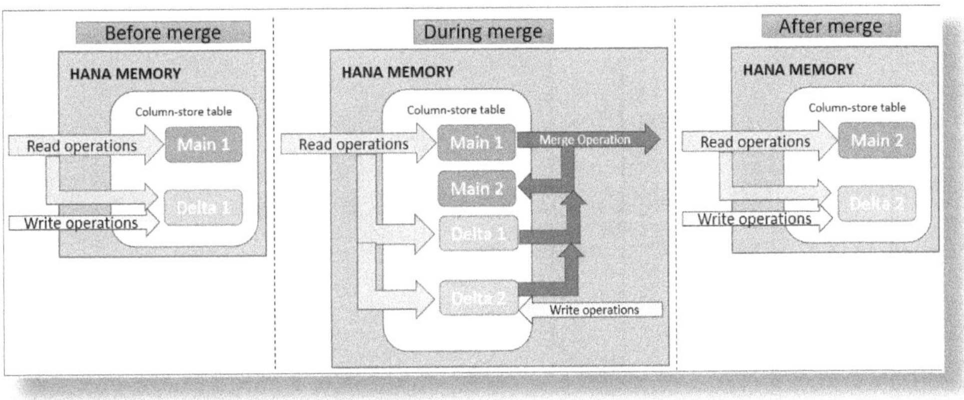

Figure 4.6: Delta merge sequence

The sequence is as follows:

1. Prior to the delta merge operation, all write operations for the specific column-store table are directed to DELTA 1 store. Read operations read data from MAIN 1 and DELTA 1 stores.
2. During the merge operation, any ongoing uncommitted changes are recorded in the newly created DELTA 2 store for that table. However, read operations continue to read table data from MAIN 1 and DELTA 1 stores, as well as DELTA 2 store. By the end of this operation, the content of

MAIN 1 store and the committed changes in DELTA 1 store are merged to form a new main storage—MAIN 2 store.

3. Upon completion of the merge operation, MAIN 1 and DELTA 1 stores are deleted, and the contents of the complete main store is persisted to disk.

In general, delta merges are triggered *automatically* by the HANA database for various reasons, known as *merge motives*. However, there are cases where a delta merge is triggered *manually* by an end user or application. Manual merges can also be initiated through HANA Studio (see Figure 4.7) or by using SQL commands (this is shown later in Figure 4.9).

Figure 4.7 shows the triggering of a manual delta merge from HANA Studio. First, find the table from the CATALOG and right-click on it. Then, choose PERFORM DELTA MERGE.

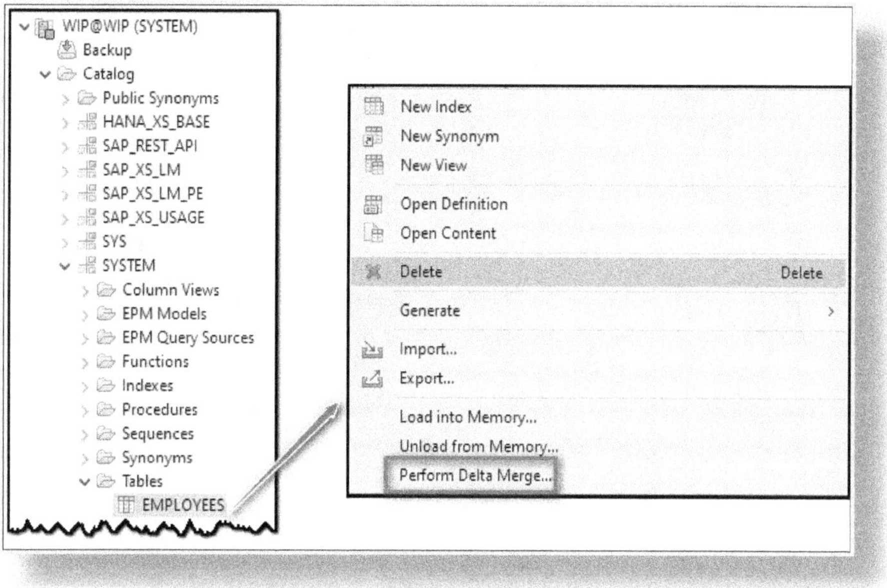

Figure 4.7: Triggering delta merge from HANA Studio

Figure 4.8 shows various merge motives that can trigger a delta merge operation.

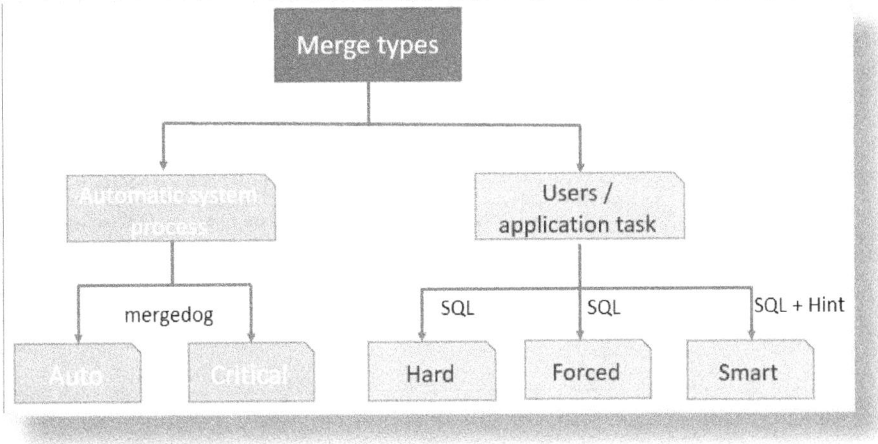

Figure 4.8: Merge motives

Let's examine the merge motives in more detail:

- An *auto merge* is the standard method for initiating a delta merge and is triggered by a system process called *mergedog*. This process periodically checks the column-store tables loaded into memory and determines whether a merge should be triggered based on configured criteria such as the size of delta store per table, available memory, time since the last merge, etc.
- A *smart merge* is triggered when an application sends a *hint* to the HANA database to check if a merge is necessary for a particular table. However, the merge is only initiated if the merge evaluation criteria is successful.
- A *hard merge* is when a delta merge operation is manually triggered using the SQL command `MERGE DELTA OF "<table_name>";`(see Figure 4.9) or via HANA Studio (see Figure 4.7).
- A *forced merge* is a type of hard merge that includes the *--FORCE REBUILD* clause with the *MERGE* command. It performs a hard merge on database memory even if there are no rows to merge in the old delta store or old rows to be deleted from the old main store. The SQL command for performing a forced merge is:

```
MERGE DELTA OF '<table_name>' FORCE REBUILD;
```

Figure 4.9 shows the execution of a forced merge on a table.

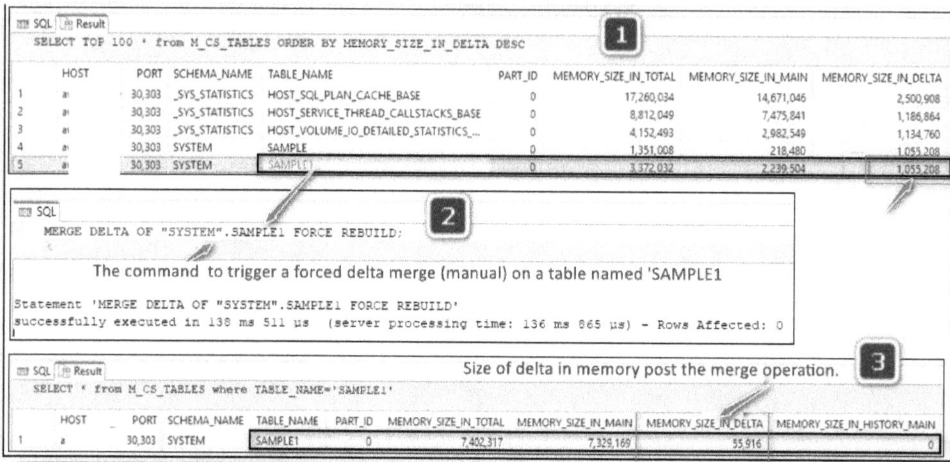

Figure 4.9: Forced manual merge on a column-store table

The numbered areas in the image are as follows:

❶ Identify the top 10 column-store tables consuming the most delta store memory using the following SQL query:

```
SELECT TOP 10 * FROM M_CS_TABLES ORDER BY MEMORY_SIZE_IN_DELTA
DESC;
```

❷ Execution of a forced merge on the table.

❸ Comparison of the size of the delta store before and after the forced merge.

A *critical merge* is a database-initiated operation that helps maintain system stability. It is automatically triggered by the database when a specific threshold is reached.

Mergedog, in the HANA database, is an internal process responsible for managing the merge of the delta store into the main store of the column-store tables. This process is crucial for maintaining performance and memory efficiency in HANA databases. When MERGEDOG • ACTIVE is set to

YES and SMART_MERGE_ENABLED is also set to YES (see Figure 4.10), mergedog actively monitors the tables and triggers merges when conditions are met. The primary objective of a *smart merge* is to ensure that merges occur only when beneficial, based on system health and workload.

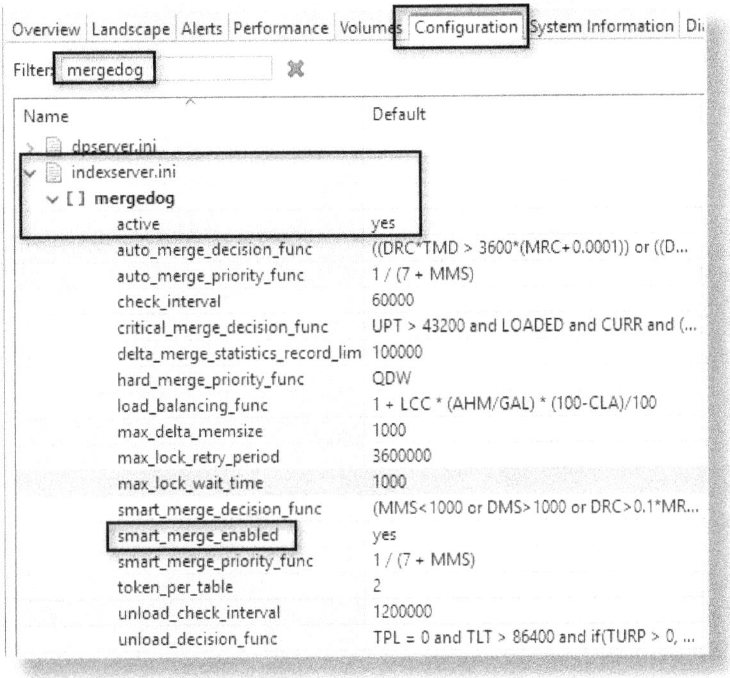

Figure 4.10: mergedog and smart merge

A detailed history of delta merges executed against a column-store table is available via:

- System views M_DELTA_MERGE_STATISTICS and _SYS_STATISTICS.HOST_DELTA_MERGE_STATISTICS.
- HANA STUDIO • SYSTEM INFORMATION • MERGE STATISTICS

These are shown in Figure 4.11.

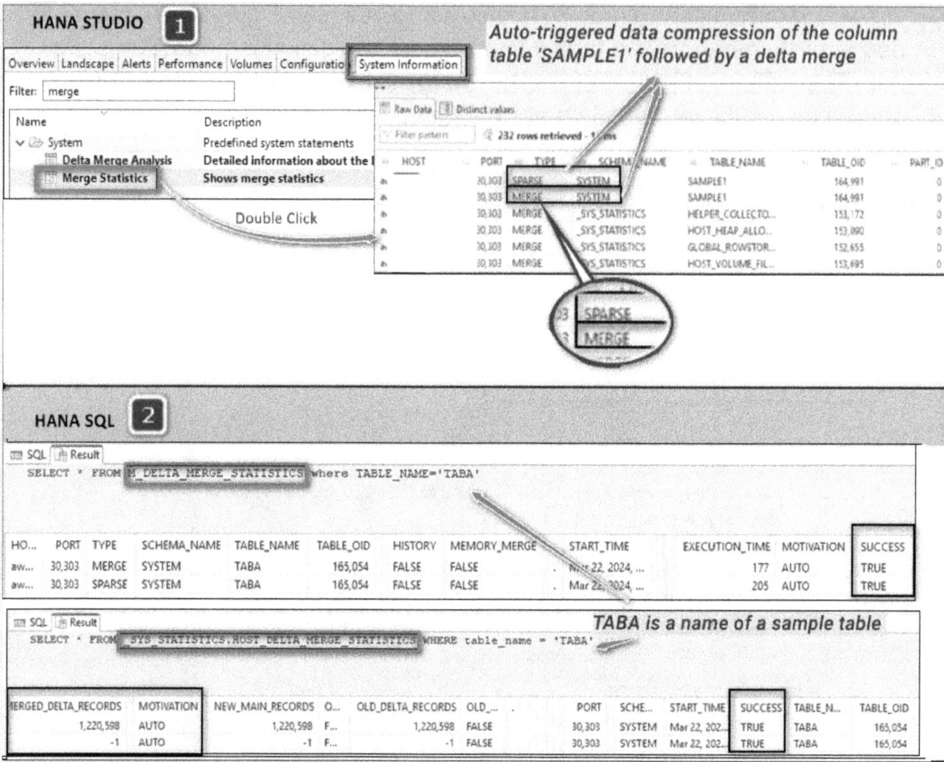

Figure 4.11: Delta merge statistics

The image shows the following:

❶ In HANA Studio, go to the SYSTEM INFORMATION tab and MERGE STATISTICS to view the list of MERGE operations executed against a table. Note that MERGE represents a delta merge, and SPARSE signifies the column-store compression that was automatically executed following the delta merge.

❷ shows the execution and output of the following queries to understand the list of MERGE operations executed against a table:

```
SELECT * FROM M_DELTA_MERGE_STATISTICS where TABLE_NAME='<table_
name>';
SELECT * FROM _SYS_STATISTICS.HOST_DELTA_MERGE_STATISTICS WHERE
TABLE_NAME='<table_name>';
```

4.1.6 Data compression in column store

In the HANA database, column-store tables are efficiently compressed in memory, enhancing search performance and calculation speed. In general, there are two levels of database compression:

- *Dictionary compression*—this default compression is applied to all columns in a column-store table and helps to effectively manage duplicate data by preventing it from consuming additional memory (see Section 2B in Figure 1.4).
- *Advanced compression*—the HANA database applies advanced compression techniques such as prefix, run-length (RLE), cluster, sparse, and indirect encoding to each column. It intelligently selects the optimal method automatically, thereby eliminating the need for manual intervention.

! Delta merge and compression

Every system-triggered delta merge operation on a table is followed by the compression optimization of the table's new main store in memory.

Figure 4.12 shows how to initiate table compression manually using SQL statements.

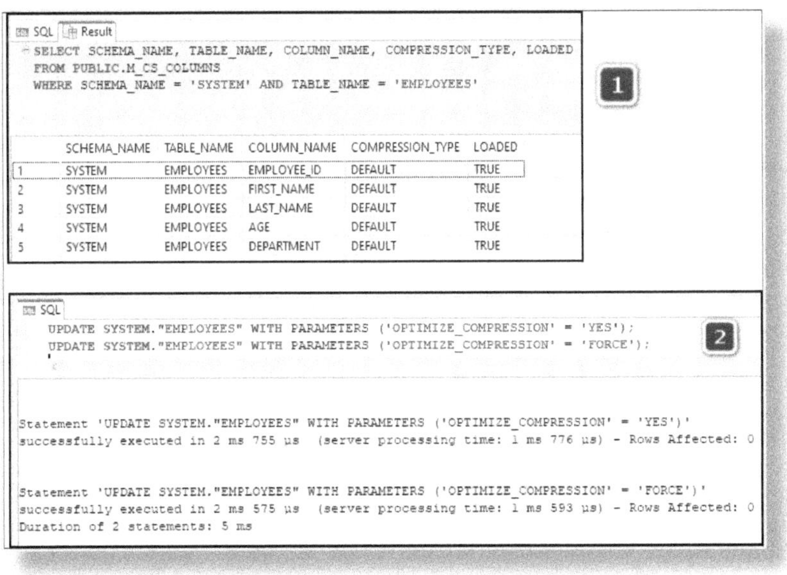

Figure 4.12: Data compression on column-store table

The image shows the following:

- Area ❶ shows the SQL to identify the type of compression that the HANA database has applied to a specific column in a table using the system view M_CS_COLUMNS. The SQL is:

```
SELECT SCHEMA_NAME, TABLE_NAME, COLUMN_NAME, COMPRESSION_TYPE,
LOADED
FROM PUBLIC.M_CS_COLUMNS
WHERE SCHEMA_NAME = '<schema_name>' AND TABLE_NAME = '<table_
name>';
```

- Area ❷ shows the SQL commands to trigger a manual data compression:

```
UPDATE <schema>."<table_name>" WITH PARAMETERS ('OPTIMIZE_
COMPRESSION' = 'YES');
UPDATE <schema>." <table_name>" WITH PARAMETERS ('OPTIMIZE_
COMPRESSION' = 'FORCE');
```

4.1.7 Table partition

The partitioning feature of the HANA database is designed to efficiently manage large column-store tables by splitting them into multiple sub-tables or partitions. Each partition contains a distinct set of rows from the original table. In a distributed HANA database, these partitions can be distributed across different worker hosts to optimize load balancing.

The logic for assigning a table's record set or row to a particular partition depends on the chosen partitioning algorithm (e.g., *hash, range*, or *round-robin*) and the column used for partitioning the table. Figure 4.13 shows a sample range-partitioned table—TEST (in area ❶)—divided into five partitions based on the value in the NUMBER column (in area ❷).

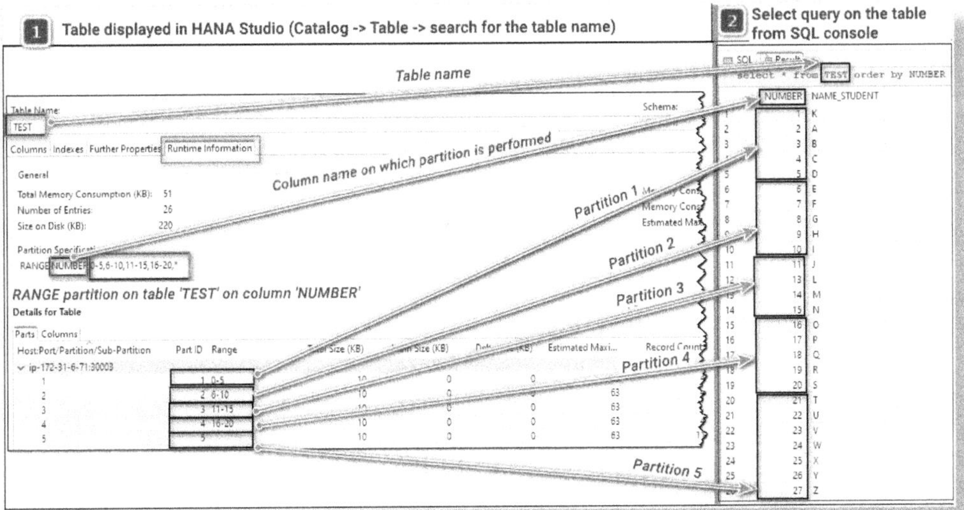

Figure 4.13: Sample range-partitioned table

Efficiently partitioned tables can limit the number of records loaded into HANA memory for query processing. This is because HANA loads column data at the individual partition level into memory, helping to reduce the table's overall memory footprint. Figure 4.14 shows a query execution on a table, resulting in PARTITION 1 specifically being loaded into memory, unlike an unpartitioned table where the entire table content might have to be loaded into memory.

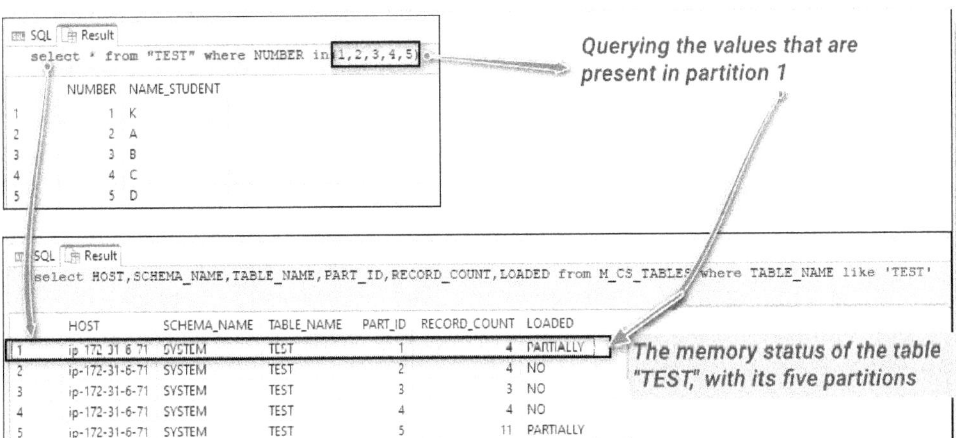

Figure 4.14: Partial memory loading of a partitioned table

Partitioning has proven to be both beneficial and memory-efficient, not only in distributed environments but also in single host setups.

To execute table partitioning, either the HANA Cockpit or the SQL console can be used. Database users performing the partitioning must have the *ALTER OBJECT* privilege for that table and *PARTITION ADMIN* system privilege. The latter privilege is required to carry out partitioning operations, such as partitioning a table, moving table partitions from one host to another in a scale-out setup, merging partitions, etc.

! Partition restriction

- The total record count of an unpartitioned table must not exceed 2 billion. To overcome this limitation, it is recommended to partition the table when its record count is close to 1.5 billion.
- In HANA, the record count per partition can also not exceed 2 billion due to memory constraints. Therefore, even fast-growing partitioned tables should be closely monitored and re-partitioned if any record count per partition nears 1.5 billion.
- The maximum number of partitions permitted per HANA database table is 16,000.

! Partition operation—online mode

Table partitioning is an online operation, meaning that the underlying table remains fully available for read operations, with only temporary blocks to write operations.

Single-level partitions

When a table is partitioned using one of the partitioning algorithms—hash, range, or round-robin—it is referred to as a *single-level partition*. Let's look at these algorithms more closely.

Hash partitioning

Hash partitioning is an algorithm that evenly distributes table rows across partitions based on one or more of the table's primary keys. The main advantage of this algorithm is that it overcomes the limit of 2 billion records per table or partition, without requiring a detailed understanding of the table content.

A sample command to execute hash partitioning on a table is:

```
ALTER TABLE <schema_name>.<table_name> PARTITION BY HASH
(<column_Name>) PARTITIONS <n>;
```

Here, <n> represents the desired number of partitions.

Figure 4.15 shows the state of a table (NAME2) before executing a hash partition.

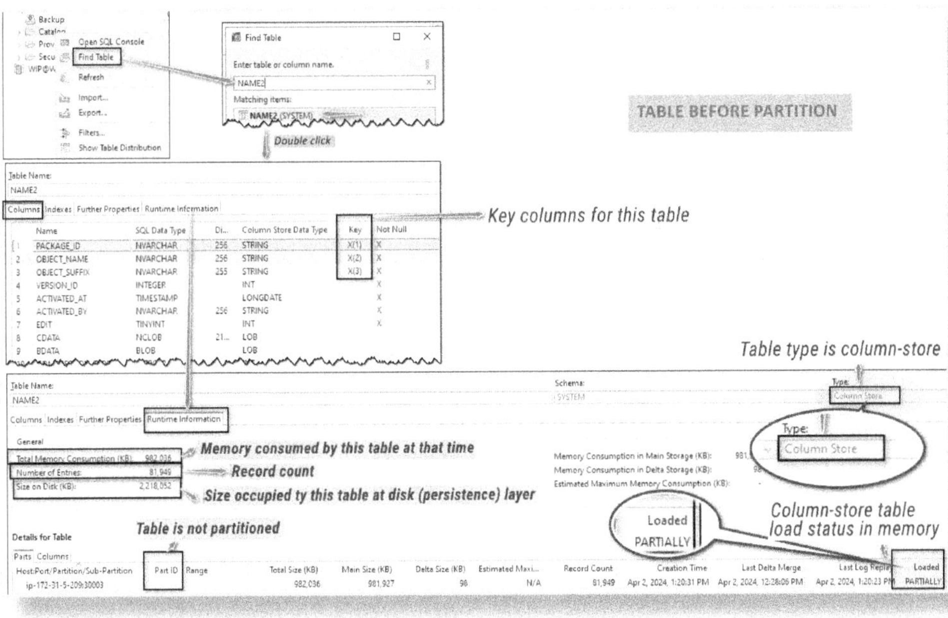

Figure 4.15: Table before hash partition

Figure 4.16 shows the execution of a hash partition on this table based on one of its primary keys—PACKAGE_ID. The table is divided into two partitions as per the SQL statement.

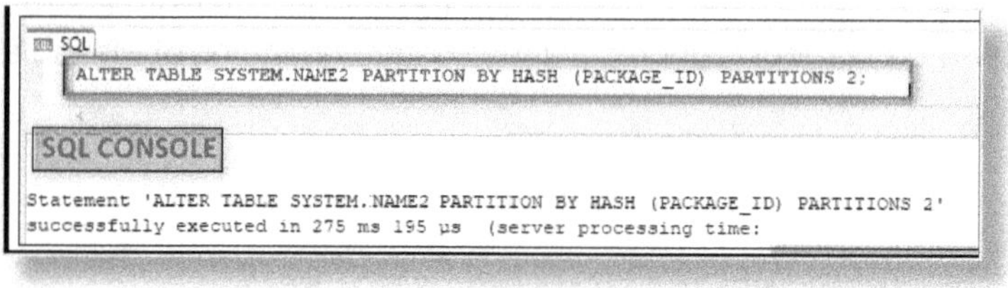

Figure 4.16: Executing hash partition on a sample table

The HANA database executes partitioning as a database job and its progress can be tracked using the JOB PROGRESS tab in HANA Studio (see Figure 4.17).

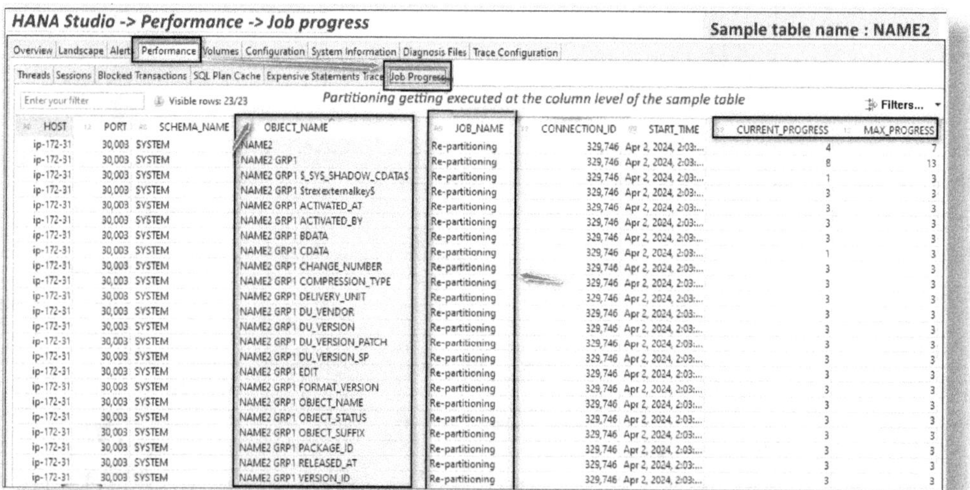

HOST	PORT	SCHEMA_NAME	OBJECT_NAME	JOB_NAME	CONNECTION_ID	START_TIME	CURRENT_PROGRESS	MAX_PROGRESS
ip-172-31	30,003	SYSTEM	NAME2	Re-partitioning	329,746	Apr 2, 2024, 2:03:...	4	7
ip-172-31	30,003	SYSTEM	NAME2 GRP1	Re-partitioning	329,746	Apr 2, 2024, 2:03:...	8	13
ip-172-31	30,003	SYSTEM	NAME2 GRP1 $_SYS_SHADOW_CDATA$	Re-partitioning	329,746	Apr 2, 2024, 2:03:...	1	3
ip-172-31	30,003	SYSTEM	NAME2 GRP1 $trexexternalkey$	Re-partitioning	329,746	Apr 2, 2024, 2:03:...	3	3
ip-172-31	30,003	SYSTEM	NAME2 GRP1 ACTIVATED_AT	Re-partitioning	329,746	Apr 2, 2024, 2:03:...	3	3
ip-172-31	30,003	SYSTEM	NAME2 GRP1 ACTIVATED_BY	Re-partitioning	329,746	Apr 2, 2024, 2:03:...	3	3
ip-172-31	30,003	SYSTEM	NAME2 GRP1 BDATA	Re-partitioning	329,746	Apr 2, 2024, 2:03:...	3	3
ip-172-31	30,003	SYSTEM	NAME2 GRP1 CDATA	Re-partitioning	329,746	Apr 2, 2024, 2:03:...	1	3
ip-172-31	30,003	SYSTEM	NAME2 GRP1 CHANGE_NUMBER	Re-partitioning	329,746	Apr 2, 2024, 2:03:...	3	3
ip-172-31	30,003	SYSTEM	NAME2 GRP1 COMPRESSION_TYPE	Re-partitioning	329,746	Apr 2, 2024, 2:03:...	3	3
ip-172-31	30,003	SYSTEM	NAME2 GRP1 DELIVERY_UNIT	Re-partitioning	329,746	Apr 2, 2024, 2:03:...	3	3
ip-172-31	30,003	SYSTEM	NAME2 GRP1 DU_VENDOR	Re-partitioning	329,746	Apr 2, 2024, 2:03:...	3	3
ip-172-31	30,003	SYSTEM	NAME2 GRP1 DU_VERSION	Re-partitioning	329,746	Apr 2, 2024, 2:03:...	3	3
ip-172-31	30,003	SYSTEM	NAME2 GRP1 DU_VERSION_PATCH	Re-partitioning	329,746	Apr 2, 2024, 2:03:...	3	3
ip-172-31	30,003	SYSTEM	NAME2 GRP1 DU_VERSION_SP	Re-partitioning	329,746	Apr 2, 2024, 2:03:...	3	3
ip-172-31	30,003	SYSTEM	NAME2 GRP1 EDIT	Re-partitioning	329,746	Apr 2, 2024, 2:03:...	3	3
ip-172-31	30,003	SYSTEM	NAME2 GRP1 FORMAT_VERSION	Re-partitioning	329,746	Apr 2, 2024, 2:03:...	3	3
ip-172-31	30,003	SYSTEM	NAME2 GRP1 OBJECT_NAME	Re-partitioning	329,746	Apr 2, 2024, 2:03:...	3	3
ip-172-31	30,003	SYSTEM	NAME2 GRP1 OBJECT_STATUS	Re-partitioning	329,746	Apr 2, 2024, 2:03:...	3	3
ip-172-31	30,003	SYSTEM	NAME2 GRP1 OBJECT_SUFFIX	Re-partitioning	329,746	Apr 2, 2024, 2:03:...	3	3
ip-172-31	30,003	SYSTEM	NAME2 GRP1 PACKAGE_ID	Re-partitioning	329,746	Apr 2, 2024, 2:03:...	3	3
ip-172-31	30,003	SYSTEM	NAME2 GRP1 RELEASED_AT	Re-partitioning	329,746	Apr 2, 2024, 2:03:...	3	3
ip-172-31	30,003	SYSTEM	NAME2 GRP1 VERSION_ID	Re-partitioning	329,746	Apr 2, 2024, 2:03:...	3	3

Figure 4.17: Hash partition—"Job Progress" tab

Figure 4.18 shows the state of the table after executing hash partitioning. It shows the table's RUNTIME INFORMATION, including the table's partitioning specification, memory consumption at the individual partition level, host server details, and more.

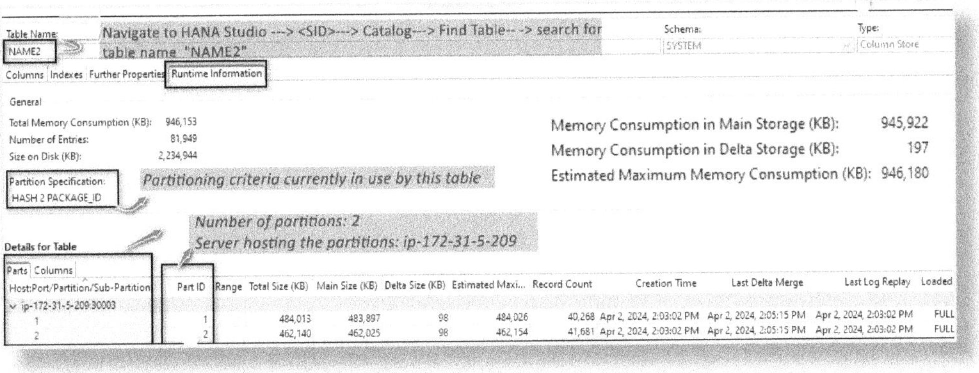

Figure 4.18: Table runtime information after partition

Round-robin partitioning

Round-robin partitioning is an algorithm that evenly distributes table rows across partitions in a rotational manner, without taking into account any column values, including the table's primary key. As a result, unlike hash partitioning, round-robin can place closely related records in different partitions, which may lead to performance issues in certain scenarios. However, this algorithm helps bypass the 2-billion-record limit per table in the HANA database and is suitable for tables without a primary key.

The command used to perform a round-robin partition is:

```
ALTER TABLE "<schemaname>"."<tableName>" PARTITION BY ROUNDROBIN
PARTITIONS <n>;
```

In this command, <n> indicates the number of partitions.

Let's look at how a table can be partitioned with the round-robin algorithm. Figure 4.19 shows the state of the table NAME3 before executing partitioning.

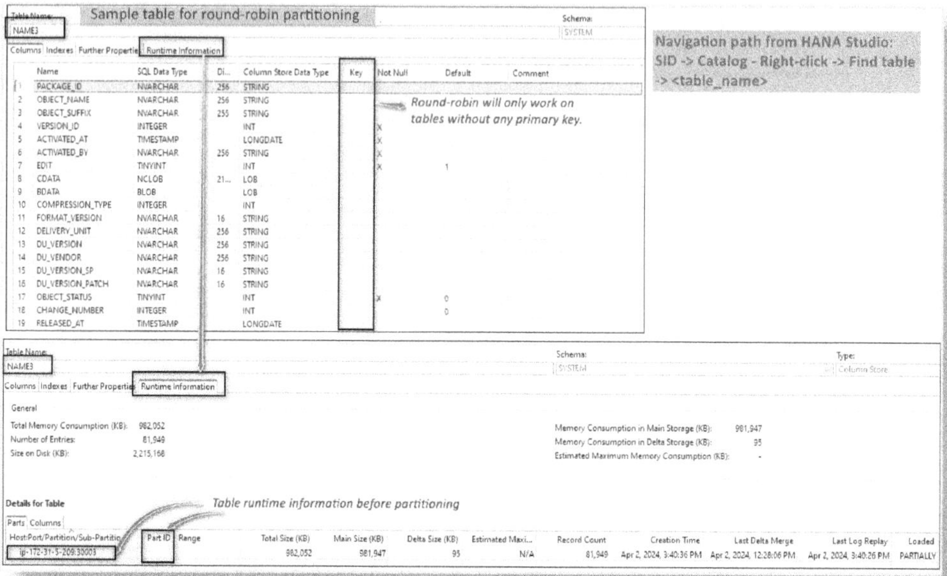

Figure 4.19: Table before round-robin partitioning

Figure 4.20 shows the execution of round-robin partitioning on the NAME3 table.

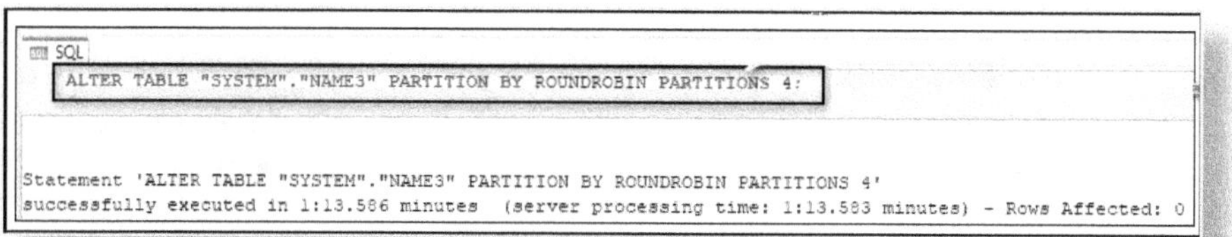

Figure 4.20: Round-robin partitioning

Figure 4.21 shows the state of the NAME3 table after executing round-robin partitioning. This algorithm has resulted in an equal distribution of table records among the partitions.

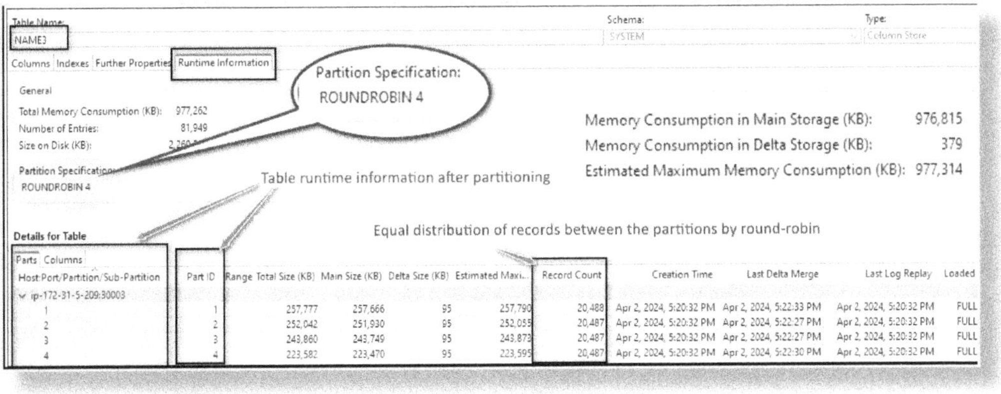

Figure 4.21: Table after round-robin partitioning

Range partitioning

The *range* partitioning algorithm creates partitions by grouping a range of values from a specific key column (usually the primary key if the table has one). For example, range partitioning can be used to group the rows of a table by month, provided the table has a dedicated column for each month. It is important to note that range partitioning requires a better understanding of column values to ensure efficient partitioning. However, it does not guarantee equal distribution (load-balancing) of records across partitions. This is mainly because the distribution is controlled by the values present in the chosen column of a table, unlike hash and round-robin partitioning.

The SQL command for range partitioning is as follows:

```
ALTER TABLE <schema_name>.<table_name> PARTITION BY
RANGE (NUMBER) (PARTITION <FromColumnValue> <= VALUES <
<ToColumnValue>, PARTITION <FromColumnValue> <= VALUES <
<ToColumnValue>....., PARTITION OTHERS);
```

The `OTHERS` clause in the above SQL signifies that any values that do not fall within the defined range can be assigned to the `OTHERS` range.

Figure 4.22 shows how a sample table—named TEST—is range partitioned.

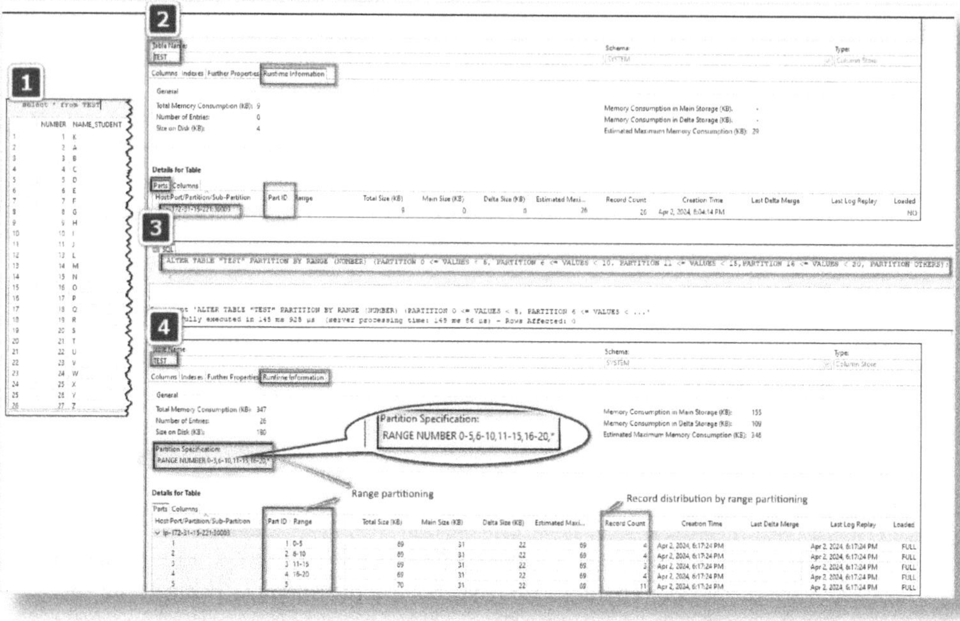

Figure 4.22: Executing range partitioning on a sample table

The numbers in the image refer to the following:

❶ Contents of a sample table (TEST) that are to be partitioned based on a specified range.

❷ The table's RUNTIME INFORMATION before partitioning.

❸ Executing range partitioning on the indicated table.

❹ The table's RUNTIME INFORMATION after range partitioning.

Moving partitions to different index servers

In a HANA database scale-out set-up, one or more partitions of a table can be moved to a different worker host with an active index server within the same SID. The command to move a table's partition from one index server to another, within a database, is as follows:

```
ALTER TABLE <Schema_Name>.<Table_Name> MOVE PARTITION <n> TO
'<host>:<indexserver port>' PHYSICAL;
```

In the above SQL, <n> represents the Part ID (partition ID) that is to be moved to a different index server.

Figure 4.23 shows a sample execution of a partition movement from one index server to another.

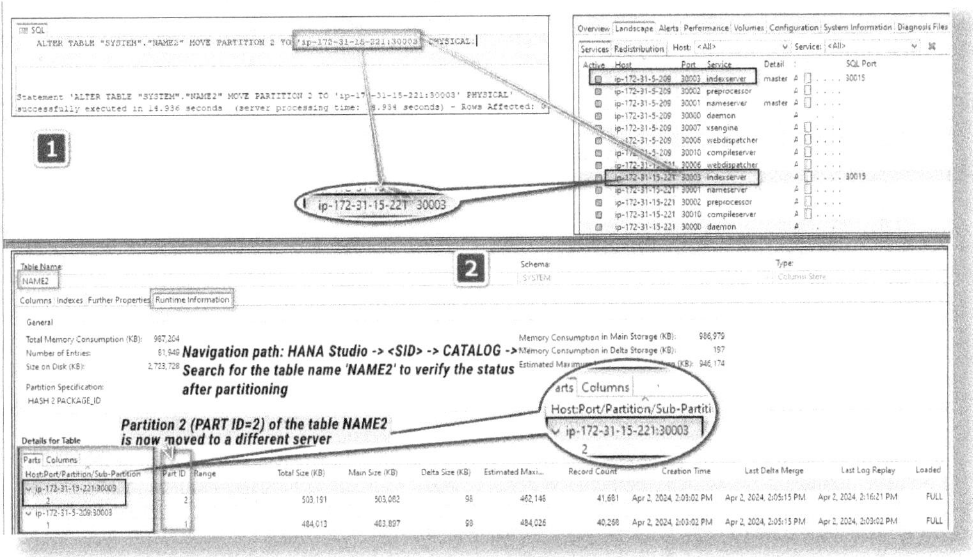

Figure 4.23: Manually moving partition to different host

The numbers in this image refer to the following:

❶ The sample partitioned table NAME2 initially had all its partitions located on *<server1>:3<nn>03*. By executing the ALTER SQL statement, the partition with PART_ID 'n' was relocated to the target server *<server2>:3<nn>03*. Here, <nn> represents the HANA database instance number, and the port *3<nn>03* refers to the index server port, which can be identified via the LANDSCAPE • SERVICES tabs in HANA Studio.

❷ This part of the image highlights the sample table's RUNTIME INFORMATION, showing that one of its partitions was successfully moved to a different host.

Altering number of partitions in a table

There could be a need to increase the number of partitions for an already partitioned table, regardless of the algorithm used. In such instances, re-executing the partition command with an increased number of partitions will yield the desired result, as shown in Figure 4.24.

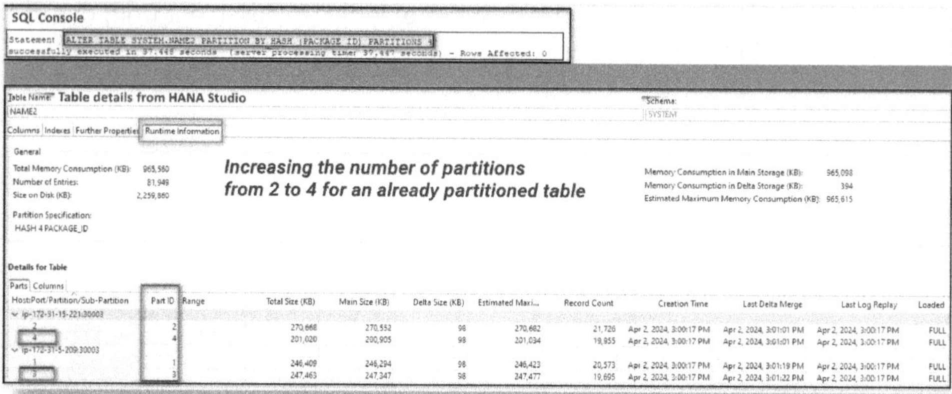

Figure 4.24: Increasing the number of hash partitions from 2 to 4

Here, the hash partition algorithm (see Figure 4.16) is re-executed with an increased number of partitions.

Multi-level partitioning

The HANA database offers *multi-level partitioning*, which enables a combination of algorithms for partitioning a table. This feature is beneficial for addressing the need for a primary key column in the case of single-level partitioning—hash and range algorithm.

Types of multi-level partitioning include:

- hash-range
- round-robin-range
- hash-hash
- range-range

For additional details, refer to the "Table Partitioning" section at the SAP Help Portal.

Uses of table partitioning

Some of the reasons to use table partitioning are as follows:

- Partitioning helps with load balancing in a distributed system, where each table partition can reside on a distinct worker host/active index server. This ensures parallel processing and equal distribution of the database load, during query processing, among all actively available hosts.
- Partitioning helps to overcome the 2-billion-record count limitation on a column-store table.
- It helps with efficient HANA memory utilization because HANA loads the column-store table at individual partition level.
- As data changes occur at the individual partition level, partitioning facilitates faster delta merges. Because fewer partitions need to be delta-merged, it also improves the performance of write operations.

System views for monitoring partitions

System views that provide information about table partitions are:

- *TABLE_PARTITIONS,*
- *M_TABLE_PARTITIONS,*
- *PARTITIONED_TABLES,*
- *TABLE_COLUMNS,*
- *M_CS_PARTITIONS,*
- *M_TABLE_PARTITION_STATISTICS,* etc.

Partitioning consistency checks

Each partition in the HANA database can be validated for its consistency and repaired wherever possible using the following SQL procedure:

```
CALL CHECK_TABLE_CONSISTENCY('<check_action>',
'<schema_name>','<table_name>');
```

Where `<check_action>` can have values such as `CHECK_PARTITIONING`, `CHECK_PARTITIONING_DATA` and `REPAIR_PARTITIONING_DATA`.

Figure 4.25 shows execution of the commands against test table NAME2.

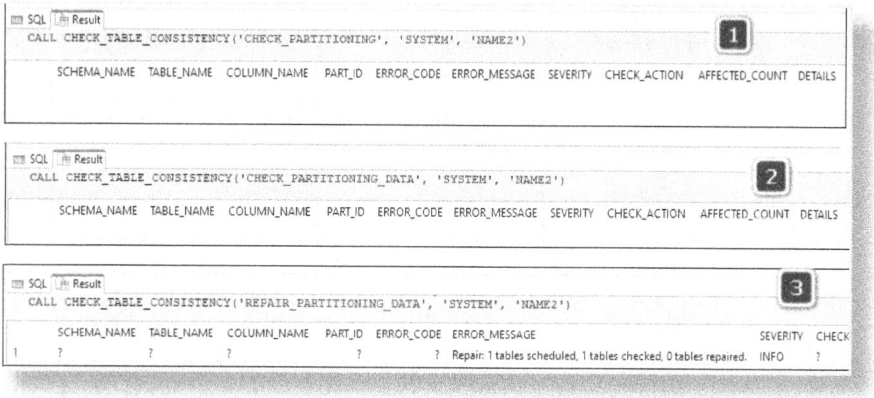

Figure 4.25: Consistency checks on partitioned tables

The numbers in the image refer to the following:

❶ Performing a general check on the partitions of a table.

❷ Conducting an extended data check on the partitions of the table.

❸ Repairing data that is incorrectly assigned to a partition.

4.1.8 Table re-distribution

In a distributed environment (scale-out), when a new host is added or an existing host is removed, tables need to be rebalanced or re-distributed. This ensures proper load balancing of the database tables across the existing HANA database host.

Re-distribution after adding a new-node:

Figure 4.26 shows a distributed HANA database with one master index server and an additional index server with host name IP-172-31-15-221, which was recently added. Because this additional index server was added after the database installation, it does not currently have any tables, unlike the other index server.

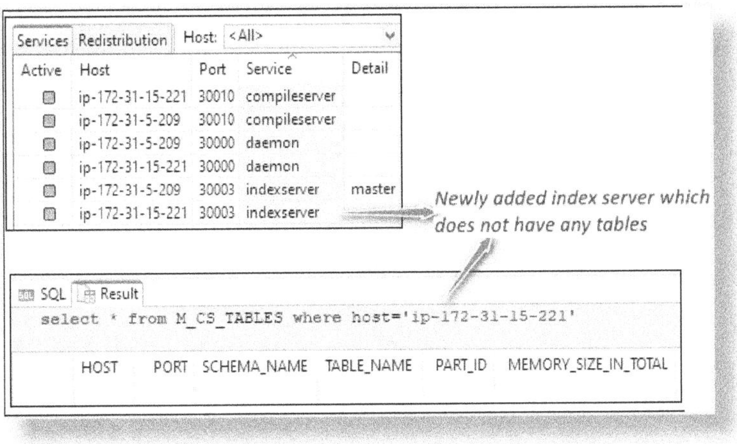

Figure 4.26: HANA system with one newly added host

For correct HANA database load distribution, the database tables must be re-distributed equally among all the available index servers. To do this, an execution plan must be generated in the database, as shown in Figure 4.27, using the following SQL procedure:

```
CALL REORG_GENERATE(1,'');
```

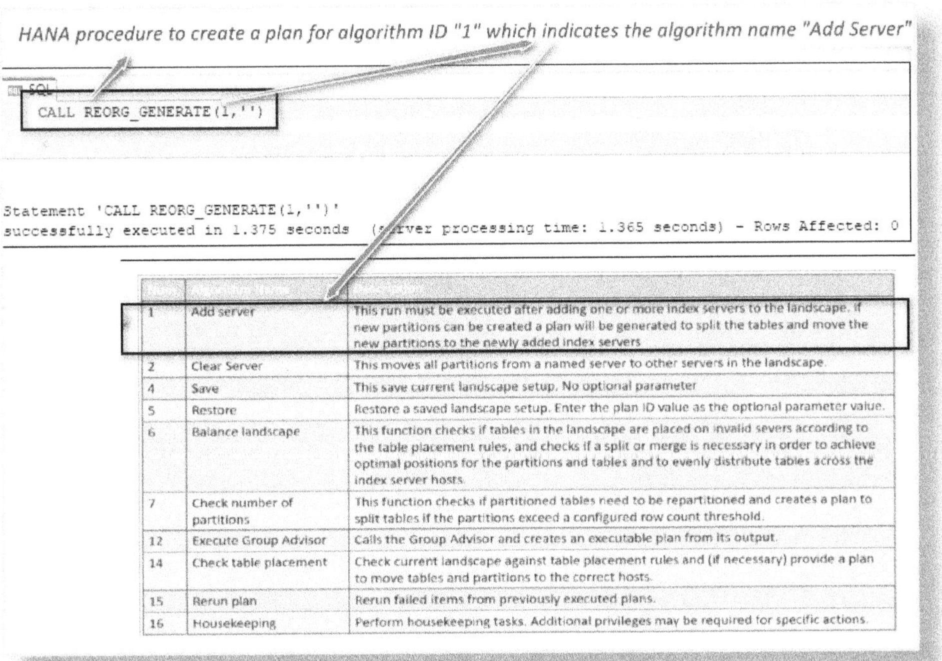

Figure 4.27: Create execution plan to redistribute tables

In this command, the value 1 represents the algorithm ID with algorithm name ADD SERVER. This SQL procedure generates a table redistribution plan which then generates a command to move some of the database tables into the newly added index server.

Once the execution plan has been created, it needs to be executed, as shown in Figure 4.28.

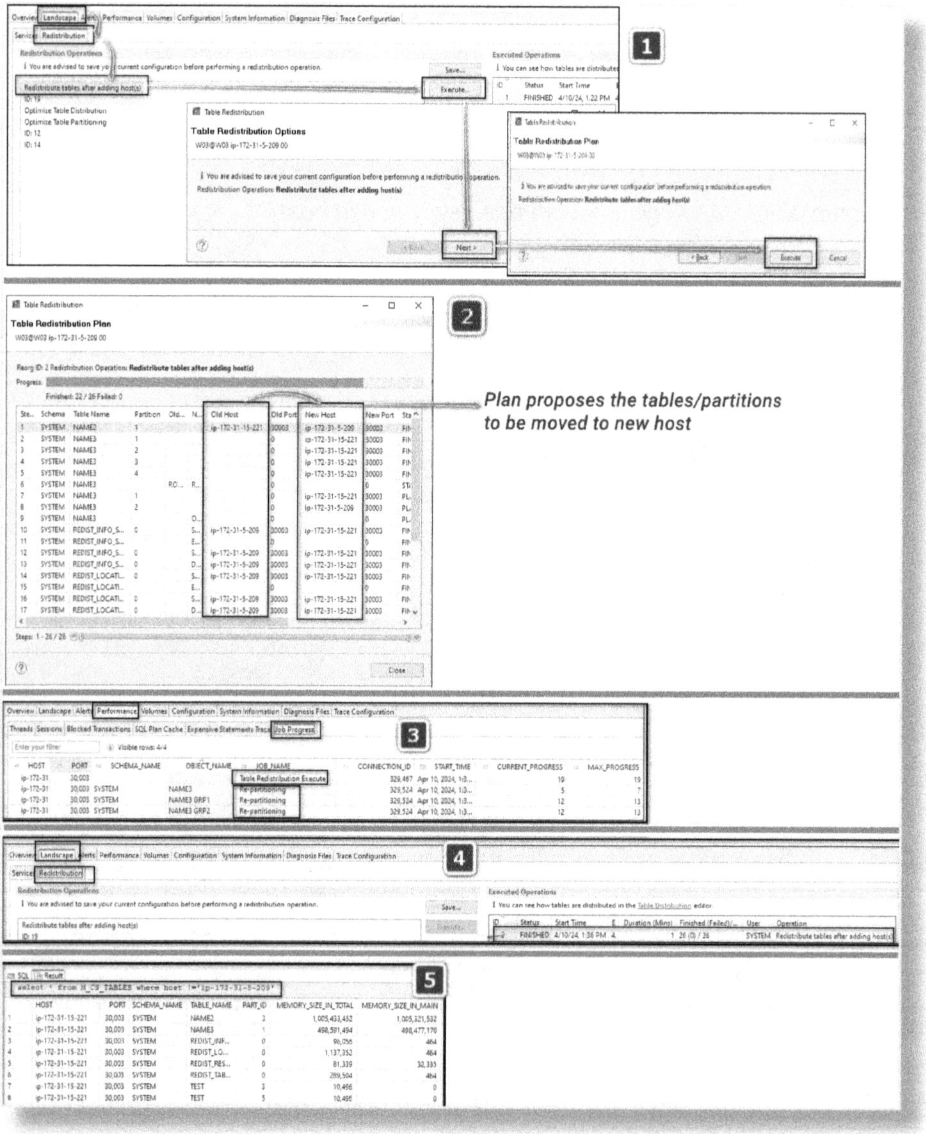

Figure 4.28: Executing re-distribution after adding new host

The steps shown in this image are as follows:

❶ Navigate to LANDSCAPE • REDISTRIBUTION in HANA Studio, select REDISTRIBUTE TABLES AFTER ADDING HOST(S), and click NEXT to view the redistribution plan. This plan specifies which tables will be moved to the newly added host. Click on EXECUTE to proceed further.

❷ Shows the execution of the table redistribution plan, where database tables are moved to the newly added server in the HANA database system.

❸ You can monitor the redistribution task via the PERFORMANCE tab, JOB PROGRESS in HANA Studio.

❹ Check for the status of the redistribution task by navigating to LANDSCAPE • REDISTRIBUTION • EXECUTED OPERATIONS.

❺ View the list of tables located in the new host using the SQL query:

```
select * from M_CS_TABLES where host = '<new_server>';
```

Re-distribution before removing a node

Before removing an index server host from a distributed HANA database, the tables from its index server must be relocated to a different host's index server within the database. This process involves generating a redistribution plan, which aims to transfer all tables from the index server of the host that is being removed to another index server in the same database.

Figure 4.29 shows the removal of a host, where the node with IP address IP-172-31-15-221 is scheduled for removal from a distributed HANA database. All the tables in this index server host are re-distributed/moved to a different index server host before removing the former host.

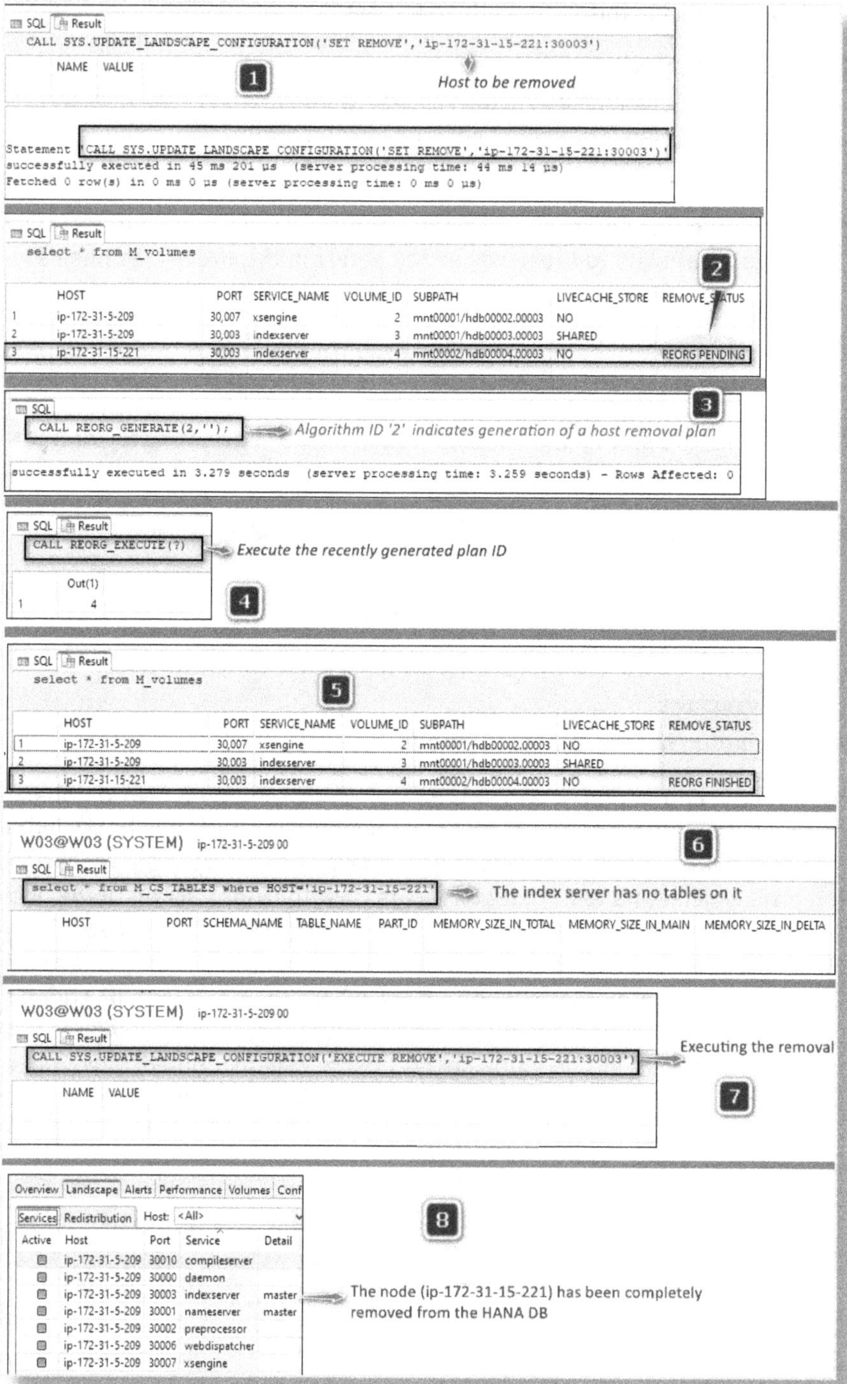

Figure 4.29: Removing a host from HANA database

The steps shown in the image are as follows:

❶ Specify the host to be removed using the following SQL procedure:

```
CALL SYS.UPDATE_LANDSCAPE_CONFIGURATION('SET REMOVE',
'<server_to_be_removed>:<indexserver_port>');
```

❷ Verify the status of M_volumes by executing the SQL query:

```
select * from M_volumes;
```

- The host marked for removal in the previous step will now have the status REORG PENDING.

❸ Execute the following SQL procedure to generate a reorganization plan for host removal (the algorithm ID 2 specifies the generation of a host removal plan, which will move all tables from the host marked in ❶ to another node):

```
CALL REORG_GENERATE(2,' ');
```

❹ Execute the plan generated in step 3 using the following SQL procedure:

```
CALL REORG EXECUTE(?);
```

- Before executing the plan, you can review its details using the following SQL queries:

```
SELECT * FROM SYS.REORG_OVERVIEW;
SELECT * FROM SYS.REORG_PLAN;
```

❺ Wait for the SQL procedure execution to finish. Check the execution status with the following SQL query:

```
select * from M_volumes;
```

- The REMOVE_STATUS column should now display REORG FINISHED.
- You can also verify the status in HANA Studio via:
  - LANDSCAPE • REDISTRIBUTION, or
  - PERFORMANCE • JOB PROGRESS.

❻ Verify that no tables remain on the host marked for removal using the following SQL query:

```
select from M CS TABLES where HOST='<host_to_b_deleted>';
```

❼ If no tables are present, proceed to delete the host with SQL query:

```
CALL SYS.UPDATE_LANDSCAPE_CONFIGURATION ('EXECUTE REMOVE',
'<host_tobe_removed>:<indexserver_port>');
```

❽ Confirm the removal by checking the LANDSCAPE • SERVICES tabs in HANA Studio.

4.1.9 Exporting and importing tables

HANA database tables, whether row-store or column-store, can be exported or imported using HANA Studio or the following SQL queries:

- To export a table:

```
EXPORT <schema>.<table_name> AS BINARY INTO '<Target export
location>' WITH REPLACE THREADS <n>;
```

- To import a table:

```
IMPORT <schema>.<table_name> AS BINARY FROM '<Target export
location>' WITH REPLACE THREADS <n>;
```

In the above commands, <n> represents the number of parallel threads working to execute the export/import database action.

Figure 4.30 shows an example of the export and import of a table called SAMPLE. The table is being exported to and imported from the specified file system location, as defined in the command.

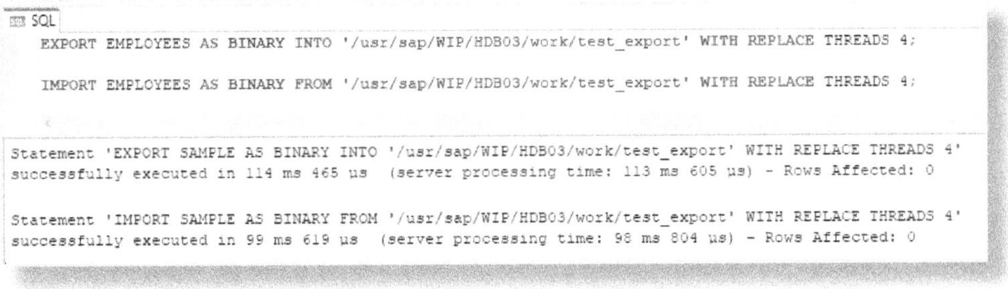

Figure 4.30: Sample export and import table commands

4.1.10 Table and catalog consistency check

HANA provides various stored procedures and commands to perform a range of consistency checks on the database catalog and database tables. It is highly recommended to include these checks in routine maintenance schedules in order to detect issues beforehand. The SQL queries to execute these checks are as follows:

- For table consistency check:

```
CALL CHECK_TABLE_CONSISTENCY ('<CheckAction1>,<CheckAction2>',
'<schema_name>', '<table_name>');
```

- For catalog consistency check:

```
CALL CHECK_CATALOG ('<CheckAction1>','<schema_name>',
'<object_name>','<catalog_object_type>');
```

Figure 4.31 shows the sample execution of some of these consistency checks.

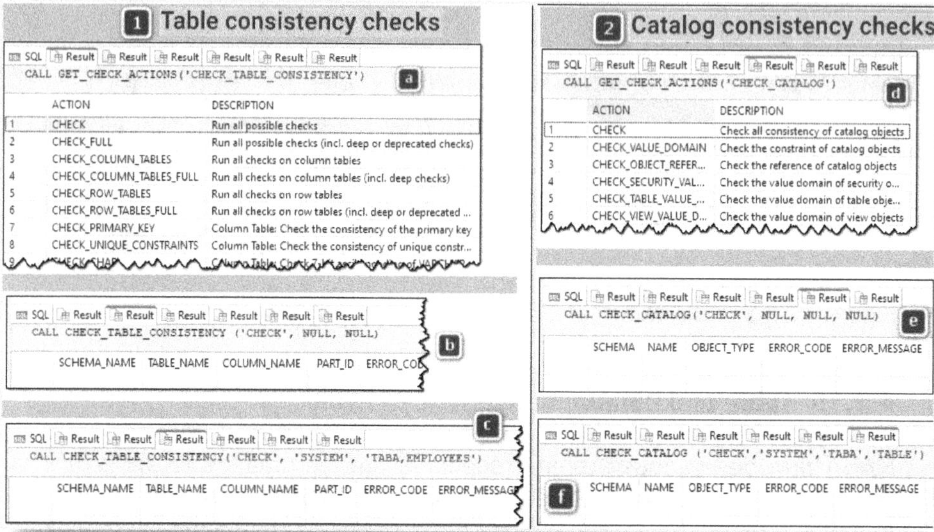

Figure 4.31: Consistency checks—table and catalog

Area ❶ shows the SQL queries for table consistency checks, as follows:

a To list the available consistency checks for tables:

```
CALL GET_CHECK_ACTIONS('CHECK_TABLE_CONSISTENCY');
```

b To check the consistency of all the database tables:

```
CALL CHECK_TABLE_CONSISTENCY ('CHECK', NULL, NULL);
```

c To check the consistency of specific sample tables:

```
CALL CHECK_TABLE_CONSISTENCY('CHECK', '<schema_name>', '<table_
name1>,<table_name2>');
```

Area ❷ shows the following:

d To list the available consistency checks for catalogs:

```
CALL GET_CHECK_ACTIONS('CHECK_CATALOG');
```

e To check the consistency of all the database catalogs:

```
CALL CHECK_CATALOG('CHECK', NULL, NULL, NULL);
```

[f] To check the consistency of a specific catalog object:

```
CALL CHECK_CATALOG ('CHECK','<schema_name>','<table_
name>','<object_name>');
```

There are system views that store the historical data of all the prior consistency check executions in the HANA database:

- *M_CONSISTENCY_CHECK_HISTORY_ERRORS*
- *M_CONSISTENCY_CHECK_HISTORY*

Some of these consistency checks can be scheduled to run periodically. For example, the SQL query to schedule periodic table consistency check is:

```
update _SYS_STATISTICS.STATISTICS_PROPERTIES set value = 'check'
where key = 'internal.table_consistency.check_actions';
```

This is shown in Figure 4.32.

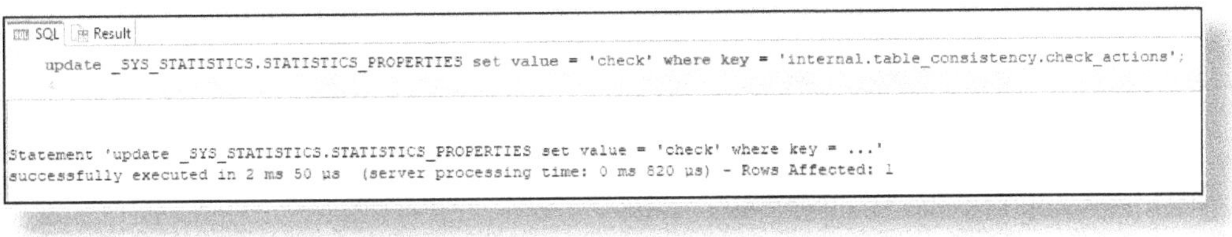

Figure 4.32: Consistency check historical information

The database user permissions required to execute these checks are:

- *CATALOG READ* for check actions
- *DATA ADMIN* for repair actions.

Figure 4.33 outlines some of the key configuration parameters in the indexserver.ini file that control the execution of table consistency checks in the HANA database. These parameters can be viewed from the CONFIGURATION tab in HANA Studio.

Section from *indexserver.ini*	Parameter Name	Description
[metadata]	enable_startup_consistency_check	Enable/disable metadata consistency check during SAP HANA startup and includes CHECK_CATALOG with check action CHECK_OBJECT_REFERENTIAL_INTEGRITY.
[row_engine]	consistency_check_at_startup	Configure row store consistency check during SAP HANA startup.
[row_engine]	startup_consistency_check_timeout	Maximum duration of consistency check at SAP HANA startup
[table_consistency_check]	check_max_concurrency_percent	This parameter controls the overall CPU and thread resource consumption of CHECK_TABLE_CONSISTENCY, defined as a percentage of max_concurrency_hint in the global.ini file which is the general limit for the number of concurrently running threads
[table_consistency_check]	max_duration	Define the maximum duration of a CHECK_TABLE_CONSISTENCY call

Figure 4.33 "indexserver.ini" consistency check parameters

4.1.11 Row-store reorganization

Unlike column-store tables, all row-store tables in a HANA database are automatically loaded into memory as part of the database startup procedure and remain there whether they are currently in use or not. Consequently, periodic reorganization of these row-store tables might be needed in order to recover memory fragments that might occur as a result of any database operations performed on these tables. The reorganization of row-store tables can be performed either in offline or online mode, as illustrated Figure 4.34.

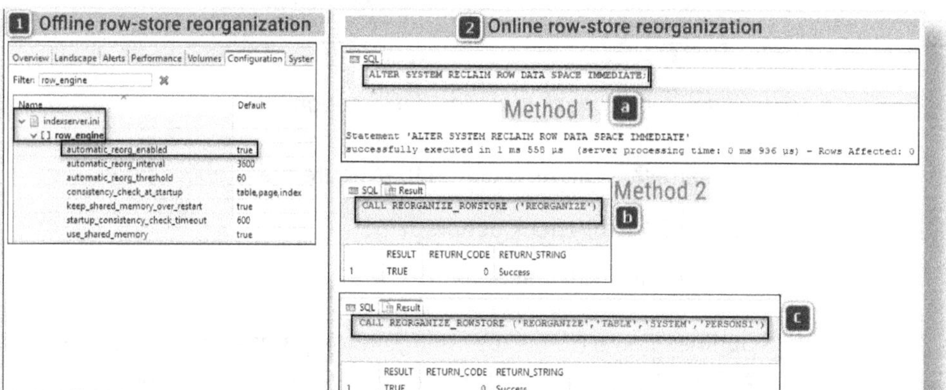

Figure 4.34: Row-store reorganization

The image shows the following:

❶ Offline row-store reorganization—to enable automatic offline row-store reorganization during database startup, set the parameter value INDEXSERVER.INI • [ ] ROW ENGINE • AUTOMATIC_REORG_ENABLED to TRUE.

❷ Online row-store reorganization—this can be triggered in different ways:

[a] Using an SQL Statement—execute the following SQL command to reorganize all row-store tables in the HANA database:

```
ALTER SYSTEM RECLAIM ROW DATA SPACE IMMEDIATE;
```

[b] Using a CALL procedure—execute the following procedure to reorganize all row-store tables.

```
CALL REORGANIZE_ROWSTORE ('REORGANIZE');
```

[c] Online row-store reorganization can also be performed at the individual table level using the following:

```
CALL REORGANIZE_ROWSTORE ('REORGANIZE','TABLE','<schema_
name>','<table_name>');
```

For more information, refer to SAP Note 1813245—"SAP HANA DB: Row Store Reorganization".

4.2 HANA memory and its types

As an in-memory database, the size of the physical memory accessible from the underlying hardware significantly influences the HANA database's available memory and its licensing. It is therefore crucial for a database administrator to understand how this memory is requested, utilized, and managed by HANA. HANA employs various terms such as *physical memory, virtual memory, resident memory, used memory, peak used memory*, and *persistent memory (PMEM)* to denote the memory available from the underlying hardware at different points during HANA database operations. The memory types are shown in Figure 4.35.

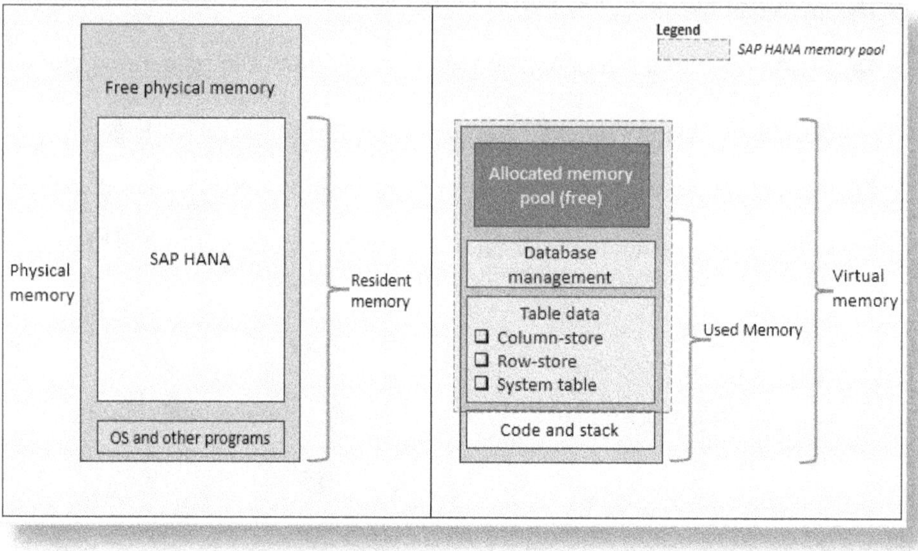

Figure 4.35: Types of HANA memory

4.2.1 Physical memory, virtual memory, resident memory, and used memory

The size of a HANA system is typically determined by the amount of physical memory (DRAM–dynamic RAM) installed on the underlying server/host. The *physical memory*, apart from hosting the HANA database, must also support the execution of Linux operating system processes and other operating system programs installed on the server.

In general, the Linux operating system allocates memory virtually for all its running processes. This virtually allocated memory, per process, is referred to as the *virtual memory* of that process. The amount of memory reserved per process increases as more memory is required than was initially assigned, and decreases when it releases unused memory. The Linux operating system treats the HANA database as a process and allocates virtual memory accordingly.

When a process requires a portion of its virtually allocated memory, it is loaded and mapped to the physical memory of the host. This physically allocated memory from the virtual memory is known as *resident memory*. This refers to the actual memory used by the respective process. However, the operating system can swap out this memory based on the least recently used (LRU) algorithm to create space for other processes and code. As a result, the size of the process's resident memory fluctuates independently of the process's virtual memory. Therefore, the term *resident memory* is more indicative from an OS perspective than that of the HANA database itself.

Used memory refers to the total amount of memory currently in use by the HANA database and can be monitored by querying the monitoring view *M_HEAP_MEMORY*. This encompasses program code and stack, all data and system tables, and the memory required for temporary computations. While this term is more specific to the database and can be considered as resident memory from the database's perspective, it is important to note that used memory is not synonymous with resident memory.

The SQL query that can be used to calculate the used memory in the HANA database at any point in time is:

```
select sum(INCLUSIVE_SIZE_IN_USE)/1024/1024/1024 as used_mry_GB
from M_HEAP_MEMORY;
```

This is shown in Figure 4.36.

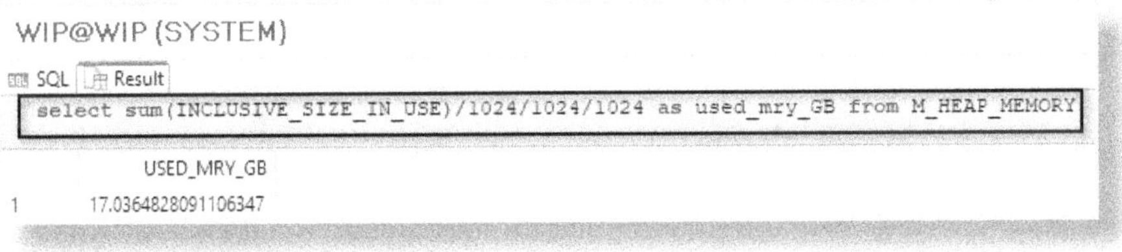

Figure 4.36: Used memory in HANA

4.2.2 Used memory, peak used memory, and allocation limit.

Used memory refers to the current total amount of memory in use by the database, and *peak used memory* refers to HANA SID's highest recorded memory usage over a period of time. The database's peak used memory value can be reset using the following SQL query:

```
ALTER SYSTEM RESET MONITORING VIEW "SYS"."M_HEAP_MEMORY_RESET";
```

Post-reset, the recording of new memory peak since that time is facilitated, as shown in Figure 4.37.

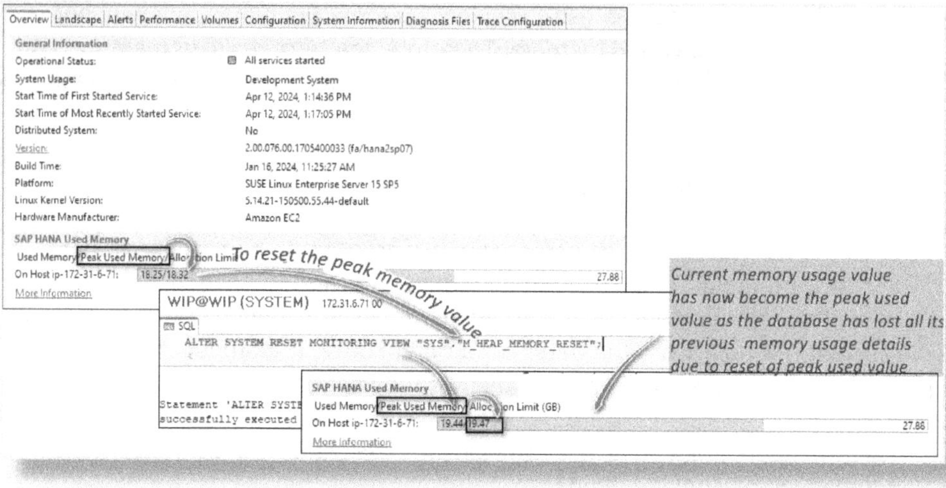

Figure 4.37: Resetting the peak used memory value

An *allocation limit* is defined as the maximum amount of virtual memory reserved from the physical memory (DRAM) for the HANA database before actual utilization. This value is determined by the HANA database parameter *global_allocation_limit*. Its default value is computed as 90% of the initial 64GB of available physical memory on the host, along with 97% of each additional GB. The HANA database is licensed based on this value.

Figure 4.35 also shows the *SAP HANA Memory pool*. SAP HANA pre-allocates and manages its memory pool with the help of the *HANA memory manager*. This pool is used for storing in-memory table data, thread stacks, temporary results, and other system data structures. When more memory is required for table growth or temporary computations, the SAP HANA memory manager obtains it from the pool. When the pool cannot satisfy the request, the memory manager increases the pool size by requesting more memory from the operating system, up to a predefined allocation limit. Upon completion of a temporary computation or the dropping of a table, the memory is released. This freed memory returns to the memory manager, which recycles it back into its pool without notifying the operating system. Consequently, from SAP HANA's perspective, the used memory amount decreases without affecting the virtual and resident memory size. This scenario can lead to the used memory value being lower than the size of SAP HANA's resident memory, which is normal.

! Resident memory and used memory

Note that the HANA database resident memory does not always match HANA used memory. HANA's resident memory is the memory usage from the operating system, whereas HANA used memory is the memory utilized from the HANA database.

It is also important to note that the memory manager might opt to return memory to the operating system, especially when the pool nears the allocation limit or when it contains substantial unused portions. If memory usage approaches or surpasses this allocation limit, SAP HANA might encounter *out-of-memory (OOM)* issues if it cannot further release any utilized memory.

It is worth noting that the code and program stack typically occupy only around 6GB, leaving most of the used memory allocated for table storage, computations, and database management purposes. Refer to Figure 4.35.

Figure 4.38 contains screenshots from HANA Studio—OVERVIEW and LANDSCAPE tabs—showing memory terminologies and their usage within a HANA system.

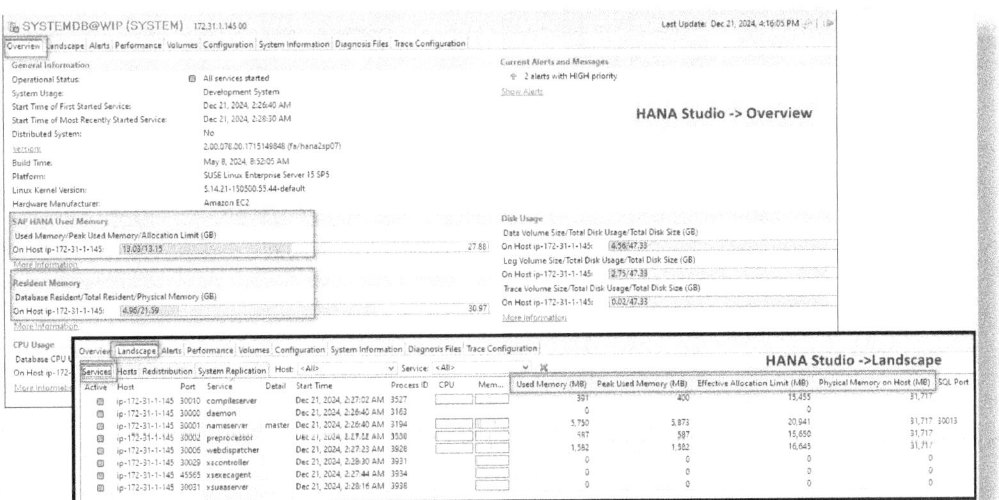

Figure 4.38: HANA memory terminologies

4.2.3 Heap memory and shared memory

As covered earlier, in Linux, the operating system (OS) is tasked with allocating memory for processes. Upon database startup, the OS reserves memory for the program code, program stack, and static data, and dynamically allocates additional memory when requested by the HANA memory manager. This dynamically allocated memory includes *heap memory* and *shared memory*, with the latter serving to cache essential data required by both the name server and the index server(s). Details about shared memory can be found in the monitoring view *M_SHARED_MEMORY*, which provides information through its columns values—*EFFECTIVE_ALLOCATION_LIMIT* and *TOTAL_MEMORY_USED_SIZE*.

4.2.4 Service used memory

As detailed previously, the SAP HANA system consists of multiple server components operating as dedicated OS processes, each independently consuming memory. However, in a HANA system, the index server process dominates memory consumption, primarily because it holds all the database tables and temporary results—this significantly influences HANA database's used memory. Therefore, if we need to restrict memory usage at individual service level, we can configure the parameter *allocationlimit* in the corresponding configuration file *<service>.ini*.

! 'allocationlimit' and 'global_allocation_limit'

The parameter *allocationlimit* controls memory allocation at the individual service level and can be configured in the dedicated configuration file for each service. However, the parameter *global_allocation_limit* indicates the maximum amount of memory that a HANA database, along with its services, can consume and is set in the global configuration file—*global.ini*.

4.2.5 Persistent memory

All references to physical memory consistently refer to DRAM (dynamic RAM), which is volatile. Because HANA stores its data in this volatile memory and synchronizes it with disk persistence through savepoints, data in memory will be lost following a server crash or database restart. Consequently, every time the database restarts, data must be reloaded into memory, leading to increased database startup times. To address this issue, the HANA database supports non-volatile memory (NVRAM) with DAX-enabled (Direct Access) file systems. Referred to as *persistent memory (PMEM)* in SAP HANA, this memory combines features of both DRAM and persistent flash storage. It is byte-addressable, like DRAM, and can be treated by the CPU as RAM.

Persistent memory is well-suited to hold the main storage from column-store tables, which is the primary memory consumer in a HANA database due to its higher latency. However, areas such as delta storage, caches, row store, and so on, can only exist on DRAM.

Using PMEM, the column-store data is preserved even during a server crash or database restart, because this data persists. Consequently, this not only decreases the total DRAM requirement but also expedites the HANA restart process.

Figure 4.39 illustrates two scenarios of a HANA database—one without PMEM and another with PMEM. With the former, both the main and delta storage reside in DRAM. However, HANA database systems with associated PMEM store their main memory contents in PMEM, while the delta memory continues to remain in DRAM.

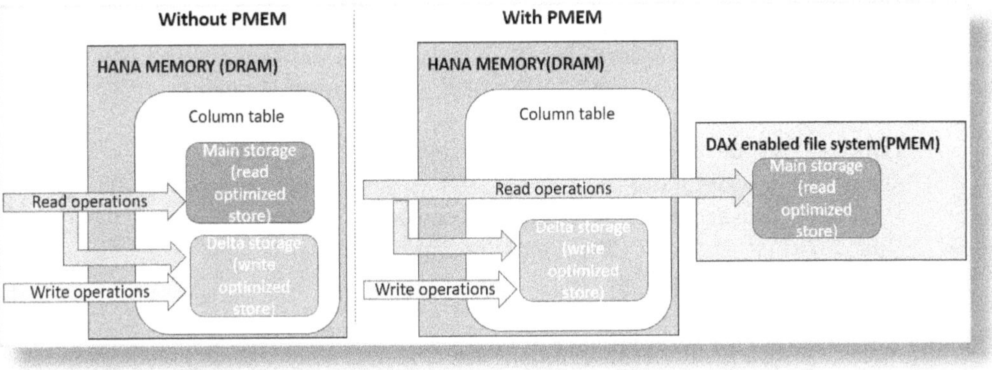

Figure 4.39: Persistent memory

For additional details, refer to:

- SAP Note 2786237—"Sizing SAP HANA with Persistent Memory"
- SAP Note 2700084—"FAQ: SAP HANA Persistent Memory"

4.3 Managing tenants

The SAP HANA tenant database serves as the foundation for multitenancy in SAP HANA. As part of HANA 2.0 database installation, a default tenant is created with the database name matching the HANA SID. To retrieve the list of tenant databases in a HANA database system, execute the query `select * from M_DATABASES` from the SystemDB, as shown in Figure 4.40.

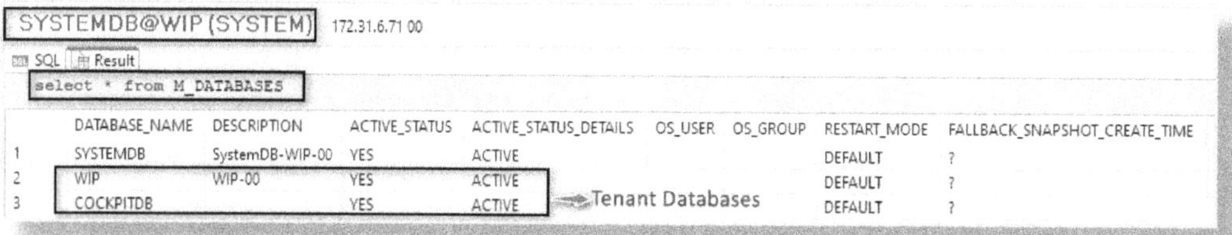

Figure 4.40: Tenant databases

Entries other than SystemDB represent tenant databases of the HANA SID.

4.3.1 Creating a tenant database

In HANA, additional tenants can be created along with the default tenant, using the following SQL statement:

```
CREATE DATABASE <database_name> [ AT [ LOCATION ]
'<hostname>[:<port_number> ] ' ]
 [ ADD '<servicetype>' [ AT [ LOCATION ] '<hostname>[:<port_
number> ] ' ] ]
 { AS REPLICA OF [ <source_database_name> ] AT [ LOCATION ]
'<hostname>[:<port_number> ]' | SYSTEM USER PASSWORD <password> }
 [ OS USER '<username>' OS GROUP '<groupname>' ]
 [ NO START ]
 [ <restart_mode> RESTART ]
```

Sample SQL queries to create a tenant are:

- `CREATE DATABASE DB1 SYSTEM USER PASSWORD Welcome1;`–this creates a tenant database with automatic host placement and automatic port assignment.
- `CREATE DATABASE DB2 AT LOCATION 'HOST_A:30147' SYSTEM USER PASSWORD Welcome1;`–this creates a tenant database on a specific host accessible via a specific SQL port (30148). The SQL port number is the internal communication port plus 1.

Figure 4.41 shows the creation of a sample tenant database.

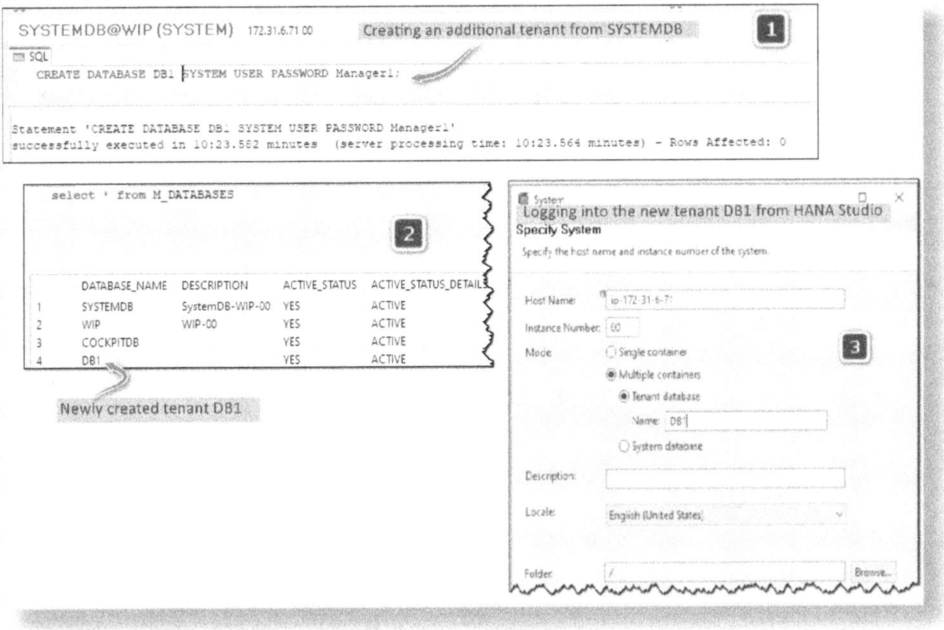

Figure 4.41: Creating a tenant database from SQL console

The numbers in the image show the following:

➊ SQL query to create a tenant database from the SystemDB.

➋ List of tenant databases associated with the HANA database system.

➌ Logging into the HANA Studio by connecting as a tenant database.

> **File system structure for a tenant database**
>
> Refer again to Figure 2.3 to identify the distinct file system structure created for the tenant database.

4.3.2 Starting and stopping tenant databases

Tenant databases can be restarted using either the HANA Cockpit or the SystemDB SQL console. The latter is shown in Figure 4.42.

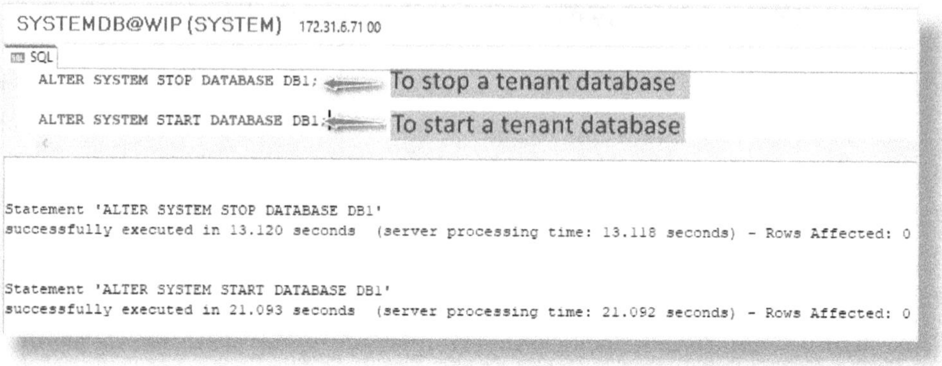

Figure 4.42: Start/stop a tenant database via SystemDB SQL console

The SQL command to stop a tenant database is:

```
ALTER SYSTEM STOP DATABASE <tenant_Database_NAME>;
```

The SQL command to start a tenant database is:

```
ALTER SYSTEM START DATABASE <tenant_Database_NAME
```

System privileges *DATABASE ADMIN* or *DATABASE START* are required to perform a database start or stop.

4.3.3 Configuring a tenant database

System configuration (**.ini*) files have a *database layer* to facilitate the configuration of system properties specific to individual tenant databases. For further information, refer to Section 4.4.

Figure 4.43 shows the SQL query that is executed from the SystemDB's SQL console to set a configuration parameter exclusively for a specific tenant database:

```
ALTER SYSTEM ALTER CONFIGURATION ('<service.ini>', 'database',
'<tenant_SID>') SET ('<layer>', '<layer_name>') = '<value>' WITH
RECONFIGURE;
```

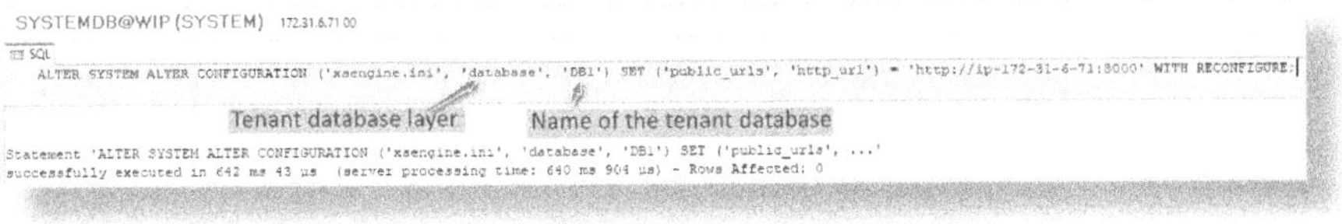

Figure 4.43: Sample SQL to configure parameters specific to tenant database

The configuration files (**.ini*) containing tenant-specific values are stored at the OS level in the directory */sapmnt/<SID>/SYS/global/hdb/custom/config/DB_<dbname>*, where *dbname* represents the name of the tenant database.

4.3.4 Monitoring tenant databases

Tenant databases can be monitored from HANA Studio or from HANA Cockpit by logging into the respective tenant databases. They can also be monitored from the SystemDB using the system view *M_DATABASES* (SYS) and database objects of schema *SYS_DATABASES*.

M_DATABASES

This system view from the SystemDB is part of *SYS* schema and offers an overview of all tenant databases in the HANA database. Access to the contents of this view is restricted to users with the system privilege *DATABASE ADMIN*.

SYS_DATABASES schema

The system views from the SystemDB's *SYS_DATABASES* schema aggregate information from the tenant database's system views from the database schemas—*SYS* and *_SYS_STATISTICS*. Each view in the *SYS_DATABASES* schema includes a DATABASE_NAME column to distinguish data from different tenant databases. Access is restricted to users with *DATABASE ADMIN* or *CATALOG READ* privileges. For example, when executed from SystemDB, the outputs of the select queries `select * from M_CONNECTIONS` and `select * from SYS_DATABASES.M_CONNECTIONS` are different because the former operates within the default schema SYS and retrieves connection information specific to the SystemDB, whereas the latter retrieves details from all the tenants. Figure 4.44 shows a sample output of a system view SYS_DATABASES.M_CONNECTIONS from the SystemDB.

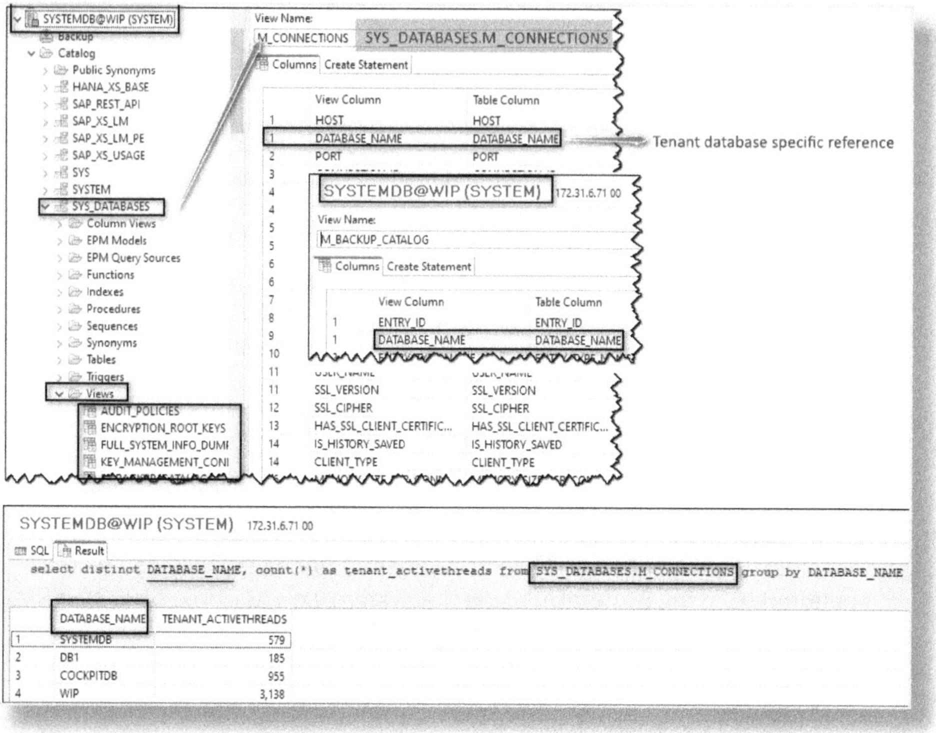

Figure 4.44: Monitoring tenant from SystemDB using views in SYS_ DATABASES

4.3.5 Memory and CPU usage for tenant database and SystemDB

In a multi-container scenario, the SystemDB and its tenant databases compete for hardware resources, such as CPU and memory because they operate on the same underlying hardware. It is therefore crucial to delineate resource consumption among these databases. System property (*.ini) files at the database layer facilitate these restrictions for individual tenant databases:

- *[memorymanager] • allocationlimit* in global.ini—this property limits the maximum amount of memory (in MB) that can be allocated to a tenant database.
- *[execution] • max_concurrency* in global.ini file—this property influences the maximum number of CPU cores that can be used by a tenant database . This is done by limiting the number of concur-

rently running threads used by the *JobExecutor* subsystem. A reasonable default value is the number of cores divided by the number of tenant databases. It is recommended to avoid specifying a value of 0.

The SQL queries to set these parameters are as follows:

```
ALTER SYSTEM ALTER CONFIGURATION ('global.ini', 'DATABASE',
'<SID>') SET ('memorymanager', 'allocationlimit') = '<memory
value>' WITH RECONFIGURE;

ALTER SYSTEM ALTER CONFIGURATION ('global.ini', 'DATABASE',
'<SID>') SET ('execution', 'max_concurrency') = '<value>' WITH
RECONFIGURE;
```

These are shown in Figure 4.45:

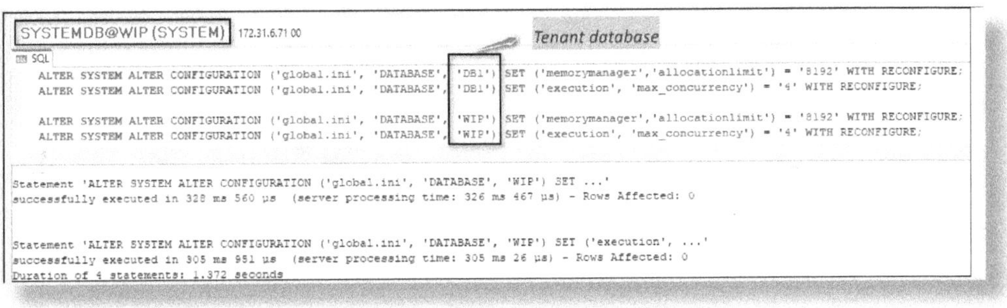

Figure 4.45: Memory and CPU usage restriction/allocation

Note that the SystemDB typically has an average consumption of 15GB, and the minimum memory consumed by the SystemDB can be reserved by configuring the parameter [ ] MULTIDB • SYSTEMDB_RESERVED_MEMORY in the GLOBAL.INI file, as shown in Figure 4.46.

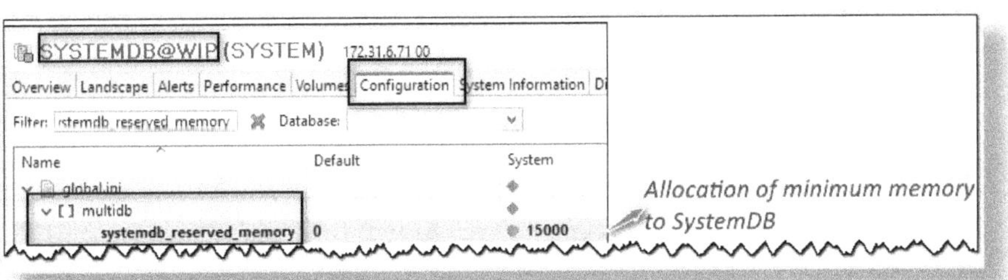

Figure 4.46: Minimum memory requirement for SystemDB

4.3.6 Resetting DB user password—SYSTEM

Resetting SYSTEM user for tenant database

There may be instances where the password for a tenant database *SYSTEM* super user is lost/forgotten, and no user with the system privilege *USER ADMIN* is available to reset the password. In such cases, the password can be reset by logging into the SystemDB and following the procedure shown in Figure 4.47.

Figure 4.47: Password reset sequence for tenant DB SYSTEM user

The steps shown in the image are as follows:

❶ Log in to the SystemDB using a database user with *DATABASE ADMIN* system privilege.

❷ Stop the tenant database from SystemDB using the SQL query:

```
ALTER SYSTEM STOP DATABASE <tenant_database_name>;
```

❸ Change the tenant database password from the SystemDB using the SQL query:

```
ALTER DATABASE <tenant_name> SYSTEM USER PASSWORD <new_password>;
```

❹ Start the tenant database from the SystemDB using the SQL query:

```
ALTER SYSTEM START DATABASE <tenant_database_name>;
```

❺ Connect to the tenant database from HANA Studio using the new temporary password. Change the password when prompted.

Resetting SYSTEM user for SystemDB

There might be situations where the *SYSTEM* user password for the SystemDB is lost/forgotten and there is no user in the SystemDB who can reset the password. In such cases, the steps to reset the SystemDB *SYSTEM* user are shown in Figure 4.48.

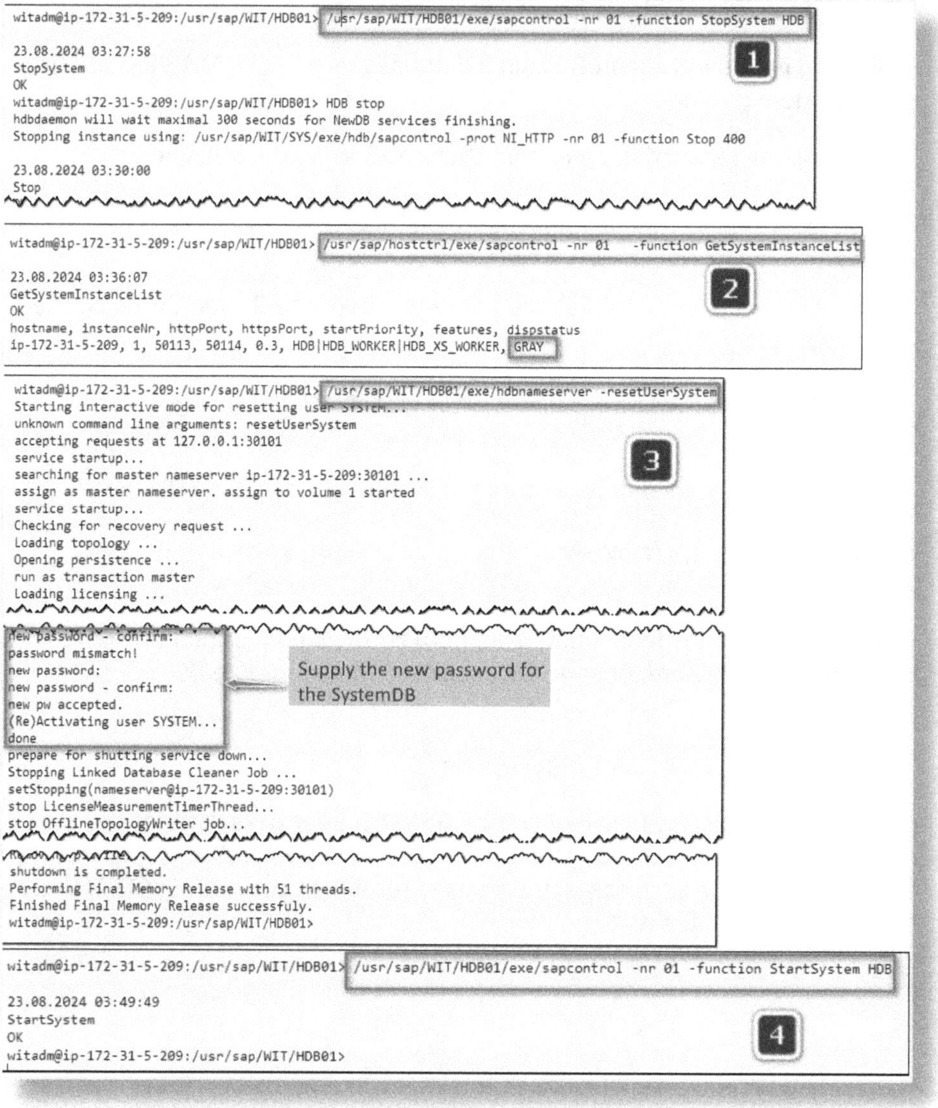

Figure 4.48: Password reset for SystemDB SYSTEM user

The steps shown in the image are as follows:

➊ Log in to the master node, which hosts the name server, as operating system user--*<sid>adm*, and shut down the database using the following command:

```
/usr/sap/<SID>/HDB<instance>/exe/sapcontrol -nr <instance>
-function StopSystem HDB
```

❷ Ensure that the database is down using the command:

```
/usr/sap/hostctrl/exe/sapcontrol -nr <instance> -function
GetSystemInstanceList
```

- All the services must be in GRAY status.

❸ In a new PuTTY session on the same host, execute the following commands to start the name server of the system database:

```
/usr/sap/<SID>/HDB<instance>/hdbenv.sh
```

```
/usr/sap/<SID>/HDB<instance>/exe/hdbnameserver -resetUserSystem
```

- Provide the new password for the *SYSTEM* database user when prompted.

❹ In another PuTTY session, start the instance by executing the following command:

```
/usr/sap/<SID>/HDB<instance>/exe/sapcontrol -nr <instance>
-function StartSystem HDB
```

4.3.7 Deleting a tenant database

Tenant databases can be deleted using the SQL queries as follows:

- To drop a tenant database, excluding its backup:

```
DROP DATABASE <tenant_name>;
```

- To drop a tenant database and discard its backup:

```
DROP DATABASE <tenant_name> DROP BACKUPS;
```

It is recommended to stop the tenant database from the SystemDB before deleting, as shown in Figure 4.49.

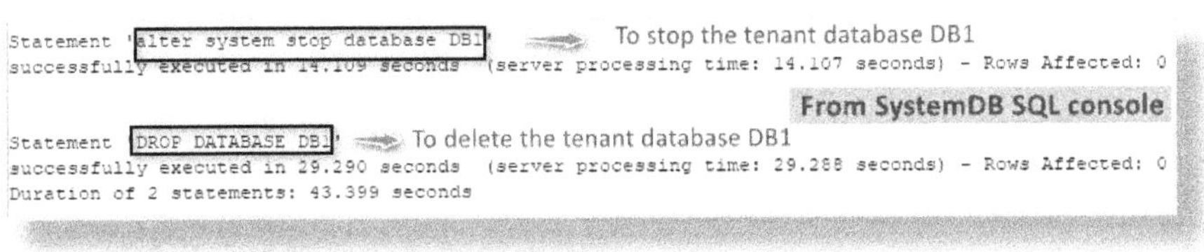

Figure 4.49: Deleting a tenant database

4.4 HANA system properties

The properties of a HANA database are governed by its parameter values, forming a layered configuration framework that enables administrators to manage and optimize the database. These parameters can be configured globally (affecting SystemDB and all tenant databases) or at the individual tenant database level.

4.4.1 SAP HANA system properties files (ini files)

All HANA database configurations are stored in **.ini* files. These files can be service-specific (e.g., indexserver.ini, compileserver.ini) or service-independent (global.ini). Within these configuration files, similar parameters are grouped together for better database parameter management.

The current value of these parameters can be viewed by querying the system view *M_INIFILE_CONTENT (SQL query: SELECT * FROM M_INIFILE_CONTENT;)*, and the historical values of these parameters are recorded in the system view *M_INIFILE_CONTENT_HISTORY*.

HANA database parameters can be configured at different layers—*system*, *database*, and *host*. These are explained in Table 4.2.

Layer	Description
Default	Holds the property's default values and are read-only parameters. These are the baseline values when the system is first installed.
System	Contains system-wide parameter values set for all tenants in a multi-tenant environment or the entire database from the SystemDB. If a system-specific value is not configured for a parameter, the default value applies.
Database or tenant	Property value is specific to the database or tenant and can be configured at either the SystemDB or tenant database level.
Host	Property value is specific to the host and can only be configured in the SystemDB.

Table 4.2: HANA DB parameter layers

The priority order for these parameters, from highest to lowest, is: *Host > Database > System > Default.*

The parameters set at a higher-priority layer override those configured at a lower-priority layer:

Figure 4.50 shows these database layers from both the SystemDB and the tenant database using HANA Studio.

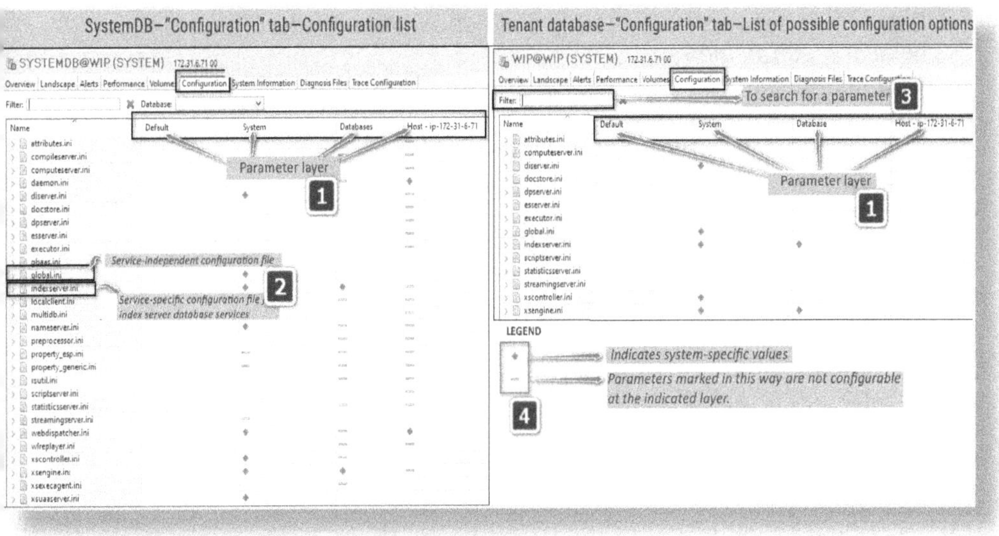

Figure 4.50: HANA database parameters

The numbers in this figure refer to the following:

❶ The parameter layers from Table 4.2.

❷ An example of service-dependent (e.g., INDEXSERVER.INI) and service-independent (e.g., GLOBAL.INI) configuration files.

❸ Search for a parameter using the filters in the HANA Studio CONFIGURATION tab.

❹ Legend showing the icons in the configuration files.

All these HANA database configurations are stored in different folder structures at OS level according to their layer. Table 4.3 outlines these layers and locations.

Layer	Location
Default layer	*/usr/sap/<SID>/HDB<nn>/exe/config/*
System layer	*/sapmnt/<SID>/SYS/global/hdb/custom/config/*
Database or tenant layer	*/sapmnt/<SID>/SYS/global/hdb/custom/config/DB_<tenant_db_name>*
Host layer	*/usr/sap/<SID>/HDB<instance>/<hostname>/*

Table 4.3: Parameter layers and file system locations

These are shown in Figure 4.51.

Figure 4.51: HANA parameter priority layers at OS level

4.4.2 Changing parameter values

The tools available for setting or modifying HANA database parameters are:

- Administration tools such as HANA Studio or HANA Cockpit
- SQL statement—`ALTER SYSTEM ALTER CONFIGURATION`
- Console Tool—`setParameter.py`

To modify parameters, the database user must have system privileges *INIFILE ADMIN* and *SESSION ADMIN*.

Modifying parameter values using SQL console

When the HANA database is online, the database parameters can be modified using the SQL query:

```
ALTER SYSTEM ALTER CONFIGURATION ( <filename>, <layer>[, <layer_
name> ] )
  { SET | UNSET } <parameter_key_value_list>
  [ WITH RECONFIGURE ]
  [ COMMENT <comment_string> ]
```

A sample SQL to modify a parameter from the SQL console is shown in Figure 4.52.

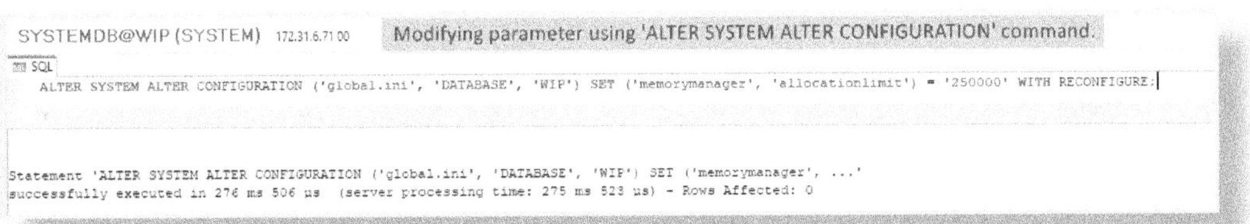

Figure 4.52: Altering a HANA DB parameter using SQL command

Modifying parameters using HANA Studio

To modify parameters using HANA Studio, navigate to the CONFIGURATION tab and search for the parameter using the FILTER field. Double-click to modify the values, as illustrated in Figure 4.53, and SAVE the changes. This method is applicable only when the database is online.

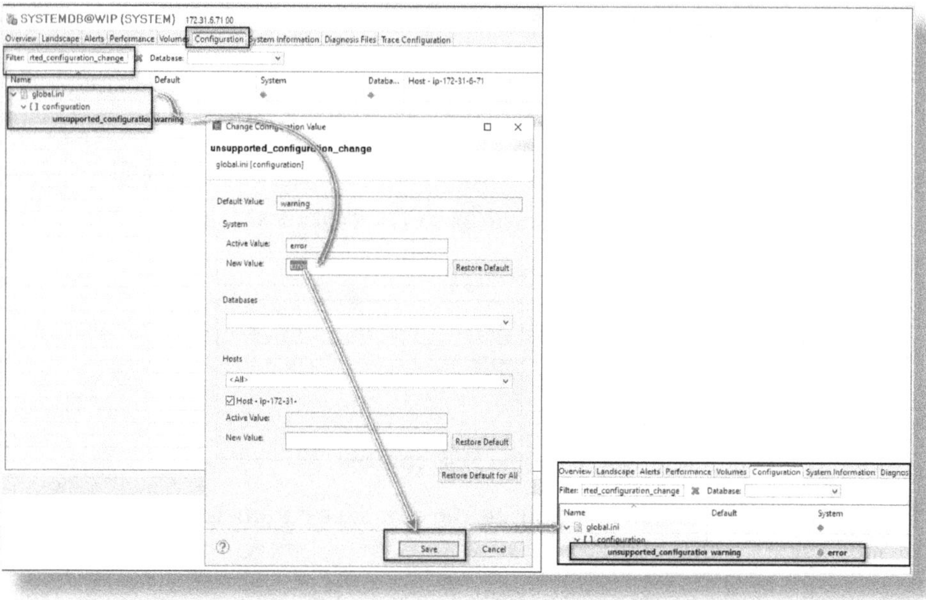

Figure 4.53: Altering a HANA DB parameter from HANA Studio

Modifying parameters using console tool setParameter.py

The console tool *setParameter.py* offers an alternative method to modify configuration parameter values, and is applicable regardless of whether the database is offline or online. The command for using this tool is as follows:

```
python setParameter.py -set(or unset)=<LAYER>/<INIFILE_
NAME>/<SECTION>/ <KEY>=<VALUE> [-comment=comment] [-reconfigure]
[-sapcontrol=1]
```

<LAYER> refers to a system, a database, or a host, as outlined in Table 4.3.

Figure 4.54 shows a sample configuration modification, on a tenant database, using this tool.

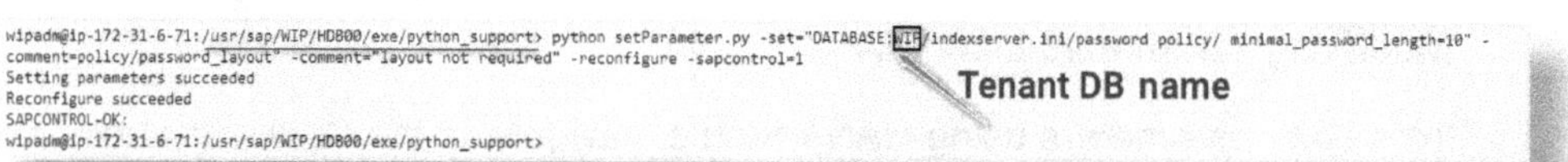

Figure 4.54: Sample execution of setParameter.py

> **! Modifying parameters at OS level**
>
> It is possible to directly edit the **.ini* files at the OS level to modify database configuration parameters, but this is not recommended.

Handling invalid parameters

When an invalid parameter is set in the HANA database, the system issues a warning by default and discards the changes without saving them. This behavior is controlled by the parameter *unsupported_configuration_change = error*.

4.4.3 Static and dynamic configuration parameters

Some parameters may require a database restart for the modified values to take effect. To determine if a restart is required for a parameter change to be effective, query the CONFIGURATION_PARAMETER_PROPERTIES table, as shown in Figure 4.55.

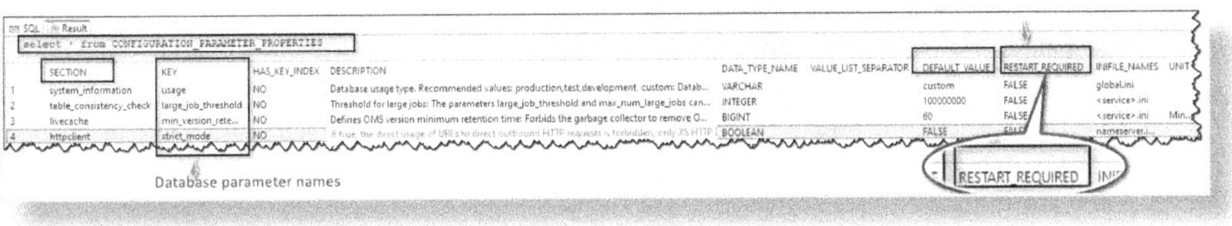

Figure 4.55: Parameter change and DB restart

4.5 Persistent data storage

Although HANA is an in-memory database, it still requires a persistence layer for data storage. This persistence layer and file system structure were discussed in earlier sections.

Let's now delve deeper into some of the persistence-related configurations and operations in the HANA database.

4.5.1 Savepoints in HANA

As detailed earlier, HANA periodically writes its in-memory data to the file system layer at regular intervals through *savepoint operations*. By default, this interval is set to 5 minutes and is controlled by the parameter *savepoint_interval_s* in *global.ini*, as shown in Figure 4.56.

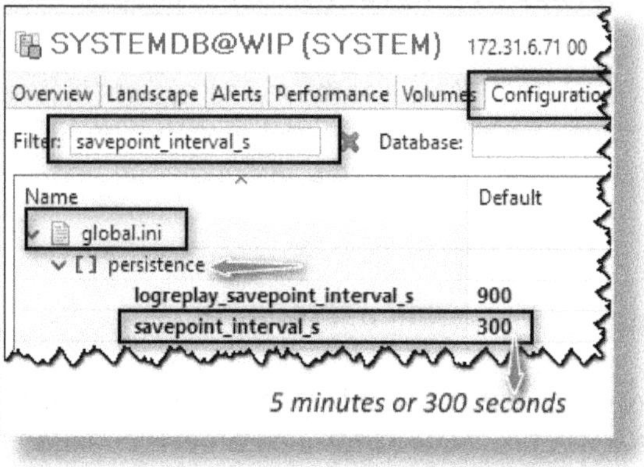

Figure 4.56: Savepoint parameter in global.ini

In the HANA database, a savepoint operation is triggered automatically during specific database operations:

- planned or unplanned shutdowns of the HANA database
- before starting a database backup
- when reaching a consistent database state during startup
- activation of snapshots (savepoints preserved for prolonged use)
- reclaiming data volume to defragment persistence (refer to SAP Note 2400005—"FAQ: SAP HANA Persistence")

Note that a savepoint operation can also be triggered manually using the following SQL command:

```
ALTER SYSTEM SAVEPOINT;
```

To obtain more information about the savepoint operations that are triggered on a HANA database, use the following systems views:

- *M_SAVEPOINTS*—contains information about current and historical savepoints.

- *M_SAVEPOINT_STATISTICS*—provides information about savepoints triggered using SQL statement `ALTER SYSTEM SAVEPOINT;`.

With a well-configured HANA database, savepoint operations have minimal impact on performance and do not affect transaction processing. For additional information, see SAP Note 2100009—"FAQ: SAP HANA Savepoints".

4.5.2 Persistence configuration

The *global.ini* file contains detailed persistence configurations under sections [ ] PERSISTENCE and [ ] FILEIO. These settings provide insights into the operating system level file system structure and its mapping to the HANA database. For example, Figure 4.57 shows that the data volume path is */hana/shared/data* and the log volume path is */hana/shared/log* for the connected HANA database.

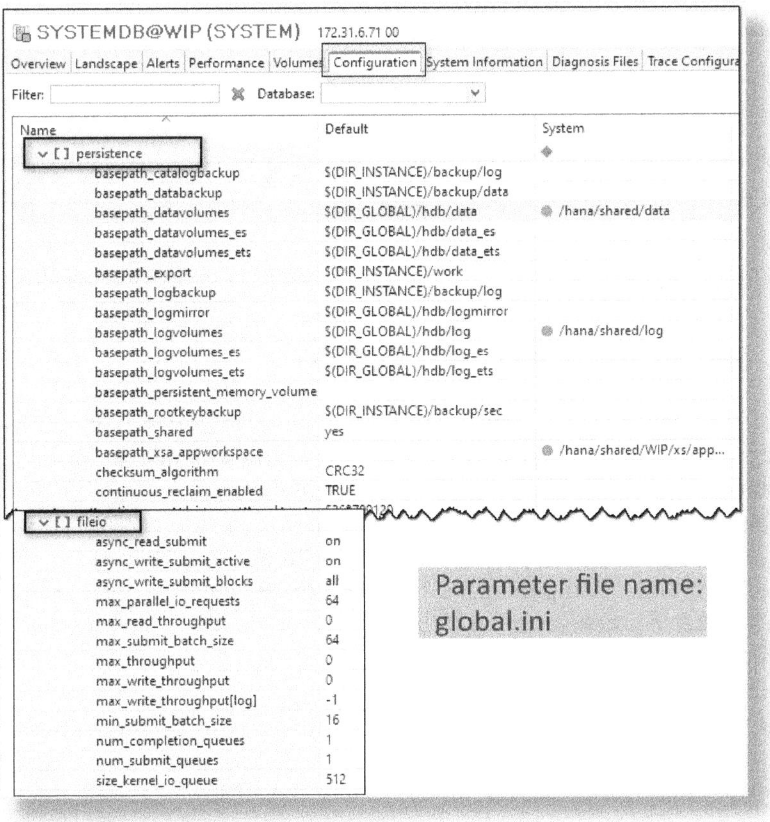

Figure 4.57: global.ini—persistence parameter settings

4.5.3 Reclaiming free log segments

Log segment files in log volumes can be cyclically overwritten based on the *log_mode* parameter. In a typical production setup (*log_mode = normal* in *global.ini*), overwriting occurs automatically in the HANA database after a successful log backup of the corresponding log segment. To free up file system space, these files can also be manually reclaimed using SQL command `ALTER SYSTEM RECLAIM LOG;`, as shown in Figure 4.58.

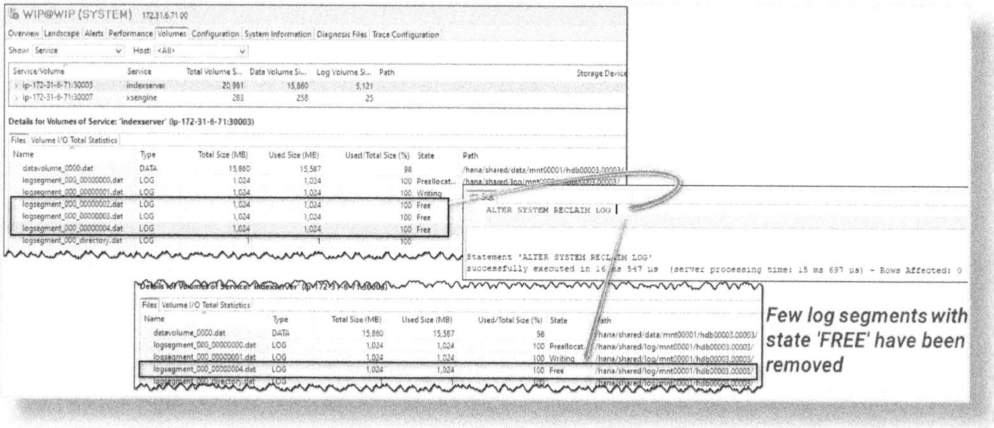

Figure 4.58: Reclaiming free log segments

Section 6.1.1 covers further information on log segments and their states.

4.5.4 Data volume defragmentation

During normal database operations, the actual data volume size might be much smaller than the total allocated size, indicating a significant amount of free, unused space within the HANA database's file system (persistence) layer. This situation, known as *data fragmentation*, can result from various scenarios, such as the reduction of business data due to archiving and deletion, table optimization processes that temporarily increase disk usage, and the long-term preservation of snapshots, which leads to a higher number of shadow pages.

Data volume fragmentation issues can be identified by running the *HANA_Disks_Overview* SQL statement, available in the *SQLStatements_MDC* zip folder in the attachment section of SAP Note 1969700—"SQL Statement

Collection for SAP HANA". This SQL statement must be executed from the SystemDB. The output value under the FRAGMENTATION_PCT column indicates the fragmentation percentage—a value below 30% is generally acceptable.

Figure 4.59 shows data volume defragmentation using the indicated statement collection.

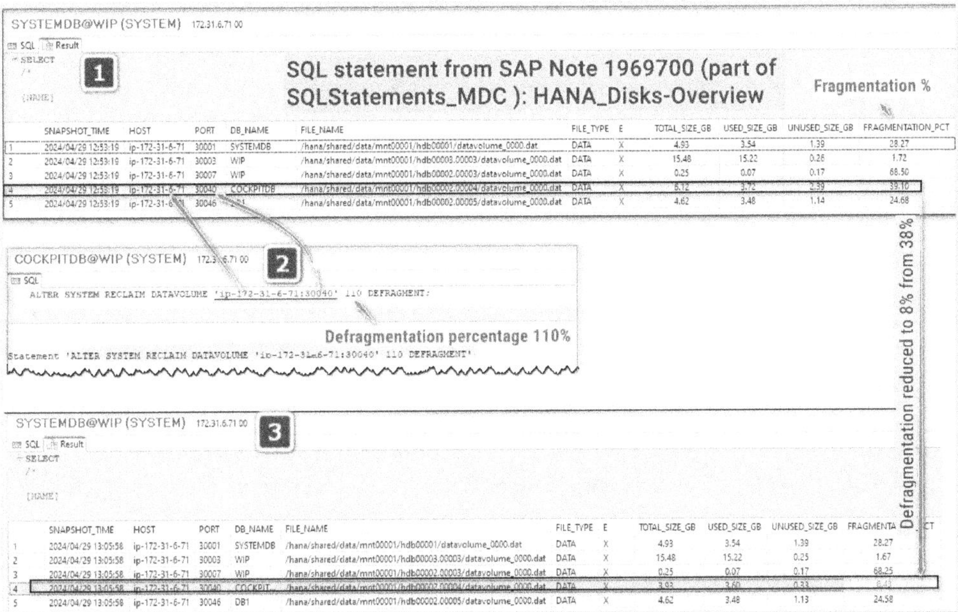

Figure 4.59: Data volume defragmentation

The steps in the image are as follows:

❶ Execute SQL statement *HANA_Disks_Overview* from the SystemDB (SAP Note 1969700).

❷ Log in to the tenant database and execute the defragmentation SQL command:

```
ALTER SYSTEM RECLAIM DATAVOLUME '<host>:<port>' 120 DEFRAGMENT;
```

❸ Re-execute the SQL statement *HANA_Disks_Overview* from the SystemDB (SAP Note 1969700).

The value of `110` in the SQL query shown here indicates 100% of data plus 10% of acceptable fragmentation. Similarly, a value of 120 means 100% data plus 20% of acceptable fragmentation. This value is deemed reasonable due to temporary space requirement for table optimizations, garbage, and so on.

! Data defragmentation

- Data defragmentation of 100% is never possible and must not be executed.
- Data defragmentation is an online operation that does not block access to tables during execution. However, it is advisable to perform this task during non-business hours.

4.5.5 Monitoring persistence

The HANA database persistence layer can be monitored using HANA Studio, HANA Cockpit, or system views—such as *M_DATA_VOLUME_STATISTICS, M_VOLUME_FILES, M_TABLE_PERSISTENCE_STATISTICS*. Figure 4.60 shows this monitoring capability using:

❶ HANA Studio—via the OVERVIEW and VOLUMES tabs.

❷ System views—using SQL queries:

```
select * from M_DATA_VOLUME_STATISTICS;
select * from SYS.M_VOLUME_FILES;
```

Another system view which helps with understanding and monitoring persistence is M_TABLE_PERSISTENCE_STATISTICS (see Figure 4.61).

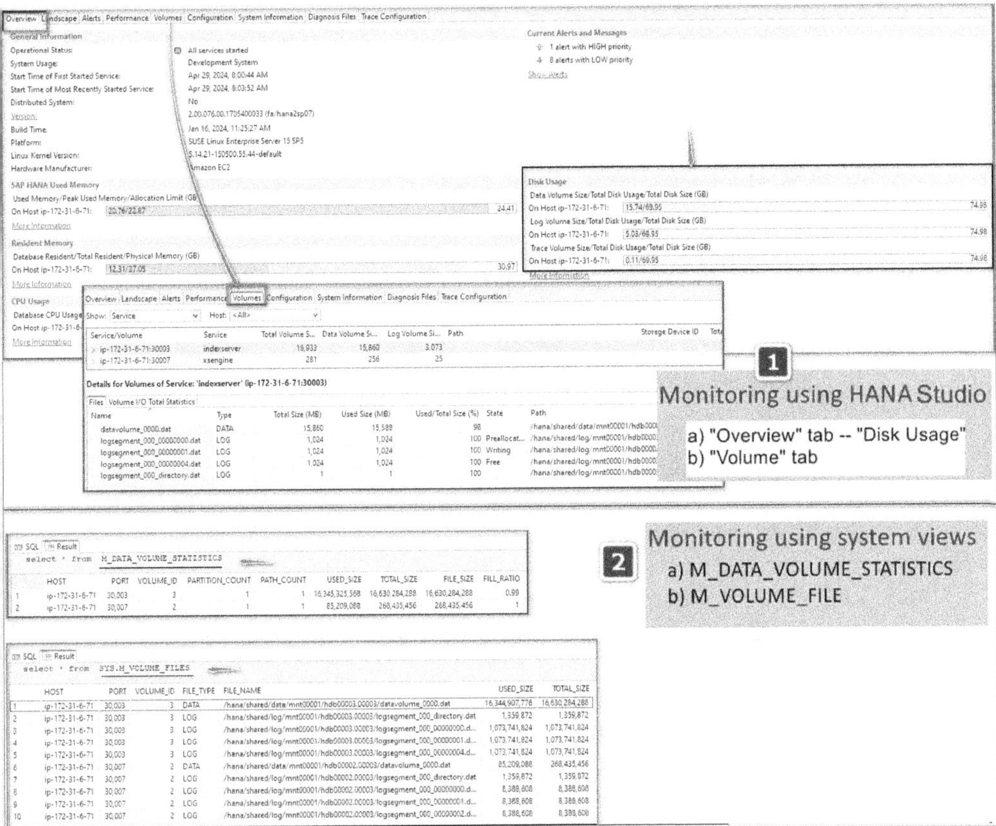

Figure 4.60: Monitoring HANA disk (persistence) layer

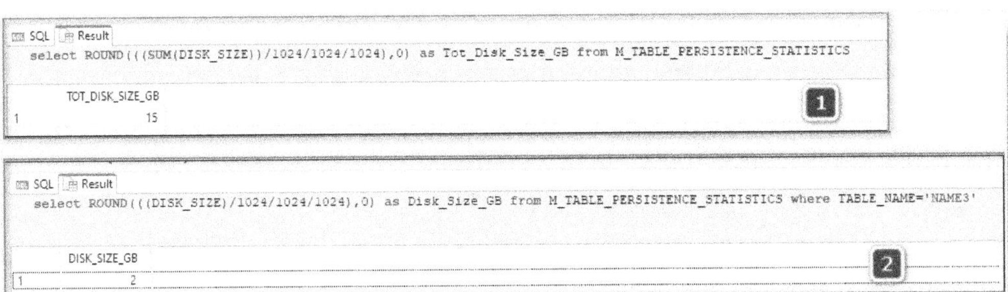

Figure 4.61: Disk size occupied by database tables

The two sections shown in Figure 4.61 are:

❶ The SQL query to identify the total disk size occupied by all the column-store tables:

```
select ROUND (((SUM(DISK_SIZE))/1024/1024/1024),0) as Tot_Disk_
Size_GB from M_TABLE_PERSISTENCE_STATISTICS;
```

❷ The SQL query to identify the disk size occupied by a specific table:

```
select ROUND (((DISK_SIZE)/1024/1024/1024),0) as Disk_Size_GB
from M_TABLE_PERSISTENCE_STATISTICS where TABLE_NAME = '<table_
name>';
```

4.6 Workload management

HANA workload management involves tools and strategies for effectively allocating system resources to ensure efficient workload and query processing. It helps to balance and optimize CPU, memory, disk I/O, and network usage between the SystemDB and tenant databases by applying selective limitations. The following sections look at various ways that workloads can be managed in the HANA database.

4.6.1 Controlling CPU consumption by NUMA mapping DB services and objects

NUMA (Non-Uniform Memory Access) is a term commonly associated with operating systems, describing the memory architecture in a multi-processor system. In a NUMA system, processors are organized into distinct units called NUMA nodes, where each node has its own dedicated CPU cores and local memory. The example in Figure 4.62 shows details of a server's NUMA nodes and its associated CPU and memory.

The SQL queries and OS commands referenced in the image are as follows:

❶ OS command `lscpu`—this provides information about the number of NUMA nodes and CPUs assigned to each node in the operating system. Here, it indicates that the system has 1 NUMA node with 8 CPUs.

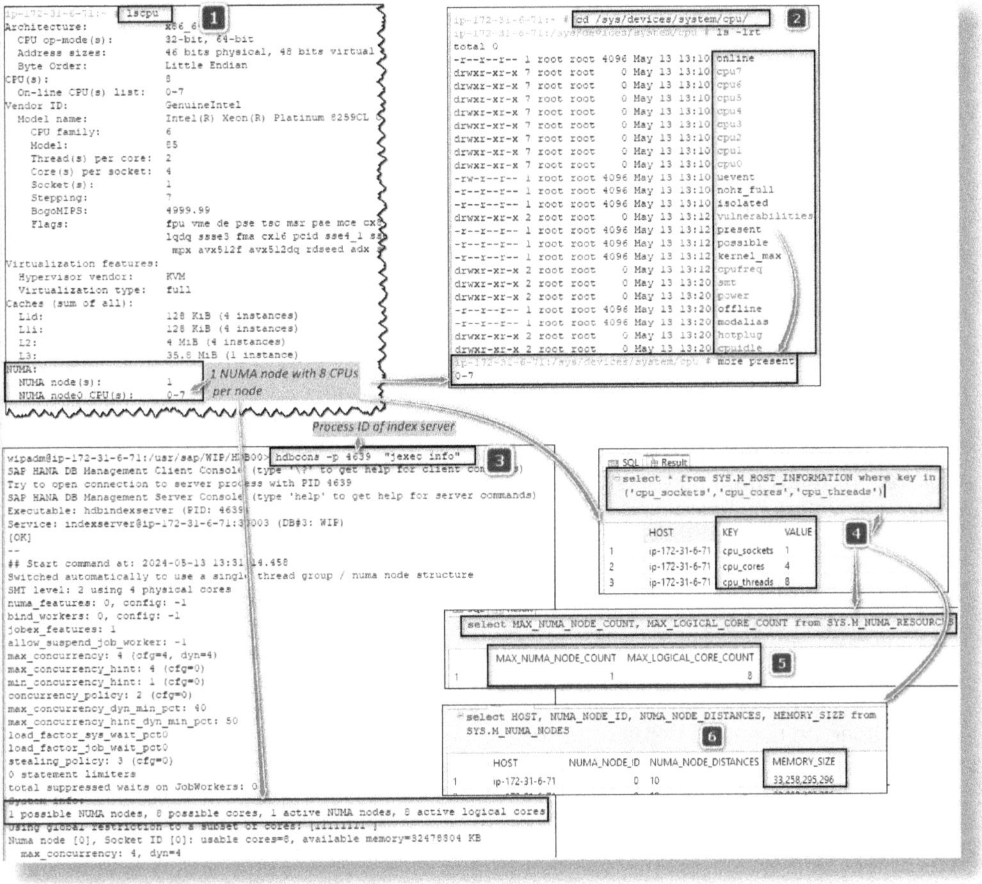

Figure 4.62: Examining database server topology

❷ OS command `more present`—accessed from the file system path */sys/devices/system/cpu*, this command indicates the number of CPU cores present in the operating system. The example shows that the system has 8 CPUs.

❸ HANA hdbcons command `hdbcons -p <process_of_indexserver>"jexec info"`. This command connects to the specified index server process and displays information about the Java virtual machine running on the process, including its memory usage, CPU usage, number of NUMA nodes, and other details.

❹, ❺, and ❻: The following SQL queries provide similar details about NUMA nodes, including their count, CPU usage, and memory allocation:

```
select * from SYS.M_HOST_INFORMATION where key in ('cpu sockets',
'cpu_cores', 'cpu_threads');

select MAX_NUMA_NODE_COUNT, MAX_LOGICAL_CORE_COUNT from SYS.M_
NUMA_RESOURCES;

select HOST, NUMA_NODE_ID, NUMA_NODE_DISTANCES, MEMORY_SIZE from
SYS.M_NUMA_NODES;
```

A thorough understanding of NUMA nodes enables complete control over CPU usage in the HANA database by mapping NUMA nodes to different levels of the database hierarchy, as follows:

- To map a tenant database to a specific CPU range:

```
ALTER SYSTEM ALTER CONFIGURATION ('daemon.ini', 'SYSTEM') SET
('indexserver.DB1', 'affinity') ='<n>-<m>';
```

With this SQL command, we can bind a specific tenant database (e.g., DB1) to a specific range of CPUs (n to m).

- To map an individual database service to a specific CPU:

```
ALTER SYSTEM ALTER CONFIGURATION ('daemon.ini', 'SYSTEM') SET
('nameserver', 'affinity') = '<n>,<m>';
```

With this command, the name server is mapped to specific CPUs (n, m) at the OS level.

- To map a specific database object to a specific CPU:

```
ALTER SYSTEM ALTER CONFIGURATION ('daemon.ini', 'SYSTEM') SET
('indexserver.DB1', 'affinity') ='<n>-<m>';
```

With this command, we can bind specific tables to a specific range of CPUs (n-m).

The above mappings ensure that each object or service is restricted to a specific CPU or CPU ranges within a NUMA node. These are shown in Figure 4.63.

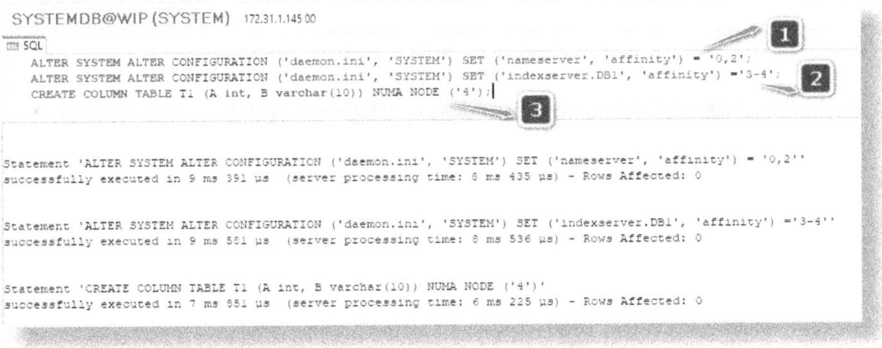

Figure 4.63: Setting up CPU affinity at different levels

4.6.2 Controlling parallel execution of SQL statements

Like any other database, the parallel execution of threads or statements must be well managed and controlled to ensure optimal database performance. In HANA, parallel statement execution is controlled by defining thread limits for two pools—SQLEXECUTOR AND JOBEXECUTOR. The parameters shown in Figure 4.64 control the respective limits for each of these pools.

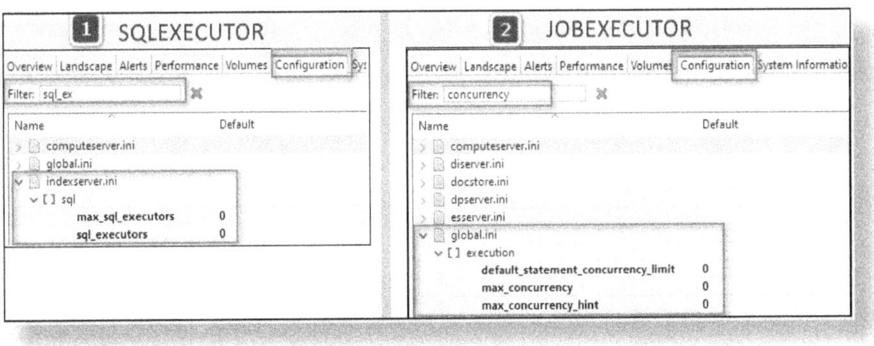

Figure 4.64: SQL Executor and Job Executor

Area ❶ in the image shows the SqlExecutor pool, which handles incoming client requests and short OLTP (or similar) statements. It can be controlled using the following parameters under the [] SQL section of INDEXSERVER.INI:

- MAX_SQL_EXECUTORS—this sets a hard limit on the maximum number of logical cores that can be used for SQL query execution, beyond which the query execution cannot continue.

- SQL_EXECUTORS—this sets a soft limit on the desired number of logical cores for the SqlExecutor pool.

Area ❷ shows the JobExecutor pool, which acts as a job dispatching subsystem and manages parallel tasks such as OLAP workloads, updates, backups, and garbage collection. It can be controlled with the help of the following parameters under the [ ] EXECUTION section of GLOBAL.INI.

- DEFAULT_STATEMENT_CONCURRENCY_LIMIT—this restricts the degree of parallel execution per connection within a statement.
- MAX_CONCURRENCY—this sets the target number of logical cores for the JobExecutor thread pool, thereby saving capacity for SqlExecutors.
- MAX_CONCURRENCY_HINT—this limits the number of logical cores for job workers.

4.6.3 Setting memory limit for SQL statements

The HANA database needs to be protected from excessive memory consumption caused by a single SQL statement or an individual user. This can be controlled by adjusting various parameters in GLOBAL.INI, in subsection [ ] MEMORYMANAGER, AS SHOWN AT ❶ IN Figure 4.65.

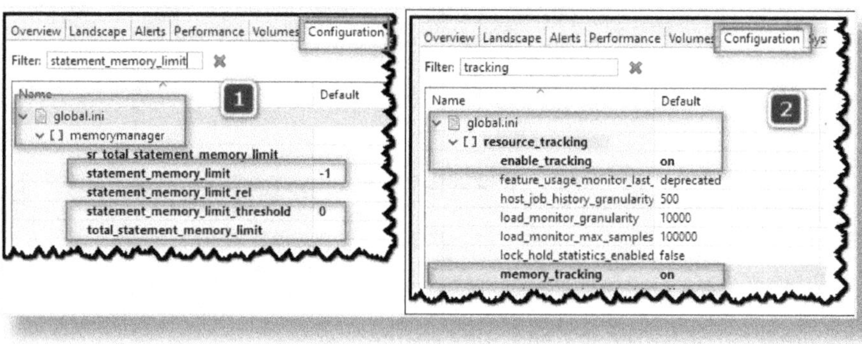

Figure 4.65: Controlling memory usage at SQL statement level

As a prerequisite, for these parameters to be effective, ENABLE_TRACKING and MEMORY_TRACKING must be set to ON in GLOBAL.INI, as shown in area ❷ of the image.

Some of the key parameters in global.ini, under [] MEMORYMANAGER ARE:

- STATEMENT_MEMORY_LIMIT—this defines the maximum memory a single SQL statement can use, preventing it from consuming excessive resources and affecting other query execution or overall system performance. The parameter's value is set in gigabytes (GB) and can range from 0 to the global allocation limit. If set to -1, the system calculates the effective limit as 25% of the smaller value between *global_allocation_limit* and *process_allocation_limit*. Statements exceeding this limit are terminated, and a dump file, labelled *compositelimit_oom,* is generated every 24 hrs by default.
- STATEMENT_MEMORY_LIMIT_THRESHOLD—this specifies the percentage of *global_allocation_limit* at which the *statement_memory_limit* becomes applicable during statement execution in SAP HANA. The latter parameter is enforced only if the total memory usage exceeds this threshold. By default, the parameter is set to 0% of the *global_allocation_limit*, meaning that the *statement_memory_limit* is always respected.
- TOTAL_STATEMENT_MEMORY_LIMIT—this specifies the maximum memory available in GB for all statements that are executed on the HANA database.

Sample calculation to explain the correlation between the parameter values

If the HANA DB's physical memory is 128GB, then the default *global_allocation_limit* will be 90% of the first 64GB of available physical memory on the host, plus 97% of each further GB. Assuming that the *statement_memory_limit_threshold* is set to 60% and *statement_memory_limit* is set to 1GB, and if a statement execution results in allocating 2GB of memory and the current used memory size in SAP HANA is 50GB, then the calculations are as follows:

- `0.9 * 128GB = 115.2 (global allocation limit)`
- `0.6 * 115.2 = 69.12 (threshold in GB)`

Because 50GB is less than 69.12GB, the threshold is not yet reached. This statement is executed, even though it exceeds the 1GB of statement memory limit. However, if the system's used memory reaches 70GB, which is more than the threshold limit of 69.12GB, the value of the *statement_memory_limit* is respected and any SQL that requests more memory than 1GB is cancelled

To understand the memory consumption details at individual statement level, use the table column *MEMORY_SIZE* from the system view *M_EXPENSIVE_STATEMENTS* using SQL query:

```
select CONNECTION_ID, DB_USER, APP_USER,MEMORY_SIZE, CPU_
TIME, RECORDS, STATEMENT_STRING, ERROR_CODE from M_EXPENSIVE_
STATEMENTS;
```

4.6.4 Managing peak load (admission control)

The HANA database uses *admission control* to manage and control new database requests when there is a system performance issue by applying certain limits. These limits can be applied in two ways:

- New requests are queued until processing capacity is available, or until a timeout occurs.
- A higher threshold is defined for rejecting new requests above a maximum workload level. If a request is rejected, a server overload error message (*1038, 'ERR_SES_SERVER_BUSY'*) is returned to the client.

Threshold values for admission control can be configured via parameters in INDEXSERVER.INI • ADMISSION_CONTROL, as shown in section ❶ of Figure 4.66.

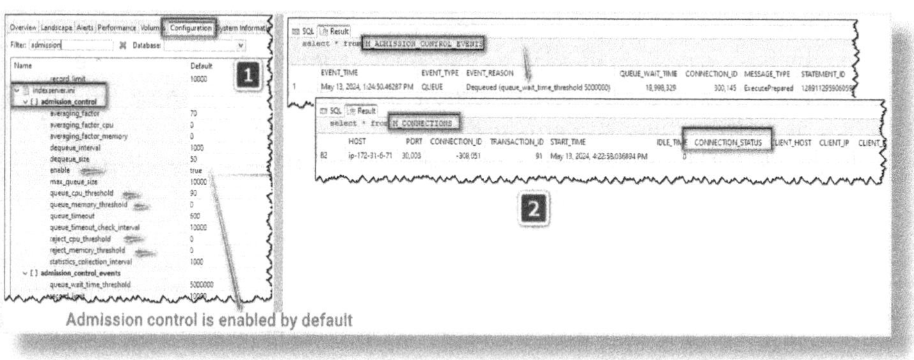

Figure 4.66: Admission control parameters

Events relating to admission control are logged in the following system views:

- *M_ADMISSION_CONTROL_EVENTS*

- *M_CONNECTIONS* (CONNECTION_STATUS column with the value *queuing*).
- *M_ADMISSION_CONTROL_QUEUES*

Some of these are shown in area ❷ of Figure 4.66.

Note that admission control should be disabled during planned maintenance events to avoid unnecessary interference during heavy database loads.

4.6.5 Setting user parameters for workload

Resource utilization at individual user level can be controlled if the parameters under section [] RESOURCE_TRACKING are enabled (see Figure 4.65).

Within workload management, there are three parameters that govern resource allocation at individual user level:

- *STATEMENT MEMORY LIMIT*
- *STATEMENT THREAD LIMIT*
- *PRIORITY*

Figure 4.67 shows a selection of SQL queries that are used for setting these user-level workload parameters.

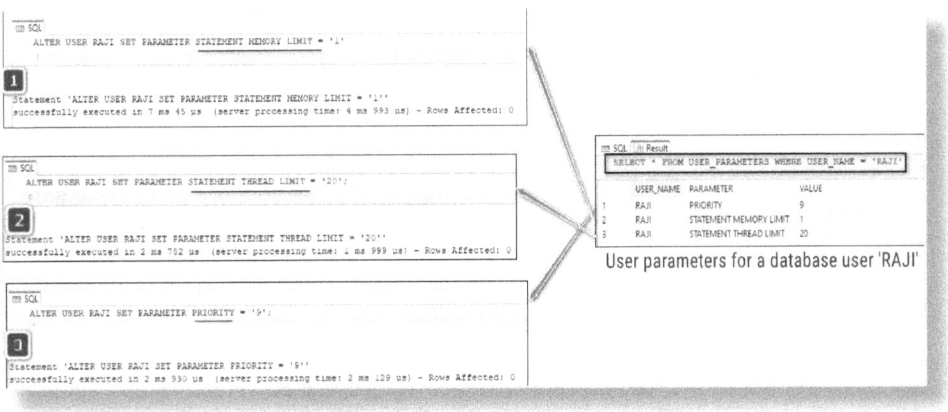

Figure 4.67: User-level workload management at (SQL)

Note that only database users with *USER ADMIN* privilege can manage these parameters.

The numbers in the image refer to the following:

❶ To restrict the user's SQL statement memory limit:

```
ALTER USER <user_name> SET PARAMETER STATEMENT MEMORY LIMIT =
'<numeric value>';
```

❷ To restrict the user's thread limit (concurrency of statements):

```
ALTER USER <user_name> SET PARAMETER STATEMENT THREAD LIMIT =
'<numeric value>';
```

❸ To set a user-level priority value for all the SQL statements—the range of possible value is 0 to 9 (default is 5):

```
ALTER USER <user_name> SET PARAMETER PRIORITY = '<numeric
value>';
```

To view the `PRIORITY` value at individual connection level, use the following SQL query and specify the appropriate *CONNECTION_ID* value:

```
SELECT PRIORITY FROM M_CONNECTIONS WHERE CONNECTION_ID='<value>’;
```

These user specific parameters can be viewed by querying the USER_PARAMETERS table (see Figure 4.67).

Another way to configure the user specific workload parameters is through HANA Cockpit, as shown in Figure 4.68.

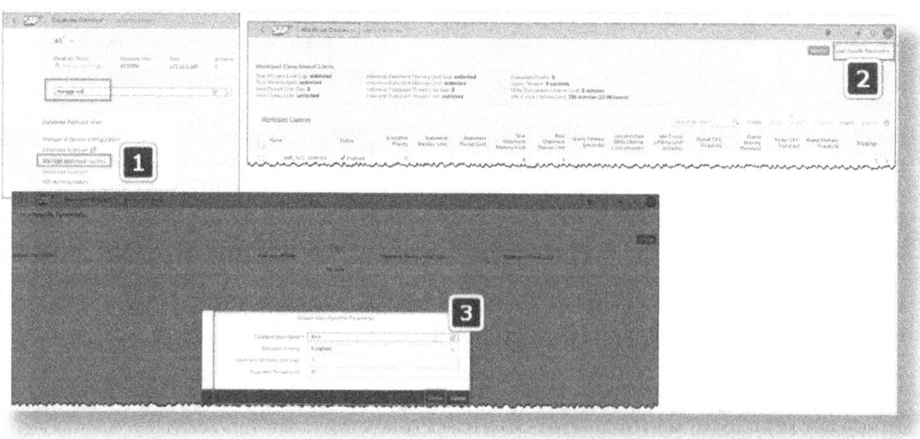

Figure 4.68: User-level workload management through HANA: Cockpit

Click on MANAGE WORKLOAD CLASSES ❶, navigate to USER SPECIFIC PARAMETERS ❷, and enter the desired values under CREATE USER-SPECIFIC PARAMETER ❸.

For further information, refer to SAP note 3202692—"How to set Memory Limit for SQL Statements".

Global and user statement memory limit

User-specific limits set at individual user level take higher precedence over limits set at global level, regardless of whether they exceed or fall below the *global_statement_memory_limit*. However, setting the statement memory limit to 0 removes any upper limit on memory usage for individual statements or user, thereby enabling them to utilize as much memory as the system can provide.

To remove the user-specific limits, a *CLEAR* clause must be used along with an *alter user* statement. The SQL query to reset a user-specific memory limit is as follows:

```
ALTER USER <user_name> CLEAR PARAMETER STATEMENT MEMORY LIMIT;
```

4.6.6 Managing workload with workload classes

HANA database workloads can be grouped into various classes known as *workload classes*. This enables database administrators to manage these classes individually by configuring resource limitations, such as *statement memory*, *thread limits*, or *priority*. These classes can then be mapped either to specific database users, clients, application names, or application users, or to application types, with the help of *workload class mappings*. This mapping results in the corresponding workload parameters being dynamically applied to each client session based on their workload class mappings.

Configurable resource limitations for workload classes include:

- `PRIORITY` (0 to 9),
- `STATEMENT THREAD LIMIT`,
- `STATEMENT MEMORY LIMIT`,
- `TOTAL STATEMENT THREAD LIMIT`,

- `TOTAL STATEMENT MEMORY LIMIT`,
- `STATEMENT TIMEOUT`,
- `WRITE TRANSACTION LIFETIME`,
- `IDLE CURSOR LIFETIME`,
- `ADMISSION CONTROL REJECT CPU THRESHOLD`,
- `ADMISSION CONTROL REJECT MEMORY THRESHOLD`,
- `ADMISSION CONTROL QUEUE CPU THRESHOLD`, and
- `ADMISSION CONTROL QUEUE MEMORY THRESHOLD`.

It is important to note that workload class settings supersede all other configuration settings (such as `*.ini` file values or user-specific parameter settings). However, workload class settings apply only for the current session, and changes applied at user-level persist even beyond the sessions.

Creating workload classes and mappings

Creating and managing workload classes and their mappings can be done using either:

1. **SQL statement:**

- A sample SQL to create a workload class with specific configuration is:

```
CREATE WORKLOAD CLASS "<WorkloadClass_name>" SET
PRIORITY = '3',
STATEMENT MEMORY LIMIT = '2',
STATEMENT THREAD LIMIT = '20',
ADMISSION CONTROL QUEUE CPU THRESHOLD = '70',
ADMISSION CONTROL QUEUE MEMORY THRESHOLD = '80',
ADMISSION CONTROL REJECT CPU THRESHOLD = '100',
ADMISSION CONTROL REJECT MEMORY THRESHOLD = '100';
```

- An SQL to create a workload class mapping:

```
CREATE WORKLOAD MAPPING "<name of workload mapping>"
WORKLOAD CLASS "<workload class name>"
SET 'APPLICATION NAME'='<applicationName>';
```

2. SAP HANA Cockpit

Figure 4.69 shows the creation of a workload class and workload class mappings through HANA Cockpit.

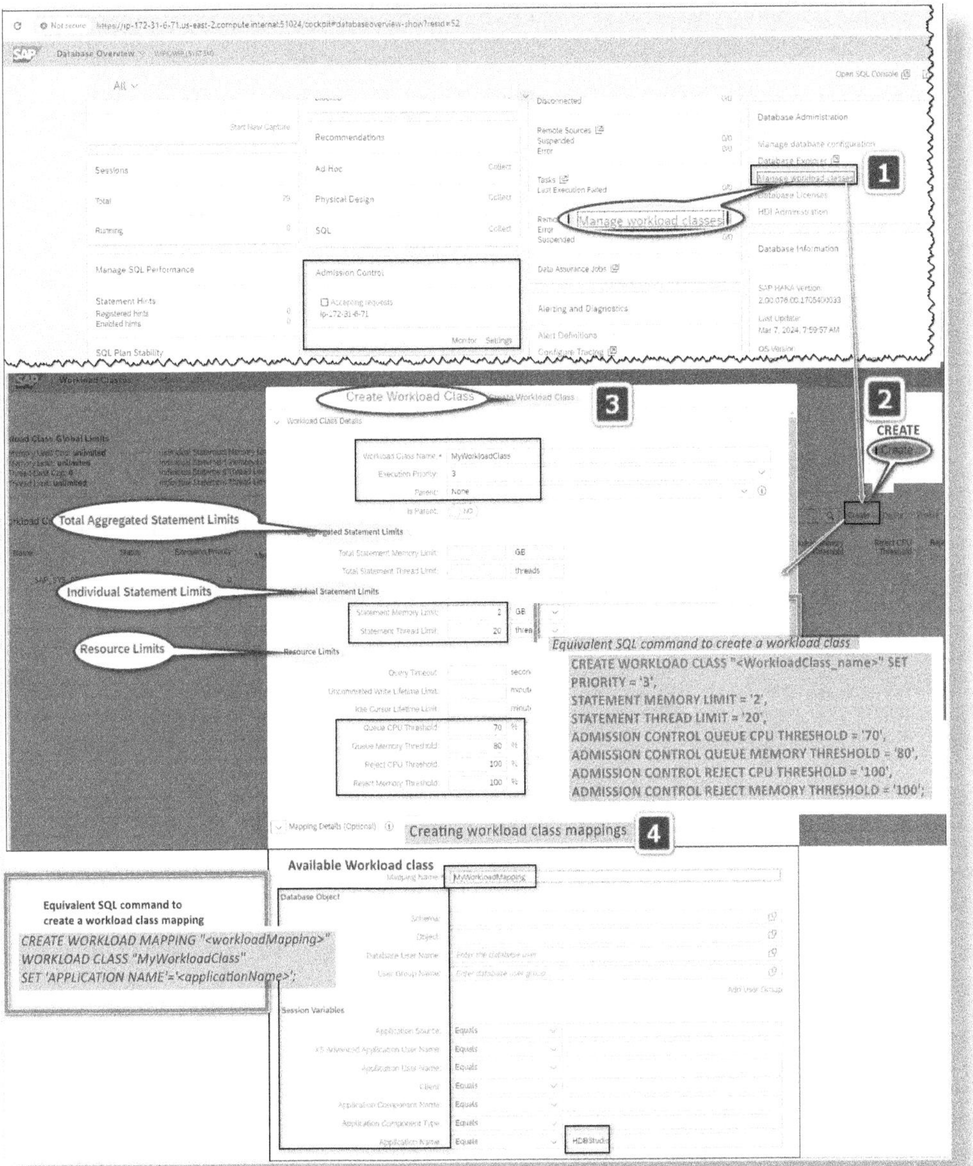

Figure 4.69: Creating workload class and mapping via SQL or HANA cockpit

The numbers in this image show the following steps:

❶ Log in to HANA Cockpit and navigate to DATABASE ADMINISTRATION • MANAGE WORKLOAD CLASSES.

❷–❸ Click on CREATE and provide the workload class name along with other required configurations.

❹ Create a workload mapping that maps the previously created workload class to the target client (here, HANA Studio) on which these settings must be applied.

We have now seen mapping that to link workload classes to client sessions based on specific client properties.

Workload class relationships can be viewed using the system view *WORKLOAD_CLASSES*.

Hints for workload classes

We can also control the execution of SQL statements dynamically, using workload classes, by specifying them as *hints*. This takes higher precedence over any previously created workload mapping.

A sample SQL query is:

```
SELECT * FROM TAB1 WITH HINT( WORKLOAD_CLASS("MY_WORKLOAD_CLASS") ); .
```

This SQL uses the resource limitations tagged against the workload class *MY_WORKLOAD_CLASS* during its execution.

4.7 HANA alert monitoring and scheduling

4.7.1 Statistics service and alerts

The primary responsibility of a database administrator is to monitor the database, manage its resource utilization, and ensure its continuous availability. To simplify this process, the HANA database includes an integrated internal database monitoring service called the *statistics service*. Apart from gathering and analyzing information regarding the database's status, performance, and resource consumption, the statistics service also conducts regular checks against predefined thresholds and generates alerts of varying criticality levels. The monitoring data and alert notifications are then stored in dedicated tables within the schema called *_SYS_STATISTICS*. The tables under this schema are accessible via HANA Cockpit or SAP HANA Studio.

Figure 4.70 shows the ALERTS tab in HANA Studio.

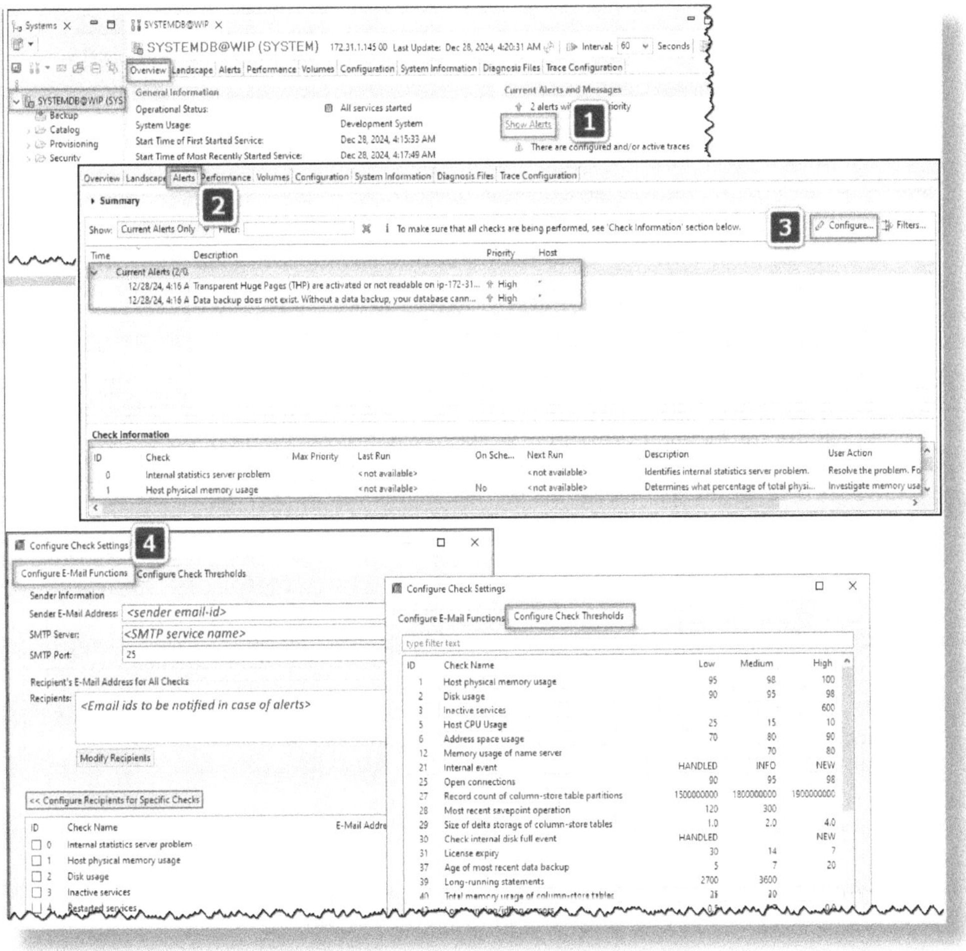

Figure 4.70: Navigating through alerts using HANA Studio

The numbers in the image refer to the following:

❶ Alerts in HANA Studio (logged in the SystemDB or tenant databases) can either be accessed via the ALERTS tab or by navigating to OVERVIEW and clicking on SHOW ALERTS.

❷ The CHECK INFORMATION section on the ALERTS tab helps to understand the Alert ID, the CHECK, the LAST RUN date (if it is scheduled to run periodically) and the frequency.

❸ Click on CONFIGURE to change or configure the alerts.

❹ The CONFIGURE CHECK SETTINGS function helps to configure email alerts and thresholds.

Some of the key statistics tables that house alert-related data are:

- *_SYS_STATISTICS.STATISTICS_SCHEDULE*
- *_SYS_STATISTICS.STATISTICS_OBJECTS*
- *_SYS_STATISTICS.STATISTICS_PROPERTIES*

The data collected by the statistics service's data collectors is automatically deleted after a retention period of 42 days. To adjust this retention period for individual data collectors, the following SQL query can be used:

```
UPDATE _SYS_STATISTICS.STATISTICS_SCHEDULE set RETENTION_
DAYS_CURRENT=<retention_period_in_days> where ID=<ID_of_data_
collector>;
```

The data collector ID used in the previous SQL query can be obtained using the following query:

```
SELECT * from _SYS_STATISTICS.STATISTICS_OBJECTS where type =
'Collector';.
```

4.7.2 Activating and scheduling individual alerts

SAP HANA Cockpit serves as the administration tool used to activate and schedule database checks, as shown in Figure 4.71.

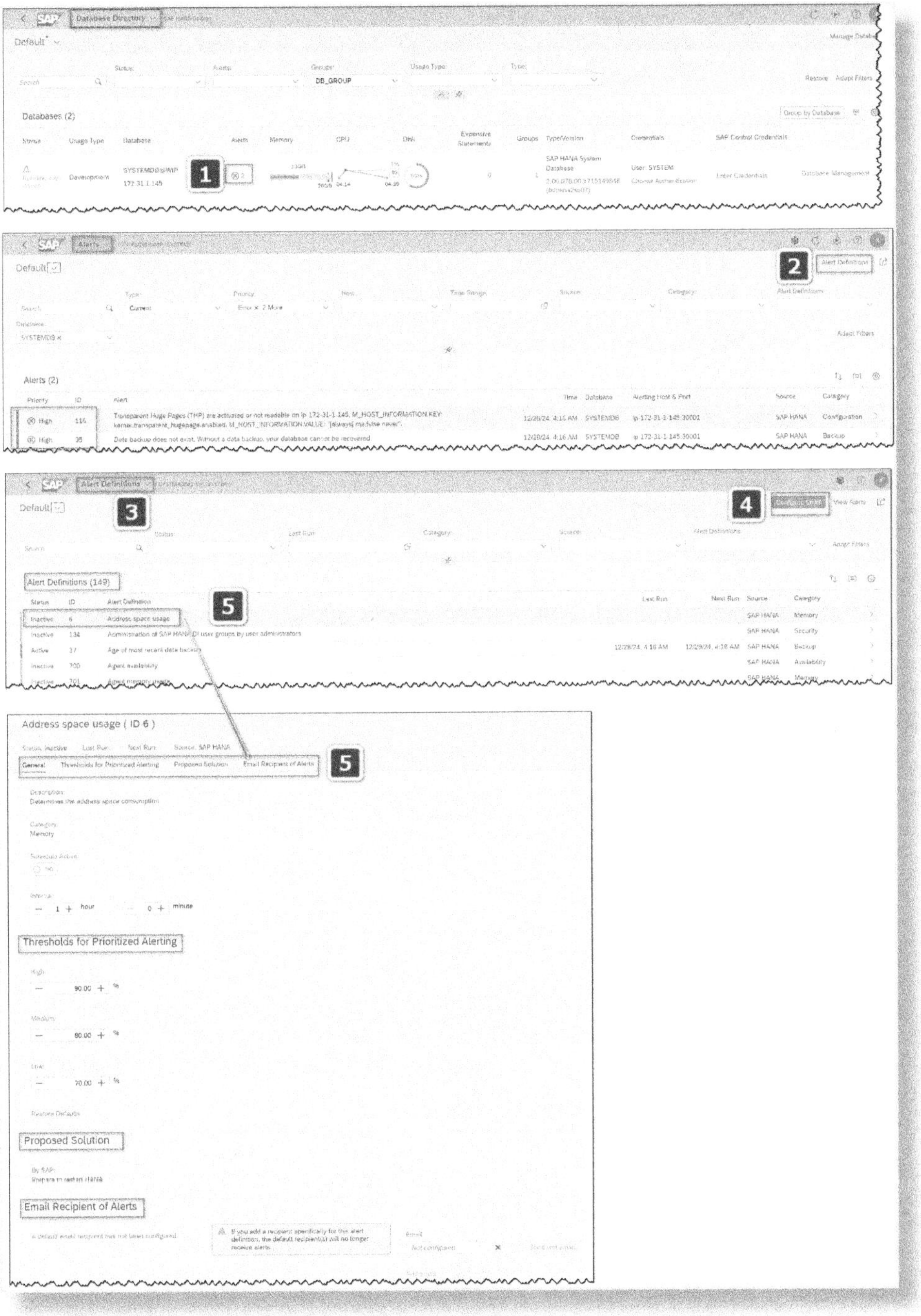

Figure 4.71: Activating and configuring alerts from the Cockpit

The numbers in this image show the following steps:

❶ Log in to the HANA Cockpit and go to the DATABASE DIRECTORY.

❷–❸ Click on ALERTS to access ALERT DEFINITIONS.

❹ Click on CONFIGURE EMAIL to set up email-based alerts.

❺ Open individual ALERT DEFINITIONS to configure them, including—enabling the alert on the database, setting the scheduling interval, adjusting the alert priority, and defining its thresholds.

The output of these checks can be analyzed and interpreted using the ALERTS function in HANA Studio.

4.8 System views

The HANA database provides pre-built *system views* for easy monitoring and administration. These views can be accessed in HANA Studio on the SYSTEM INFORMATION tab, as shown in Figure 4.72.

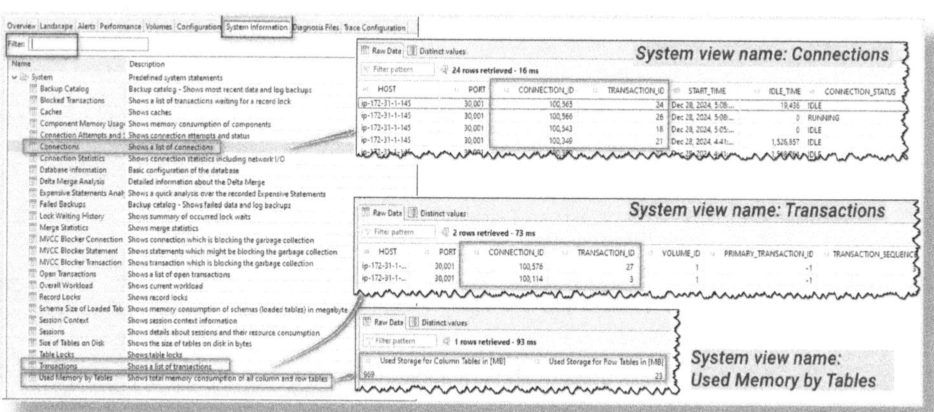

Figure 4.72: SYSTEM INFORMATION in HANA Studio

Some of the system views that are available are CONNECTIONS, TRANSACTIONS and USED MEMORY BY TABLES. The relationship between the CONNECTIONS and TRANSACTIONS SYSTEM views is shown in the CONNECTION_ID and TRANSACTION_ID columns. The screenshots also show the use of the USED MEMORY BY TABLES system view to analyze the total memory consumption of both column-store and row-store tables.

4.9 Limitations

When administering a HANA database, it is crucial for an administrator to understand the database limitations. Most of the predefined system limits can be viewed by querying the system view M_SYSTEM_LIMITS, as shown in Figure 4.73.

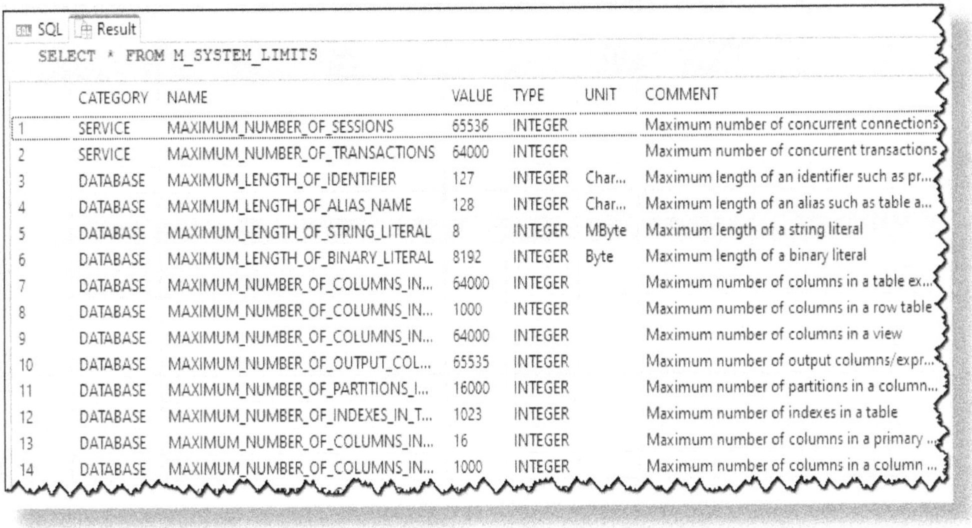

	CATEGORY	NAME	VALUE	TYPE	UNIT	COMMENT
1	SERVICE	MAXIMUM_NUMBER_OF_SESSIONS	65536	INTEGER		Maximum number of concurrent connections
2	SERVICE	MAXIMUM_NUMBER_OF_TRANSACTIONS	64000	INTEGER		Maximum number of concurrent transactions
3	DATABASE	MAXIMUM_LENGTH_OF_IDENTIFIER	127	INTEGER	Char...	Maximum length of an identifier such as pr...
4	DATABASE	MAXIMUM_LENGTH_OF_ALIAS_NAME	128	INTEGER	Char...	Maximum length of an alias such as table a...
5	DATABASE	MAXIMUM_LENGTH_OF_STRING_LITERAL	8	INTEGER	MByte	Maximum length of a string literal
6	DATABASE	MAXIMUM_LENGTH_OF_BINARY_LITERAL	8192	INTEGER	Byte	Maximum length of a binary literal
7	DATABASE	MAXIMUM_NUMBER_OF_COLUMNS_IN...	64000	INTEGER		Maximum number of columns in a table ex...
8	DATABASE	MAXIMUM_NUMBER_OF_COLUMNS_IN...	1000	INTEGER		Maximum number of columns in a row table
9	DATABASE	MAXIMUM_NUMBER_OF_COLUMNS_IN...	64000	INTEGER		Maximum number of columns in a view
10	DATABASE	MAXIMUM_NUMBER_OF_OUTPUT_COL...	65535	INTEGER		Maximum number of output columns/expr...
11	DATABASE	MAXIMUM_NUMBER_OF_PARTITIONS_I...	16000	INTEGER		Maximum number of partitions in a column...
12	DATABASE	MAXIMUM_NUMBER_OF_INDEXES_IN_T...	1023	INTEGER		Maximum number of indexes in a table
13	DATABASE	MAXIMUM_NUMBER_OF_COLUMNS_IN...	16	INTEGER		Maximum number of columns in a primary ...
14	DATABASE	MAXIMUM_NUMBER_OF_COLUMNS_IN...	1000	INTEGER		Maximum number of columns in a column ...

Figure 4.73: SAP HANA limitations

5 Security administration and user management

This chapter deals with user management and security in the HANA database.

Figure 5.1 provides a comprehensive view of HANA database SECURITY AND USER MANAGEMENT in the HANA Cockpit DATABASE OVERVIEW. It has various sub-sections such as DATA ENCRYPTION, AUTHENTICATION, AUDITING, ANONYMIZATION REPORT, USER & ROLE MANAGEMENT and TRUST CONFIGURATION.

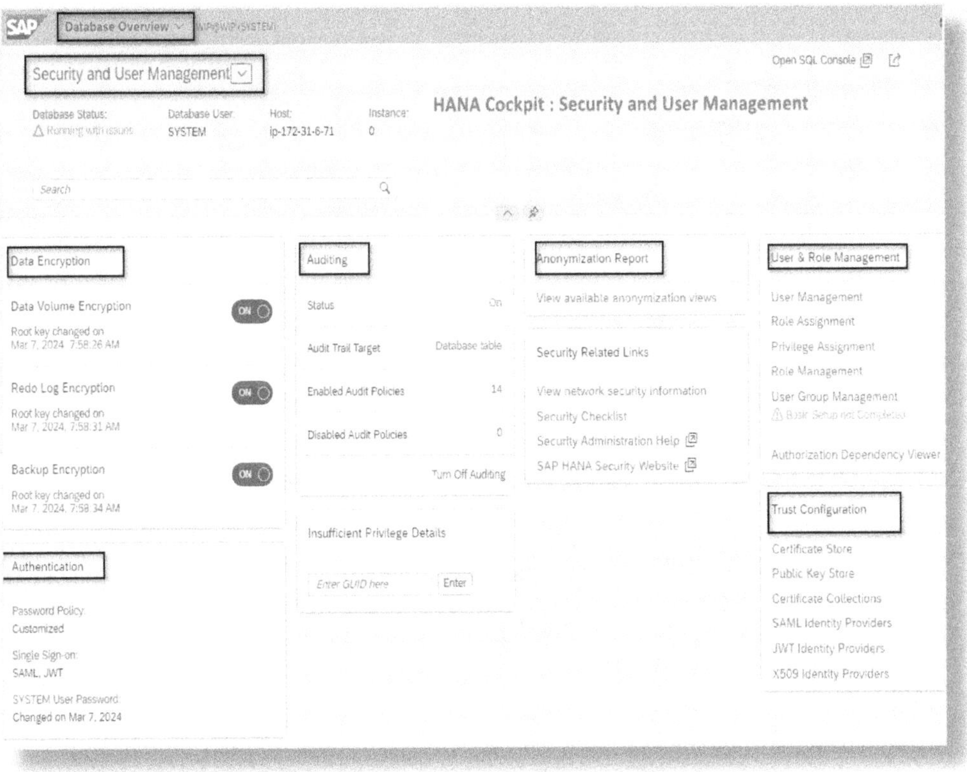

Figure 5.1: Security and User Management in HANA Cockpit

5.1 User management

SAP HANA database users can be categorized into two types:

- *Technical users*—such as administrators, modelers, and developers, who handle technical and functional database activities, and

- *Named end-users*—non-technical business users that access the database output either directly from the database or indirectly through applications connected to it. In most cases, these named users will have a 1:1 mapping between their personal name and their database username.

HANA database users (technical or end users) can be further classified as *standard users* or *restricted users*. Figure 5.2 illustrates the options of creating a standard database user and a restricted database user using HANA Studio and HANA Cockpit.

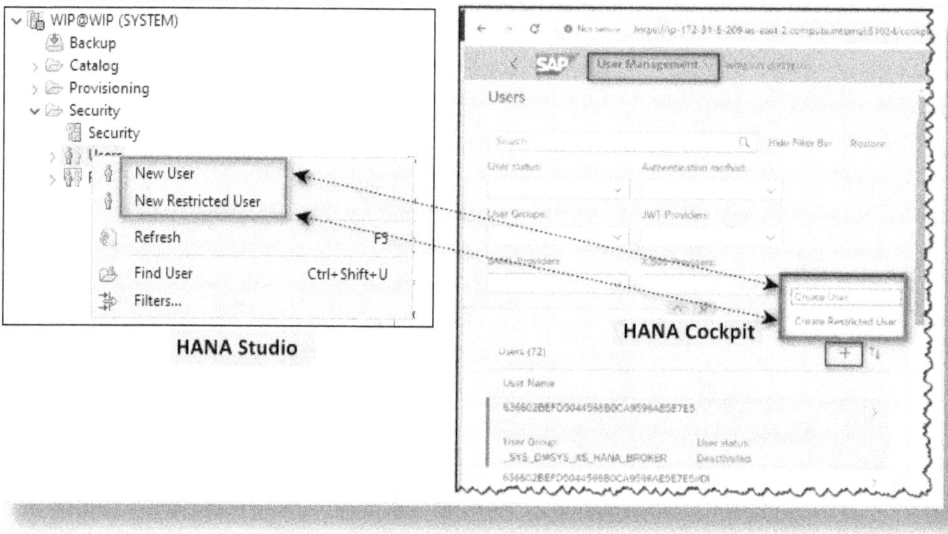

Figure 5.2: User creation in HANA Studio and HANA Cockpit

Standard users can create objects in their own schema and read data from system views due to their default assigned role—*PUBLIC*.

Restricted users, on the other hand, have no privileges. This classification is intended for users who access the HANA database through client applications.

Any database user who is not a named end user is considered a *technical database user*. In addition to these users, several predefined users are created by default during installation, such as *SYSTEM*, *SYS*, and *_SYS_AFL*.

When users log in to the database directly or indirectly via an application, they are authenticated against the database. The nature and type of database operations they can perform are determined by their assigned roles/privileges.

User provisioning and management in the HANA database can be performed using the HANA Cockpit, HANA Studio, or via SQL statements. Figure 5.3 shows some of the basic user management tasks—copying a user, setting the validity of the user, resetting passwords, granting authorizations such as roles and privileges, adding user-specific parameters, etc.

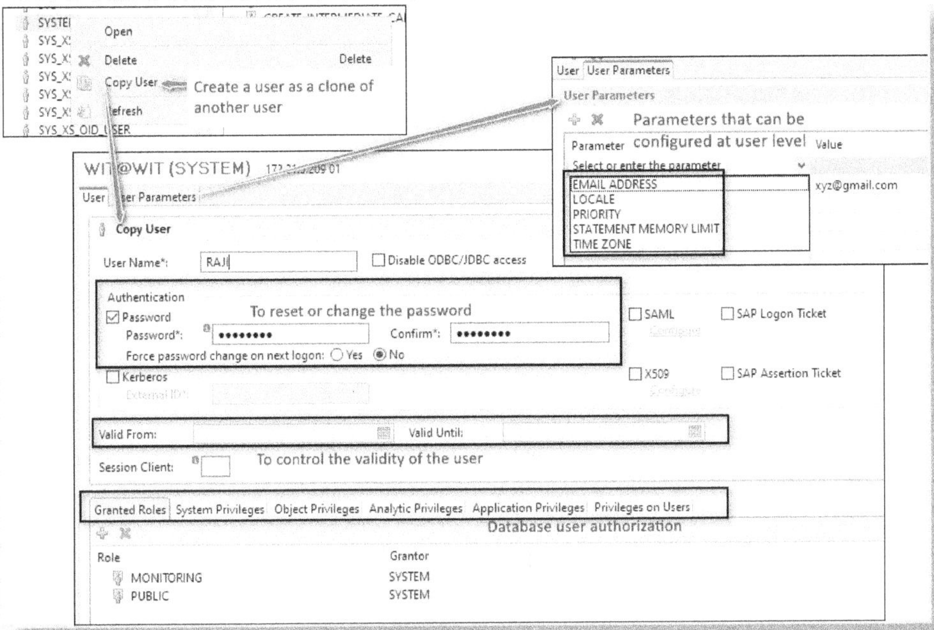

Figure 5.3: Creating user as a copy of another user

HANA database users can be activated or deactivated, as shown in Figure 5.4. Deactivating a database user stops that user from logging into the database.

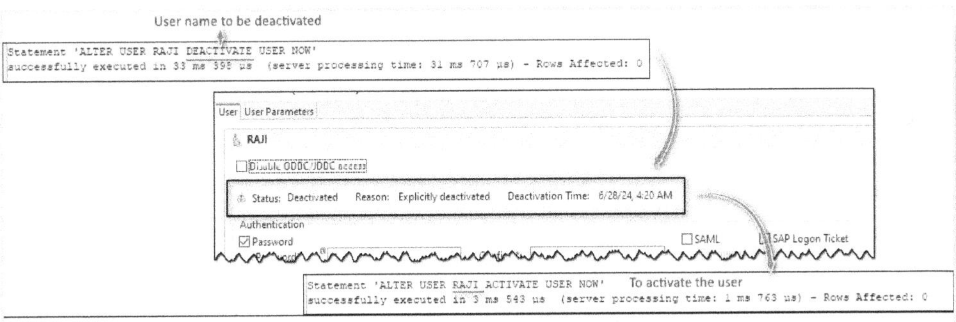

Figure 5.4: Command to activate/deactivate users

The SQL statement to deactivate a user, including a SYSTEM user, is:

```
ALTER USER <user_name> DEACTIVATE USER NOW;
```

The SQL statement to activate a database user is:

```
ALTER USER <user_name> ACTIVATE USER NOW;
```

In HANA, database users can be grouped and administered together using *user groups* (see Figure 5.5).

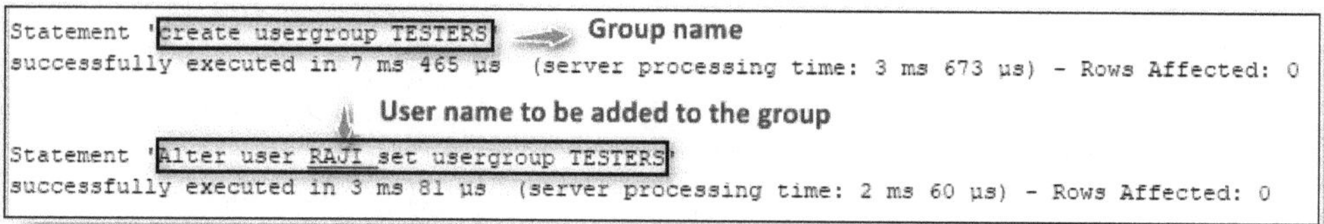

Figure 5.5: User group in HANA Database

The SQL commands to create a user group and add a user to the group are:

▶ To create a user group in HANA:

```
CREATE USERGROUP <group_name>;
```

▶ To add a database user into an existing user group:

```
ALTER USER <user_name> SET USERGROUP <group_name>;
```

5.2 Password policy

The *password policy* governs the password properties for a HANA database user. This policy encompasses a set of rules and guidelines which dictate various characteristics of the database user password, such as password complexity, password length, password expiration, prohibited passwords, account lockout duration, and so on, and are designed to enhance the strength of the password. These properties can be configured through various means, as shown in Figure 5.6.

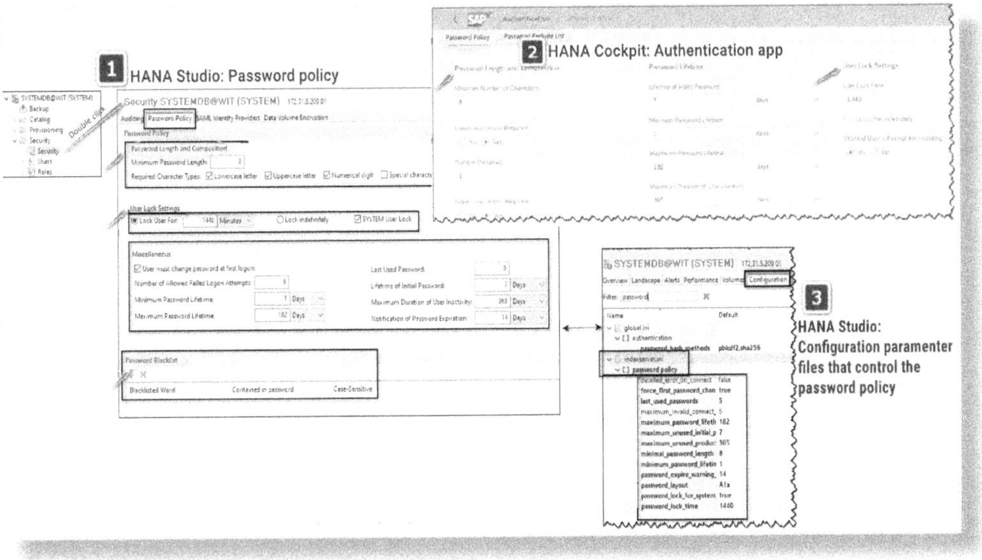

Figure 5.6: HANA database password policy

The numbers in the image refer to the following:

1. To configure the password policy in HANA Studio, navigate to SECURITY and click on PASSWORD POLICY.

2. To configure the password policy in HANA Cockpit, navigate to AUTHENTICATION (in HANA Cockpit) and click on PASSWORD POLICY and PASSWORD EXCLUDE LIST.

3. To configure the password policy using a configuration file, go to HANA Studio CONFIGURATION tab and navigate to INDEXSERVER.INI • [ ] PASSWORD POLICY.

The current HANA database password configurations can be viewed via system view *M_EFFECTIVE_PASSWORD_POLICY*.

The SQL statement to view the password configuration of a database user is:

```
SELECT * FROM "PUBLIC"."M_EFFECTIVE_PASSWORD_POLICY" WHERE USER_
NAME = '<username>';
```

5.3 HANA authorization—privileges and roles

When a database user is authenticated against a HANA database, their ability to perform a database operation on that database is determined by the *privileges* assigned to them.

5.3.1 Privileges

Privileges are the building blocks of HANA database authorization and can be assigned directly as privileges or indirectly as roles to database users (see Figure 5.7). Privileges cannot be specifically denied; however, once a requested privilege is found, the system skips all further checks and grants access to the object.

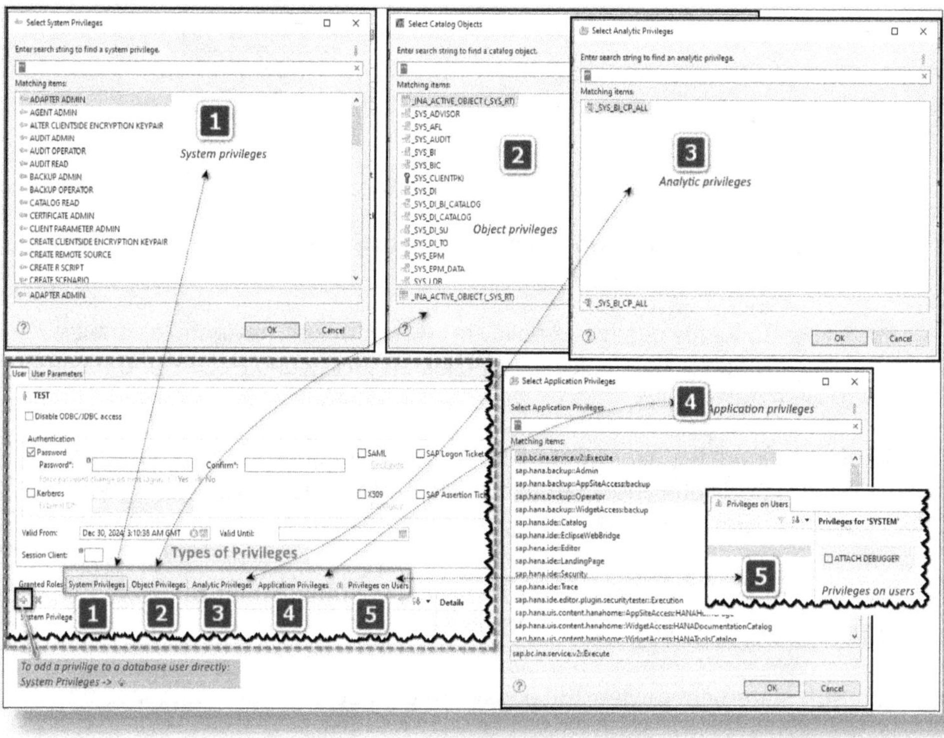

Figure 5.7: Types of privileges in the HANA database

The screenshots show the following privileges in HANA:

❶ SYSTEM PRIVILEGES—to control the SystemDB and tenant database activities. They are primarily used for administrative purposes by administrators and developers. Examples include *CATALOG READ, AUDIT ADMIN, CREATE SCHEMA, DATA ADMIN, INIFILE ADMIN*, and *MONITOR ADMIN*.

❷ OBJECT PRIVILEGES—apply to database objects such as tables, schemas, views, etc., and control access to these objects. Examples include *SELECT, CREATE ANY, ALTER*, and *DROP*. These privileges are intended for end users and technical users.

❸ ANALYTIC PRIVILEGES—allow read access to data in SAP HANA information models and apply to analytic views.

❹ APPLICATION PRIVILEGES—provide authorization to SAP HANA XS classic applications.

❺ PRIVILEGES ON USERS—a special privilege that can be granted to users. The only privilege that can be granted to a user is *ATTACH DEBUGGER*.

5.3.2 Roles

Roles are collections of one or more privileges that can be assigned to a user or another role at runtime. These predefined privilege sets allow users to perform specific tasks.

Roles can be either a standard pre-defined database role or user-defined roles. HANA includes many standard roles by default, such as *CONTENT_ADMIN, MODELING, MONITORING, PUBLIC*, and *SAP_INTERNAL_HANA_SUPPORT*. User-defined roles can be created using the following SQL statement:

```
CREATE ROLE <role_name> NO GRANT TO CREATOR;
```

Figure 5.8 shows steps to grant a pre-defined database role to a database user using the '+' icon.

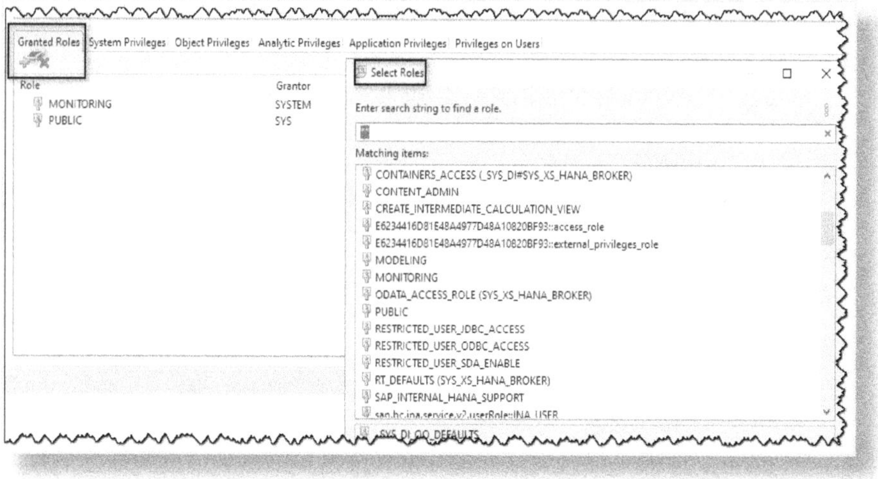

Figure 5.8: "Granted Roles" in HANA

SAP_INTERNAL_HANA_SUPPORT role

The *SAP_INTERNAL_HANA_SUPPORT* role includes system privileges (such as *CATALOG READ*) and object privileges (such as *SELECT*, on the *SYS* schema). These provide access to specific, low-level internal system views that are required by SAP's HANA development support team when analyzing database bugs and issues. Because all access granted by this role is read-only, it does not provide access to customer data.

5.4 Encryption

SAP HANA ensures secure encryption for both data at rest and data in transit. It uses encryption services to protect data on disk, including data volumes, log volumes, and backups. It also provides an internal encryption service for applications with specific encryption needs.

5.4.1 Encryption keys in HANA

In HANA, *root keys* are used for data-at-rest encryption and internal application encryption. To safeguard these keys, HANA uses *instance SSFS (Secure Storage in the File System)* or *LSS (local secure store)*. These mechanisms securely store the root keys, ensuring their protection even if the physical storage is compromised.

HANA uses *system PKI (public-key infrastructure) SSFS* to protect the system-internal root certificates. With this security mechanism, data transmitted within the database is encrypted and remains safe from interception or tampering. In addition, SAP HANA protects the instance SSFS and system PKI SSFS with individual *SSFS master keys*.

This comprehensive approach enhances the security of both data and communication within SAP HANA.

Encryption services and the corresponding keys are illustrated in Figure 5.9.

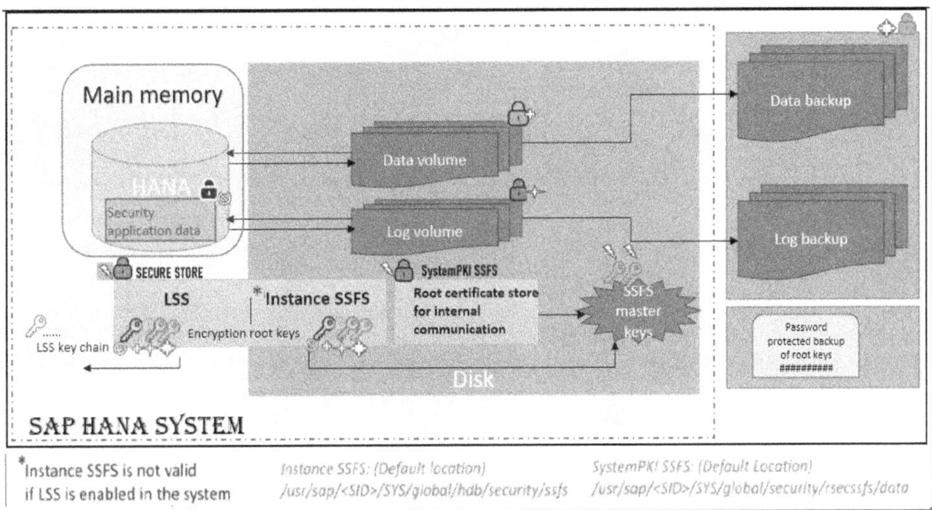

Figure 5.9: Encryption services and keys in HANA DB

The symbols in the image refer to the following:

- encryption key for the database's security application data
- lock and key of the data volume file system
- log volume file system encryption key
- backup file system encryption key
- SSFS master encryption key (protects HANA database secure store and SystemPKI SSFS)

5.4.2 Local secure store (LSS)

As an alternative to instance SSFS, SAP introduced LSS to protect server data from unauthorized access. LSS is a separate, lightweight utility used for securely storing and managing encryption keys, root keys, and other sensitive data and configurations. It functions as a separate database service with its own persistence, managed by its own operating system user *<sid>crypt*. It stores the encryption keys (PSE files) required to access the encrypted LSS database files in the local file system. These database files contain the *payload* (i.e., the SAP HANA encryption root keys) and *configuration* information of the individual tenant databases. These files are stored in the shared file system.

Figure 5.10 shows the LSS file system structure installed on a HANA database. By default, it is installed at */usr/sap/<SID>/lss*.

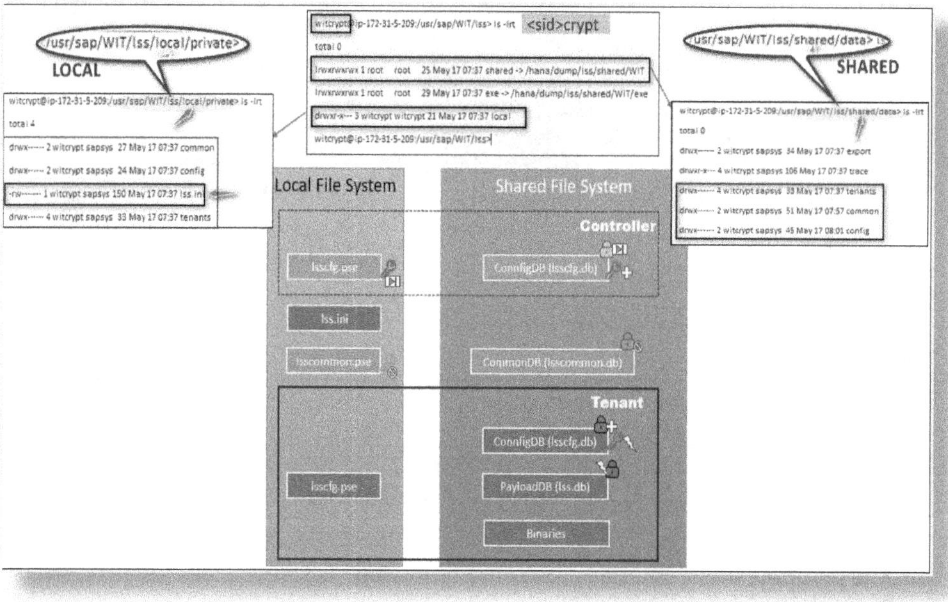

Figure 5.10: LSS file system structure

Within this directory, there are two primary folders, LOCAL and SHARED, along with their sub-folder structures and key files:

- LSS.INI—contains the settings needed to initialize the LSS.
- LSSCFG.PSE—contains the key to open the controller's configuration database file

- LSSCFG.DB (and a copy of this)—stored in the tenant-specific local file system.
- LSSCOMMON.PSE—contains the key to open the CommonDB file (LSSCOMMON.DB).

Tenant-specific LSSCFG.DB contains the key for the tenant-specific payload database file, LSS.DB:

- LSS.DB—contains the HANA database encryption root keys and HANA database encryption configuration of the tenant database or SytemDB.
- LSSCFG.DB—the key to open the PAYLOADDB file is stored in this tenant's configuration database file.

5.4.3 Changing SSFS master key

If you receive a pre-installed HANA database from a hardware vendor or hosting partner, it is strongly recommended to change the master key. These keys are usually located in the folder structure configured against the parameter *global.ini • cryptography • ssfs_key_file_path*. This change must only be made once per HANA database system, and not per tenant.

Figure 5.11 shows the steps to change the SSFS master key.

The steps are as follows (logging into the database server as operating system user *<sid>adm)*:

❶ Stop the HANA database using command `HDB stop`.

❷ Change the master key of instance SSFS by executing the following commands:

```
export RSEC_SSFS_DATAPATH=/usr/sap/<SID>/SYS/global/hdb/security/
ssfs

export RSEC_SSFS_KEYPATH=/usr/sap/<SID>/SYS/global/hdb/security/
ssfs

rsecssfx changekey $(rsecssfx generatekey
-getPlainValueToConsole)
```

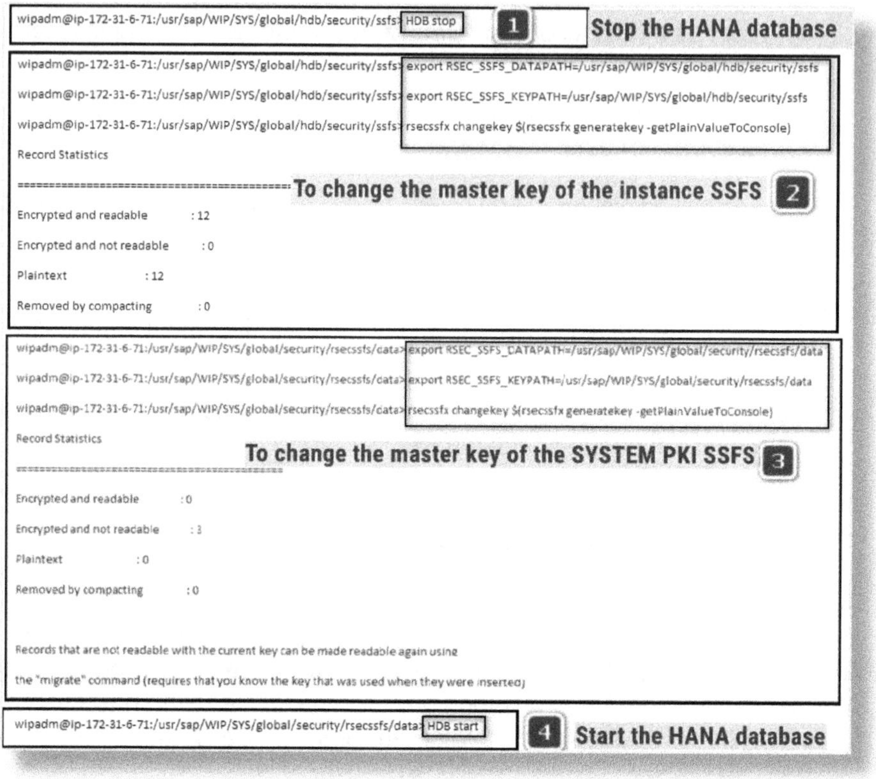

Figure 5.11: Changing the SSFS master key

❸ Change the master key of the system PKI SSFS by executing the following commands:.

```
export RSEC_SSFS_DATAPATH=/usr/sap/<SID>/SYS/global/security/
rsecssfs/data

export RSEC_SSFS_KEYPATH=<path to current key file>

rsecssfx changekey $(rsecssfx generatekey
-getPlainValueToConsole)
```

❹ Start the HANA database using the command `HDB start`.

☛ SSFS with LSS

In the case of SSFS with LSS, instance SSFS master key is not active. Also note that it is not necessary to specifically save the system PKI SSFS key file, because the system generates a new system PKI SSFS automatically if required.

5.4.4 Enabling encryption in HANA

In HANA, encryption can be enabled for data volumes, log volumes, and backup volumes. System privilege *ENCRYPTION ROOT KEY ADMIN* is required to enable or disable encryption. Note that if encryption is activated on an operational database, only the pages currently in use in the data volumes will be encrypted; other pages will be overwritten and encrypted over a period of time. Similarly, only redo log entries created after encryption is enabled will be encrypted. Redo log files created before encryption will not be encrypted. Figure 5.12 shows the commands to enable encryption.

Figure 5.12: Enabling encryption in HANA DB

The commands to enable various types of encryption in the SystemDB are:

```
ALTER SYSTEM PERSISTENCE ENCRYPTION ON;
ALTER SYSTEM LOG ENCRYPTION ON;
```

```
ALTER SYSTEM BACKUP ENCRYPTION ON;
```

The SQL to enable the SystemDB to control the encryption of a tenant database (e.g., <SID>) (executed from the tenant database) is:

```
ALTER SYSTEM ENCRYPTION CONFIGURATION CONTROLLED BY SYSTEM
DATABASE;
```

The SQLs to enable encryption in a tenant database from the SystemDB are:

```
ALTER DATABASE <SID> PERSISTENCE ENCRYPTION ON;
ALTER DATABASE <SID> LOG ENCRYPTION ON;
```

It is also possible to disable encryption. The command to disable data volume encryption is:

```
ALTER SYSTEM PERSISTENCE ENCRYPTION OFF;
```

The command to disable redo log encryption is:

```
ALTER SYSTEM LOG ENCRYPTION OFF;
```

The command to disable backup encryption is:

```
ALTER SYSTEM BACKUP ENCRYPTION OFF;
```

The encryption status of the data, log volume, and backup can be checked using the system view M_ENCRYPTION_OVERVIEW, as shown in Figure 5.13.

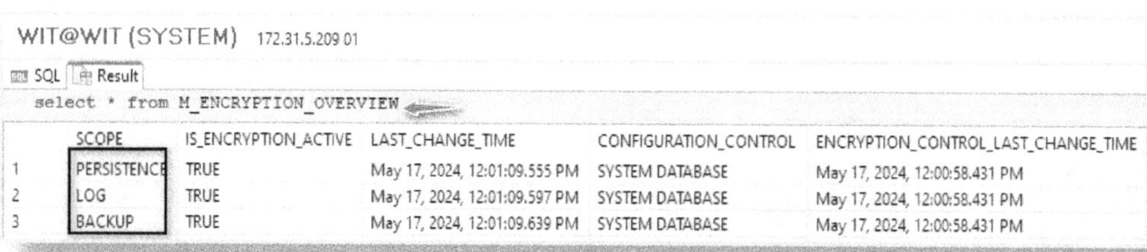

WIT@WIT (SYSTEM) 172.31.5.209 01

SQL | Result

select * from M_ENCRYPTION_OVERVIEW

	SCOPE	IS_ENCRYPTION_ACTIVE	LAST_CHANGE_TIME	CONFIGURATION_CONTROL	ENCRYPTION_CONTROL_LAST_CHANGE_TIME
1	PERSISTENCE	TRUE	May 17, 2024, 12:01:09.555 PM	SYSTEM DATABASE	May 17, 2024, 12:00:58.431 PM
2	LOG	TRUE	May 17, 2024, 12:01:09.597 PM	SYSTEM DATABASE	May 17, 2024, 12:00:58.431 PM
3	BACKUP	TRUE	May 17, 2024, 12:01:09.639 PM	SYSTEM DATABASE	May 17, 2024, 12:00:58.431 PM

Figure 5.13: Encryption status

5.5 Handling encrypted backup and restore

Before restoring an encrypted backup to the target database, the backup key from the source must be exported and then imported into the target tenant database. This ensures a smooth decryption of the source backup file used for restoring in the target database.

Figure 5.14 shows an example of exporting and importing backup encryption keys from the source tenant database to the target tenant database before triggering the database restore from the source (SID *WIB* in the example) to the target (SID *WIT*).

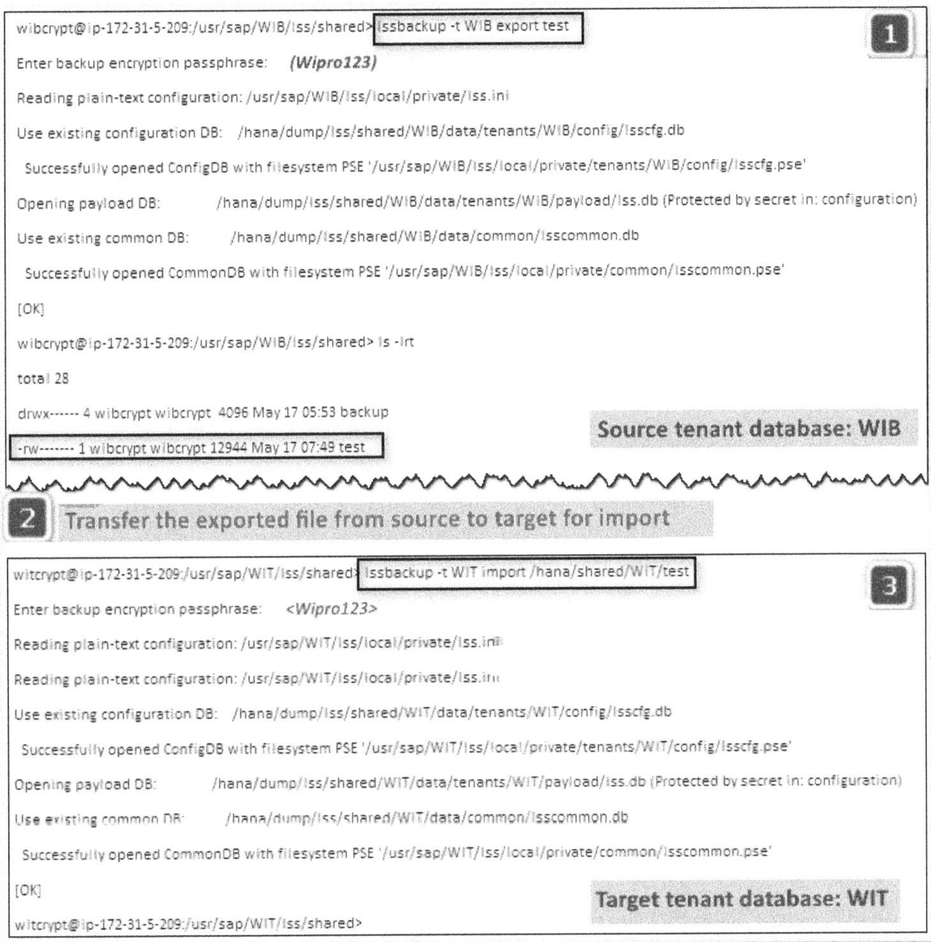

Figure 5.14: Exporting and importing backup key for restore

First, export the key from the source tenant database. To do this, log in to the source database server as *<source_sid>crypt*. Go to */usr/sap/<source_tenant_SID>/lss/shared* and execute the following command ❶:

```
lssbackup -t <source_tenant_SID> export <name_of_key_export>
```

Next, transfer the exported key file from the source to the target tenant for import ❷.

Import the previously exported key from the source to the target before triggering the restore in the target. To do this, log in to the target database server as *<target_sid>crypt*. Navigate to */usr/sap/<target_tenant_SID>/lss/shared* and execute the following command ❸:

```
lssbackup -t <target_tenant_SID> import <location_of_transferred_
exported_key>/<name_of_key_export>
```

If a restore is triggered before importing the backup encryption key from the source to the target, the restore will fail with the error message shown in Figure 5.15.

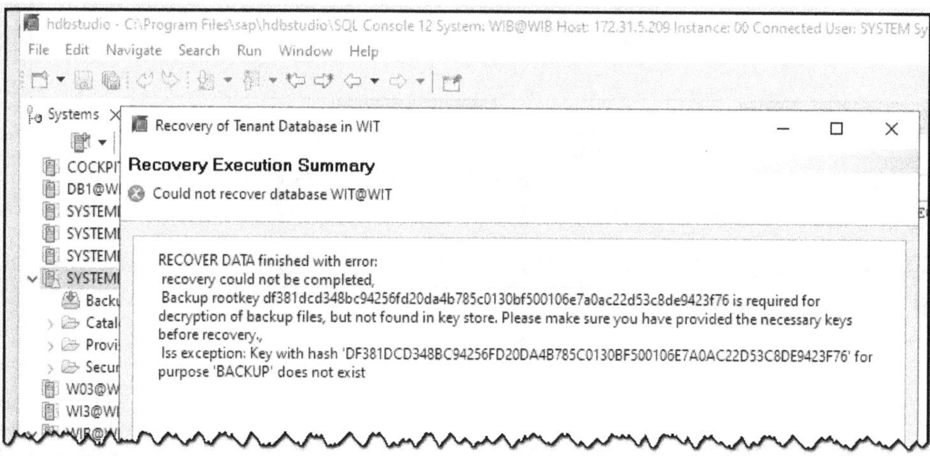

Figure 5.15: Error—missing source backup key in target tenant database during recovery

5.6 Auditing

Auditing is essential for all databases hosting critical production applications. Changes to the database must be closely monitored and recorded, for all sensitive data, to ensure compliance. HANA provides database administrators with auditing capabilities to monitor and log specific database actions, including details of who performed them, on which object, and when. Audit configurations can be managed either through HANA Studio or HANA Cockpit, as shown in Figure 5.16.

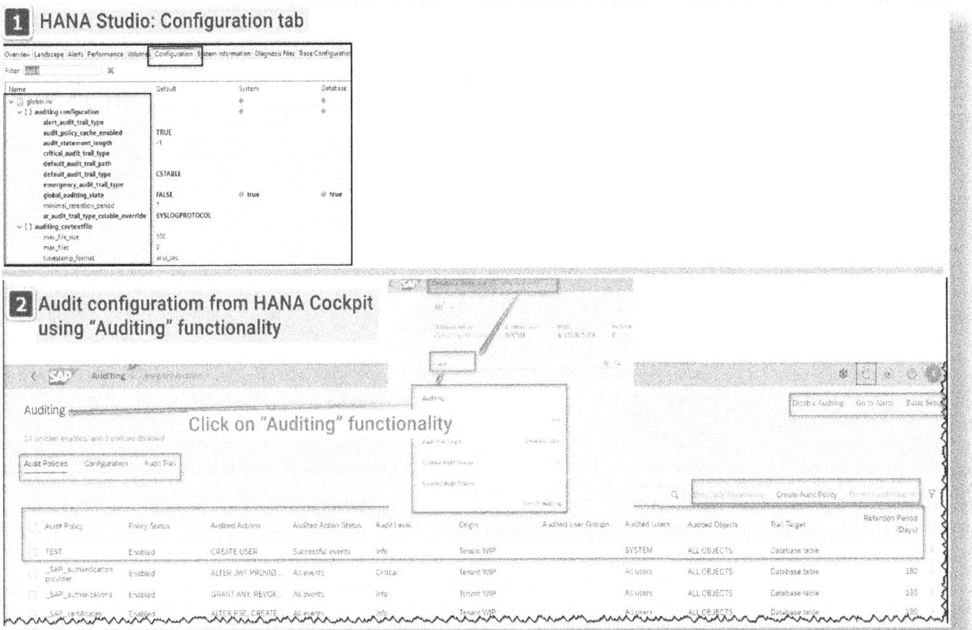

Figure 5.16: Auditing functionality—HANA cockpit and audit configuration

Note that events occurring outside the database engine cannot be audited; for example, database upgrades, HANA DB configuration changes using OS commands, and similar actions.

An *audit policy* within the HANA database specifies which database actions should be audited and the conditions under which auditing is triggered and recorded. When a specified action which is to be audited occurs in the database, it triggers the respective audit policy, and an audit event is recorded in the *audit trail*. These audit trails can be stored in an internal database table (see Figure 5.17), in a system log at the OS level, or as a CSV text file.

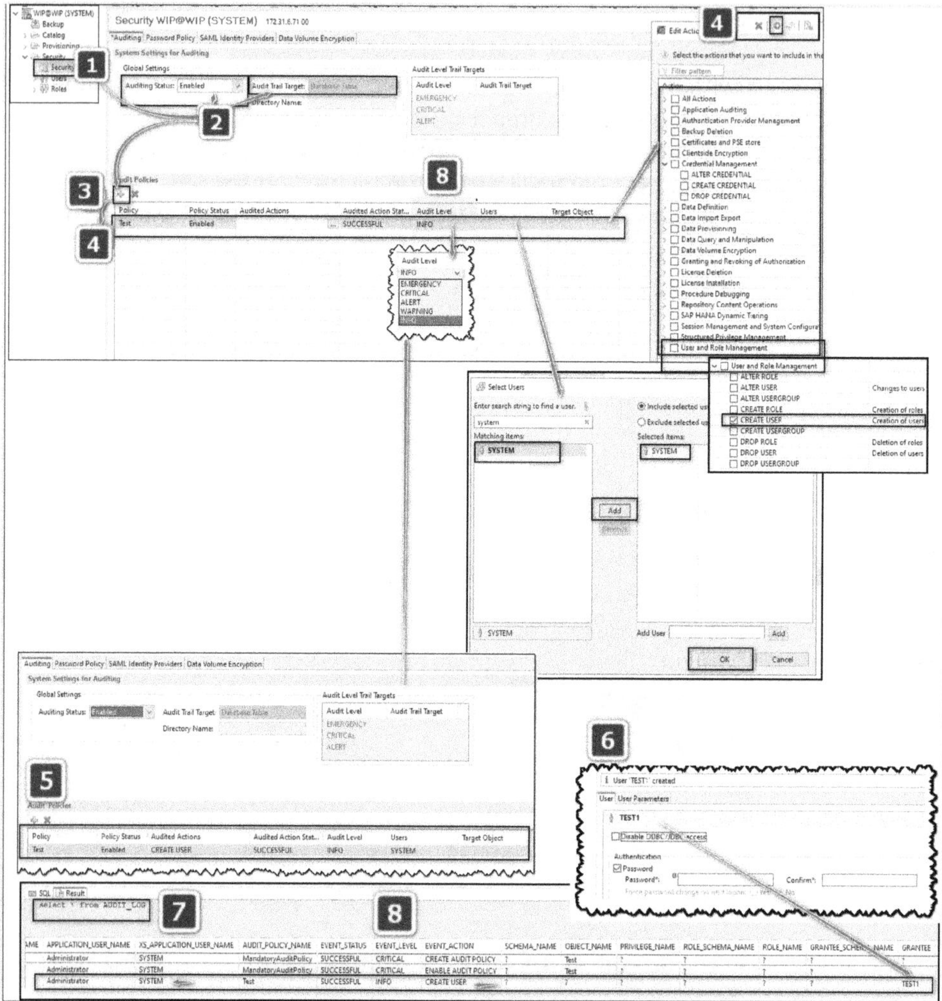

Figure 5.17: HANA audit log using HANA Studio

The numbers in the image refer to the following:

➊–➋ Enable the audit for HANA database by choosing option ENABLED in the AUDITING STATUS dropdown list. Set DATABASE TABLE as the AUDIT TRAIL TARGET.

➌, ➍,and ➎ Create an audit policy to audit all user creation actions by user *SYSTEM*.

❻ Create a test user (TEST1) by logging in as database user *SYSTEM*.

❼ Browse the audit log table, which will have captured the previous user-creation activity, by executing SQL command:

```
SELECT * FROM AUDIT_LOG;
```

❽ Shows the available audit levels in decreasing order of importance, such as EMERGENCY, CRITICAL, ALERT, WARNING, and INFO.

5.7 Authentication in HANA database

The SAP HANA database offers various authentication mechanisms to ensure secure access to the database. Figure 5.18 shows the available authentication mechanisms using HANA Studio.

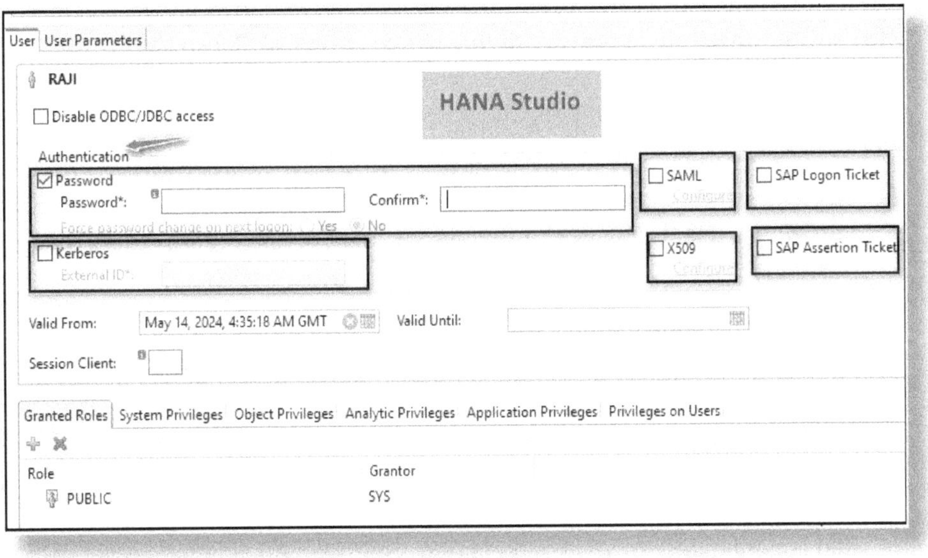

Figure 5.18: HANA database user authentication in HANA Studio

Figure 5.19 shows the available authentication mechanisms using HANA Cockpit.

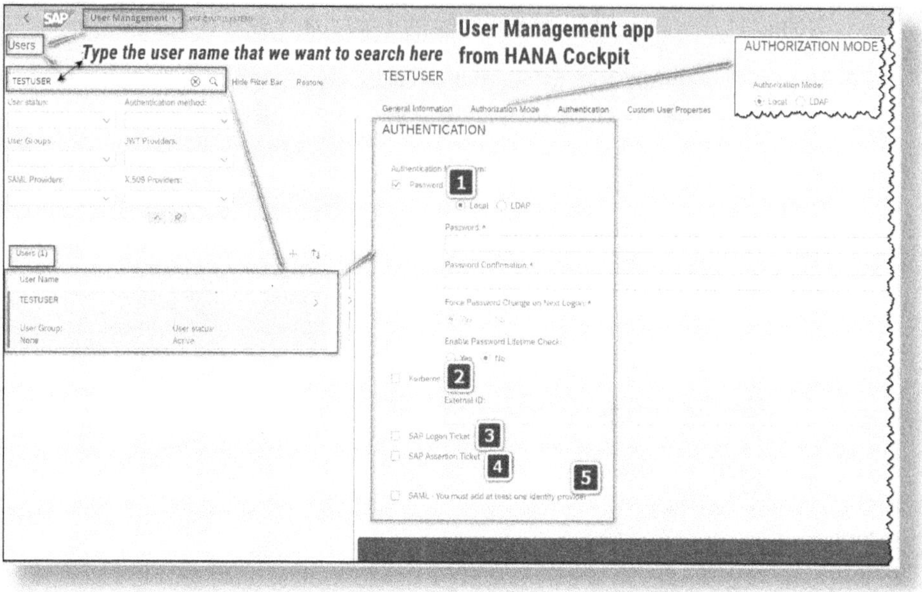

Figure 5.19: HANA database user authentication in HANA Cockpit

The authentication mechanisms shown in Figure 5.18 and Figure 5.19 are as follows:

❶ PASSWORD /database username—the most basic form of authentication where users connect to the HANA database using a predefined username and password.

❷ KERBEROS—a network authentication protocol designed to provide strong authentication for client-server applications. It requires users in all databases to be mapped to users in the Key Distribution Center (KDC).

❸-❹ SAP LOGONTICKET and SAP ASSERTION TICKET—users are authenticated by SAP logon or assertion tickets issued through the SAP system that is configured to create tickets (e.g., SAP Web Application Server or Portal).

❺ SAML (Security Assertion Markup language)—a standard for exchanging authentication and authorization data between parties. It supports *single sign-on (SSO)* by using tokens that assert the user's identity. Different trust stores with certificates can be configured for each database to validate the SAML tokens. Configuration for SAML can be set up per database for JDBC/ODBC client access.

There is also X509 (see Figure 5.18), whereby users are authenticated by client certificates that are signed by a trusted Certification Authority (CA) for HTTP/HTTPS or JDBC/ODBC client access.

5.8 Monitoring security settings

Certain HANA database settings are crucial for safeguarding against vulnerabilities. SAP provides standard recommendations for many of these configurations through the SECURITY CHECKLIST app in HANA Cockpit (see Figure 5.20). Some of these settings can also be addressed and remedied directly from within this HANA Cockpit application.

Figure 5.20: HANA Cockpit—"Security Checklist" app

6 Backup, restore and refresh

This chapter discusses HANA database backup and restore processes, along with methods for refreshing the HANA database. Backup and restore functionalities safeguard against data loss, ensure business continuity, uphold legal compliance, maintain data integrity, and support disaster recovery. Database refresh functionality involves utilizing backup to clone a database for testing and simulations.

6.1 Basics of HANA backup

In a HANA database, the data volume maintains a consistent state through its last savepoint. During a restart (see Figure 1.10), consistent data from the data volume is read, followed by the replay of redo log segments. This brings the database to its last consistent state during start-up. Figure 6.1 illustrates the relationship between the data and log volumes and their corresponding data and log backups.

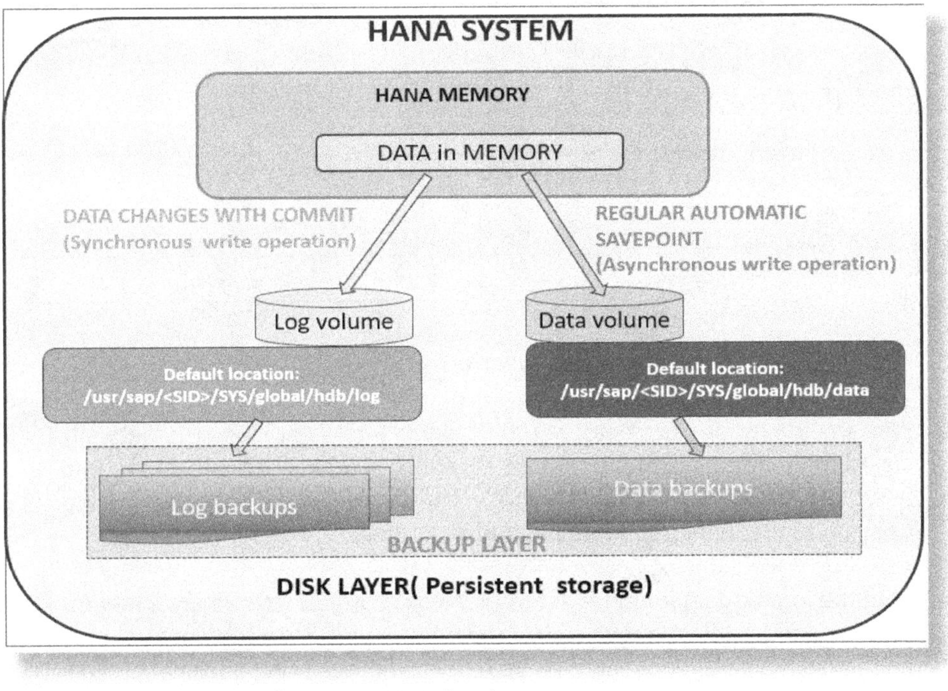

Figure 6.1: Backup layer in HANA database

If the data or log volume becomes inaccessible or corrupt, the database cannot start and will become inconsistent. In such scenarios, it must be restored to the last point-in-time (PIT) using data and log backups. These backups are therefore essential because they serve as a reliable fallback mechanism.

6.1.1 Log segments and log backups

Log segments are committed changes in HANA memory and are persisted to log volumes before the corresponding changes reach the data volumes through a savepoint. As soon as a savepoint is reached, data changes from memory are flushed to the data volume, and the log segments containing these committed changes are no longer needed and can be overwritten. This behavior is controlled by the *log_mode* and *enable_auto_log_backup* parameters. When LOG_MODE is set to NORMAL and ENABLE_AUTO_LOG_BACKUP is set to YES (see Figure 6.2 and Figure 6.5), log segments are not overwritten until they have been backed up to the log-backup file system.

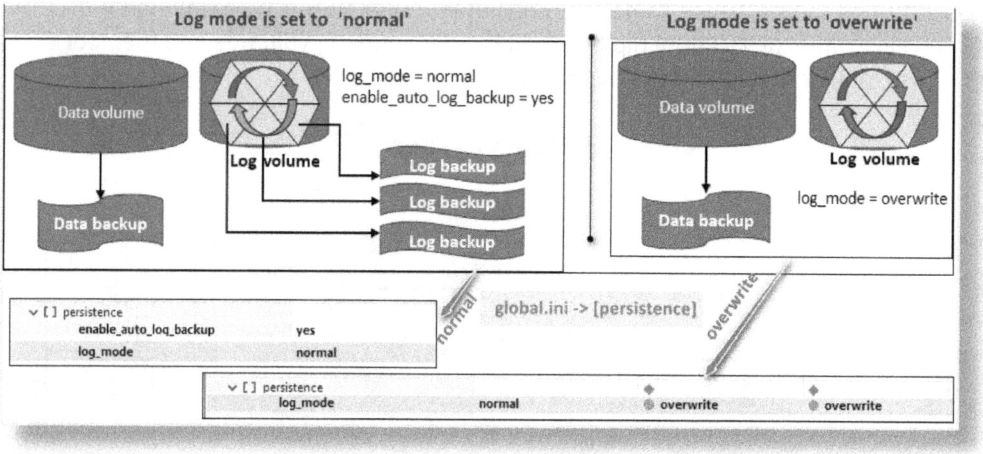

Figure 6.2: Log mode: normal versus overwrite

With the log mode parameter set to NORMAL, the log area is automatically saved to the log backup file system at regular intervals. This is configured using parameter *log_backup_timeout_s*. However, this recording of the log backup is independent of data backup execution.

With the log mode parameter set to OVERWRITE, log segments are overwritten as soon as the changes from memory are written to the data volume, and these log segments can then be reused without being backed up.

Figure 6.3 illustrates various log segment states, from recording a data commit in the *Writing* state, to transitioning to the *Free* state, thereby making the log segment available for use in the next database write and commit operation.

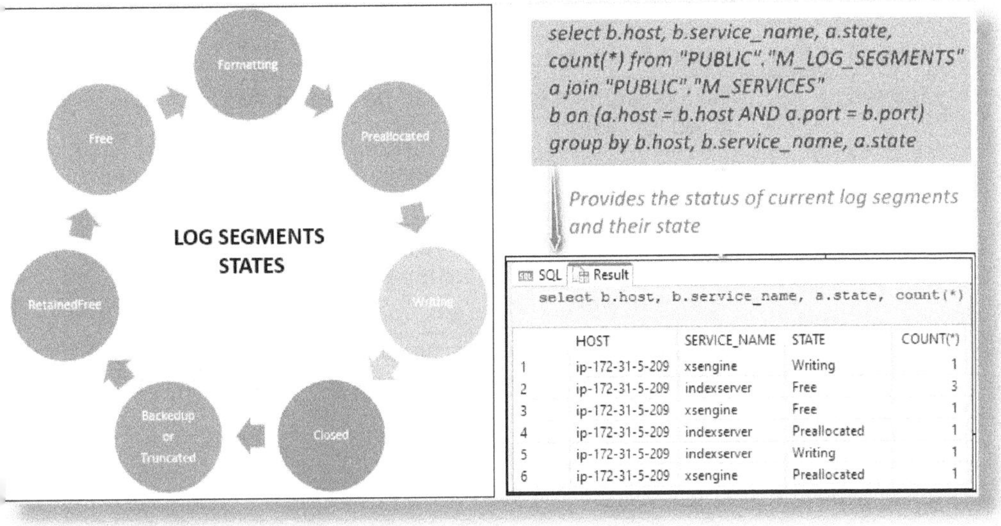

Figure 6.3: Log segments states

The SQL query used to identify the number of current log segments and their state, per HANA database service, is:

```
select b.host, b.service_name, a.state, count(*) from
"PUBLIC"."M_LOG_SEGMENTS" a join "PUBLIC"."M_SERVICES" b on
(a.host = b.host AND a.port = b.port) group by b.host, b.service_
name, a.state;
```

! Log segment state—BackedUp or Truncated

BackedUp and *Truncated* states are invalid when the *log_mode* parameter is set to *overwrite* because this mode does not back up the log segment. Instead, these log segments are directly overwritten and are made available for re-use by the HANA database.

Table 6.1 outlines the list of possible HANA database log segment states.

State	Description
Formatting	The log segment is being formatted and not yet used.
Preallocated	The log segment has been preallocated, but never used.
Writing	Currently writing to this segment.
Closed	The log segment is closed, not backed up, and is still required for restart.
Truncated	Truncated, but not yet backed up. Backup will change the segment state to BackedUp.
BackedUp	Segment is already backed up, but a savepoint has not yet been written. Therefore it needs to be kept for instance recovery.
RetainedFree	The log segment has been backed up and is not required for restart, but is required to resync the system replication sites.
Free	Segment is free for reuse.

Table 6.1: Log segment states

! Log segment—truncated state

If a log segment is in *Truncated* state, it means that the segment is awaiting backup, even though the respective changes have already been transferred from memory to the data volume through a savepoint. The presence of many log segments in this state might indicate a slow-running log backup or that the log backup file system is full, which prevents successful execution of further log backups. When the log backup file system is full, it will lead to a database freeze when the *log_mode* is set to *normal*.

In addition to regular interval-based log backups, log backups are also auto-triggered when a log segment reaches its maximum size. The size of a log segment is controlled by the parameter *log_segment_size_mb* in the *persistence* section of global.ini.

6.1.2 Data volume and data backup types

Data volume in the HANA database is protected through a data backup. This backup saves the payload in the data area of the HANA database. HANA supports different types of data backups, as illustrated in Figure 6.4.

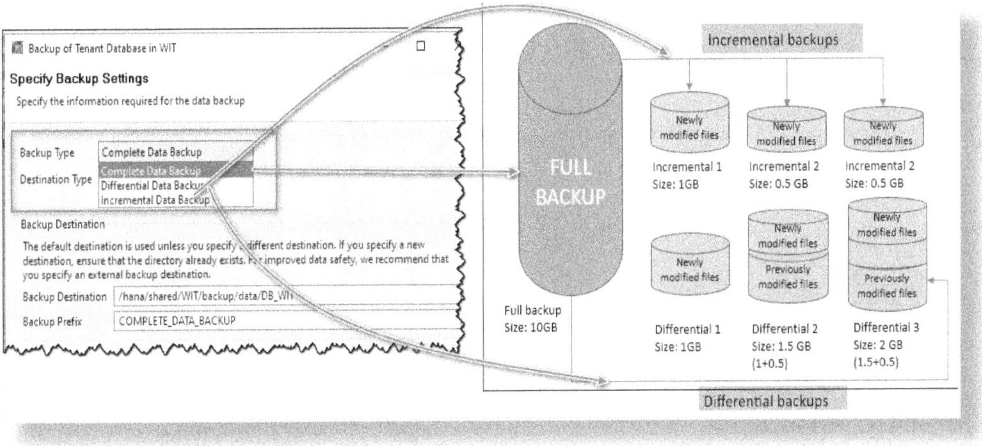

Figure 6.4: HANA backup types

The data backup types are as follows:

- COMPLETE DATA BACKUP—includes all the data payload required to recover the database.
- DIFFERENTIAL DATA BACKUP—stores all the data changes made since the last full data backup.
- INCREMENTAL DATA BACKUP—the data changes made since the last full data backup or the last delta backup (incremental or differential).

6.1.3 Backup configuration

The first step after installing the HANA database is to configure the backup settings. This can be done using either HANA Studio or HANA Cockpit. In HANA Studio, the backup configuration can be done either from the backup console or from the CONFIGURATION tab in HANA Studio, as shown in Figure 6.5.

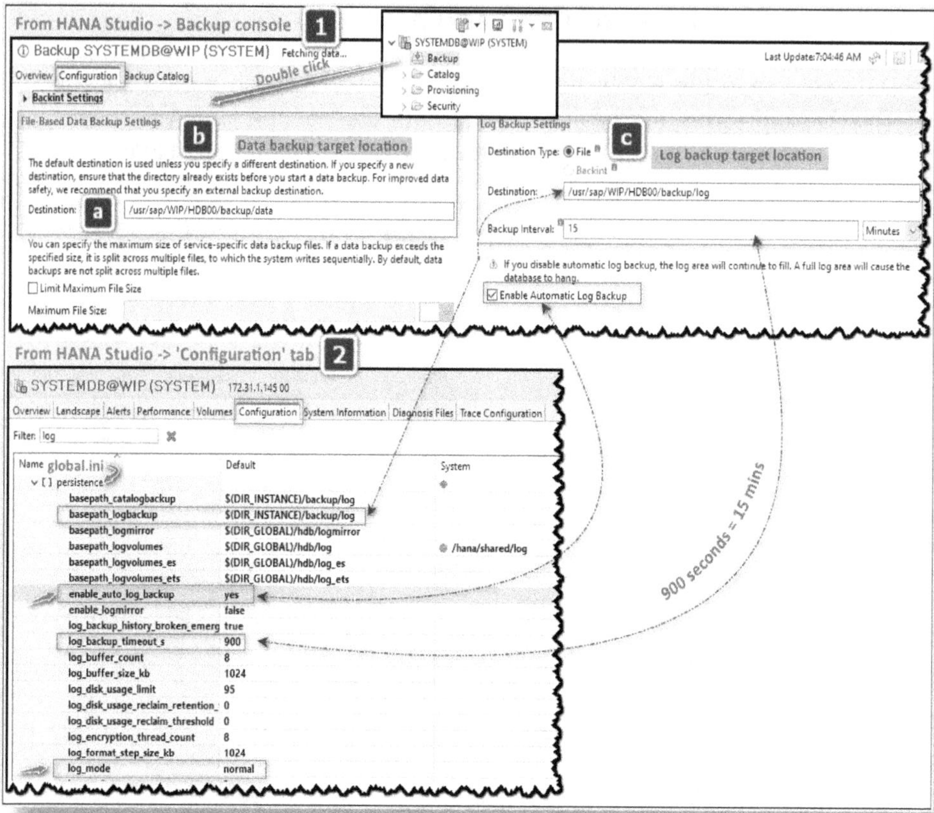

Figure 6.5: Ways to configure HANA backup

Area ❶ in the image shows backup configuration in the backup console. Area ❷ shows backup via the CONFIGURATION tab.

☛ Log backup configuration—recommendation

For log backups in a production environment, it is recommended to set LOG_MODE to NORMAL and ENABLE_AUTO_LOG_BACKUP to YES. From the backup console, we can also control the frequency of log backups using the parameter LOG_BACKUP_TIMEOUT_S, as shown in Figure 6.5.

HANA backups can be stored at:

- file system level, or
- a third party location using the third-party backup tool via the database backup interface *backint*.

To configure file system backups, the DESTINATION [a] parameter under FILE-BASED DATA BACKUP SETTINGS [b] for data backups, and LOG BACKUP SETTINGS [c] for log backups, must be configured as shown in Figure 6.5 and Figure 6.6. Figure 6.5 also shows the equivalent parameter values that can be configured to reflect their respective details in the backup console.

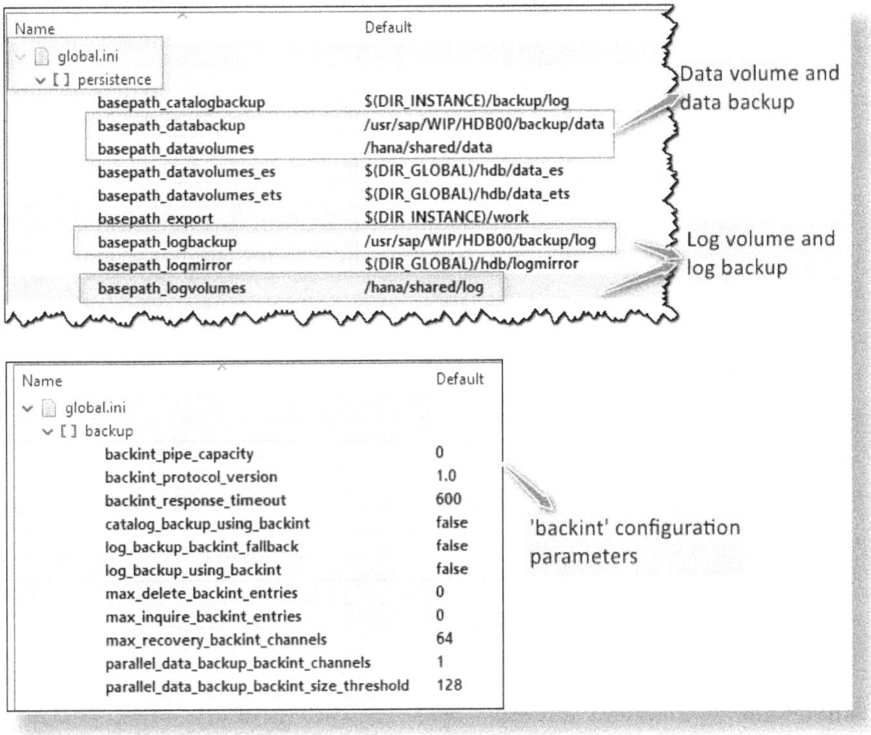

Figure 6.6: HANA database backup configuration

Backup configuration based on *backint* is specific to the third-party backup tool being used. However, some of its properties can be controlled from HANA using backint based parameters, as shown in Figure 6.6.

! HANA backint features

This book does not cover HANA database backup using third-party tools with the backint interface because each third-party backup provider has their own methods of integration with the HANA database. Refer to the provider's documentation for the relevant configuration instructions.

6.2 Executing a HANA database backup

HANA database backups can be executed via:

- HANA Cockpit
- HANA native SQL statements
- HANA Studio

In HANA Cockpit , execute the database backup by going to BACKUP CATALOG and CREATE BACKUP, as shown in Figure 6.7.

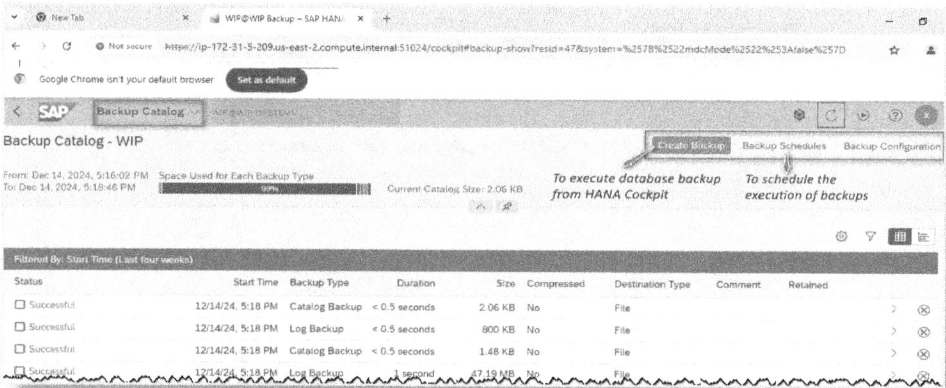

Figure 6.7: Executing backup via HANA Cockpit

Executing database backups via HANA native SQL statements is shown in Figure 6.8.

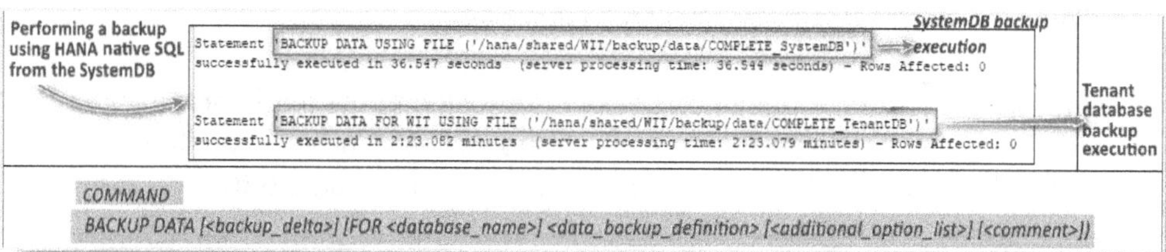

Figure 6.8: Executing backup using SQL command

A database backup in HANA Studio is shown in Figure 6.9.

The numbers in the image show the following steps:

❶ Log in to the SystemDB from HANA Studio, right-click on the system, and select BACKUP AND RECOVERY.

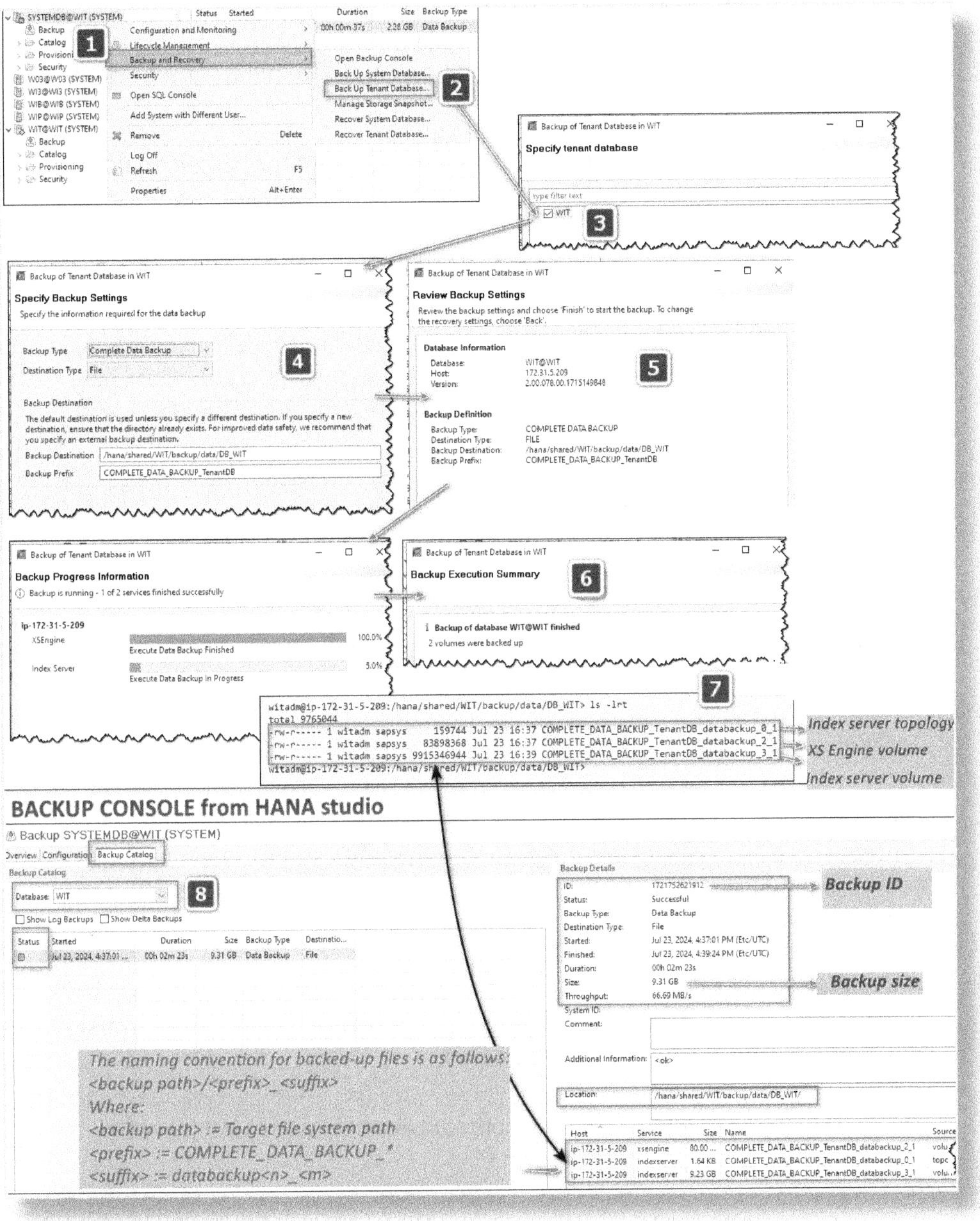

Figure 6.9: Executing Tenant DB backup from HANA Studio

❷ Select the tenant for which the backup must be triggered using the BACK UP TENANT DATABASE option.

❸ Choose the required tenant database.

❹ Validate the BACKUP PREFIX name and the BACKUP DESTINATION.

❺ Review the backup settings and click on FINISH to initiate the backup execution.

❻ Backup progress is shown on-screen, and a summary is provided upon completion.

❼ After the backup has completed successfully, verify the target backup dump at file system level.

❽ Recheck the backup details in the backup console. You will also be able to view the unique backup ID, backup SIZE, THROUGHPUT, LOCATION, service mapping for the backed-up files, backup execution DURATION, and more.

The SQL command to execute backup for the SystemDB is:

```
BACKUP DATA USING FILE ('<backup path>/<prefix>_<suffix>');
```

The SQL command to execute a tenant database backup is:

```
BACKUP DATA FOR <tenant_SID> USING FILE ('<backup
path>/<prefix>_<suffix>');
```

The default value for <prefix> is COMPLETE_DATA_BACKUP and for <suffix> it is databackup_<n>_<m> where *n* refers to volume ID and *m* refers to partition ID. The suffix is automatically added by the HANA database with the backup name.

The primary prerequisite before executing a HANA database backup is that all its services must be up and running. In other words, the database must be online throughout the backup operation.

The system privileges required to execute a HANA database backup are

- *BACKUP ADMIN*
- *BACKUP OPERATOR*
- *DATABASE ADMIN*

The *CATALOG READ* privilege is needed to perform backups using HANA Studio.

Note that HANA database backups can also be encrypted.

6.2.1 HANA database backup dump

A sample execution of a HANA backup and its output from HANA Studio is shown in Figure 6.10.

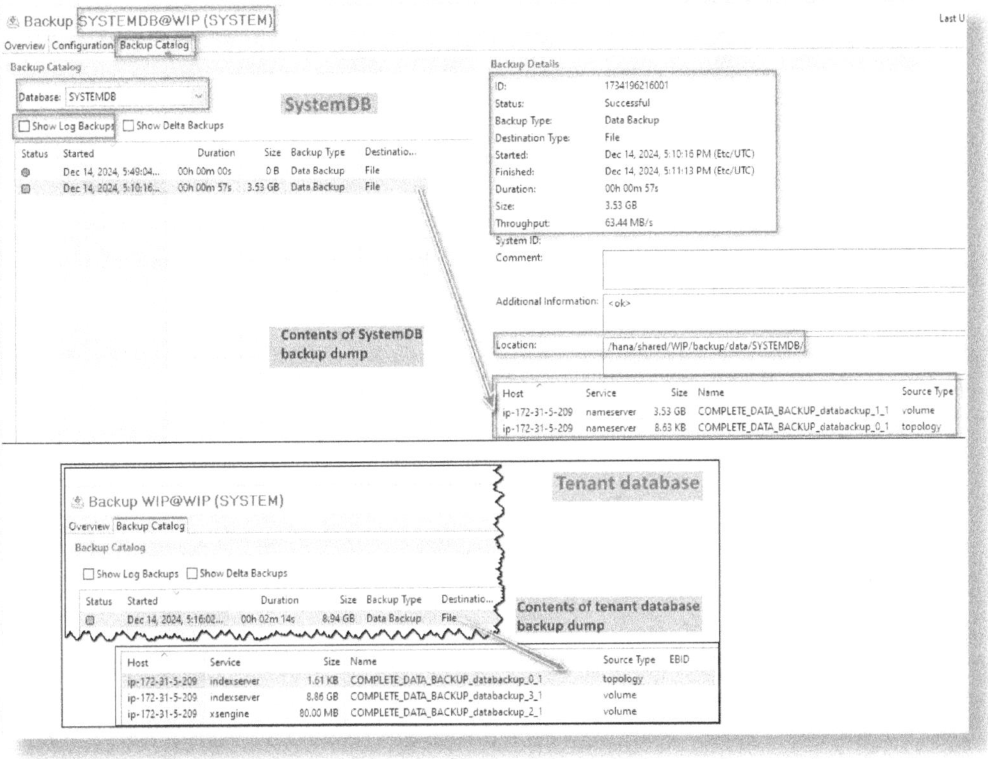

Figure 6.10: Backup dump of a SystemDB

From these examples, we can see that every HANA database service that persists data (as listed in Table 1.3), has its own backup file. For example, the SystemDB produces two backup files—one for system topology information, and the other for nameserver service. Likewise, the tenant database produces three backup files—one for topology information and other two for service-specific files relating to index server and xsengine.

It is important to note that, by default, only the data area is included in the HANA database backup, while the database configuration (*.ini) files are not backed up. This behavior can be altered by setting the *include_configuration_backup* parameter to *true* in the global.ini.

! Partial restore of HANA database

Individual database objects or services cannot be restored from a HANA database backup. The database backup enables restoration of the entire data payload only.

6.2.2 Backup catalog

HANA maintains a history of all its backups through the HANA *backup catalog*. This catalog is useful for assessing a system's recoverability to a specific PIT by checking the availability of the respective data and log-backup files for restore.

With the system privilege *CATALOG READ*, system view M_BACKUP_CATALOG and M_BACKUP_CATALOG_FILES can be queried to understand more details about the backed-up files and backup catalogs (see Figure 6.11).

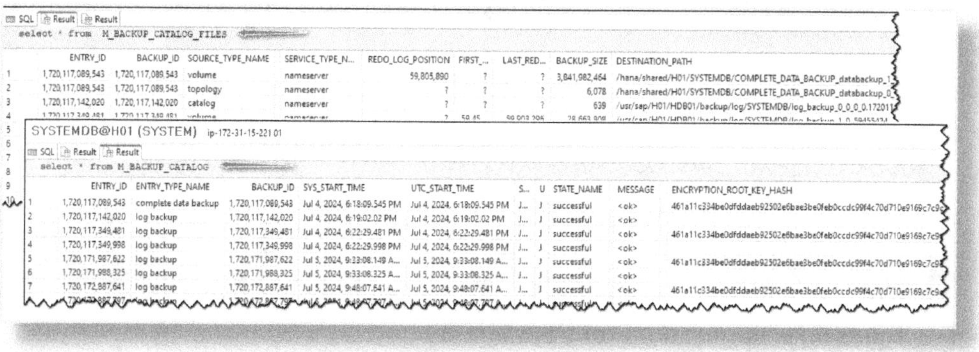

Figure 6.11: Understanding the backed-up files

It is worth noting that the backup catalog is saved along with the log backups, with proper versioning.

6.2.3 System view for HANA database backup

HANA provides several system views that offer comprehensive information about HANA database backups. These include *M_BACKUP_CONFIGURATION, M_BACKUP_HISTORY_BROKEN, M_BACKUP_PROGRESS*, and *M_BACKUP_SIZE_ESTIMATIONS*. In addition, the system view *M_CONVERTER_*

STATISTICS can be used to estimate the size of the next complete backup using the SQL query:

```
SELECT SUM(allocated_page_size) / 1024 / 1024 / 1024 AS size_gb
FROM M_CONVERTER_STATISTICS;
```

This is shown in Figure 6.12.

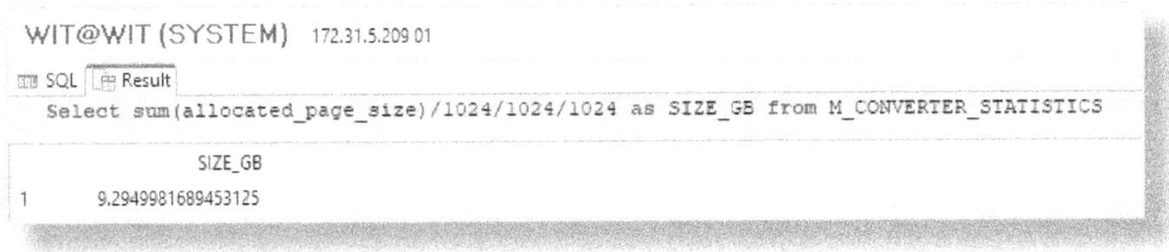

Figure 6.12: Estimate the backup size

6.2.4 Cancelling a HANA backup

A running HANA database backup can be canceled using the following SQL:

```
BACKUP CANCEL <backup_ID>;
```

The backup ID can be found in the backup console or backup catalog. It is important to note that only one data backup can run at a time. Any attempt to initiate another data backup simultaneously will fail unless the previous backup is completed or cancelled. However, the execution of a data backup is independent of a running log backup.

6.3 Restoring a HANA database

Figure 6.13 illustrates a scenario where two successful data backups were triggered at B0 and B1, alongside a regular automatic log backup running from L1 to L9.

If a database inconsistency occurs after L9, the database can be restored to the last consistent state using:

- B0 with all log backups from L1 to L9, or
- B1 with log backups from L7 to L9.

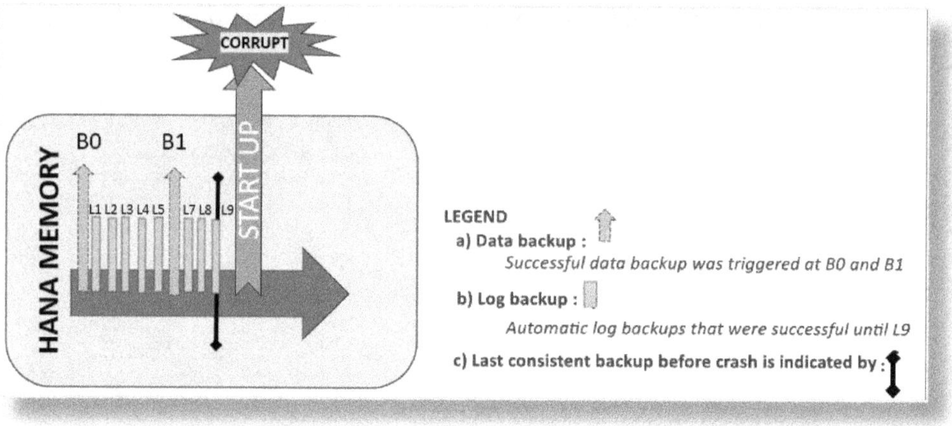

Figure 6.13: HANA database restore

The latter option is preferred because fewer log backups have to be replayed on top of the full data backup B1 during the database restore. Therefore, a well-designed backup strategy is essential for faster recovery with minimal data loss. This includes determining the frequency of full backups, along with incremental or differential backups, and setting appropriate intervals between consecutive log backups. Shorter intervals between log backups help minimize potential data loss. This interval value can be configured using the parameter LOG_BACKUP_TIMEOUT_S, as shown in Figure 6.5.

6.4 Refreshing a HANA database

A HANA database backup also facilitates cloning of one tenant database with another. The newly created or refreshed tenant database will inherit data from its source tenant database (mostly the production database) and can be used for testing purposes.

There are several methods for performing a HANA tenant database refresh:

1. Native HANA database backup and restore
2. Storage snapshot
3. HANA System Replication (HSR)
4. Tenant copy function

6.4.1 Method 1—Native HANA database backup and restore

Let's look at how to perform a native tenant database restore from a source to a target database.

Prerequisites

Before copying/refreshing one HANA tenant database to another, certain prerequisites must be met between the source and target database:

1. The target database version must be equal to or higher than that of the source database.
2. The number and the type of services in the source and target database must be the same.
3. The data volume in the target must be large enough to accommodate the size of the source database.
4. The password for the *SYSTEM* user of the source tenant must be available for login to the target after the refresh.
5. The credentials of the *<sid>adm* operating system user on the target database server are required for troubleshooting during restore.
6. The timestamp, up to which the target database must be restored from the source database, must be finalized.
7. The necessary source database backups required for recovery must be accessible from the target HANA database operating system.
8. As part of a HANA database backup, the source database's license is included and is reinstalled automatically in the target database during a restore. However, since the source and target databases are different, the source HANA license will not be valid for the target database. As a result, after the restore, the target HANA database will be in locked state, awaiting a valid target database license. To address this, the HANA database restore process provides a prompt to supply the target database license well in advance—while initiating a restore. This new target database license is applied automatically after the successful completion of the database restore. The target HANA database license should be readily available to be supplied during the restore.
9. Ensure that the backup is consistent before triggering a restore using the tool *hdbbackupcheck*. For further details, refer to SAP Note 1869119—"Checking backups with 'hdbbackupcheck'".

Executing a refresh

This section covers a HANA database tenant refresh from a source tenant database WIP to a target tenant database H01. Further details of this refresh is provided in Table 6.2.

Description	Source DB	Target DB
Tenant database SID	WIP	H01
Instance number	00	01
Number of services	preprocessor – 1 indexserver – 2 scriptserver – 1 nameserver – 1 compileserver – 1 webdispatcher – 1 xsengine – 1	preprocessor – 1 indexserver – 1 scriptserver – 0 nameserver – 1 compileserver – 1 webdispatcher – 1 xsengine – 1
PIT for restore	2024-07-24 GMT 07 :11 :00	
Backup location in target (data and log backup)	/hana/shared/H01/backup	

Table 6.2: Source and target tenant database for restore—example

Aligning the number of services

Before triggering a restore, the number and type of services in the source database must be the same as the target database. According to the information provided in Table 6.2, the target tenant database does not have the same number of index servers or script servers as the source database. This is also shown in Figure 6.14.

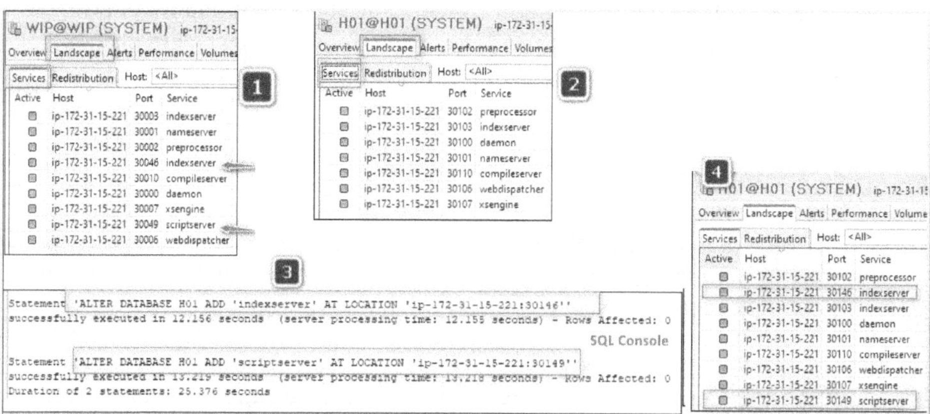

Figure 6.14: Matching HANA services target tenant database

The image shows these differences and also the procedure to match the number of services between the source and tenant databases:

❶ The number of services in the source tenant database.

❷ The number of services in the target tenant database.

❸ The SQL statements used to add an additional pseudo index sever and a new script server to the target tenant database:

```
ALTER DATABASE <SID> ADD 'indexserver' AT LOCATION
'<host>:<port>';
ALTER DATABASE <SID> ADD 'scriptserver' AT LOCATION
'<host>:<port>';
```

❹ Target tenant database after adding the missing services.

The SQL command for adding an additional service to a HANA database is:

```
ALTER DATABASE <SID> ADD '<service_name>' AT LOCATION
'<host>:<port>';
```

After matching the number of services in the source and target tenant databases, we can proceed with the next steps of the restore process.

Files required for restore

For any restore activity, you need to determine the PIT up to which the target database must be restored from the source database. Once this PIT has been finalized, the files required for the restore can be identified in the source using HDBBACKUPDIAG, as shown in Figure 6.15. These backup files must be made accessible on the target server, either by manually copying them from the source or by placing them on a shared file system.

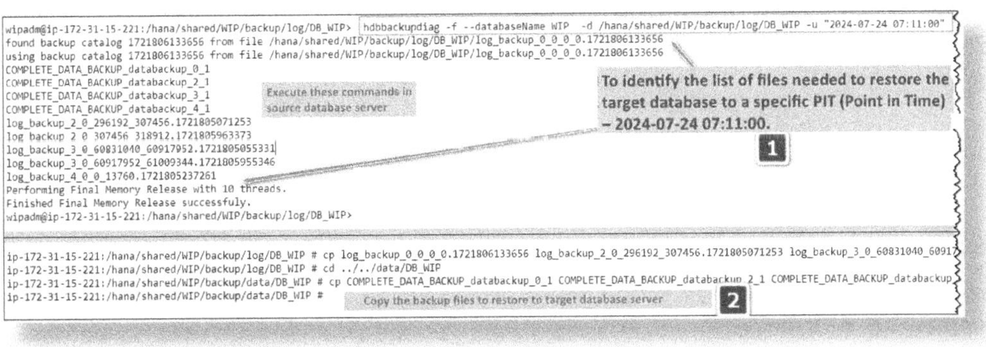

Figure 6.15: Database backup files required from the source

The HDBBACKUPDIAG command is:

```
hdbbackupdiag -f --databaseName <source_SID> -d <source_log_
backup_location> -u "<point-in-time>"
```

Source backup encryption key

If the source database uses LSS for backup encryption, the source backup key must be exported from the source database and imported into the target database before triggering the restore. This step was covered in Section 5.5.

Triggering the restore

The restore activity for a target tenant database can be executed via HANA Cockpit, HANA Studio, or at OS level. Figure 6.16, Figure 6.17 and Figure 6.18 show the steps involved in recovering a tenant database (H01) from the source database (WIP).

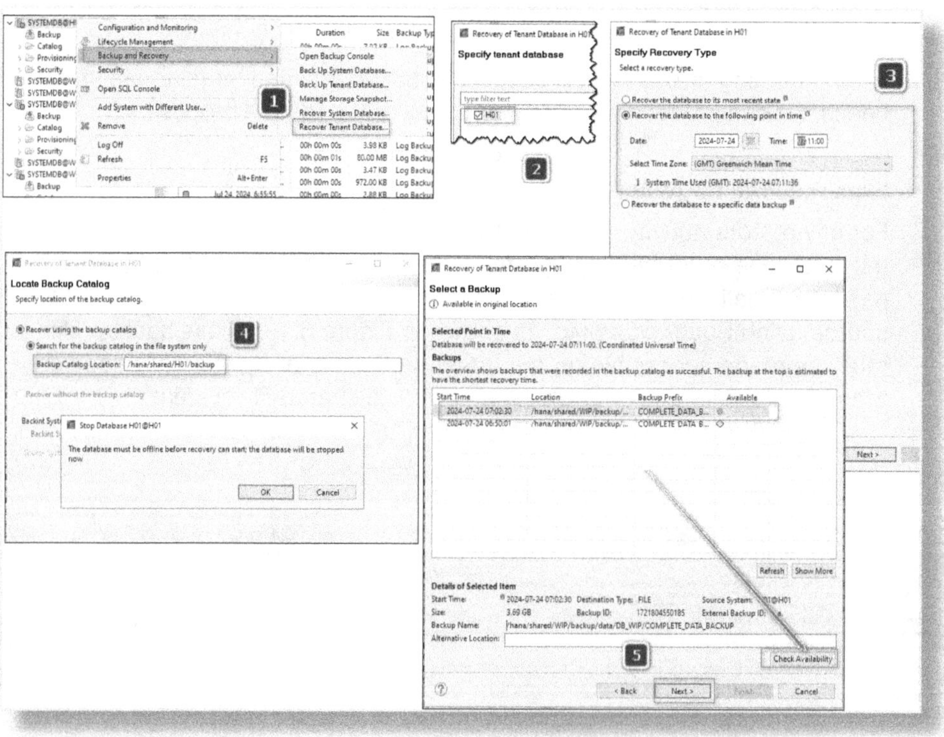

Figure 6.16: HANA database restore from WIP to H01 (1/3)

The numbers in Figure 6.16 refer to the following steps:

❶ Trigger the restore by right clicking on the source database SystemDB. Choose BACKUP AND RECOVERY • RECOVER TENANT DATABASE.

❷ Choose the tenant database to be restored.

❸ Adjust the PIT (point in time) to the required TIME for the restore process.

❹ Specify the location on the target server that contains the source database backup.

❺ Select the appropriate backup to be used for the restore and click on CHECK AVAILABILITY.

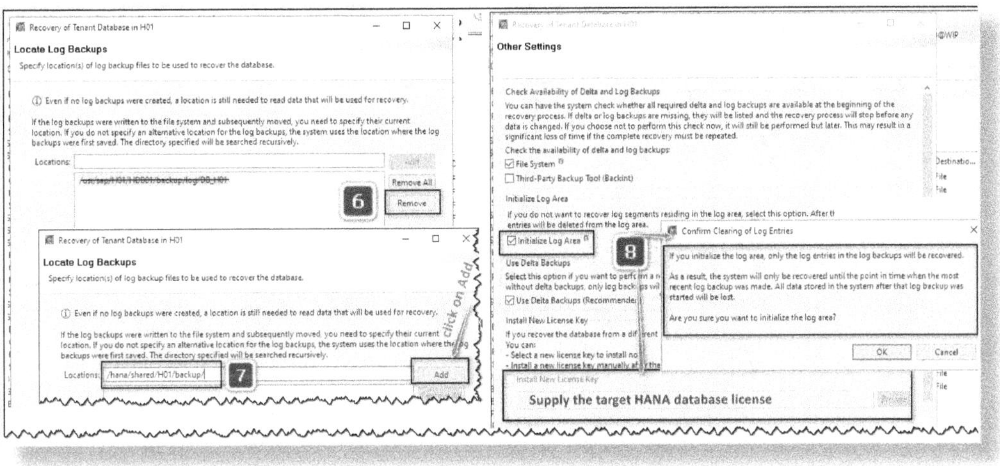

Figure 6.17: HANA database restore from WIP to H01 (2/3)

The numbers in Figure 6.17 show the next steps:

❻ Remove the default log backup LOCATION that was auto-populated.

❼ Add the correct log backup LOCATION.

❽ Select the INITIALIZE LOG AREA checkbox and provide the target HANA database license. This license will be auto-installed as part of restore.

Selecting the INITIALIZE LOG AREA checkbox is mandatory when the source and target databases are different. Failure to do so will cause the target tenant database to apply the old log segments from the target database after full backup restore from the source database, resulting in target database inconsistency.

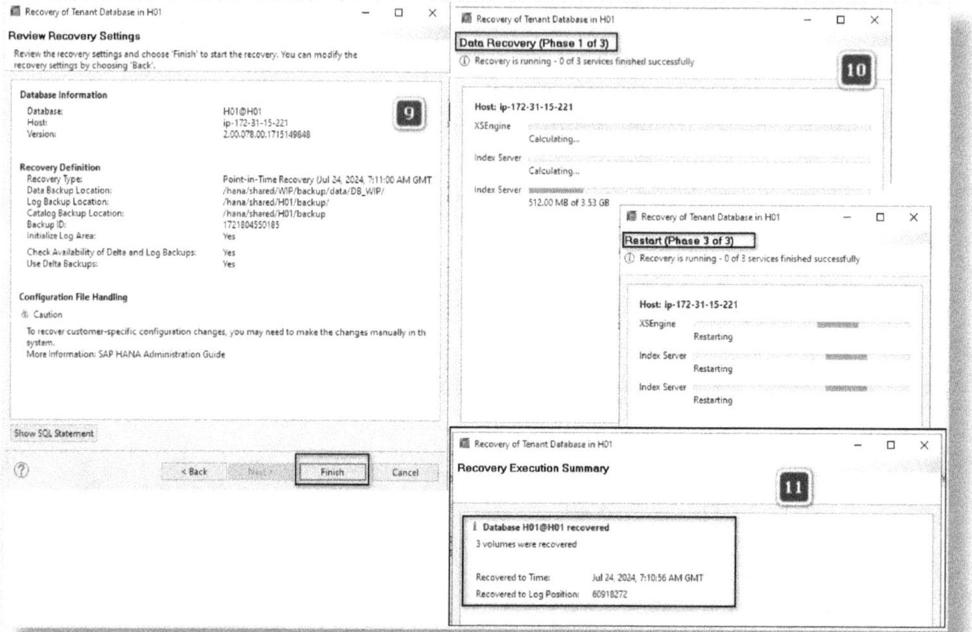

Figure 6.18: HANA database restore from WIP to H01 (3/3)

The numbers in Figure 6.18 show the following steps:

❾ Click on FINISH after cross validating the supplied details.

❿ Monitor the database recovery process and its phases.

⓫ After successful recovery, a message appears indicating that the database was recovered.

Troubleshooting—logfiles and dignostics tools

The HANA database generates trace files specific to backup and restore—*backup.log* for file system-based backups and restore (see Figure 6.19), and *backint.log* for third-party backups and restore.

```
h01adm@ip-172-31-15-221:/usr/sap/H01/HDB01/ip-172-31-15-221/trace> ls -lrt back*
-rw-r----- 1 h01adm sapsys 221553 Jul 24 10:16 backup.log
h01adm@ip-172-31-15-221:/usr/sap/H01/HDB01/ip-172-31-15-221/trace>
```

Figure 6.19: backup.log in HANA trace folder

HANA also provides various diagnostic tools relating to backup and restore, as listed below:

- *hdbbackupdiag*—identifies the backups needed to recover to a specified PIT and verifies their availability and accessibility (refer back to Figure 6.15 for an example).
- *hdbrecovercheck*—available as of HANA 2.0 SP05, this Python tool validates the consistency and recoverability of backups to a specific PIT (see Figure 6.20).

Figure 6.20: hdbrecovercheck tool—example

As *<sid>adm*, at execution path */usr/sap/<SID>/HDB<n>/exe/python_support*, the command is:

```
python hdbrecovercheck.py checkBackupConsistency -c <log_backup_location> --database <SID>
```

- *hdbbackupcheck*—used to check the integrity of individual data backups and log backups for both file system-based backups and backups created using third-party tools. It can also be used outside of the HANA database. The command for this is as follows:

```
hdbbackupcheck <backup file>
```

6.4.2 Method 2—Storage snapshots

SAP HANA storage snapshots provide the fastest way to perform data backups with negligible impact on the network, I/O, or database performance. However, unlike regular backups, this process does not verify the database's internal integrity during creation.

The creation of a snapshot involves the following steps:

1. The HANA database needs to be prepared for the storage snapshot using the SQL command shown in Figure 6.21:

```
BACKUP DATA FOR FULL SYSTEM CREATE SNAPSHOT COMMENT '<comment>';
```

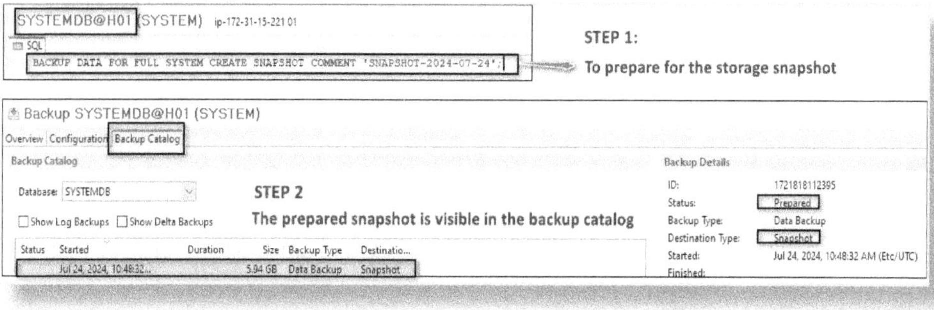

Figure 6.21: "Prepare" statement for HANA database storage snapshot

2. This *prepare* statement generates a system-wide savepoint, creating an internal snapshot of the database. This snapshot status can be identified under BACKUP CATALOG, as shown in Figure 6.21 .

3. The storage snapshot of the entire data area must now be created using the storage system's functionality at the storage layer, according to the hardware. As this is a storage level activity, it varies based on the provider, and is not shown here.

4. Once the storage snapshot has been completed, its status must be reported back to the HANA database, as shown in Figure 6.22.

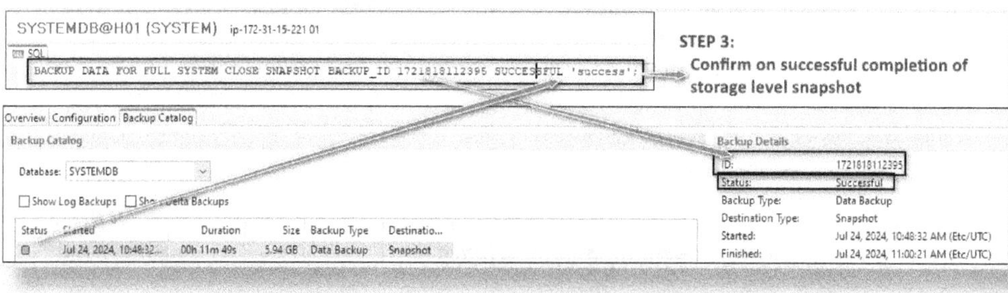

Figure 6.22: Confirming successful completion of storage snapshot

The SQL statements to report a successful and unsuccessful storage snapshot are:

```
BACKUP DATA FOR FULL SYSTEM CLOSE SNAPSHOT BACKUP_ID <backup_id>
SUCCESSFUL '<comment>';

BACKUP DATA FOR FULL SYSTEM CLOSE SNAPSHOT BACKUP_ID <backup_id>
UNSUCCESSFUL '<comment>';
```

In these statements, <backup_id> refers to the unique identifier of the backup snapshot, and <comment> is a descriptive comment explaining the backup.

6.4.3 Method 3—HANA System Replication

Another way to restore a HANA database to a new instance is through HANA System Replication (HSR). While this method is mainly intended for high availability and disaster recovery, it can also be used to create a database copy.

SAP HANA System Replication (HSR) continuously replicates one HANA database to another. When configured, the target initially receives a full load of the source database, followed by ongoing replication of delta changes from the source system, as shown in Figure 6.23. The target HANA database is kept up to date with changes from the source system until the replication connection is interrupted.

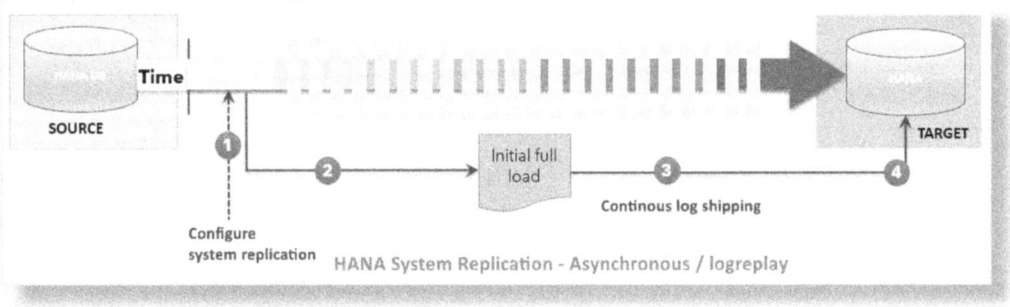

Figure 6.23: Refresh using HSR

Prerequisites for HSR

The primary prerequisites for executing HSR between two HANA database systems include the prerequisites covered in Section 6.4.1 along with some additional requirements:

1. The target system must have the same instance number and SID as the source system. If needed, the target database SID and instance number can be changed/renamed after refreshing it through HSR.

2. Both the source and target databases must be running on a different physical host.

3. For HSR, a port offset value of 10,000 must be configured to reserve ports for system replication communication. Refer to Figure 6.24.

4. The password for the operating system user *<sid>adm* is required for both the source and target systems.

5. The system PKI SSFS key and data files specified below must be copied from the source system to the target system: */usr/sap/.../SYS/global/security/rsecssfs/data/SSFS_.DAT/usr/sap/.../SYS/global/security/rsecssfs/key/SSFS_.KEY*

Ports used for replication

For HSR or tenant copy (see Section 6.4.4), the additional ports listed in Figure 6.24 are used.

System type	Port	System replication port	Details	Example
Multitenant	3<inst_id><service_port>	4<inst_id><service_port>	service port	30140 -> 40140
		4<inst_id>(<service_port>+1)	cross-site TrexNet request	30101 -> 40102
		4<inst_id>(<service_port>+5)	cross-site TrexNet request with SSL	30101 -> 40106

Figure 6.24: Ports used during HSR or tenant copy

The cross-site TrexNet request and service ports must be opened between the primary and secondary HANA databases. The service port offset is controlled with the parameter *global.ini • [system_replication] • replication_port_offset*, and it should be set to 10,000 for a multi-tenant system.

High-level steps for HSR

The high-level steps in using HSR for performing a database refresh are as follows:

1. Configure HSR from the source system to the target system with the *operation mode* as *asynchronous* and the *log mode* as *logreplay*. This configuration triggers a full data payload transfer from the source database to the target database.

2. Once the full data transfer is complete, the source system continuously replicates its delta data changes to the target system.

3. A takeover can be executed on the target database anytime during the delta data transfer. This command in the target database breaks the replication between the source and target systems and puts the target database into a standalone mode.

After performing these steps, the target database will now have the data from the source database up to the point of takeover.

Technical steps involved with using HSR for database refresh

Figure 6.25 and Figure 6.26 show a sample HSR execution for performing a database restore from a source database to a target database. In this case, the source and target have a HANA database installation with the same SID and instance number as per the HSR prerequisite.

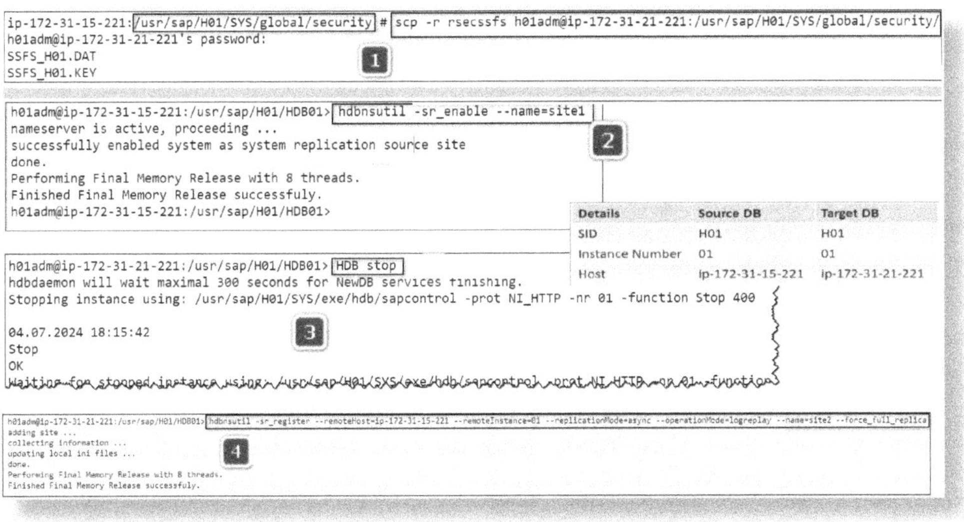

Figure 6.25 Restoring the target database using HSR (1/2)

The numbers in the image indicate the following steps:

❶ From the source HANA database server, transfer the source system PKI `SSFS_<sid>.KEY` and `SSFS_<sid>.DAT` to the target HANA database server from and to the locations shown. As *<sid>adm* from */usr/sap/<SID>/SYS/global/security*, execute the following command:

```
scp -r rsecssfs h01adm@ip-172-31-21-221:/usr/sap/H01/SYS/global/
security/
```

❷ From the source HANA database server, execute the following command to enable the source HANA database as the source of replication:

```
hdbnsutil -sr_enable --name=<Source_site_name1>
```

❸ Stop the target HANA database server using the command:

```
HDB stop
```

❹ From the target HANA database server, enable the replication between source and target HANA databases using the command:

```
hdbnsutil -sr_register --remoteHost=<souce_host>
--remoteInstance=<instance_numer> --replicationMode=async
--operationMode=logreplay --name=<target_site_name> --force_full_
replica
```

The callout numbers in Figure 6.26 refer to the following steps:

❺ From the target HANA database server, start the target HANA database using the command:

```
HDB start
```

❻ Log in to the SystemDB of the source HANA database to verify the replication status.

❼ Wait until the system displays the replication status ALL SERVICES ARE ACTIVE AND IN SYNC.

❽ Take over the target database in standalone mode using the command `hdbnsutil -sr_takeover`. This will disconnect the target database from the source database and break the replication from the source. Once the takeover is successful, the target database becomes independent and is an exact copy of the source system.

❾ The status of the source and target HANA databases after takeover is displayed.

For more information on HSR, including its operation mode and log mode, refer to SAP Note 1999880—"FAQ: SAP HANA System Replication".

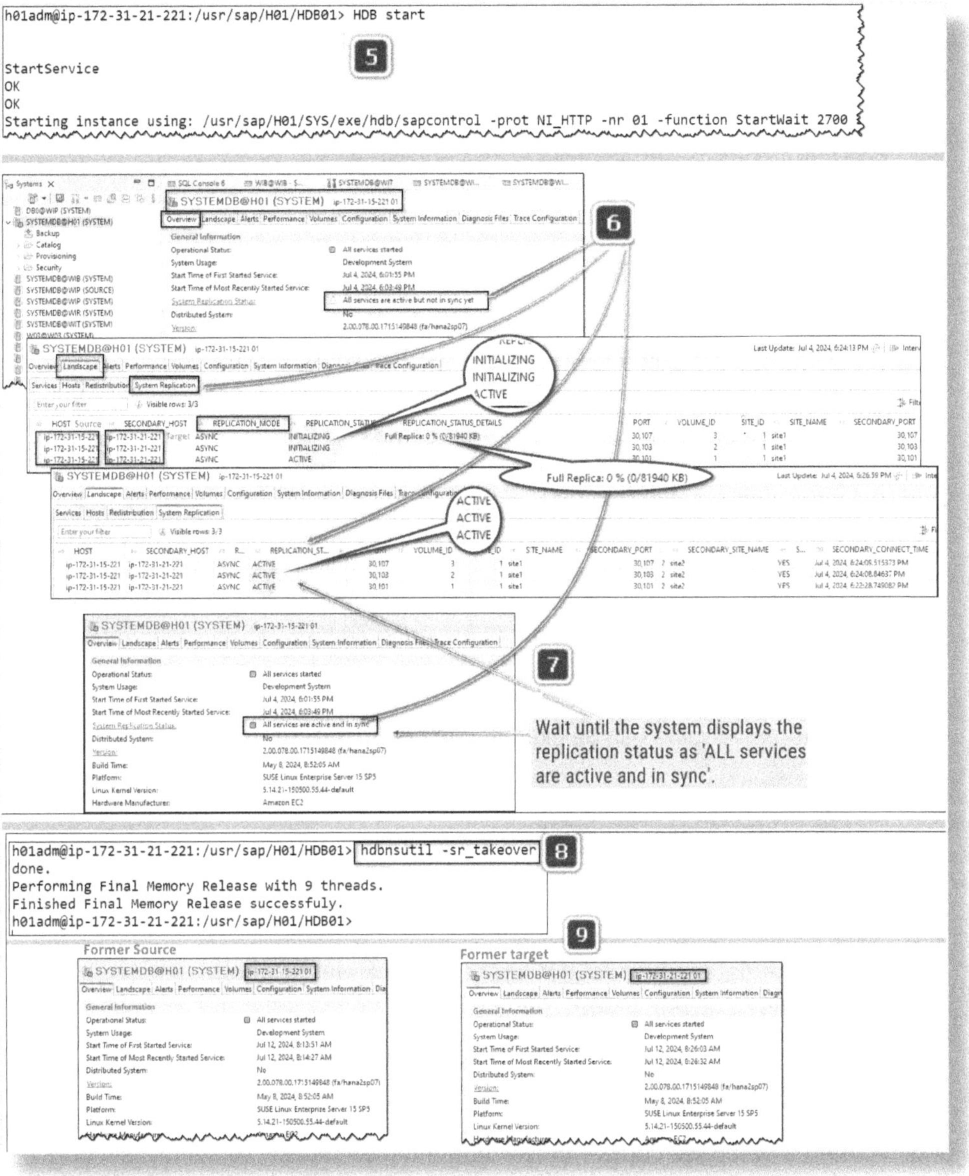

Figure 6.26: Restoring the target database using HSR (2/2)

6.4.4 Method 4—Tenant copy

Tenant copy is another method for performing a system refresh or migration, or for cloning a HANA database. With HANA tenant copy, one or more

HANA tenant databases can be individually moved or copied from one HANA database system to another—either on the same host or on a different host, with near-zero downtime.

Tenant copy or move can be used in various scenarios:

- to load balance tenants between available hosts—for example, a tenant database that requires more memory and CPU can be moved to a host that can better accommodate the load.
- to execute tenant-specific upgrades by moving the tenant database to a different HANA database system, leaving the parent database system undisturbed.
- to clone or create template tenant databases.

With tenant copy replication, the source system's data volumes, log volumes, and in-database certificates and their collections are copied or replicated to the target database, excluding trace files, log files, data backups, encryption root keys, application function libraries, and other configurations present at the following location: *$DIR_INSTANCE/../SYS/global/hdb/custom/config/<DB>*.

Note that tenant copies can be executed even on an HSR-enabled system.

Tenant copy/move—prerequisites

The prerequisites that must be met for a successful tenant copy/move are as follows:

1. The target database must not already have a tenant with the same SID as the one to be replicated from the source.
2. The software version of the target must be equal to or higher than that of the source database.
3. During a database copy or move, data must be replicated using a secure (SSL/TLS) network connection by default.
4. There must not be any changes to the source topology during the tenant copy operation.
5. The source system must be disabled from having the host auto-failover option.

6. The source must not have the following components configured:
    - Rserver
    - SAP HANA dynamic tiering
    - SAP HANA Accelerator for SAP ASE
    - SAP HANA Streaming Analytics
7. The ports detailed in Figure 6.24 must be opened between the source and target HANA tenant databases.

Tenant copy—phases and steps

Figure 6.27 shows the high-level phases involved with tenant copy.

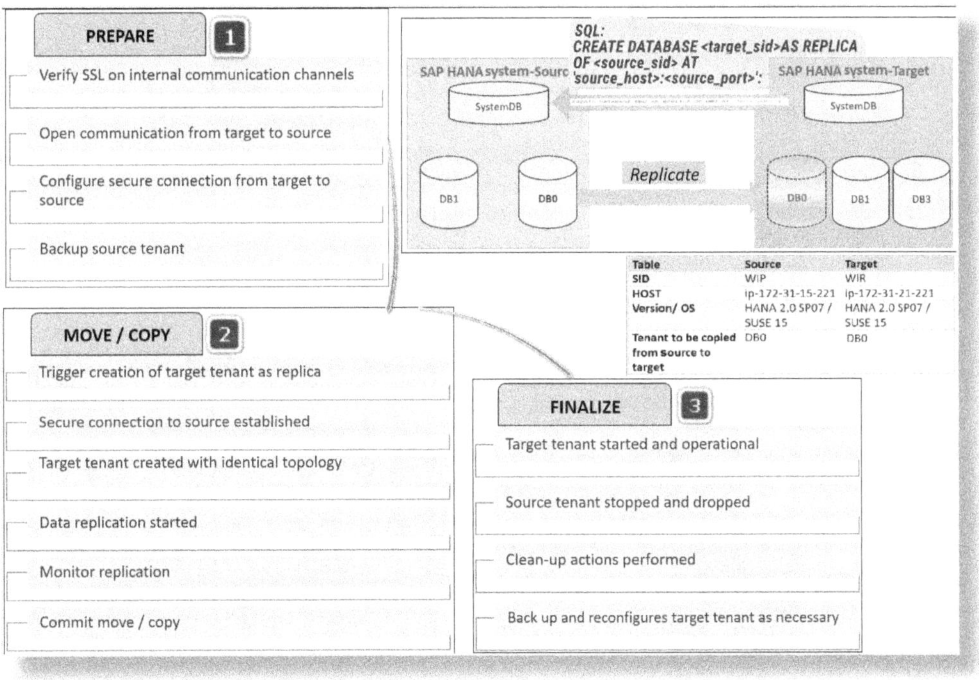

Figure 6.27: Tenant copy/move

We will now take a closer look at the steps in this process.

Phase 1—Prepare

The source and target databases must be prepared before executing the tenant copy.

First, ensure that TLS/SSL is enabled on internal communication channels based on the system public key infrastructure (system PKI) in both the source and target HANA databases. Refer to steps 1 to 3 in Figure 6.28 and Figure 6.29.

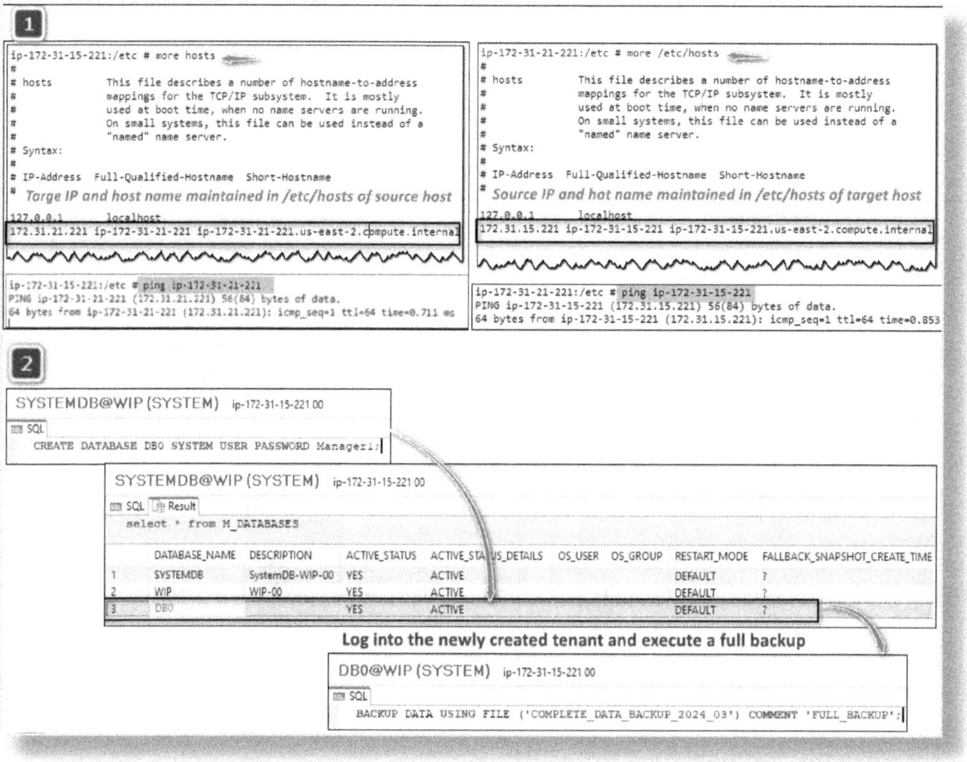

Figure 6.28: Tenant copy (1/10)

The numbers in Figure 6.28 refer to the following steps:

❶ Ensure that the source and target hosts can communicate with each other by adding their IP addresses and hostnames to each other's */etc/hosts* file.

❷ (valid only for this tenant copy process simulation) Create a test tenant database that will serve as the source tenant that must be replicated to the target through tenant replication. Execute the following command from the SystemDB to create the test tenant database (source):

```
CREATE DATABASE DB0 SYSTEM USER PASSWORD <system_DB_password>;
```

- The successful creation of a test tenant database can be verified by executing the SQL query:

```
select * from M_DATABASES;
```

(Note that, in the example scenario, the source tenant already exists and does not need to be created.)

- Trigger a backup on the source tenant database before proceeding further. This can be done using the following SQL statement:

```
BACKUP DATA USING FILE ('<backup_name>') COMMENT '<comment>';
```

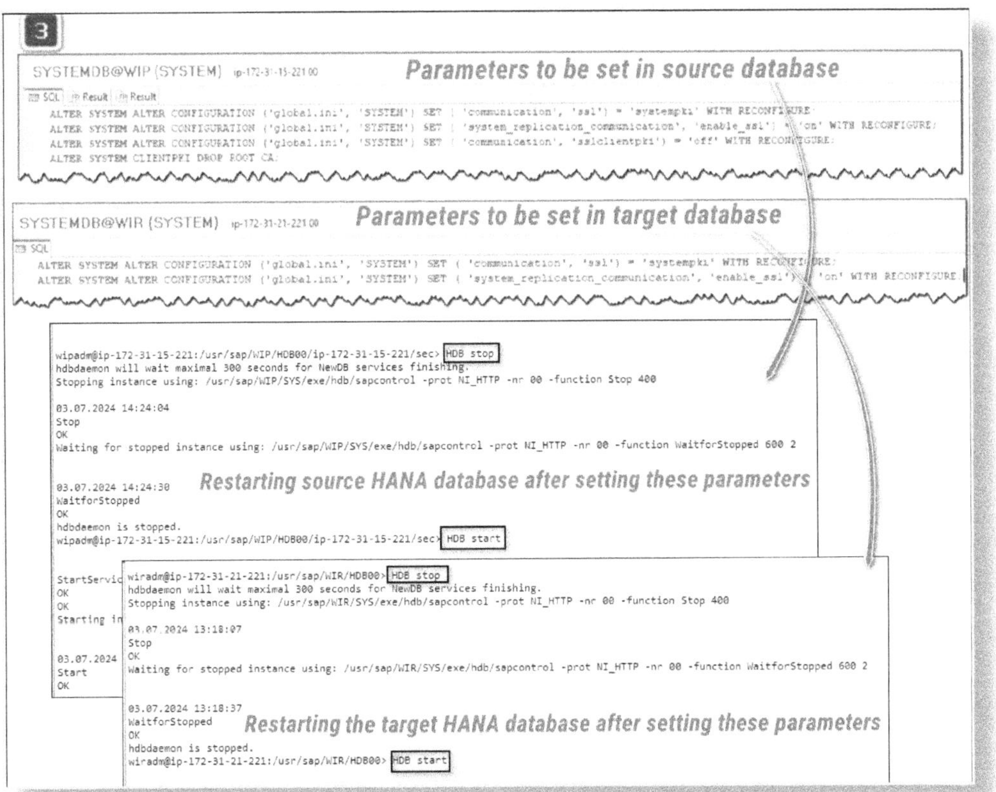

Figure 6.29: Tenant copy (2/10)

The step shown in Figure 6.29 is as follows:

❸ Ensure that TLS/SSL is enabled on internal communication channels based on the system PKI in both the source and target HANA databases by setting the parameters shown below. Also, disable the client PKI and drop the root CA certificate in the source SystemDB.

- Parameters to be set in the source SystemDB:

```
ALTER SYSTEM ALTER CONFIGURATION ('global.ini', 'SYSTEM') SET (
'communication', 'ssl') = 'systempki' WITH RECONFIGURE;
ALTER SYSTEM ALTER CONFIGURATION ('global.ini', 'SYSTEM') SET (
'system_replication_communication', 'enable_ssl') = 'on' WITH
RECONFIGURE;
ALTER SYSTEM ALTER CONFIGURATION ('global.ini', 'SYSTEM') SET (
'communication', 'sslclientpki') = 'off' WITH RECONFIGURE;
ALTER SYSTEM CLIENTPKI DROP ROOT CA;
```

- Parameters to be set in the target SystemDB:

```
ALTER SYSTEM ALTER CONFIGURATION ('global.ini', 'SYSTEM') SET (
'communication', 'ssl') = 'systempki' WITH RECONFIGURE;
ALTER SYSTEM ALTER CONFIGURATION ('global.ini', 'SYSTEM') SET (
'system_replication_communication', 'enable_ssl') = 'on' WITH
RECONFIGURE;
```

- After setting these parameters, restart the SystemDB of both the source and target databases.

Next, set up a trust relationship between the target and source database servers (see steps 4 to 9 in Figure 6.30 and Figure 6.31).

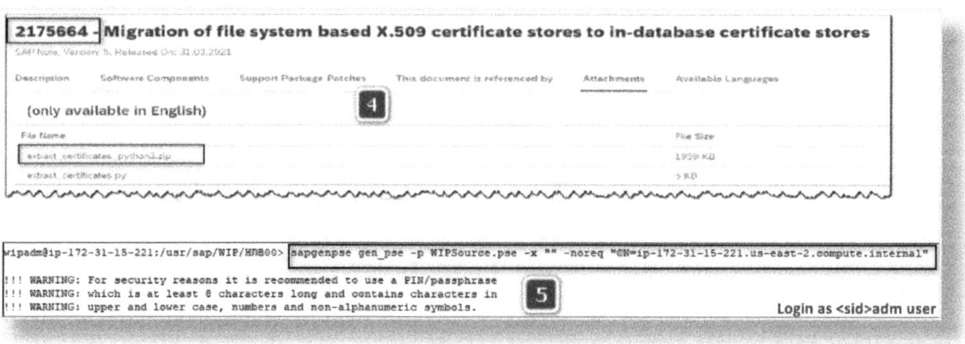

Figure 6.30: Tenant copy (3/10)

Steps 4 to 5 are as follows:

❹ Download the EXTRACT_CERTIFICATES_PYTHON3.ZIP from SAP Note 2175664—"Migration of file systems based X.509 certificate stores to in-database certificate stores"—and place it in *$SECUDIR* path as user *<sid>adm*.

❺ Create a new self-signed certificate using the following command:

```
sapgenpse gen_pse -p <path>/<file name>.pse -x "" -noreq
"CN=<hostname_FQDN_source_host>"
```

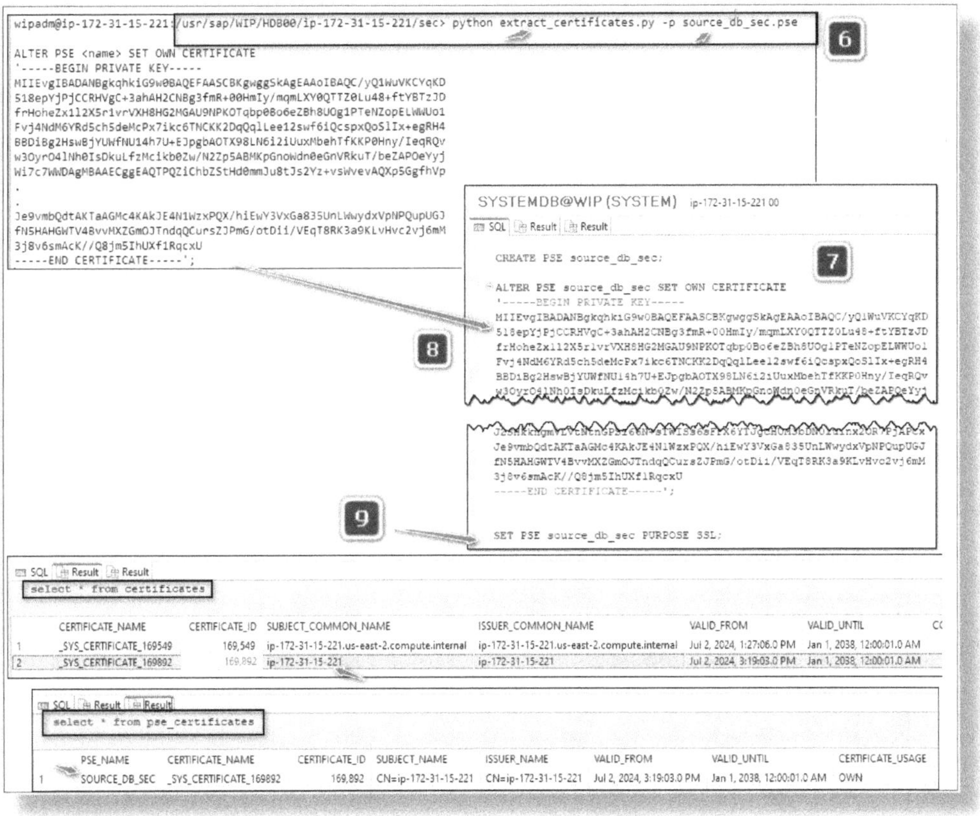

Figure 6.31: Tenant copy—source database system activities (4/10)

Steps 6 to 9, are as follows:

❻ Extract the generated private key and the self-signed certificate from the PSE file using the EXTRACT_CERTIFICATES.PY script. The output of this script is an SQL statement which will be executed in the next step. The command is:

```
python extract_certificates.py -p source_db_sec.pse
```

❼ From the SQL console of the source SystemDB, create a certificate collection:

```
CREATE PSE <collection_name_source>;
```

❽ Execute the SQL statement from step ❻ after replacing the *<name>* with the previously created certificate collection name *<collection_name_source>*.

❾ Set the *PURPOSE* of the PSE collection as *SSL* using the following SQL statement:

```
SET PSE <collection_name_source> PURPOSE SSL;
```

▶ The created certificates can be queried using the following SQLs

```
SELECT * FROM certificates;
SELECT * FROM pse_certificates;
```

The next steps are shown in Figure 6.32 and Figure 6.33.

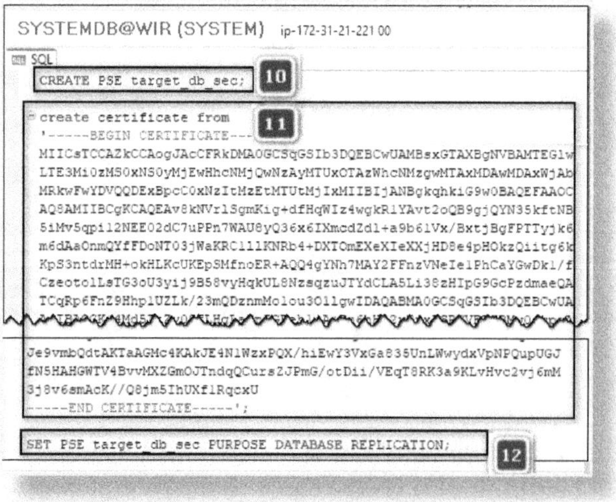

Figure 6.32: Tenant copy—target database system activities (5/10)

Steps 10 to 12 are as follows:

❿ From the SQL console of the target SystemDB, create a certificate collection using the following command:

```
CREATE PSE <collection_name_target>;
```

⓫ Import the source server certificate to the target server. To do this, use only the certificate section from the output from step ❻ and create the certificate using the name *<collection_name_target>* from step ❿.

⓬ Set the *PURPOSE* of the PSE collection as `DATABASE REPLICATION` using the SQL statement:

```
SET PSE <collection_name_target> PURPOSE DATABASE REPLICATION;
```

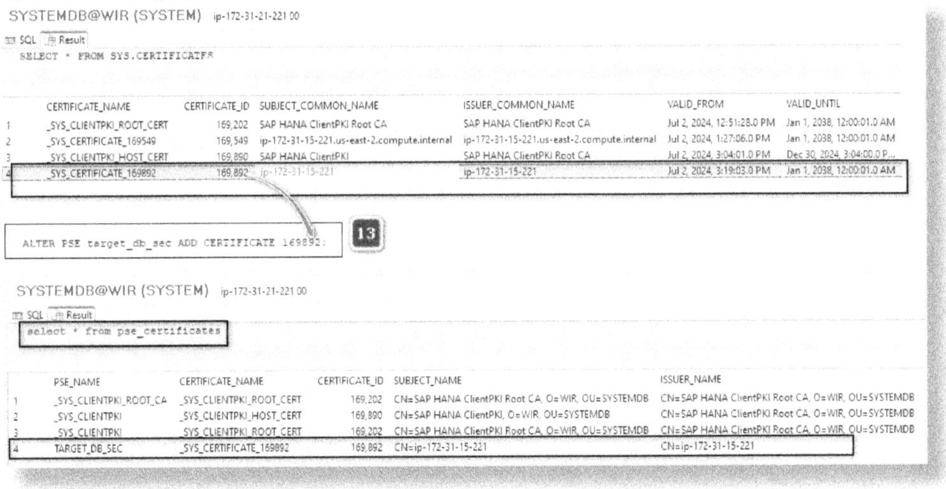

Figure 6.33: Tenant copy—target database system activities (6/10)

⓭ Add the certificate that was created in step ⓫ to the new collection, as follows:

- Verify and note the CERTIFICATE_ID of the previously imported certificate using the SQL query:

```
SELECT * FROM SYS.CERTIFICATES;
```

- Add the previously identified CERTIFICATE_ ID to the certificate collection using SQL query:

```
ALTER PSE < collection_name_target > ADD CERTIFICATE
<certificate_id>;
```

Open the communication channel from the target to the source system by enabling services in the source system to listen on all network interfaces (see Figure 6.34).

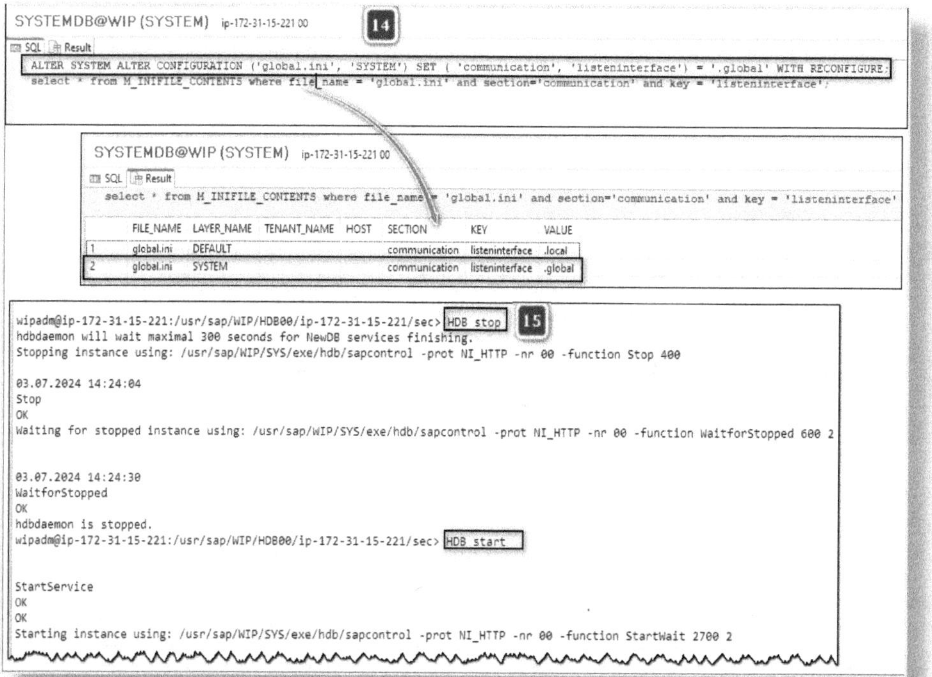

Figure 6.34: Tenant copy—enabling source network interfaces (7/10)

Steps 14 to 15 are as follows:

⓮ Configure the source SystemDB LISTENINTERFACE using the following SQL statement:

```
ALTER SYSTEM ALTER CONFIGURATION ('global.ini', 'SYSTEM') SET (
'communication', 'listeninterface') = '.global' WITH RECONFIGURE;
```

⓯ Restart the HANA database source system.

Create credentials for authenticated access to the source system database from the target SystemDB. Create a user in the source SystemDB with *EXECUTE* privilege for the stored procedure *GET_DATABASE_REPLICATION_PSE*.

Similarly, create a user in the target SystemDB with the system privilege *CREDENTIAL ADMIN*.

Note that in Step 16 (see Figure 6.35), the user *SYSTEM* is used without creating a new user, because it has all the required privileges in both the source and target databases.

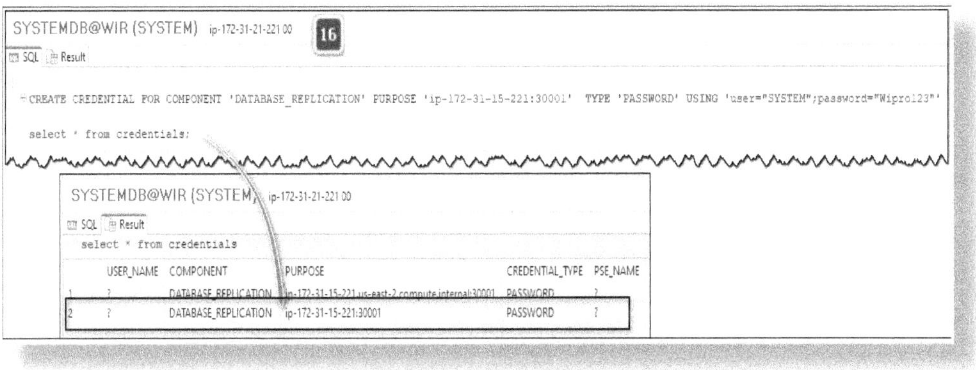

Figure 6.35: Tenant copy—credentials for authentication (8/10)

Step ⓰ uses the following SQL statement in the target SystemDB to create *CREDENTIAL* mapping of *SYSTEM* user source SystemDB in the target SystemDB:

```
CREATE CREDENTIAL FOR COMPONENT 'DATABASE_REPLICATION' PURPOSE
'<source_host:3nn01>' TYPE 'PASSWORD' USING 'user="<Source_
system_user>";password="<respective password>"';
```

Here, *<nn>* indicates the source system instance number.

To verify the creation of the credential in the target SystemDB, use SQL query:

```
select * from credentials;
```

Ensure that the backup triggered in the source tenant database in step ❷ is successful.

Phase 2—Move/copy

To perform a tenant copy, create a replica of the source tenant database in the target database, as depicted in Figure 6.36.

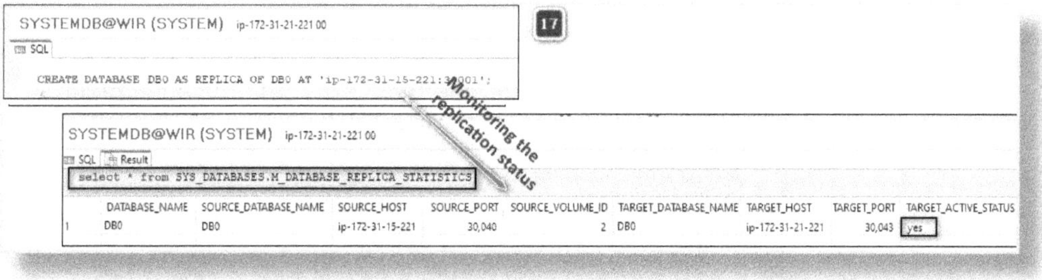

Figure 6.36: Tenant copy—create replica (9/10)

Step ⓱ shows the following SQL statement for replica creation in the target database:

```
CREATE DATABASE <SID_to_be_moved> AS REPLICA OF <SID_source> AT
'<source_host>:3nn01';
```

This action requires a database user with system privileges *DATABASE ADMIN* and *CATALOG READ*

The on-going replication and its status can be monitored using SQL query:

```
select * from SYS_DATABASES.M_DATABASE_REPLICA_STATISTICS;
```

Note that the progress of tenant replication can also be monitored using the *REPLICATION_STATUS* column from the system view *SYS_DATABASES.M_DATABASE_REPLICAS*.

To summarize, the replication process establishes a secure connection between the target SystemDB and the source SystemDB. It then creates a new tenant database with the same topology as that of the source tenant database and replicates data between the respective services of the source and target databases. Table 6.3 outlines the possible replication statuses during tenant replication. *Primary system* refers to the source system and *secondary system* refers to the target system.

Status	Description
UNKNOWN	The secondary system has been unable to connect to the primary system since the primary system's last restart.
INITIALIZING	Data transfer has been initiated. In this state, the secondary system is unavailable for use.
SYNCING	The secondary system is resynchronizing (e.g., after a temporary connection loss or a restart of the secondary system).
ACTIVE	Initialization or synchronization with the source system is complete, and the target system is now continuously replicating. In SYNC mode, no data is lost in the event of a crash.
ERROR	Indicates a connection error. Further details can be found in REPLICATION_STATUS_DETAILS.

Table 6.3: SYS_DATABASES.M_DATABASE_REPLICAS statuses

Once the replication status changes to *ACTIVE*, the replication to the target database can be stopped and finalized, as shown in Figure 6.37 in step 18.

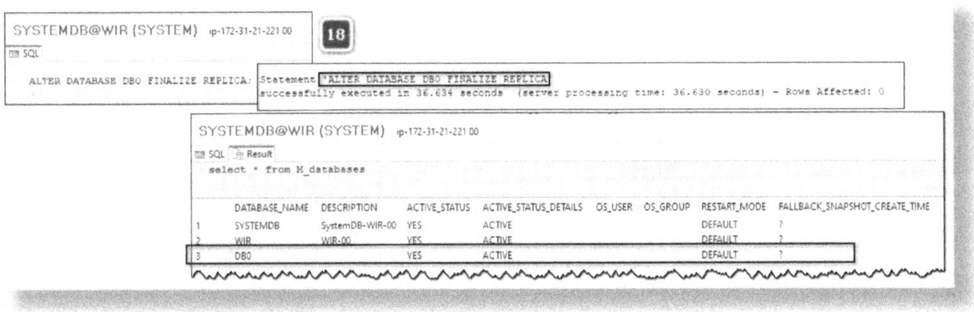

Figure 6.37: Tenant copy—finalize replica (10/10)

The SQL statement to break the replication is:

```
ALTER DATABASE <SID_that_was_moved> FINALIZE REPLICA;
```

In the case of an error, the replication can also be cancelled with the following SQL statement:

```
ALTER DATABASE CANCEL REPLICA;
```

Phase 3—Finalize

Once the tenant copy/move is finalized, the target SystemDB starts the new tenant database, updates the root key for data volume encryption, and re-encrypts data in the new database if data volume encryption is enabled. In addition, it deletes database users' remote identities if the original tenant database was configured for cross-database access.

> **Tenant move**
>
> Unlike the tenant copy process described earlier, with a tenant move, the source tenant can be dropped using the following SQL command as the final step, along with the steps from tenant copy:
>
> ```
> DROP DATABASE <tenant_database_name>;
> ```

Advantages

Copying/migrating a HANA database using a tenant copy offers distinct advantages over a native HANA database restore or HSR, primarily due to its zero-downtime capability. Additionally, unlike HSR, which requires the entire HANA system—including the SystemDB and all its tenant databases—to be replicated to the target system, tenant copy enables migration via replication of individual tenants. Also, tenant copy does not involve the transfer of database backup dumps between source and target servers, making it more secure. However, to copy/move a tenant database within the same HANA database system, backup and restore is generally more effective than tenant copy.

7 Troubleshooting

This chapter provides general guidance for troubleshooting HANA database issues which were not specifically covered in previous chapters.

7.1 Classifying the issue

In general, HANA database issues can be user-specific, statement-specific, region-specific, or global, affecting the entire database and all users.

- User-specific issues are often due to user-specific parameter configuration (see Section 4.6.5) or missing authorizations.
- Region-specific issues usually point to network problems affecting a specific area.
- Statement-specific issues may arise from problems relating to the underlying table that is being queried, complex loops or joins involved with the statement being executed, or the workload class associated with the statement (refer to Section 4.6).
- Global issues could arise due to either a hardware issue (abnormal CPU and RAM consumption, file system full issues, problematic network, etc.) or an underlying software issue such as bugs or a misconfigured database.
- These issues mostly result in memory, CPU or file system problems, causing performance issues in the HANA database.
- Memory issues often arise from a column-store table, report, or query that is consuming excessive memory from an incorrectly configured HANA database, or due to improper garbage collection.

Garbage collection in HANA

The term *garbage collection* typically refers to the HANA database process that automatically cleans up unused memory or disk space. The *M_GARBAGE_COLLECTION_STATISTICS* system view provides details of the garbage collection processes executed by the database. For more information, refer to SAP Note—"2169283 – FAQ: SAP HANA Garbage Collection".

CPU issues typically occur when a query or user triggers too many threads, exhausting CPU resources.

A disk-full situation can freeze the database, blocking database and user logins or actions.

As a first step in troubleshooting, it is critical to identify the affected area and proceed with the analysis accordingly.

7.2 HANA Studio "Overview"

The starting point in troubleshooting any HANA database issue is to check the OVERVIEW tab in HANA Studio (see Figure 3.7—CURRENT ALERTS AND MESSAGES) or the DATABASE OVERVIEW in the HANA Cockpit (see Figure 7.1).

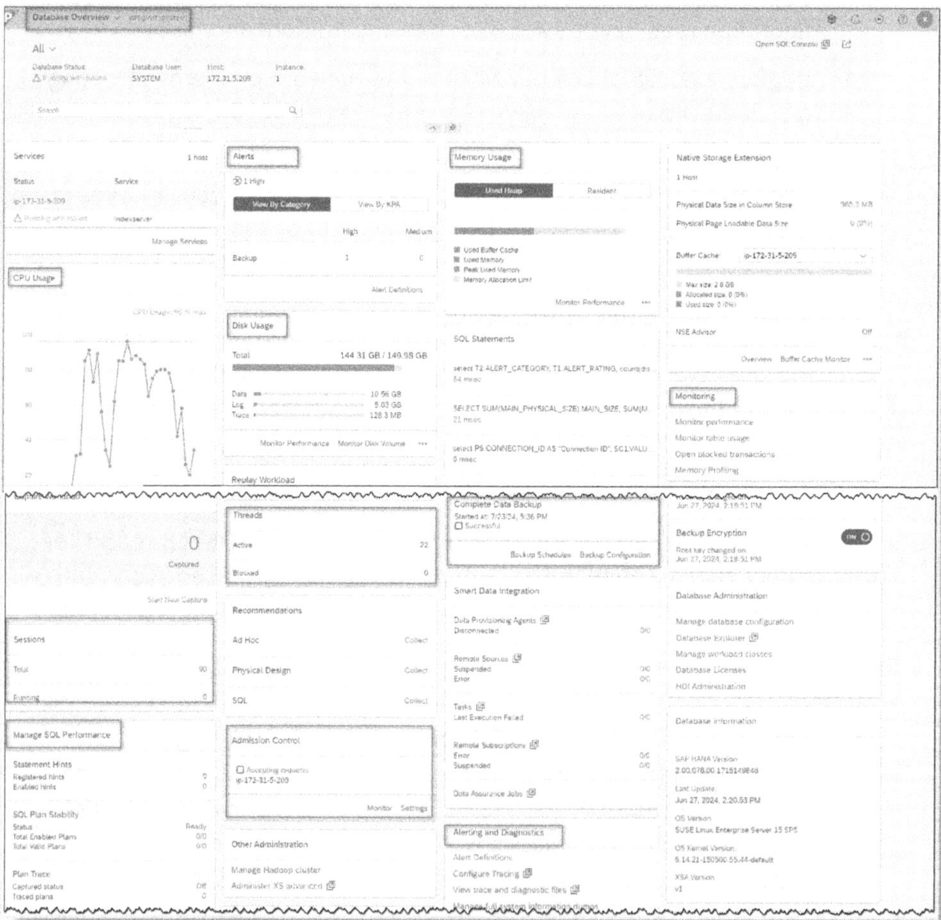

Figure 7.1: SAP HANA cockpit—"Database Overview"

These provide a concise summary of the current database status, including memory, CPU, and disk usage. The ALERTS sections on these screens provide a list of current and historical alerts, which serve as the starting point for analyzing HANA database issues.

7.3 SQL statement collection

The next step in troubleshooting HANA database issues is to run the *HANA_Configuration_MiniChecks* script, which can be found in the *SQLStatements.ZIP* file attached to SAP Note 1969700, as shown in Figure 7.2.

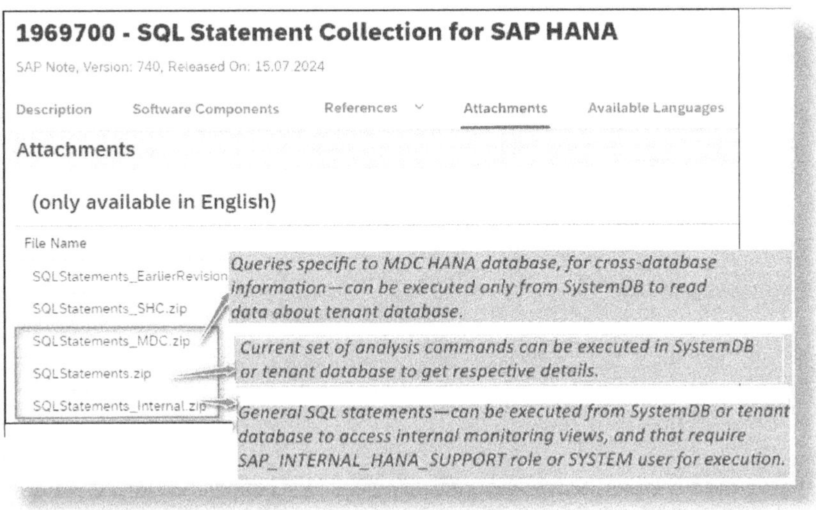

Figure 7.2: "SQL Statement Collection for SAP HANA"

The output of this script helps administrators to verify whether the database has been configured according to recommended values, with discrepancies shown in column C (see Figure 7.3).

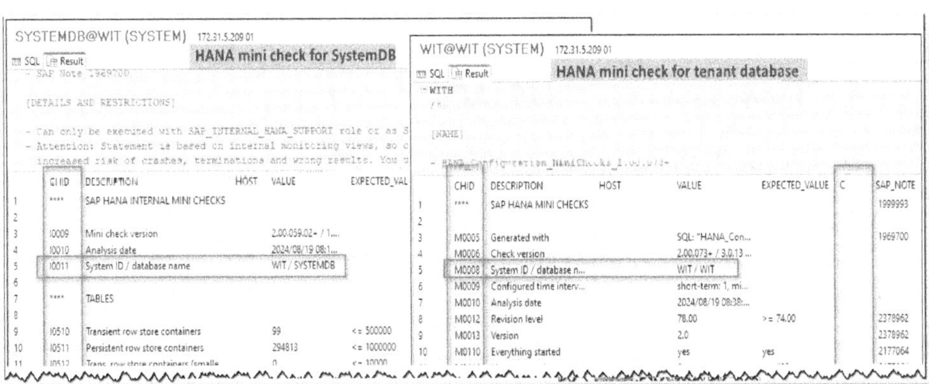

Figure 7.3: HANA_Configuration_MiniChecks

SAP Note 1969700 also provides an extensive collection of predefined, customizable SQL statements for analyzing HANA database issues that are crucial for daily monitoring. Note that most of these SQL scripts are specific to certain HANA database versions and hence a suitable version of these must be selected for successful execution. In addition, these scripts include a modification section, which enables output to be customized based on the requirement, as shown in Figure 7.4.

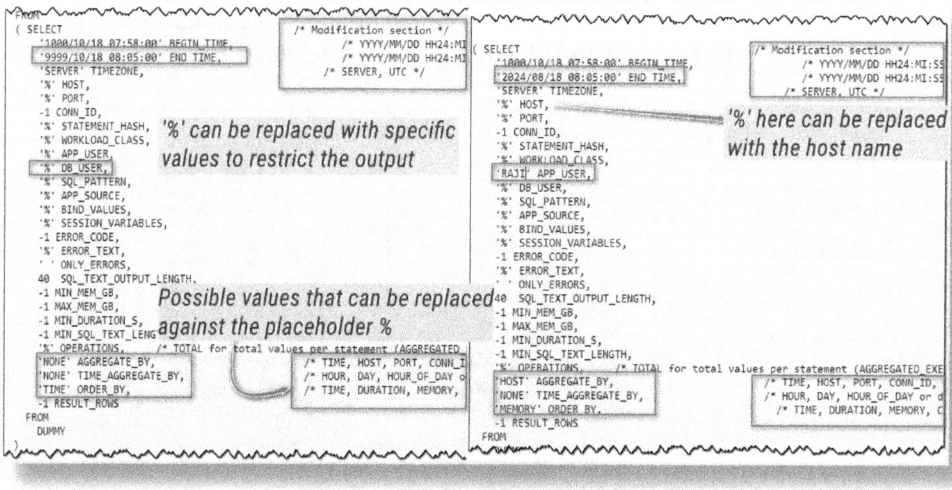

Figure 7.4: Sample modification section in SQL Collection

Refer to SAP Note 3311408—"Bookmark of SQL Statement Collection Reports for SAP HANA"—which can help in understanding the purpose of most of these SQL statement collections.

For more detailed information and a deeper understanding of the *HANA_Configuration_Minichecks* report, refer to SAP Note 3284834-SQL Statement Collection: "HANA_Configuration_Minichecks" report for SAP HANA.

7.4 "Guided Answers" and FAQs

The third troubleshooting step is to use SAP's GUIDED ANSWERS, an interactive support tool that employs decision trees to help diagnose and solve issues (see Figure 7.5).

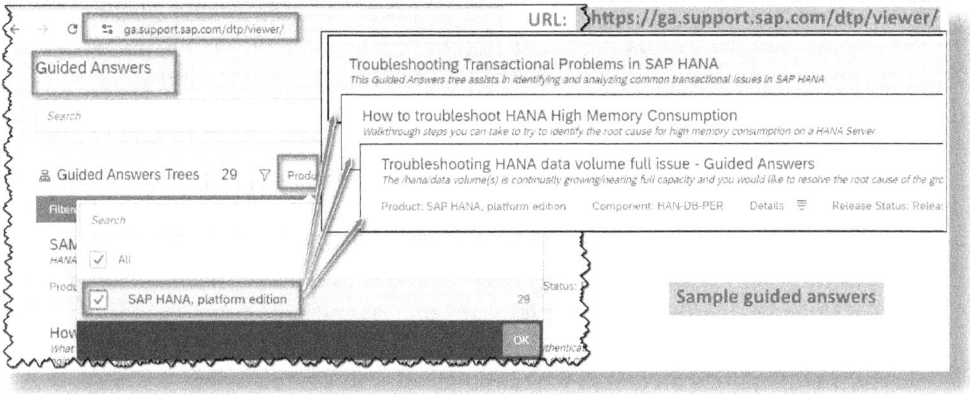

Figure 7.5: Guided answers

GUIDED ANSWERS covers various SAP products, including SAP HANA, and provides a step-by-step analysis approach. In addition, it provides the necessary SAP SQL collection script and the relevant SAP notes for resolution. This page can be found at: *https://ga.support.sap.com/dtp/viewer/*.

Some of the important guided answers on this site include:

- Troubleshooting performance issues in SAP HANA
- How to troubleshoot HANA high memory consumption
- Troubleshooting HANA upgrade issues
- How to troubleshoot HANA high CPU utilization

Further detailed information on HANA database issues can be found in the form of FAQs (Frequently Asked Questions). A comprehensive list of these can be found in SAP Note 2000003—"FAQ: SAP HANA"—which can help you to analyze database administration issues.

7.5 Analyzing disk-full situations

A HANA database might become unresponsive due to data volume, log volume, a log backup, or a HANA shared file system (*/hana/shared*) disk-full situation. This can be identified using the operating system command `df -h`.

The first step to resolve such issues is to extend the file system. Do not delete files directly, as this will cause database inconsistency. In the case of a log volume full situation, it can be helpful to either extend the log volume file system or reclaim free log segments using the SQL command `ALTER SYSTEM RECLAIM LOG;`, as per SAP Note 2821539—"Volume /hana/log is full with log segments in status RetainedFree". If the file system cannot be extended, and freeing up log segments does not provide enough free space in the log volume, a temporary workaround is to create soft links to a file system with more space, after shutting down the database. This is covered in SAP Note 1679938—"DiskFullEvent on Log Volume".

For further guidance on disk-full situations, refer to the following:

- SAP Note 2083715—"Analyzing log volume full situations"
- Guided Answers—"Troubleshooting HANA data volume full issue"
- SAP Note 2988616—"/hana/shared volume full or growing"

7.6 Collecting and analyzing database dumps

The next step towards issue resolution involves collecting HANA database dumps, such as *full system dumps (FSD)* and *runtime dumps (RTE)*. FSDs and RTEs are generally collected when an SAP support case is raised. RTEs can also be used for initial analysis by anyone, including SAP, by loading it into the HANA Dump Analyzer, which we will look at more closely in Section 7.6.3.

7.6.1 Full system dumps

Whenever an SAP support ticket is raised with SAP for any database-specific issue resolution, it is highly recommended to automatically collect an FSD and attach it to the support ticket. This helps the SAP team to better understand the current state of the database as it automatically includes current trace files, configurations, backup logs, performance traces, and hardware information on CPU and memory. However, this dump does not include runtime dumps.

FSDs can be collected using:

- HANA Studio (see Figure 7.6)
- Python script—FULLSYSTEMINFODUMP.PY (see Figure 7.7)

The default location where the generated FSD is stored is: */usr/sap/<SID>/SYS/global/sapcontrol/snapshots/*.

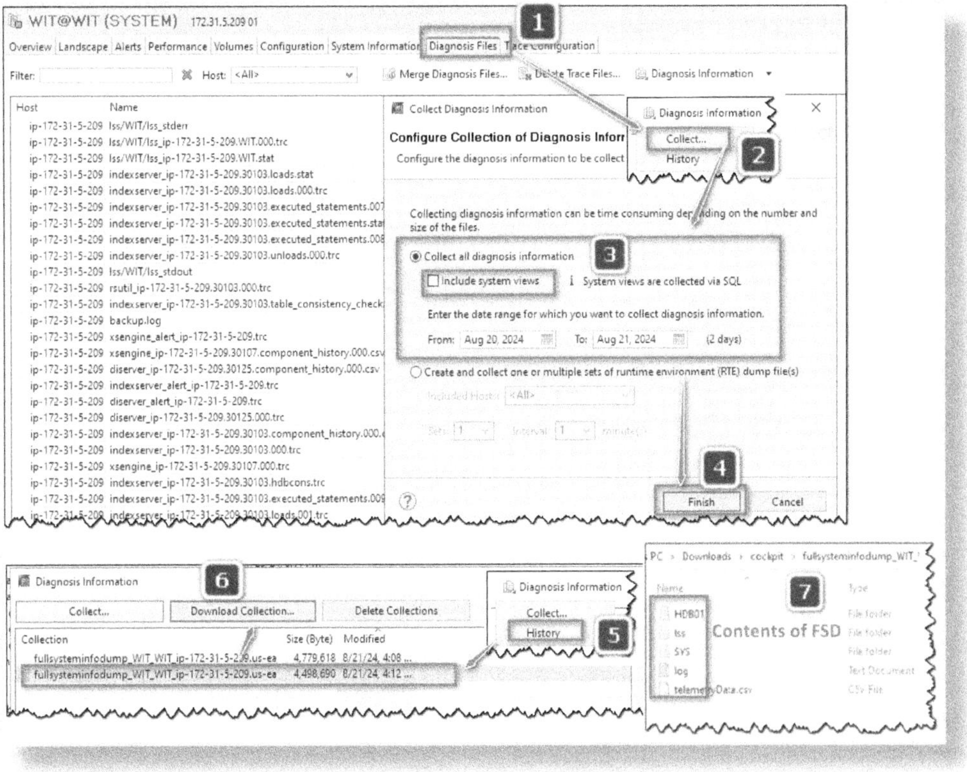

Figure 7.6: Steps for collecting FSD using HANA Studio

To collect the FSD from HANA Studio, follow the steps shown in Figure 7.6:

❶ Log in to the database and navigate to the DIAGNOSIS FILES tab.

❷ Click on the DIAGNOSIS INFORMATION dropdown and choose COLLECT.

❸ Select the COLLECT ALL DIAGNOSIS INFORMATION radio button, select the INCLUDE SYSTEM VIEWS checkbox, and enter the required date range for which the dump needs to be collected.

❹ Click on FINISH.

❺-❻ After successfully collecting the FSD, it can be downloaded by selecting HISTORY from the DIAGNOSIS INFORMATION dropdown list. Click on DOWNLOAD COLLECTION to save it in the local desktop.

❼ Shows the contents of the FSD zip folder.

Figure 7.7 uses a Python script to collect the FSD from the database operating system level via operating system user *<sid>adm*. The command to trigger FSD is:

```
python fullSystemInfoDump.py
```

The verbose output also provides the location where this FSD is saved.

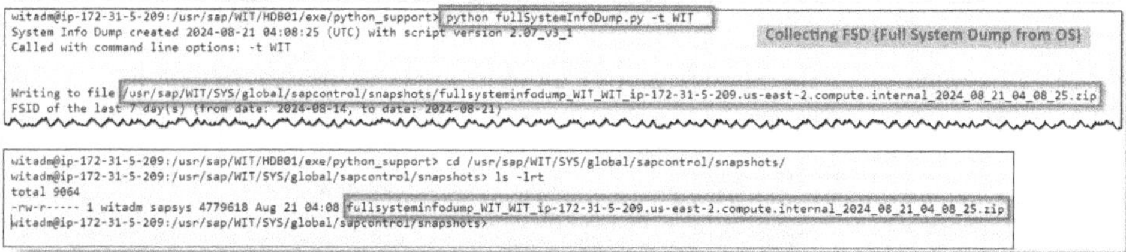

Figure 7.7: Collecting FSD using python script

For more information, refer to SAP Note 2573880—"FAQ: SAP HANA Full System Info Dump".

7.6.2 Runtime dumps (RTE dumps)

HANA database runtime dumps are text files that can be created manually or automatically by the HANA database to indicate the current state of the database. These dumps provide more focused traces when they are created during ongoing database issues and help to analyze high-memory consumption, lock contention, blocked savepoint phases, high CPU consumption, and more. These traces are stored by default in the HANA trace directory */usr/sap/<sid>/HDB<inst>/<host>/trace*.

Figure 7.8 shows three ways to generate a runtime dump in a HANA database.

The various methods are:

❶ Use the following OS command by logging into the HANA database server as *<sid>adm*:

```
python fullSysteminfoDump.py --tenant <SID>--rtedump --sets
<number of sets> --interval=<duration>
```

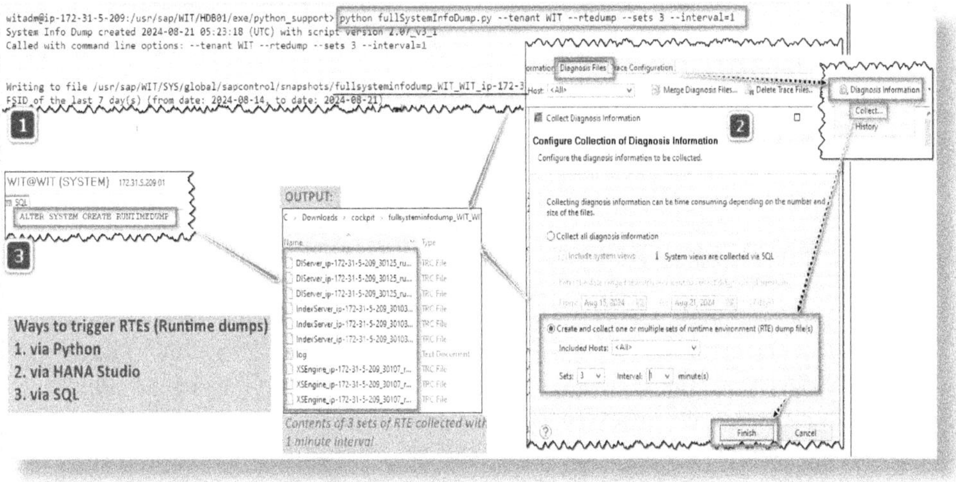

Figure 7.8: Three methods to trigger runtime dump

❷ On the HANA Studio's DIAGNOSIS FILES tab, go to DIAGNOSIS INFORMATION • COLLECT, and choose the required option.

❸ Use SQL statement:

```
ALTER SYSTEM CREATE RUNTIMEDUMP;
```

The naming convention for the RTE dump text file is *<service>_<host>.<port>.rtedump.<timestamp>.<issues>.trc*. Figure 7.9 shows some of the RTE dump files from a HANA database system.

```
witadm@ip-172-31-5-209:/usr/sap/WIT/HDB01/ip-172-31-5-209/trace/DB_WIT> ls -lrt *rte*
-rw-r--r-- 1 witadm sapsys 4788587 Aug 21 04:49 indexserver_ip-172-31-5-209.30103.rtedump.20240821-044929.0003554.trc
witadm@ip-172-31-5-209:/usr/sap/WIT/HDB01/ip-172-31-5-209/trace/DB_WIT> cd ..
witadm@ip-172-31-5-209:/usr/sap/WIT/HDB01/ip-172-31-5-209/trace> ls -lrt *rte*
-rw-r--r-- 1 witadm sapsys 1219885 Aug 21 04:49 nameserver_ip-172-31-5-209.30101.rtedump.20240821-044946.0003133.trc
witadm@ip-172-31-5-209:/usr/sap/WIT/HDB01/ip-172-31-5-209/trace>
```

Figure 7.9: RTE dump files

The *<issues>* clause is optional and can include:

- *after_oom_cleanup*, *compositelimit_oom* (statement-specific out-of-memory), *oom_memory_release*, etc., for memory issues,
- *deadlock* to indicate a transactional deadlock, or
- *savepoint_blocked* for savepoint issues.

For more details on the *<issues>* clause, refer to SAP Note 2400007—"FAQ: SAP HANA Runtime Dumps".

RTE dump collection can also be automated using HANASitter (see Section 7.9.2) or by using *rtescript.sh*, as described in SAP Note 3265717—"Periodic Scheduling of Runtimedumps".

7.6.3 HANA Dump Analyzer

HANA runtime dumps are long, verbose text files and are generally difficult to analyze. To assist with this, SAP provides a tool called the *HANA Dump Analyzer*. This portable software can be downloaded using the link provided in SAP Note 2498739—"How-To: Analyzing Runtime Dumps with SAP HANA Dump Analyzer". As a prerequisite, Java(TM) Platform SE Binary must be installed. This tool is a standalone software and does not connect to the database; therefore, RTE dumps need to be downloaded from the database and imported into the tool for further analysis (see Figure 7.10).

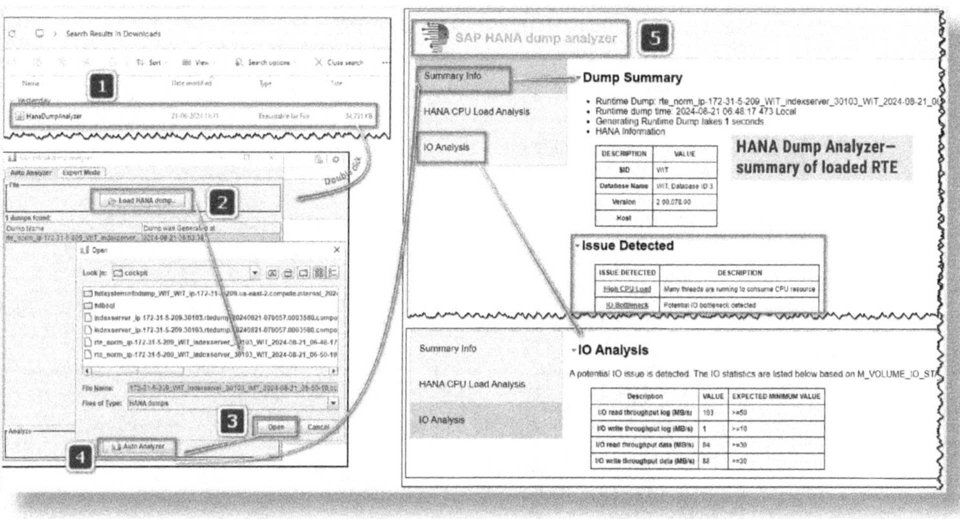

Figure 7.10: HANA Dump Analyzer

The numbers shown in the image indicate the following:

❶ ❷ and ❸—Upload an RTE dump.

❹ Analyze the RTE dump by clicking on AUTO ANALYZER.

❺ View the dump summary for detailed information about the system state when the dump was generated.

For larger RTE dumps, the tool might require a higher Java heap and can be started using the command:

```
java -Xmx1G -jar HANADumpAnalyzer.jar.
```

This tool helps to narrow down the database issue to a memory, CPU, I/O, lock wait, or delta merge issue, etc.

7.6.4 SQL error code and knowledge base search

Database errors are usually accompanied by SQL *ERROR_CODES* that hint at the cause of the failure. These codes are either returned to the user or recorded in trace and alert files. The system view *M_ERROR_CODES* provides a comprehensive list of these codes and their descriptions. These codes can be used as keywords in the *SAP for Me* portal to find relevant SAP Notes for resolution (go to: *https://me.sap.com/notes/*).

7.6.5 Analyzing out-of-memory RTE

Analyzing RTE dumps relating to out-of-memory (OOM) issues is generally straightforward, because the dump identifies the exact cause (e.g., user or statement). All OOM issues are recorded in the *M_OUT_OF_MEMORY_EVENTS* system view along with the reason, in the EVENT_REASON column, as shown in Figure 7.11.

Figure 7.11 shows an example where an OOM RTE was caused by a user-specific memory restriction of 1GB. The letters in the image indicate the following:

[a] The error thrown by the database when the user attempted to execute an SQL procedure.

[b] The system view M_OUT_OF_MEMORY_EVENTS has recorded the error along with details such as CONNECTION_ID (303,148) and STATEMENT_ID, etc. The EVENT_REASON column in this system view indicates that the error was due to the parameter value. STATEMENT_MEMORY_LIMIT for this specific user

[c] Similar information can also be observed in the RTE dump generated for this issue.

[d]–[e] Additional details about the exact statement that caused the issue can be obtained by querying the STATEMENT_ID in the system view M_OUT_OF_MEMORY_EVENTS.

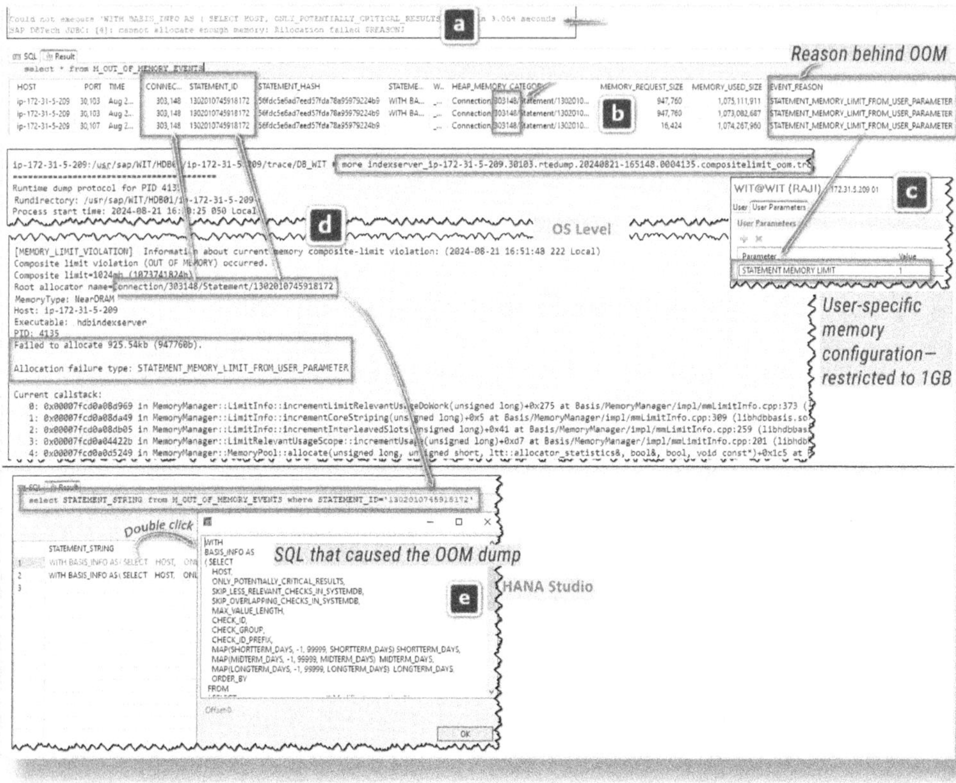

Figure 7.11: OOM analysis

In the example, the STATEMENT MEMORY LIMIT user parameter was restricted to 1GB usage, so when the user attempted to exceed this limit, the database cancelled the session and terminated the SQL execution with an OOM RTE.

7.7 Analyzing SQL statement issues

7.7.1 SQL statements and plan caches

When a database issue arises due to the execution of a specific SQL statement, it is crucial to identify the problematic SQL. Trace files typically provide a *STATEMENT_ID* or *STATEMENT_HASH*. Using the *M_SQL_PLAN_*

CACHE or *HOST_SQL_PLAN_CACHE* system views, we can identify the SQL statement and obtain details about the user, memory usage, CPU, number of records queried, etc. Figure 7.12 shows a sample output to obtain the SQL statement when we know the problematic STATEMENT_HASH with the help of system view M_SQL_PLAN_CACHE.

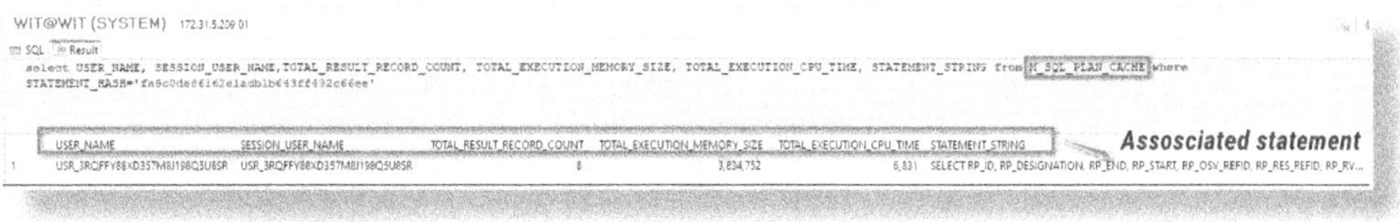

Figure 7.12: Identifying SQL details using STATEMENT_HASH

The SQL query used here is:

```
select USER_NAME, SESSION_USER_NAME,  TOTAL_RESULT_RECORD_
COUNT, TOTAL_EXECUTION_MEMORY_SIZE,  TOTAL_EXECUTION_CPU_TIME,
STATEMENT_STRING from M_SQL_PLAN_CACHE where STATEMENT_
HASH='<statement_hash>';
```

A similar result can be obtained by querying system view *_SYS_STATISTICS"."HOST_SQL_PLAN_CACHE.*

Sometimes, a database issue may be related to a specific table. This can affect all SQL statements that use that table. We can find all such SQL statements that are executed against a specific table using the following SQL query:

```
select * from M_SQL_PLAN_CACHE where ACCESSED_TABLE_NAMES like
'%<TABLE_NAME>%'.
```

7.7.2 System views for analyzing the workload

In many database issues, the *STATEMENT_HASH* involved can be identified from RTE dumps or from the *M_OUT_OF_MEMORY_EVENTS* system view. With this *STATEMENT_HASH*, additional details can be retrieved by querying the system views listed in Table 7.1 along with a *WHERE* clause against the *STATEMENT_HASH*.

Task	System views
To identify problematic statements	▶ *M_ACTIVE_STATEMENTS* ▶ *M_PREPARED_STATEMENTS* ▶ *M_EXPENSIVE_STATEMENTS*
To identify database operations, threads, or applications that are causing high CPU utilization.	▶ *M_SERVICE_THREAD* ▶ *M_SERVICE_THREAD_SAMPLES,* ▶ *M_EXPENSIVE_STATEMENTS.CPU_TIME (column)* ▶ *M_SERVICE_THREAD_CALLBACKS (stack frame information for service threads)* ▶ *M_JOBEXECUTORS (job executor statistics).*

Table 7.1: System views to analyze workload in HANA

7.8 Traces in HANA database

To identify the root cause of an issue, it is recommended to review the trace file from the time the issue occurred because it might reveal the cause of the underlying problem. For this purpose, HANA provides several types of trace files in its trace directory, as shown in Figure 7.13.

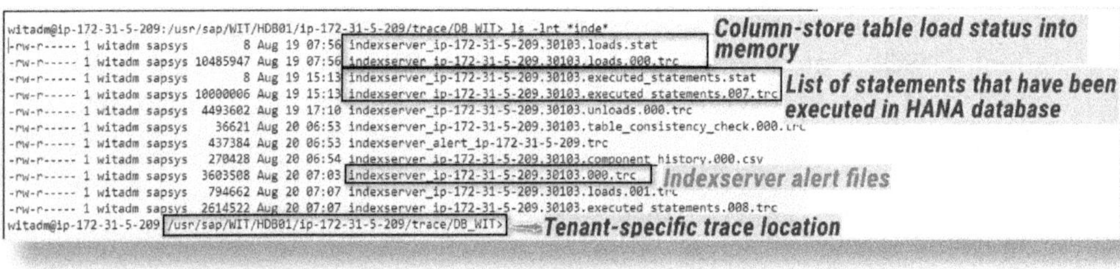

Figure 7.13: HANA database trace file location

The SystemDB-specific trace files are stored at location */usr/sap/<SID>/HDB<nn>/<server>/trace/*.

The tenant database specific trace files are stored at location */usr/sap/<SID>/HDB<nn>/<server>/trace/DB_<SID>/*

The HANA database has different types of trace files, such as DATABASE TRACE, SQL TRACE, PERFORMANCE TRACE, USER-SPECIFIC TRACE, etc., as shown in area ❶ in Figure 7.14.

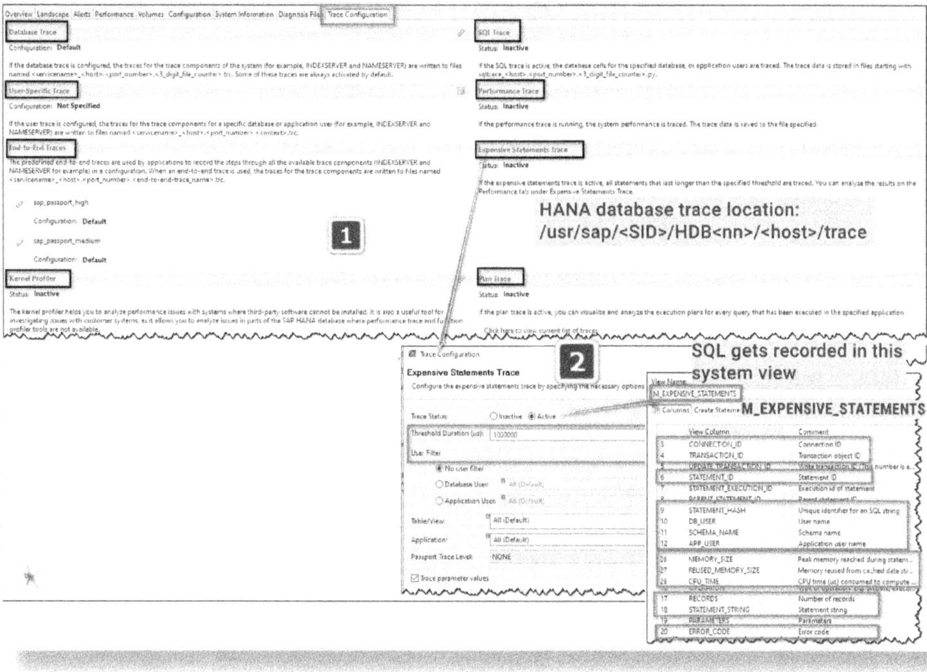

Figure 7.14: HANA database and trace files

These files can be configured from HANA Studio using the TRACE CONFIGURATION tab. Note that only the DATABASE TRACE is activated by default—other traces have to be specifically activated if needed. Instructions and reasons for activating these traces can be found in SAP Note 2119087—"How-To: Configuring SAP HANA Traces".

Area ❷ in Figure 7.14 shows how to activate and configure the EXPENSIVE STATEMENTS TRACE. It is generally recommended to keep this trace active in a production database because it enables database administrators to backtrack all database operations in accordance with the configured threshold for this trace. All SQL statements that exceed the specified threshold are recorded in the system view *M_EXPENSIVE_STATEMENTS* and are also captured in the trace directory as expensive statement traces. By querying the system view *M_EXPENSIVE_STATEMENTS*, database administrators can obtain a detailed overview of memory usage, CPU consumption, execution duration, errors, the number of records, and more, for a specific SQL statement.

A sample query on *M_EXPENSIVE_STATEMENTS* to obtain the desired output is:

```
select CONNECTION_ID, DB_USER, APP_USER,MEMORY_SIZE, CPU_TIME,
RECORDS, STATEMENT_STRING, ERROR_CODE from M_EXPENSIVE_STATEMENTS
where STATEMENT_HASH='<statement_hash>';
```

Note that there is also a system view called *M_EXECUTED_STATEMENTS*, which records most DDL (data definition language) operations (e.g., *CREATE, DROP*) that occur in the database by default. This is in contrast to the *M_EXPENSIVE_STATEMENTS* system view, which focuses on tracking DML (data manipulation language) operations (e.g., *SELECT, UPDATE, EXECUTE*).

7.9 Troubleshooting tools

SAP provides many additional tools for optimal HANA database management and troubleshooting. Let us take a closer look at these.

7.9.1 HANACleaner

HANACleaner is a Python script designed to manage and automate tasks such as the cleanup of backup catalog entries, backups, trace files, logs, SAP HANA alerts, free log segments, and much more. A full list of HANACleaner capabilities are available in SAP Note 2399996—"How-To: Configuring automatic SAP HANA Cleanup with SAP HANACleaner". The script and a detailed configuration guide can be downloaded at: *https://github.com/chriselswede/hanacleaner*.

Figure 7.15 shows installation and some of the cleanup functionality that is possible with this tool.

The numbers in this image refer to the following:

❶ Download and transfer HANACLEANER.PY to the Python directory in the HANA database server.

Figure 7.15: Implementing HANACleaner

❷ Create a database user with the required privileges:

```
CREATE USER HANACLEANER PASSWORD <password> NO FORCE FIRST
PASSWORD CHANGE;
ALTER USER HANACLEANER DISABLE PASSWORD LIFETIME;
GRANT SELECT, DELETE ON _SYS STATISTICS.HOST_OBJECT_LOCK_
STATISTICS_BASE TO HANACLEANER;
GRANT SELECT, DELETE ON SYS STATISTICS.STATISTICS ALERTS BASE TO
HANACLEANER:
GRANT SELECT, DELETE ON SYS REPO. OBJECT HISTORY TO HANACLEANER;
GRANT SELECT ON SYS STATISTICS.STATISTICS_EMAIL PROCESSING TO
HANACLEANER;
GRANT audit admin, audit operator, backup admin, catalog read,
log admin, monitor admin, resource admin, trace admin to
HANACLEANER;
```

❸ Store the database user and password in the hdbuserstore using the following command (where, `<hanacleaner_key>` refers to the user store key and `<nn>` indicates the database instance number):

```
hdbuserstore SET <hanacleaner_key> <host>:3<nn>15 HANACLEANER
<password>
```

❹ Some of the cleanup that can be executed from this tool is as follows:

- To clean up the trace files older than 10 days:

```
python hanacleaner.py-k <hanacleaner_key> -tc 10 -tf 10
```

- To reclaim free log segments for the HANA process with more than one free log segment:

```
python hanacleaner.py -k <hanacleaner_key> -lr 1
```

In Figure 7.15, we can see that the input for the required cleanup operations were passed as part of the Python command. However, all such inputs can be stored in a single configuration file and passed to HANACleaner for execution, as depicted in Figure 7.16.

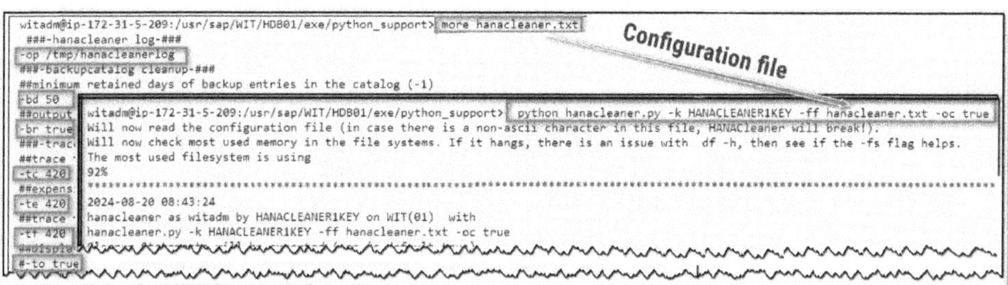

Figure 7.16: Triggering HANACleaner using configuration file

The command used in this figure is shown below (where the file HANACLEANER.TXT contains all the configuration specific to the cleanup to be executed through HANACleaner):

```
python hanacleaner.py -k <hanacleaner_key> -ff hanacleaner.txt
-oc true
```

For more information, refer to:

- SAP Note 2399996—"How-To: Configuring automatic SAP HANA Cleanup with SAP HANACleaner".
- SAP Note 2695950—"HANACleaner Fails to Connect HANA Database Using hdbuserstore Key".

7.9.2 HANASitter

During performance issues, it is crucial to collect dumps and traces while the problem still exists. *HANASitter* is a Python script that can automatically create trace files when the configured performance thresholds are exceeded. Some of these threshold configurations are: monitoring HANA database availability, responsiveness, CPU, memory usage, and so on. The collected traces can then be used for further analysis. The trace files that can be configured and automatically collected varies—call stacks, runtime dumps, indexserver gstacks, kernel profiler traces, etc. The script, along with its documentation, can be downloaded at: *https://github.com/chriselswede/hanasitter*.

Figure 7.17 shows a HANASitter installation.

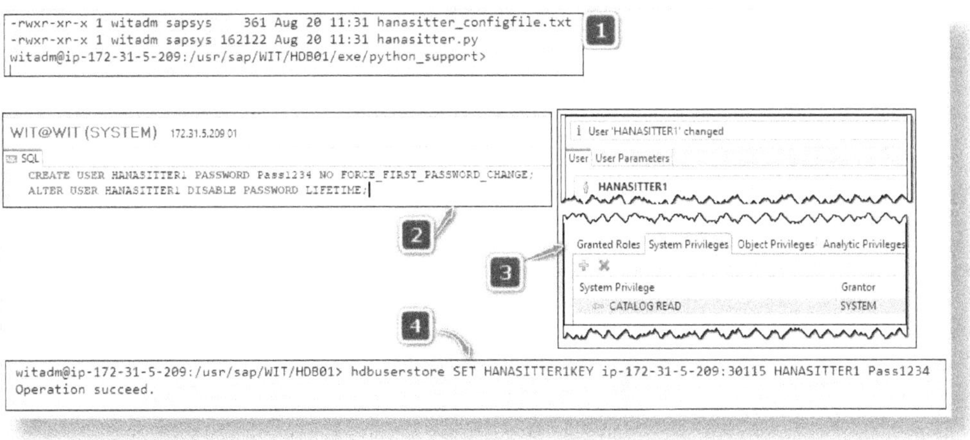

Figure 7.17: HANASitter installation

The numbers in the image refer to the following steps:

❶ Transfer the downloaded Python script to the database server.

❷ Create user *HANASITTER1* in the database:

```
CREATE USER HANASITTERI PASSWORD <password> NO FORCE_FIRST_
PASSWORD_CHANGE;
ALTER USER HANACLEANER DISABLE PASSWORD LIFETIME;
```

❸ Add *CATALOG READ* system privilege to the user.

❹ Create a userstore for HANASitter using the previously-created user:

```
hdbuserstore SET <hanasitter_key> <host>:3<nn>15 HANASITTER1
<password>
```

Figure 7.18 shows a sample execution of HANASitter using the following command to trigger a HANA dump collection if the database does not have at least 10 active indexserver threads:

```
python hanasitter.py -cf "M_SERVICE_THREADS,WHERE,IS_
ACTIVE='TRUE' and SERVICE_NAME='indexserver',>10" -nc 1 -k
<userstorekey>
```

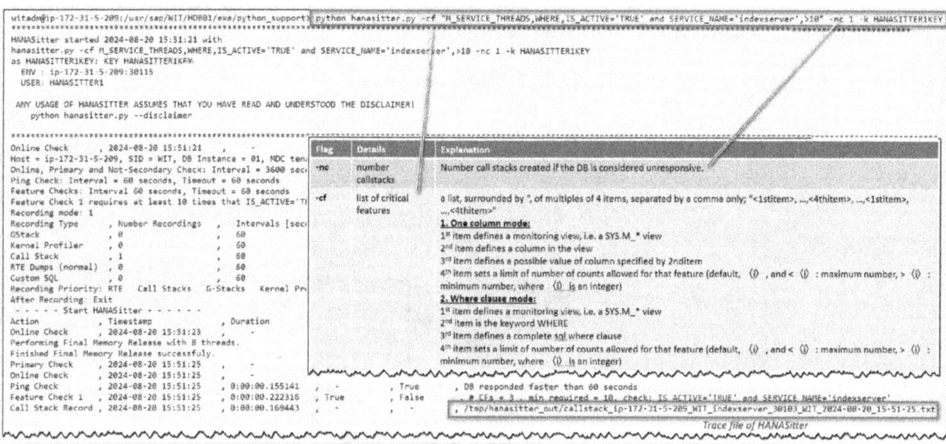

Figure 7.18: HANASitter—sample execution

Once installed, HANASitter must be configured as a cron job for continuous database monitoring to enable automatic recording of database dumps. Figure 7.19 shows the steps to schedule HANASitter as a cron job.

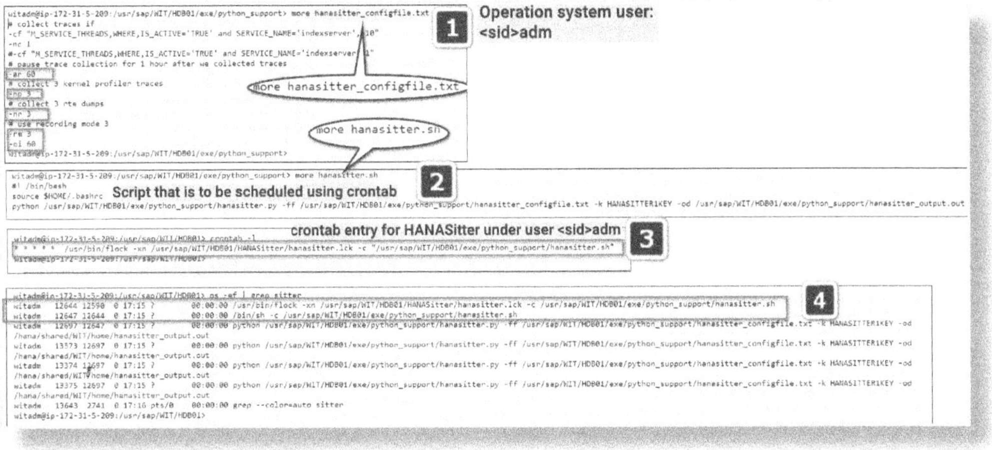

Figure 7.19: HANASitter through cron jobs

Log in to the database server as *<sid>adm* and proceed with the following steps:

❶ Create the configuration file with respect to the threshold that has to trigger the trace file collection.

❷ Create an OS script named *hanasitter.sh* with the required configuration to call HANASitter by passing the previously created configuration file as input.

❸ Schedule the cron job. The specified configuration ensures that multiple instances of HANASitter are not triggered simultaneously. The crontab entry is:

```
* * * * * /usr/bin/flock
-xn /usr/sap/<SID>/HDB<nn>/HANASitter/hanasitter.lck -c "/usr/
sap/<SID>/HDB<nn>/exe/python_support/hanasitter.sh"
```

❹ HANASitter has started to monitor the database against the conditions dictated and is collecting the trace file accordingly.

Further information is available in SAP Note 2399979—"How-To: Configuring automatic SAP HANA Data Collection with SAP HANASitter".

7.9.3 GraphViz tool

While *HANASitter* records kernel profiler traces for analyzing high CPU issues, the *GraphViz* tool helps to decode these traces. This tool can be downloaded at:

https://graphviz.gitlab.io/_pages/Download/windows/graphviz-2.38.zip.

Areas ❶ and ❷ in Figure 7.20 show the downloading and triggering of this tool from the executable GVEDIT.

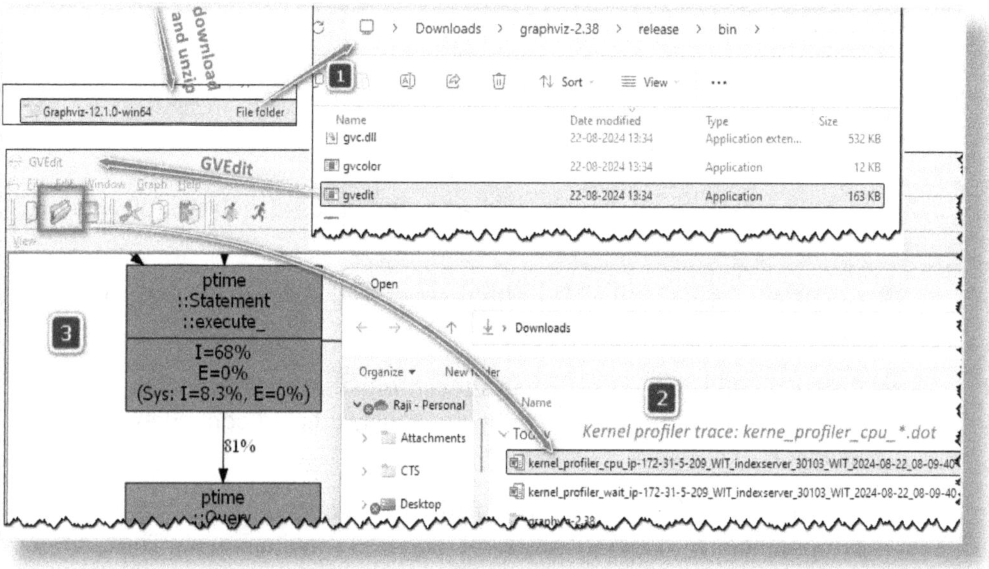

Figure 7.20: GVEdit for analysing Kernel profiler trace

The kernel profiler trace that was captured earlier can be analyzed further by uploading it to this tool, as shown in area ❸. The box shows the problematic thread which caused the CPU issue.

For further details, refer to SAP Note 1875973—"SAP HANA Studio: Kernel Profiler Trace" and the SAP Guided Answers page.

7.10 Raising a support case with SAP

As a final step in troubleshooting database issues, it is recommended to raise a support ticket with SAP, following the instructions in SAP Note 1296527—"How to create a support case for SAP Support – SAP for Me". It is advisable to have the HANA database connection accessible via router by opening the required ports (see Figure 7.21 and also Table 2.6). It is also recommended to provide a read-only user with the role *SAP_INTERNAL_HANA_SUPPORT* to assist SAP in analyzing the issue.

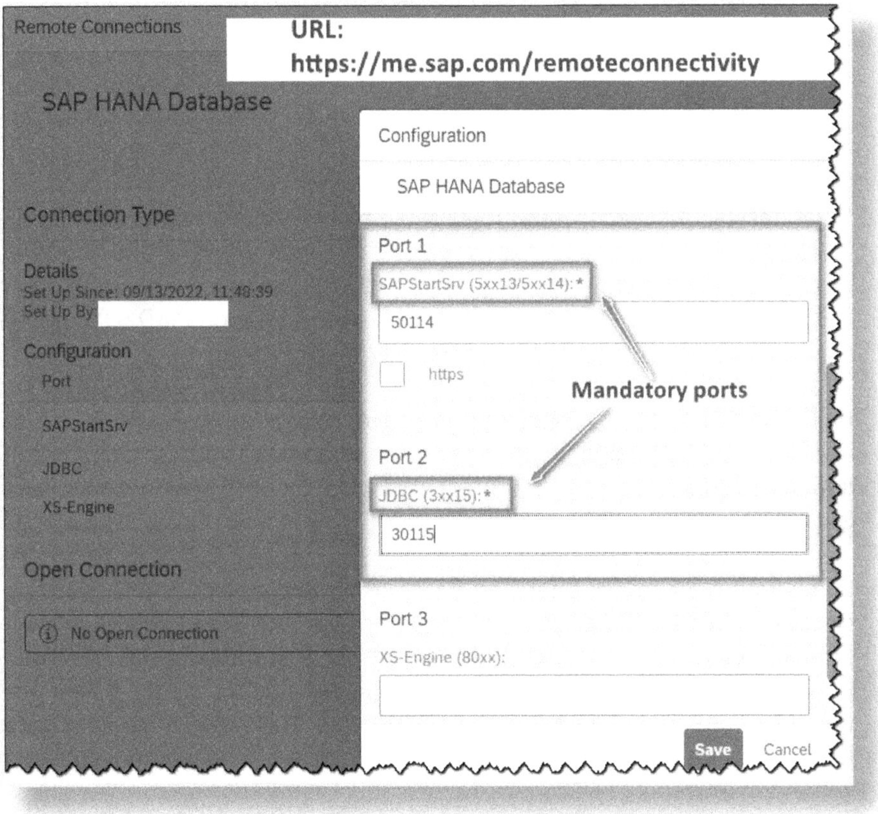

Figure 7.21: Ports to be opened for remote support

A About the Author

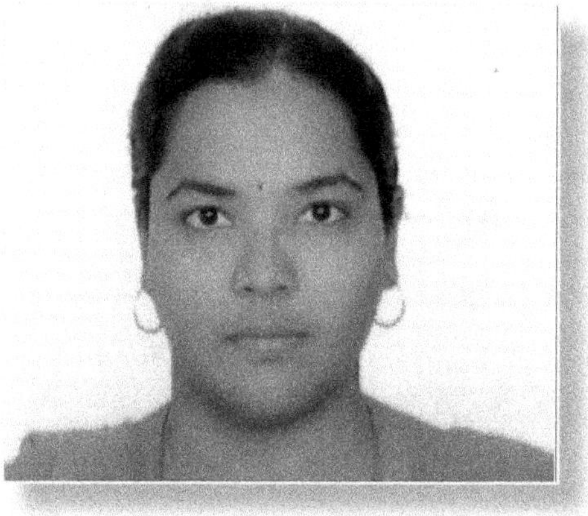

Rajarajeswari Kaliyaperumal (Raji) is a Solution Architect, specializing in HANA and SAP Cloud. She has 15 years of experience in SAP and has been involved in implementation, migration, and support teams throughout her SAP career journey. Raji has worked for IBM, HP Enterprise (DXC), and Accenture. As an author, she has written over 60 SAP blogs.

Raji is an SAP-certified consultant in HANA, Migration, SAP Activate Methodology, and SAP Basis. In addition, she has attained various cloud certifications, including Associate, Professional, SAP on AWS specialization, and SAP on Azure.

She currently works for Wipro, an SAP partner and leading SAP consulting company based in India, where she is part of the SAP Cloud Migration Competency Team. In this role, Raji aids SAP customers worldwide in their cloud transformation journeys, giving her a unique perspective on the challenges faced by both consultants and their customers. Raji holds a bachelor's degree in Information Technology from SSN College of Engineering, affiliated with Anna University in Chennai, Tamil Nadu.

B Index

A

ACID 12
admission control 234
advanced compression 175
allocation limit 202, 204
analytic privilege 253
application privilege 253
audit levels 265
audit policy 263
audit trail 263
authentication 265
auto merge 171
AWS 15
Azure 15

B

backint 274, 275
backup catalog 280
backup console 133
backup key 261
brownfield migration 52
BYOL 16

C

cluster manager 106
column-store 17, 19
complete data backup 273
critical merge 172

D

database limitation 245
DATABASE_NAME 152
database role 252, 253
database trace 323
data defragmentation 226
data fragmentation 224
DDL 26
delta area 168
delta merge 20, 23, 169
dictionary compression 175
differential data backup 273
disk full 314
distributed system 112
DML 26
document store 161
DRAM 205
dynamic RAM 24, 200

E

E_HANAINS 16
encryption 254, 259
enforced license 117
error_code 319
ETL 14
execution plan 190
expensive statement trace 323
expert sizing guidelines 57

F

failover 106
fencing 106
file-based data backup 275
forced merge 171
FSD 314, 316
full system dump 314

G

garbage collection 309
GCP 15
global_allocation_limit 202, 204
GraphViz 330
greenfield implementation 52
Guided Answers 312

H

HANA 9
HANACleaner 324
HANA client 157
HANA Cockpit 141
HANA Configuration MiniChecks 311
HANA Dump Analyzer 318
HANA Express Edition 149
HANA preferences 132
HANA prespective 131
HANA revision strategy 122
HANASitter 327
HANA Studio 96, 103, 130, 133, 149
HANA System Replication 282, 291
hard merge 171
hash partitioning 179
hdbbackupcheck 283
HDBLCM 75
HDBSQL 151
hdbuserstore 155, 156
heap memory 204
HEC 16
HINT 240
Host Agent 75
host group 115
HSR 134, 292, 294
HTAP 11, 17
HWCCT 16
hybrid LOB 57, 168

I

IaaS 38
IMCE 23
IMDB 9
incremental data backup 273
instance SSFS 254
ITOA 160

J

JobExecutor 231
job progress 180

K

KDC 266
kerberos 266
KPI 64, 66

L

LaMa 160
lazy loading 26
LMDB 160
LOB 57
log backup 270, 281
log mode 224
log_mode 270, 274
log segment 270, 271, 272
log volume 25, 50
LRU 21, 200
LSS 71, 122, 254, 256

M

main storage 169
master key 257
MCOD 41, 45
MCOS 41, 45
MDC 32
memory manager 166, 202, 232, 233
memory pool 202
mergedog 171
merge motives 170
merge statistics 173
multi-level partitioning 186
multiple-container mode 46
MVCC 23

N

native backup 282, 283
network ports 98
NSE 13
NUMA 228
NVRAM 205

O

object privilege 253
OLAP 9, 10
OLTP 9, 10
OOM 319
OS 34
out-of-memory 203

P

PaaS 16
password policy 250
peak used memory 201
permanent license 117
persistence layer 47
persistent memory 199, 205
physical memory 200
PIT 270
Platform LCM 77
PMEM 205
privilege 252

Q

Quick Sizer 52

R

range partitioning 183
recovery 282
redo log 26
refresh 282
resident HDBLCM 77, 91, 120
resident memory 200, 203
restricted users 248
root key 254
round-robin partitioning 181
row-store 17, 19
row-store reorganization 198
RPO 13
RTE 314, 318
RTO 13
runtime dump 316

S

S/4 HANA 14
SAML 266
SAP 9
SAPCAR 73
SAP HANA Hardware and Cloud Measurement Analysis 64
SAP HANA Hardware and Cloud Measurement Tool 64
SAP HANA Hardware Configuration Check Tool 16
SAP HANA Platform Edition 71
SAP HANA XS Advanced server 36
SAP Host Agent 90, 123
SAP_INTERNAL_HANA_SUPPORT 254, 331
SAPS 55, 60
savepoint 25, 28, 222, 269
savepoint_interval_s 222
schemas 161
SCOS 41, 45
security checklist 267
shadow paging 29

shared memory 204
SID 29, 152
single-container mode 46
single-host 43, 91
single-level partition 178
single tenant database 42
slave 106
slave node 106
SLD 159, 160
smart merge 171
snapshot 224
SOLMAN 158
SQL console 249
SqlExecutor 231
SQL port 103, 151
SSD 50
SSFS master keys 255
SSH 90
standard users 248
standby 44, 105
STANDBY 106
STATEMENT_HASH 320, 321
statement_memory_limit 233
statistics service 240
storage snapshot 289
support pack stack 122
SWPM 158
SystemDB 29
system PKI SSFS 255
system privilege 178, 253
system property 210
system view 162, 321
system views 244

T

table partition 177, 178
table redistribution 188
TDI 15, 16, 45
technical users 247
temporary license 117
tenant copy 282, 295, 297
tenant database 29
topology 31
trace file 322

U

undo log 27
unenforced license 117
uninstall 118
unload priority 166
used memory 201
user group 250

V

virtualized platforms 39
virtual memory 200

W

WinSCP 123
worker host 106
workload class 237, 240
workload class mappings 237
workload management 228
workspaces 131

X

X509 267
XSA 13

C Disclaimer

This publication contains references to the products of SAP SE.

SAP®, ABAP®, ExpenseIt®, Joule, OpenSAP®, SAP ActiveAttention®, SAP® Adaptive Server® Enterprise, SAP® Advantage Database Server®, SAP® AppGyver®, SAP Ariba®, SAP Business ByDesign®, SAP® Business Explorer®, SAP® Bex, SAP® BusinessObjects, SAP® BusinessObjects Explorer®, SAP® BusinessObjects Web Intelligence®, SAP Business One®, SAP Business Workflow®, SAP BW/4HANA®, SAP Concur®, SAP® Crystal Reports®, SAP EarlyWatch®, SAP® Emarsys®, SAP Fieldglass®, SAP Fiori®, SAP Garden®, SAP® Global Trade Services (SAP® GTS®), SAP HANA®, SAP® Jam, SAP Lumira®, SAP MaxAttention®, SAP® MaxDB®, SAP NetWeaver®, SAP® PartnerEdge®, SAP® Sapphire®, SAP® PowerBuilder®, SAP® PowerDesigner®, SAP® R/3®, SAP® Replication Server®, SAP® Roambi®, SAP S/4HANA®, SAP S/4HANA® Cloud, SAP Signavio®, SAP® SQL Anywhere®, SAP Strategic Enterprise Management® (SAP® SEM®), SAP SuccessFactors®, SAP Vora®, Taulia®, The Best Run SAP®, TripIt®, and other SAP products and services mentioned herein as well as their respective logos are trademarks or registered trademarks of SAP SE in Germany and other countries.

SAP SE is neither the author nor the publisher of this publication and is not responsible for its content. SAP Group shall not be liable for errors or omissions with respect to the materials. The only warranties for SAP Group products and services are those that are set forth in the express warranty statements accompanying such products and services, if any. Nothing herein should be construed as constituting an additional warranty.

More Espresso Tutorials Books

Julie Hallett, Sarah Hallett Reeves:

A Practical Guide to Cybersecurity Governance for SAP®

- Introduction to cybersecurity framework compliance for SAP software
- SAP-centric deep dive into controls
- How to create a cyber risk ruleset in SAP GRC
- Implementing a cyber framework for your SAP landscape

https://es-tu.de/hDcMR1

Fernando Roque:

A Practical Guide to SAP S/4HANA® Administration: Monitoring and Optimizing Performance

- Impact of database design on HANA processing performance
- SAP HANA architecture: system database and multi-tenant topology
- Monitoring SAP HANA infrastructure: services, CPU, memory, and disk usage
- SAP HANA user roles and privileges in a multi-tenant environment

https://es-tu.de/Zsgopy

Aušra Gustainienė, Damian Jordan:

SAP S/4HANA® Rollout Strategies and Best Practices

- Complete guide to SAP S/4HANA roll-out projects
- Choosing the right approach for your organization
- Global template
- Implementation guidelines

http://5518.espresso-tutorials.com

Anurag Barua:

Robotics Process Automation in SAP S/4HANA®

- The basics of Intelligent Robotics Process Automation in S/4HANA
- Use cases and success stories with SAP automation capabilities
- Business Technology Platform (BTP)
- Bot creation design and deployment

https://es-tu.de/UWuJ7y

Aušra Gustainienė, Domantas Mincė:

Practical Guide to Using Focused Build for SAP® Solution Manager

- Introduction to Focused Build for SAP Solution Manager
- Key features and benefits of Focused Build
- End-to-end requirements definition, project scoping, and build management
- Configuration overview and best practices

https://es-tu.de/L9c8

Santosh Kumar, Kai Zhang:

Practical Guide to SAP® Entitlement Management with SAP S/4HANA®

- SAP S/4HANA Entitlement Management models and functionality
- Configuration and deployment options
- Creating and changing entitlements
- Splitting and merging entitlements

https://es-tu.de/cC89ho

www.ingramcontent.com/pod-product-compliance
Lightning Source LLC
Chambersburg PA
CBHW071425230926
51846CB00001B/118
* 9 7 8 3 9 6 0 1 2 4 4 2 9 *